CONFRONTATIONAL READINGS
LITERARY NEO-AVANT-GARDES IN DUTCH AND GERMAN

LEGENDA

LEGENDA is the Modern Humanities Research Association's book imprint for new research in the Humanities. Founded in 1995 by Malcolm Bowie and others within the University of Oxford, Legenda has always been a collaborative publishing enterprise, directly governed by scholars. The Modern Humanities Research Association (MHRA) joined this collaboration in 1998, became half-owner in 2004, in partnership with Maney Publishing and then Routledge, and has since 2016 been sole owner. Titles range from medieval texts to contemporary cinema and form a widely comparative view of the modern humanities, including works on Arabic, Catalan, English, French, German, Greek, Italian, Portuguese, Russian, Spanish, and Yiddish literature. Editorial boards and committees of more than 60 leading academic specialists work in collaboration with bodies such as the Society for French Studies, the British Comparative Literature Association and the Association of Hispanists of Great Britain & Ireland.

The MHRA encourages and promotes advanced study and research in the field of the modern humanities, especially modern European languages and literature, including English, and also cinema. It aims to break down the barriers between scholars working in different disciplines and to maintain the unity of humanistic scholarship. The Association fulfils this purpose through the publication of journals, bibliographies, monographs, critical editions, and the MHRA Style Guide, and by making grants in support of research. Membership is open to all who work in the Humanities, whether independent or in a University post, and the participation of younger colleagues entering the field is especially welcomed.

ALSO PUBLISHED BY THE ASSOCIATION

Critical Texts
Tudor and Stuart Translations • *New Translations* • *European Translations*
MHRA Library of Medieval Welsh Literature

MHRA Bibliographies
Publications of the Modern Humanities Research Association

The Annual Bibliography of English Language & Literature
Austrian Studies
Modern Language Review
Portuguese Studies
The Slavonic and East European Review
Working Papers in the Humanities
The Yearbook of English Studies

www.mhra.org.uk
www.legendabooks.com

GERMANIC LITERATURES

Germanic Literatures includes monographs and essay collections on literature originally written not only in German, but also in Dutch and the Scandinavian languages. Within the German-speaking area, it seeks also to publish studies of other national literatures such as those of Austria and Switzerland. The chronological scope of the series extends from the early Middle Ages down to the present day.

Managing Editor
Dr Graham Nelson, 41 Wellington Square, Oxford OX1 2JF, UK
www.legendabooks.com

Confrontational Readings

Literary Neo-Avant-Gardes in Dutch and German

❖

EDITED BY INGE ARTEEL,
LARS BERNAERTS AND OLIVIER COUDER

l

LEGENDA

Germanic Literatures 21
Modern Humanities Research Association
2020

Published by Legenda
an imprint of the Modern Humanities Research Association
Salisbury House, Station Road, Cambridge CB1 2LA

ISBN 978-1-78188-401-0 (HB)
ISBN 978-1-78188-404-1 (PB)

First published 2020

Copy-Editor: Dr Birgit Mikus

CONTENTS

❖

INTRODUCTION

❖

Literary Neo-Avant-Gardes in Confrontation

Inge Arteel (Vrije Universiteit Brussel) &
Lars Bernaerts (Ghent University)

This book explores the manifold relationships between neo-avant-garde literature in Dutch and in German, adjacent literatures with remarkable parallels as well as a distinct identity when it comes to the rise of neo-avant-garde. In the geographical areas represented in this study (mainly Flanders, the Netherlands, Germany, and Austria), there is a surge of literary and artistic experimentation after World War II. These forms of experimentation share a number of preoccupations, on an ideological as well as a formal level. It is noteworthy that similar stylistic procedures and radical ideas about literature were circulating concurrently across Europe and worldwide. Often in the wake of the historical avant-garde, writers develop a scepticism toward language, political authority, bourgeois ideology, and toward the authority of traditional literary genres. Experimental authors from several countries face similar ideological tensions (e.g., the attraction of radical leftist thought) and institutional challenges (e.g., publication strategies and the social status of the artist). Many of them oscillate between the collective identity of a group or movement (Wiener Gruppe in Austria, Gruppo 63 in Italy, Vijftigers in the Low Countries, etc.) and a more individual profile as an isolated artist. They explore the same stylistic, narrative, and intermedial techniques, channelling their scepticism in a poetry and a prose that challenge familiar boundaries. Their texts undermine the dominant genres and blend together literary genres and media. Indeed, genre principles are central among the many conventions that are being targeted by the authors of the neo-avant-garde. We can think of the concrete poetry of Gerhard Rühm, montage fiction by J.F. Vogelaar, or the radio essay under the editorial guidance of Helmut Heißenbüttel. In view of this genre transgression, *texts* is a more appropriate label than *novels*, *stories*, *essays*, or *poetry*. Interart and multimedial transgressions are explored too, e.g. in the visual poetry of Gerhard Rühm and Paul de Vree, in the pop poetics of Rolf Dieter Brinkmann and Patrick Conrad, or in Lucienne Stassaert's poetic affinity with jazz music.

Experimental authors also share the same perspective when it comes to the relationship between literature and reality. This line of thought surfaces in the opposition between concreteness (as in 'concrete poetry') and abstraction, or between the objectivity of calculation, which crystallizes for example in permutational series of linguistic elements or in camera-eye narration, and the subjectivity of spontaneity, which is apparent in strategies of improvisation. These texts challenge the idea that literature integrates and generates a certain knowledge of reality and develop a shared notion of authenticity. Authenticity, it seems, does not imply a direct connection between the subject and reality. Instead, authentic writing springs from a singular textual remodelling of reality, as in ready-mades. For the very first time the present volume examines some of these many parallels and meaningful differences between the literary experiments in Dutch and in German.

What holds these experiments together is a view of literature, art, and society related to that of the historical avant-garde and clearly aware of that radical tradition. At the same time, the literary experiments we are discussing are diverse. That is why we prefer the plural term *literary neo-avant-gardes*. We consider the *neo-avant-garde* as a useful category for thinking about the radical literary innovations in the post-war period that refer back to the historical avant-garde in a broad sense, as the authors in our corpus do. The neo-avant-garde cannot be reduced to the climate of artistic protest in the 1960s (as Szabolcsi (1984) does), nor to Peter Bürger's pessimistic interpretation of the neo-avant-garde (1984 [1974]) as 'a manifestation that is void of sense' (1984: 61). According to Bürger, the neo-avant-garde acts counter to the rejection of art as an institution that inhered in the historical avant-garde. In that view, the neo-avant-garde is a failing avant-garde. Many critics, such as Buchloh (1986), Perloff (1989), Foster (1996), and Scheunemann (2005), have attacked and corrected this view (see also Bürger's response in 2010). Bürger's concept of the avant-garde and the neo-avant-garde favours some movements (such as Dada and surrealism) and ignores others, such as Cubism and Futurism (Scheunemann 2005: 19). Furthermore, Bürger's theory reduces the variety of contexts and intentions to the idea that the avant-garde attempts to integrate art into life (1984: 20). A more positive approach to the neo-avant-garde can reveal how it resists mimetic representation in new ways, as Dietrich Scheunemann (2005) argues, by taking avant-garde practices such as ready-made and collage to a new level. Similarly, Hal Foster's theory of the neo-avant-garde (1996) acknowledges the potential of the post-war return of the avant-garde. Foster reads the neo-avant-garde as a repetition that offers an insight impossible for the original, a dynamics for which he uses the Freudian term *Nachträglichkeit* [deferred action]. The readings in this book side with these affirmative views on the relation of the neo-avant-garde with the historical avant-garde.

There are good reasons for the particular comparison between the literary neo-avant-gardes in Dutch and in German. They emerge from geographical as well as linguistic neighbours. In terms of language as well as landscape the Dutch and the German area form a more or less continuous space within Europe. This vicinity entails that there is a lot of traffic across the borders of the countries (Austria, Belgium, Germany, and the Netherlands in particular, but also Switzerland), including interartistic, translational and intertextual traffic. As the chapters in this book will show, Dutch and Flemish authors were reading the experimental work of their German-speaking colleagues and they met each other at international arts and literary festivals and exhibitions.

In the cross-border circulation of the literary neo-avant-garde translations played a key role on a short as well as a longer term. The Dutch and Flemish neo-avant-garde appeared in German anthologies such as *Between Eyes and Breath: Dutch Poetry since 1945* [1964, *Zwischen Augen und Atem: Niederländische Lyrik seit 1945*], *Dutchmen Telling Stories* [1969, *Niederländer erzählen*], *Flemish Lyric Poetry* [1970, *Flämische Lyrik*], *Unknown Vicinity: Modern Dutch Poetry until 1980* [1985, *Unbekannte Nähe: Moderne niederländische Lyrik bis 1980*] and *Time Crystals: Dutch Short Stories* [1991, *Zeitkristalle: Erzählungen aus dem Niederländischen*], or in magazines such as *Akzente* (Munich), *Drehpunkt* (Basel) and *Schreibheft* (Essen). In the Low Countries, magazines such as *Raster* (The Netherlands) and *Yang* (Flanders) discussed and translated German experimental literature. To list only a few examples: *Raster* published translations of work by Konrad Bayer, Ernst Jandl and Gerhard Rühm; *Yang* translated Elke Erb, Friederike Mayröcker and Arno Schmidt. The Flemish-Dutch periodical *Randstad* published parts of Jürgen Becker's *Felder* and works by Hans Magnus Enzensberger. *Randstad* also positioned itself as a neo-avant-garde magazine with a special issue on 'Manifesten en manifestaties' [Manifestoes and Demonstrations] in 1966. Featuring texts by Hugo Ball, Tristan Tzara, Paul van Ostaijen, as well as Andy Warhol, Nam June Paik, and John Cage, this theme issue programmatically brought together the historical and the neo-avant-garde. Lastly, we should not underestimate the individual efforts of publishers and translators. German and Austrian innovative literature was made accessible to a Dutch-speaking audience through the work of translators such as Lucas Hüsgen, Jan H. Mysjkin, and Erik de Smedt.

The chapters of this book shed light on these cultural dynamics, explaining the circulation of the neo-avant-garde and exploring the unexpected affinities between writers. Since some of these authors are not yet familiar to readers interested in avant-garde literature, each chapter also offers accessible introductions to the authors and their work. In other words, the purpose of the book is both comparative — or confrontational, as we will see — and introductory. A limited selection of authors that we consider representative of Dutch-speaking and German-speaking neo-avant-garde will allow for in-depth comparisons. By confronting each Dutch-speaking writer with a German-speaking writer, this study not only sketches the general consensus about their works, but it also offers new perspectives as each of the authors and each of the pairs under discussion gives an outlook on particular aspects of the neo-avant-garde. The chapter on Gerhard Rühm and Paul de Vree as well as that on Helmut Heißenbüttel and Mark Insingel draw attention to the way the visual and material nature of poetry are exploited in the long 1960s. While the work of Oswald Wiener and Jacques F. Vogelaar opens up the discussion of ideology and science in the neo-avant-garde, Friederike Mayröcker and Lucienne Stassaert's work reflects upon female authorship and generic hybridity. Both women belong to the few female authors who were recognized by colleagues and critics as important contributors to a neo-avant-garde aesthetics. In general, women writers were less visible and less frequent in neo-avant-garde circles, magazines, and other publications. The chapter on Rolf Dieter Brinkmann and Patrick Conrad reminds us of the importance of pop and intermediality in the 1960s, whereas the confrontation between Alexander Kluge and Armando zooms in on the impact of World War II and on neo-avant-garde documentary aesthetics.

The book presents a first elaborate comparison between individual authors who have hitherto been considered key contributors to their particular neo-avant-garde context. Other authors who have been decisive in the literary neo-avant-garde and who could certainly make for rewarding comparative readings include Eugen Gomringer, Max Bense, Konrad Bayer, Franz Mon, Arno Schmidt, Elke Erb, and Ernst Jandl; Sybren Polet, Ivo Michiels, Lucebert, Bert Schierbeek, and Simon Vinkenoog. As the individual chapters of the book at hand make clear, the potential for further and more encompassing comparative study is substantial, but our volume does not aim or claim to discuss the top most important figures of the literary neo-avant-gardes.

The present volume is intended for scholars and students interested in the context, the dynamics, and the features of the literary avant-garde and neo-avant-garde, and more generally for anyone interested in modern Dutch and German literature. It offers readers both accessible introductions to neo-avant-garde authors and a deeper insight into their poetics. What is more, the volume facilitates first-hand acquaintance with the literary neo-avant-garde by including longer excerpts of literary prose and poetry in the chapters. In the remainder of this introduction, we outline our approach and our historical and conceptual framework, before detailing the structure and contents of the chapters.

Confrontational Readings

Confrontational Readings intends to go beyond traditional philological views according to which authors and their works are studied in their local literary-historical, biographical, and geographical contexts with special emphasis on the material traces (manuscripts, letters, editions) that can document these contexts. Also, the volume goes beyond the concept of influence, which establishes clear and verifiable links between authors. Implicitly, the notion of influence leans toward a belief in intentions, hierarchies and origins, although there have been several theoretical proposals to rethink the concept in more productive terms (see e.g. Clayton and Rothstein 1991). In the present study, an argument for influence could be made in some cases, e.g. the relation between Helmut Heißenbüttel and Mark Insingel, but such an argument would obscure the actual dynamic, which is more complex and not purely intentional. Nor do we feel bound to notions of intertextuality, even though a broad interpretation of intertextuality can illuminate the circulation of the literary neo-avant-garde. In our usage, the notion of *circulation* echoes Stephen Greenblatt's theory of culture (see also Herman and Vervaeck 2017). In Greenblatt's (2005) understanding, literary works participate in the 'circulation of cultural materials', which implies that they 'shape the forces of their culture in novel ways so that elements powerfully interact that rarely have commerce with one another in the general economy' (16). Experimental literature in the 1960s responds to and plays a role in the anti-authority and emancipatory movements, for example. Scholars observe a surge of avant-garde practices in this context across the arts and across Europe, in the Balkans (Djurić and Šuvaković 2003; Hamalidi et al. 2011), the Nordic Countries (Ørum and Olsson 2016), France, Italy (Picchione 2004; Chirumbolo et al. 2010), and Eastern Europe (Piotrowski 2009). The perspective that guides us is the idea that under similar historical and sociological conditions literary innovations may assume similar forms and may share a focus, techniques, preoccupations, and so on. A confrontational reading reveals these threads and highlights aspects that seemed marginal or did not attract attention, while at the same time acknowledging the singularity of individual writers and works. Indeed, divergent aesthetic manifestations under similar conditions can just as well shed a light on the heterogeneity of neo-avant-garde literature and confront us with the question what we mean when we assume an author to be neo-avant-garde. In that way, the book wants to contribute to the understanding of the European literary neo-avant-garde.

What these similar conditions are, is clarified in general terms in this introduction and in specific terms in each separate chapter. The starting point is twofold. First, we are dealing with geographical and linguistic neighbours: the Dutch language area and the German language area. And so there are obviously a number of shared linguistic, geographical, even political and cultural constraints and affordances. Second, we focus on the long 1960s, a period that stretches out from the mid-1950s to the early 1970s, in which Western European countries faced a surge of emancipatory movements and anti-establishment activity. The 1960s are defined by processes of economic globalization, mass consumption, mediatization and a general shift in attention to individual freedoms (e.g. sexual freedom) and individual needs. Literature and the arts respond to those developments. In several European countries, this is a period of increased literary experimentation; or more accurately: it is a period in which literary experimentation could circulate more freely because of the changing social, political, and cultural circumstances in the Western world (see Marwick 1998; DeGroot 2008; Strain 2016; Buelens 2018).

Our view of the 1960s as having loose temporal boundaries enables us to see how literary experiments both partake in the aftermath of World War II and lead up to diverse emerging phenomena of the 1970s such as new subjectivity and computational poetry. Furthermore, it avoids an all too mechanical notion of generations that focuses mainly on dates of birth. The age of the authors presented in this volume differs considerably. Yet, for all of them the long 1960s prove to be formative years, a decisive period in the development of their oeuvres, regardless of their biological age.

Are the chapters in this volume a site of violence and aggression? The title of this book, *Confrontational Readings*, and the nature of our approach, may arouse expectations in that respect. The word *confrontation* has the connotation of hostile collision. According to the *Oxford English Dictionary*, a confrontation is:

> 1. The bringing of persons face to face; esp. for examination and eliciting of the truth. 2. The action of bringing face to face, or together, for comparison. 3. The coming of countries, parties, etc., face to face: used of a state of political tension with or without actual conflict.

From these definitions one can already derive why the title is appropriate for the project of this book, as we are bringing together face to face authors from different countries for comparison, perhaps to elicit (and certainly to investigate) some 'truth' about the transnational neo-avant-garde. The action of bringing together creates a tension in which telling similarities and equally meaningful differences can surface.

And indeed, a certain degree of 'aggression' is involved in this project. First, on the level of the *authors and texts* we are examining. It will become clear that these oeuvres are characterized by 'negativity' in Adorno's terms (2002), negativity in relation to the conventional, in relation to the bourgeois capitalist society and all its excrescences. Second, on the level of our *approach*, the aggression resides in the fact that we are emphasizing the particular aspects that come into focus when two oeuvres are compared. We are imposing a view on a particular oeuvre from a new angle, namely that of another oeuvre. Along these lines, the confrontational readings in this volume will highlight, for the first time, the affinities between literary neo-avant-gardes in the Dutch and in the German language.

Finally, the 'confrontation' in this book also lies on the level of *collaboration* between scholars. This may seem trivial, but the dynamics of collaboration is integral to the fruitful comparison. The collaboration also entails a confrontation between national or language-bound philological traditions, which are often still the direct context of author studies. Dutch literary studies (*neerlandistiek*) and German literary studies (*Germanistik*) are also brought face to face here, certainly not for the first time in general terms, but probably for the first time in this kind of constellation. In sum, the principle of the *confrontation* runs as a thread through the book on the level of the corpus, the approach, and the type of collaboration.

Structure and Outline of the Chapters

Each chapter of the book stages a confrontation between the oeuvres of two authors and discusses the same contextual and textual aspects. In that way, the comparison is not only possible between the authors of a particular chapter, but also between the chapters, making the whole greater than the sum of its parts. The structure of the chapters allows the reader to easily jump from one chapter to another to compare, for example, the career development or the literary practice of author A in chapter 1 with that of author X in chapter 2. Within that structure, the contributors sometimes elaborate on a particular aspect rather than other aspects when it was more relevant to the discussion. In some cases, for example, the section on reception will be brief whereas others chapters devote more detailed attention to the way authors are read and received. In that way too, the chapters do justice to the singularity of oeuvres.

First, each chapter discusses the biographical and institutional context. The reader learns about relevant events in the writers' lives, where they worked, and with whom they worked, and gets an insight into the particular importance of the 1960s. Were they involved as editors in magazines and where did they publish? Did they practice other arts and did they participate in decisive literary events? This information serves as a background for the discussion of the writers' views of literature and art. In the second paragraph we delve into their dominant views of literature and the world, literature and the self, literature and ideology. In this volume, we use the term *poetology* for the explicit and implicit literary theories writers hold. Also at issue is the way these views evolve, the way the author articulates them in essays, interviews and so on. In that way, we can compare the various strategies with which neo-avant-garde writers fashion and position themselves as literary authors.

Whereas the second paragraph thus deals with the authors' self-positioning, the third one foregrounds the positioning of the authors by critics and scholars. How were the experiments received in literary criticism and how did the reception of their work evolve? What is the current dominant image of the authors in literary history? Finally, each chapter offers a confrontational in-depth reading of selected literary texts. By looking at stylistic features, narrative strategies, the integration of techniques from other media, and recurring themes, the chapters chart the literary preoccupations shared by authors from different countries and traditions. Since so much weight falls on language in the poetology and literary practice of the neo-avant-garde, we decided to provide the original text in an endnote. Also, the titles of literary works are translated, with original titles in parentheses. In exceptional cases the contributors deliberately refrained from translation, for example when the visual, aural effects or the nonsensical nature of the words would be lost in translation.

The first chapter of *Confrontational Readings* is devoted to two figures who are central in their neo-avant-garde networks of the post-war decades: the Belgian Paul de Vree (1909–1982) and the Austrian Gerhard Rühm (1930). Dirk De Geest and Michael Fisch draw a sharp picture of De Vree and Rühm as internationally oriented innovators of the genres and media of poetry. As a proponent of international as well as Dutch experimental poetry and an editor of the avant-garde magazine *The Round Table* (De Tafelronde), De Vree was strongly perceived by writers as an authority and was also criticized for that reason. In his essays and his own poetry, he constructs a clear affiliation between contemporary experiments and the historical avant-garde, Paul van Ostaijen in particular. Building on this tradition, De Vree starts writing concrete poetry. De Geest's discussion shows how De Vree is constantly exploring new terrain, retaining a certain 'fluidity' as an artist. The relentless fascination with the sound and shape of words and the inspiration from the historical avant-garde are shared by Gerhard Rühm. In his essays, we can find reflections on transgressions and blends of genres and media, with a particular interest in 'the expansion of material and consciousness'. Not just literary conventions but also the basic conventions of language are abandoned in his work, in favour of a meticulous exploration of visual effects or sound patterns in speech and in favour of the concomitant musical dimension of language. While De Vree becomes increasingly invested in the political potential of poetry (as in *poesia visiva*), Rühm continues to challenge the boundaries between media and between genres to this day.

A persistent interest for genre transgression and for the material qualities of literature is also characteristic of the literary works produced by the Belgian Mark Insingel (1935) and the German Helmut Heißenbüttel (1921–1996) in the long 1960s. Their work is discussed by Lars Bernaerts and Johanna Bohley in the second chapter. Both Insingel and Heißenbüttel are inspired by the historical avant-garde and by authors such as Gertrude Stein and Paul van Ostaijen. Both of them develop a version of literary abstraction and investigate the tension between the abstract and the concrete in their texts of the long 1960s. In that process, any display of subjectivity is treated with suspicion and their texts aspire to the unattainable ideal of radical objectivity (or so it seems). Insingel is known for his concrete and visual poetry, which relies on procedures of repetition and variation. In particular, his poetry as well as his novels deploy the circle as a central principle of composition. The linearity of the text is countered by circularly shaped poems, circular patterns of reasoning, and plot lines returning to the same point. Heißenbüttel too replaces conventional plot and familiar genres with more abstract principles of writing. Like Insingel, he isolates and repeats ordinary language or the discourse of certain groups to critically examine hollowed out uses of languages. In sum, Bernaerts and Bohley show that Heißenbüttel and Insingel are sceptical of the way language is used in society and in conventional literature. The two writers trade on the auditory and visual dimensions of language in similar ways and evacuate affect and subjectivity from the text while foregrounding objective patterns, which reflects their alternative aesthetic ideals.

The third chapter discusses the Austrian Friederike Mayröcker (1924) and the Belgian Lucienne Stassaert (1936), whom critics often considered as the only women authors with a distinct profile in their respective experimental contexts. As Inge Arteel and Jeroen Dera show, this allegedly similar position in the literary field does not originate in similar biographies; the poetics it leads to also displays some remarkable differences. Stassaert's poetology of the 1960s is greatly informed by an anti-establishment sentiment, whereas Mayröcker refrains from any anti-bourgeois stance. Stassaert also explicitly situates herself in a female mystical discourse, concerned with unearthing an authentic aesthetic voice that predates any female stereotyping. Mayröcker at that time does not openly address the gender question, though many of her texts can be read as touching on gender in a parodic way. Important affinities can be identified as well. Both authors definitely share a preference for *Einzelgängertum* [going it alone], not wanting to align themselves with a particular experimental circle or program of the time, and mixing seemingly opposed poetological positions. Stassaert's work of the 1960s displays an evolution from vibrant experimentalism in the early prose texts to a more communicative and sober style in the later poems. Still, all of her texts conflate oppositions such as *open* versus *hermetic*, or *expressive* versus *autonomist*. On a thematic level, the texts share a striking endeavour to revolt against death. Mayröcker's texts also testify to a remarkable poetological development, condensed in only a few years: her anarchic and intermedial genre experiments at the end of the 1960s make way for a less experimental narrative prose around 1971. However, the shift is not a radical one: the early experimental calculation is infused with transgressive lyrical pathos, and the later prose is quite unconventional in its reworking of conventions of narrativity.

In the fourth chapter of *Confrontational Readings*, Sven Vitse and Thomas Eder confront the work of the Dutch writer Jacq Firmin Vogelaar (1944–2013) with that of the Austrian Oswald Wiener (1935). As the biographical and institutional background sketched by Eder and Vitse shows, Vogelaar and Wiener are leading figures in their respective network of experimental literature and they give articulate expression to their views on artistic innovation. Wiener plays a key role in the Wiener Gruppe [Vienna Group] and participates in the 'literary cabarets' of the late 1950s and happenings of Viennese actionism in the 1960s, providing theoretical ammunition for these avant-garde activities. As a critic, Vogelaar opposes anecdotal realism in Dutch literature and develops a distinct Marxist critical approach. In his view, literature should divulge and rework the socioeconomic and ideological foundations of reality. As a consequence, his own fiction does not allow the reader easy consumption, which is already apparent in the early fiction analysed by Vitse. While Wiener is interested in philosophy, linguistics, and ideology as well, his orientation differs. His approach can be called scientific, as he examines the cognitive foundations of aesthetics. By manipulating language in literary experiments, the writer can facilitate a thorough understanding of how thought and language work, Wiener suggests. In the 1969 novel *The Improvement of Central Europe* (*Die Verbesserung von Mitteleuropa*), however, Wiener goes in another direction. As Eder explains, the novel conceptualizes language as 'social consciousness and even as the memory of humanity'.

The fifth chapter confronts the work of two highly multimedial authors, the Dutchman Armando (1929–2018) and the German Alexander Kluge (1932). Jaap Grave and Gunther Martens discuss Armando's membership as a visual artist of the international artistic network ZERO and Kluge's role as a film director in the development of New German Cinema. Armando and Kluge can be situated in a shift in documentary practices. Whereas documentary writings used to make strong pretensions of objectivity, they become increasingly embedded in committed forms of authorship. Both in their visual art works and in their literary texts, Armando and Kluge tackle the complex status of the documentary and its relation to the notion of authenticity. Of particular importance in both oeuvres is the reflection on the violence of World War II. Armando's writings present extreme situations in times of war as moments of sublime experiences. The formal principle of the fragmentary collage, in which he uses for instance original words of former SS members, aims at aesthetically intensifying the extreme experiences. In that way, key notions of Early Romanticism are adapted. Kluge for his part, addressing the emancipatory potential of popular culture, works at establishing a proletarian *Gegenöffentlichkeit* in his cinematic work. Aesthetically, it harks back to the historical avant-garde and the *Neue Sachlichkeit* and thematically it addresses the aftermath of the war in post-1945 Germany. His ultra-short stories of the 1960s are essentially by-products of these film projects. These texts too can be linked to the notion of the sublime: they are full of factual information and documentary material that is presented in an 'evident' way, a principle that Umberto Eco relates to the postmodern sublime.

The Belgian Patrick Conrad (1945) and the German Rolf Dieter Brinkmann (1940–1975), whose respective works are the topic of the sixth chapter, are intermedial artists and writers too. In their readings of these authors' poetological essays and selected poems, Hans Vandevoorde and Thomas Ernst observe manifest theoretical, poetological and ideological similarities. Both are influenced by American pop culture and explore the ambivalent relation between pop art and consumer society. Also, they both reject *littérature engagée* even though they recognize the critical potential of apolitical art and literature. Both Conrad and Brinkmann are positive towards countercultures and pre-official publishing, and they both develop an emphatically intermedial and (sexual) provocative artistic practice. They prove to be comparable in their fusion of mimetic realistic forms with intermedial practices undermining mimetic representation. The textual analyses also reveal important differences. Whereas Conrad refers to literary traditions, to *the lie* as an aesthetic principle, and while he lives as a dandy in the spirit of Decadentism, Brinkmann is in search of a 'new subjectivity', the liberation of perception, and the materialization of the present moment in poems. Brinkmann moreover plays a much more prominent role in the cultural transfer of American pop culture and aesthetic debates to West Germany, for instance by contributing to the Fiedler-debate on postmodernism. Conrad for his part may well be regarded as a predecessor of the Flemish postmodern poets of the eighties in view of his highly citational and mannered writing style.

The connections not just within the chapters but also between them are varied and telling. On a general level, these writers share an interest in the historical avant-garde, in the revolutionary potential of literature, in the visual and auditory dimensions of literature, in genre transgression and literary abstraction. More particularly, there are striking convergences ranging from the emphatic admiration of certain authors (Samuel Beckett, Gertrude Stein, Paul van Ostaijen) and the ludic but critical dialogue with popular culture to the development of genres and techniques such as concrete poetry, collage, and montage. What emerges from this volume through the method of *confrontation*, then, is the image of a diversified field of connections, which is to say relationships both varied but also limited in their variations. The confrontational reading of authors and works contributes to a detailed mapping of the European, transnational neo-avant-garde.

Acknowledgements

The project is an initiative of the research groups Olith, ENAG and SEL (Center for the Study of Experimental Literature, Ghent University & Vrije Universiteit Brussel). Olith was an interuniversity collaboration that studied the theory and practice of the dynamics of literature. ENAG (European Neo-Avant-Gardes) is a research community based at the University of Leuven which brings scholars together from universities in Brussels, Ghent, Leuven, Liège, Paris, and Vienna, and is funded by the Research Foundation Flanders (FWO). ENAG investigates the transnational literary neo-avant-garde from 1945 to the present.

Works Cited

ADORNO, THEODOR W. 2002. *Aesthetic Theory*, ed. by Gretel Adorno and Rolf Tiedemann, trans. by Robert Hullot-Kentor (London: Continuum)

BUCHLOH, BENJAMIN. 1986. 'The Primary Colors for the Second Time: A Paradigm Repetition of the Neo-Avant-Garde', *October*, 37: 41–52

BUELENS, GEERT. 2018. *De jaren zestig: Een cultuurgeschiedenis* (Amsterdam: Ambo)

BÜRGER, PETER. 1974. *Theorie der Avant-Garde* (Frankfurt a/M: Suhrkamp)

———. 1984. *Theory of the Avant-Garde*, trans. by Michael Shaw (Minneapolis: University of Minnesota Press)

———. 2010. 'Avant-Garde and Neo-Avant-Garde: An Attempt to Answer Certain Critics of *Theory of the Avant-Garde*', *New Literary History*, 41: 695–715

CHIRUMBOLO, PAOLO, MARIO MORONI, and LUCA SOMIGLI (eds). 2010. *Neoavanguardia: Italian Experimental Literature and Arts in the 1960s* (Toronto: University of Toronto Press)

CLAYTON, JAY, and ERIC ROTHSTEIN (eds). 1991. *Influence and Intertextuality in Literary History* (Madison: University of Wisconsin Press)

DEGROOT, GERARD J. 2009. *The Sixties Unplugged: A Kaleidoscopic History of a Disorderly Decade* (Cambridge: Harvard University Press)

DUBRAVKA, DJURIĆ, and MIŠKO ŠUVAKOVIĆ (eds). 2003. *Impossible Histories: Historical Avant-gardes, Neo-avant-gardes, and Post-avant-gardes in Yugoslavia, 1918–1991* (Cambridge, MA: MIT Press)

FOSTER, HAL. 1996. *The Return of the Real: The Avant-Garde at the End of the Century* (Cambridge, MA: MIT Press)

GREENBLATT, STEPHEN. 2005. 'Culture', in *The Greenblatt Reader*, ed. by Michael Payne (Malden: Blackwell), pp. 11–18

HERMAN, LUC, and BART VERVAECK. 2017. 'A Theory of Narrative in Culture', *Poetics Today*, 38.4: 605–34

HAMALIDI, ELENA, MARIA NIKOLOPOULOU, and REA WALLDÉN. 2011. 'A Second Avant-Garde without a First: Greek Avant-Garde Artists in the 1960s and 1970s', in *Regarding the Popular: Modernism, the Avant-Garde and High and Low Culture*, ed. by Hubert van den Berg, Sascha Bru, Benedikt Hjartarson, Peter Nicholls, Laurence van Nuijs, and Tania Ørum (Berlin: De Gruyter), pp. 425–44

MARWICK, ARTHUR. 1998. *The Sixties: Cultural Revolution In Britain, France, Italy, and the United States, c. 1958 — c. 1974* (Oxford: Oxford University Press)

ØRUM, TANIA, and JESPER OLSSON (eds). 2016. *A Cultural History of the Avant-Garde in the Nordic Countries 1950–1975* (Leiden: Brill)

PERLOFF, MARJORIE. 1989. 'Music for Words Perhaps: Reading/Hearing/Seeing John Cage's *Roaratorio*', in *Postmodern genres*, ed. by Marjorie Perloff (Norman: University of Oklahoma Press), pp. 193–228

PICCHIONE, JOHN. 2004. *The New Avant-Garde in Italy: Theoretical Debate and Poetic Practices* (Toronto: University of Toronto Press)

PIOTROWSKI, PIOTR. 2009. *In the Shadow of Yalta: Art and the Avant-Garde in Eastern Europe, 1945–1989* (London: Reaktion)

SCHEUNEMANN, DIETRICH. 2005. 'From Collage to the Multiple: On the Genealogy of Avant-Garde and Neo-Avant-Garde', in *Avant-Garde/ Neo-Avant-Garde*, ed. by Dietrich Scheunemann (Amsterdam: Rodopi), pp. 15–48

STRAIN, CHRISTOPHER B. 2017. *The Long Sixties: America, 1955–1973* (Chichester: Wiley)

SZABOLCSI, MIKLÓS. 1984. 'La néo-avant-garde: 1960–', in *Les avant-gardes littéraires au xxe siècle*, ed. by Jean Weisgerber, 2 vols (Budapest: Akadémiai Kiadó), I: *Histoire*, pp. 573–608

CHAPTER 1

❖

'i do not only commit myself — in making art — to one option': Confronting Paul de Vree and Gerhard Rühm

Dirk de Geest (Katholieke Universiteit Leuven) &
Michael Fisch (Hebrew University Jerusalem)

This chapter discusses the various manifestations of so-called 'experimental' literature in the domains of poetry and especially auditory, visual, and concrete poetry in Paul de Vree's and Gerhard Rühm's work of the 1960s. Confronting Gerhard Rühm and Paul de Vree, as typical examples of a specific form of neo-avant-garde, is both an easy and a difficult task. On the one hand, there are various reasons to consider the two protagonists together. Both poets are prestigious representatives of the so-called neo-avant-garde, within the specific context of their own literary traditions, but also in an explicitly international (European and even global) context. Both practised their own version of the so-called 'concrete' or 'visual' poetry, but neither Rühm nor De Vree ever limited themselves to a mechanical application of those programmatic principles. Quite on the contrary, they experimented continuously with different conceptions of literature, with various media and art forms (visual art, music, film, etc.), with numerous forms and meanings in order to explore a broad array of experiences and aesthetic ideas in their own literary work. Moreover, their reflections resulted in some major essays, on their own creative impulses as well as on the work of colleagues, which were subsequently translated and distributed internationally in circles of visual poets and critics.

Yet, at the same time there are some crucial differences which complicate our confrontation. First of all, there has never been a personal relationship between the two poets. Their acquaintance, if one can use such a term at all, was rather superficial, based on occasional meetings at poetry festivals and on an occasional reading of each other's work. De Vree mentions Rühm a few times in his essays, but only in very general terms. Rühm has never quoted De Vree. This relative non-confrontation may be partly accounted for by their clear difference in age, which cannot be overlooked. Rühm was born in 1930 while De Vree was born in 1909; as such, he actually belongs to an older generation. In fact, his literary career had already started in the 1930s, when Rühm presumably only started to decipher letters for the very first time. This difference in age also has substantial repercussions on the development of their respective careers. Rühm started publishing poetry and experimenting with various media (among others music and performances) during the 1960s, whereas De Vree at that time already had a literary career spanning three decades. Moreover, despite their unmistakably international profile both writers belong, first and foremost, to a specific national climate and tradition. This entails obvious linguistic differences. De Vree, for instance, is very aware of the limitations of his small native language (Dutch) and starts to incorporate other languages in his poetry. For Rühm, on the other hand, German remains his dominant language. Gradually, both writers gained significant international prestige within the circles of the neo-avant-garde, especially concrete poetry, which contrasts with their somewhat eccentric position in their respective national literary traditions, where neoclassicist literary conceptions still continued to prevail.

Discussing Rühm and De Vree together thus results in a 'meeting', but inevitably also in a 'confrontation'. In this chapter, in order to avoid large (and hence very vague) generalizations, we focus mainly on the crucial years of the mid-1960s.

1. Background

Paul de Vree

Paul de Vree is much older than Gerhard Rühm. Born in 1909, De Vree had already started his literary career during the interwar period, writing a semi-autobiographical psychological novel (1938), a number of classicist poetry collections — later collected in *Song in the Meadows* (1941, *Zang in de landouw*) — and various essays on the newest Dutch prose (1933; 1936b). During World War II, however, De Vree's romantic ideology led him to a certain lenience of the German occupier's ideas. As a result, in his post-war poetics, he refused any political involvement of literature, looking for a way to explore literary language on its own. This led to a modernist (at some time even surrealist) re-orientation of his poetry. During the 1950s and 1960s, De Vree thus became the major spokesman of the neo-avant-garde. He was very active as a poet, publishing collections of his own but above all contributing to numerous modern literary periodicals, both in Belgium and abroad. Even more important was his role as a critic and an organizer of literary manifestations, but also of film festivals and art exhibitions. At that time, De Vree was actively involved in almost every avant-garde literary and artistic initiative. Photographs dating from that period often show an enormous contrast between the young beatniks, dressed accordingly (with sunglasses, jeans and dark jumpers), and their nestor De Vree in his classic suit.

Yet, around 1965, De Vree's position in the Belgian neo-avant-garde scene became rather ambiguous and even controversial. On the one hand, he was still generally considered one of the most prominent and most enthusiast critical voices.

Aspiring young poets hoped to get discussed in his (Antwerp) radio talks, his critical essays and, above all, his influential avant-garde magazine *The Round Table* (*De Tafelronde*). On the other hand, however, his symbolic prestige was no longer self-evident to young writers and artists. Some objected to his constant search for 'new' forms of art and literature, his authoritative position and his partial behavior.

This institutional debate came to a climax in the summer of 1963, when some of De Vree's closest friends and collaborators — among whom the poets Ben Klein, Adriaan de Roover, and Adriaan Peel — distributed a stenciled leaflet which proclaimed 'the death of the critic Paul de Vree'. The group criticized among others De Vree's favoritism of the monochrome paintings by Jef Verheyen and the sound poetry by Henri Chopin. Although the pamphlet was rather marginal, it forced De Vree to re-orient his magazine. Due to the fervent inner opposition, *The Round Table* grew into a major forum for international neo-avant-gardism, promoting all kinds of concrete poetry, visual poetry and sound poetry.

In several respects, the institutional turbulence merely reinforced a crisis which the poet De Vree himself had been struggling with for quite some time. Gradually, De Vree had come to realize that the traditional conception of poetry as exclusively printed language had come to an end. Even the revolutionary impulses of the historical avant-garde, which continued to inspire him, had not been able to overcome these limitations: avant-garde poets still respected poetry as a discursive practice, and their typographical experiments remained all in all very moderate (and quickly became conventional). Instead, De Vree began to search for new innovative ways to rethink his own literary practice, a search which led him to the contemporary arts (especially the Zero-movement) and to intense contacts with neo-avant-garde colleagues from all over the world. In fact, the first issue of *The Round Table* after the pamphlet-affair was entitled *New Tendencies in Poetry* (*Nieuwe tendenzen in de poëzie*). From then on, De Vree's own literary creations became heavily influenced by international avant-garde groups. He experimented with various forms of concrete poetry, but ultimately opted for the Italian *poesia visiva*, which combined visual material (often taken from photographs, newspapers and advertisement) with an explicitly leftist political involvement.

Gerhard Rühm

Gerhard Rühm was born in Vienna on 12 February 1930. He grew up in a musical parental home as the son of Otto Rühm, a member of the philharmonic orchestra. He studied the piano and composition at the University of Music and Performing Arts in Vienna. In addition, he took private lessons with Joseph Matthias Hauer (Rühm 1983; see also Lichtenfeld 1964), composer and founder of twelve-tone music. Indeed Hauer — and not Arnold Schönberg, as is generally assumed — was demonstrably the first composer to invent, generate and publish a new twelve-tone compositional method (Hauer 1920; Fisch 2010: 49). His twelve-tone technique shaped both the musical and the sound-poetic work of Rühm. Hauer's twelve-tone plays, their easy characteristic style and their peculiar meaninglessness positively influenced Rühm's own compositional method.

In the 1950s, the young and radical composer Gerhard Rühm became acquainted with the poets Hans Carl Artmann and Konrad Bayer, with architect Friedrich Achleitner and jazz musician Oswald Wiener in the artistic circles of Vienna's subculture. The joint works of this circle soon found their way into the Wiener Gruppe [Vienna Group] (Rühm 1985: 17), which was founded on 13 December 1954, at first as a club called 'Exile'. However, three years earlier, a variable formation of Viennese writers had already been having regular meetings in the art-club below the Kärntner bar. Moreover, Andreas Okopenko had published a hectographed journal entitled *Publications of a Vienna Group of Young Writers* (*publikationen einer wiener gruppe junger autoren*) from 1951 until 1953. For more than a decade, members of the former as well as of the subsequent Wiener Gruppe distanced themselves from a generally conservative characteristic climate in Austria through transdisciplinary and intermedial compositions of text and image and trans-media performances, which resulted in a remarkable group identity.

In 1966 Peter Handke, who was admired and praised by some, challenged and criticized by others, wrote ironically: 'Gerhard Rühm was looking for his salvation in experiments by creating new images through the graphic arrangement of words. In doing so, he was certainly no longer able to disguise a conventional basic attitude' (2015: 13).[1] However, it should be stressed that, in the same year, Handke also used the characterization of 'description impotence' [Beschreibungsimpotenz] for the members of the Gruppe 47 [Group 47]: 'It is realized that literature is made with language and not with things that are described by language' (2007: 47).[2] Handke's medium and object of enlightenment was language, focusing especially on the relation between linguistic and actual reality and on the production of reality through linguistic communication, i.e. the established classification and ruling system of language: 'From literature, I expect a shattering of all seemingly definite world images' (2007: 38).[3] In this respect, Handke's intentions were not so different from Rühm's.

Elfriede Jelinek suggested that the playful, indeed anarchic dealing with language was typical for writers such as Rühm, who also became a role model for her. Her orientation on the conceptual Austrian literature — thus, on the Wiener Gruppe and its milieu — became clear already in her first prose texts, as, for instance, in the Rowohlt volume *we are decoys, baby!* (1970, *wir sind lockvögel baby!*). Specific influences include the artificialities of language, for instance, a consequent use of small letters, a lack of punctuation, a decomposition of syntax and of grammatical as well as orthographic rules. In fact, even concrete poetry such as Rühm's visual poems influenced Jelinek's texts, too. The Wiener Gruppe became generally known to a larger public through spectacular happenings such as the 'literary cabarets' (1958/1959) and a 'children's opera' (1964). However, the group lost one of their most significant members when Konrad Bayer committed suicide on 10 October 1964. It was Rühm who edited the work of Bayer (1966; 1968; 1992; 1996; see also Rühm 1981) as well as texts of the Wiener Gruppe (Rühm 1967). All these works were initially published by Rowohlt publishing house, making those texts accessible to a larger reading public.

Only two days after the premiere of the 'children's opera', on 12 April 1964, Gerhard Rühm moved from Vienna to Berlin and started publishing his own works by means of small publishing houses and art editions. These works were of particular importance during the 1960s in Berlin: *the pegnitz sleepers* (1964, *die pegnitz schläfer*), *propositions on the universe* (1965, *lehrsätze über das weltall*), *poem of colours* (1965, *farbengedicht*), *contemplation of the horizon* (1965, *betrachtung des horizonts*), *suicide wreath* (1966, *selbstmörderkranz*), *home* (1967, *daheim*), *rhythm r* (1968, *rhythmus r*), *a small compendium of billiards* (1968, *kleine billardschule*), *hans and helga* (1969, *hans und helga*). In retrospect, a new poets' collective emerged: the so-called Berlin Circle [Berliner Kreis] (see Rühm in Breicha 1992: 13–48). Rühm (1985: 596) stated: 'the friendly contact between former group members was not cut off after bayer's death; the contacts even intensified from time to time again in berlin resulting in a close cooperation of a new, loose formation, which now included above all dieter roth and günter brus.'[4]

When Gerhard Rühm was offered a professorship for free graphic art at the University of Fine Arts of Hamburg in 1972, he moved from Berlin to Hamburg. In 1977, his new destination became Cologne, where he still lives today. For seventy years now, this artist has felt at home in almost all areas of artistic creation. The former enfant terrible — to put it another way — has long since reached the international art, literature, and music canon through pioneering works.

2. Poetology

Paul de Vree

The various shifts in De Vree's longstanding literary career can be observed first of all in his numerous essays, most of which were first published in periodicals but later collected into books, which led to them being distributed more widely. These essays are testament to an impressive number of fundamental re-orientations: first of all from a classicist to an avant-garde poetics, and subsequently from word to image and from a national to an international perspective. In order to analyze the poetological premises of De Vree's work, it seems most appropriate to have a look at some of his seminal texts. As a prolific literary critic, De Vree wrote numerous contributions in each issue of his own periodical, *The Round Table*, but he was also omnipresent on other forums as well: in newspapers and virtually all Belgium literary periodicals (both in Dutch and in French), as well as in numerous exhibition catalogues and anthologies, both in a national context and abroad.

However, around 1965, De Vree brought together a number of his contributions and stray ideas in a deliberate attempt to present a more comprehensible and more encompassing overview of the literary neo-avant-garde, both from a contemporary and a historical point of view. In 1965, he published a general essay on the Flemish avant-garde from a historical point of view (De Vree 1965b). A few years later, in 1968, De Vree collected his critical reviews in a lengthy volume called *Under Experimental Fire* (1968b, *Onder experimenteel vuur*). In the same year, his book-length essay *Poetry in Fusion* (1968c, *Poëzie in fusie*) attempted to chart all variants of contemporary international avant-garde poetry. Taken together, these books offer a fascinating view of De Vree's poetological ideas.

Under Experimental Fire can be regarded as a retrospective view of De Vree's poetology. The book collects a substantial amount of critical reviews and shorter essays from the period between 1953, the start of *The Round Table* and the poet's radical shift to an avant-garde literature, until 1967. In its subtitle, the book is presented to the reader both as a kind of encyclopaedic *vade mecum*, offering ample relevant historical information, and as a kind of still ongoing documentary, *transit documenta*. This reflects De Vree's double ambition. The critic posits himself first and foremost as a kind of historian, of the literary past but also of the contemporary, someone who endeavours to characterize all kinds of experimental new publications by linking them both to historical and contemporary trends. In this strong historical awareness, especially the link with the historical avant-garde is stressed time and again in order to prove the permanent relevance of the ongoing neo-avant-garde and the alternative canon on which all new experiments are ultimately based. The ideas of struggle and revolution hence are considered permanent forces of opposition within modern society, and they function as the main impetus for innovative literature. Yet, at the same time this general dynamic has to be actualized time and again in order to function optimally within an ever changing societal and cultural constellation. In this respect, De Vree's literary conception is frequently framed within an overall sociological approach of society, more specifically relating literary changes to recent technological evolutions and to the contestation of younger generations.

On the other hand, De Vree tries to maintain his own position as a major literary critic and even as a prominent spokesman of the younger generation in a changing context. His historical *vade mecum* thus not only intends to inform his readers of the recent evolution in Dutch (mostly Flemish) poetry, but also to position himself as a competent, well-informed and objective literary critic. Moreover, in his reviews, he endeavors to present as many neo-avant-garde realizations as possible, even books which were published marginally or privately, intended only for a few insiders. Thus, De Vree's literary criticism may be described as a deliberate strategy to inform the broader public of the merits of neo-avant-garde poetry but also as an attempt to legitimize that perspective on literature within the literary field.

Next to this collection of shorter reviews, which offers mainly 'momentary' descriptions and evaluations, De Vree published two essays which were clearly intended to present a more synthetic view on avant-garde literature, both from an historical and a contemporary point of view.

In 1965, De Vree published a general essay on the Flemish avant-garde (*Vlaamse avant-garde (1921–1964)*), which discusses both prose and poetry and which tries to chart various tendencies within non-classical literature. This essay is primarily conceived as a historiography of a past period, although a number of footnotes were added in order to demonstrate the explicit links with the ongoing neo-avant-garde. Most attention is given to the poetical evolutions (and revolutions), which are presented chronologically. Primordial in De Vree's view is the importance of collective enterprises: the emergence of particular groups on the basis of a collective manifesto, the institutional impact of specific manifestations and, above all, of literary magazines. Instead of formulating his personal views as a literary critic, however, in this monograph De Vree opts for a rather objective tone; he obviously tries to present a comprehensive cartography of post-war experimental tendencies as such, bringing together all sorts of relevant information in a quasi-encyclopedic manner. Yet, on closer consideration, some symptomatic poetological aspects can be discerned. For instance, it is fascinating to see how De Vree considers the Flemish expressionist poet Paul van Ostaijen not only the most prominent representative of the historical avant-garde, particularly with his poetry collection *Occupied City* (1921, *Bezette stad*), but also the most prominent representative of avant-garde practice as such. *Occupied City* is considered unique in two respects: because of its explicit involvement with the traumatic reality of World War I and, even more, because of its radical preoccupation with the visual form, realized by means of an innovative 'rhythmic typography'. This poetry volume is praised extensively, in contrast with most other critics who favor especially Van Ostaijen's last, more mystical and more autonomous texts.

Both the critical involvement with reality and the fascination for the visual dimension of language dominate De Vree's ambitious essay *Poetry in Fusion* (*Poëzie in fusie*), which was published in 1968. In contrast to the rather detached, retrospective tone of the essay on the Flemish avant-garde, this book displays a more outspoken literary ambition. *Poetry in Fusion* inventories diverse manifestations of avant-garde poetry, arranged according to the medium at stake in those experiments: its subtitle is in fact 'visually, concretely, and phonetically'. The book itself consists of two parts: an essayistic overview and an anthology. The anthology offers a broad spectrum, which is intended to demonstrate convincingly the international success of the movement. Illustrations include Belgian representatives, but also many poets from abroad, ranging from America and Italy to France and Germany, including some material from Gerhard Rühm. However, considering De Vree's subsequent development as a critic and as an artist, the omission of the so-called *poesia visiva* is striking.

In *Poetry in Fusion*, De Vree distinguishes between various trends, taking into account the historical evolution as well as the diversity of the media involved. To articulate these specificities, he uses some insights among others from the semiotic and cybernetic theories by the German influential semiotian Max Bense. In his overview, the main focus lies on the enormous richness of the concrete-visual poetry, but the phonetic poetry gets a separate chapter as well. Again, De Vree demonstrates his erudition and his enormous documentation by mentioning many dozens of tendencies within the overall field of concrete poetry. In this context, the Wiener Gruppe is given some attention as well. Briefly summarizing Rühm's influential anthology (and offering a few extensive quotes), the Wiener Gruppe is associated mainly with the innovative use of dialect within the context of visual and phonetic poetry (De Vree 1968c: 30–31). Yet, this particular reference is hardly remarkable, since the literary historian De Vree tries to incorporate as many references as possible in order to demonstrate the worldwide vitality of visual and phonetic poetry. Thus, in contrast with De Vree's former book on the Flemish avant-garde, *Poetry in Fusion* offers a broad internationalist overview, in the context of which the Flemish and Dutch poets are considered interesting but by no means prominent representatives.

In addition to these descriptive considerations, both diachronically and synchronically, the future possibilities of visual and phonetic poetry are discussed theoretically as well. More particularly, De Vree endeavours to analyze the complex relation between form and meaning in conceptual terms, introducing such semiotic terms as *iconic* and *symbolic*. These theoretical remarks not only function as a background for the historical overview, they also point at De Vree's personal need to deepen his own poetic insights. *Poetry in Fusion* may indeed be linked closely to the ongoing developments in his periodical *The Round Table* and to his own poetry collections. In this respect, it may be interesting to quote some of De Vree's ultimate statements about the possible outcome of the neo-avant-garde movement. In the final pages of his study, De Vree advocates what he calls 'evolutive poetry', a kind of poetry which attempts to take into account societal actuality as much as possible. This programmatic choice will lead him inevitably towards the political Italian *poesia visiva*. However, De Vree connects this re-orientation to the experimental exploration of new technological media and even to the end of the classic book. He boldly states: 'Gutenberg's era is running to an end' (1968c: 45), instead opting for what we would nowadays call a multimedia approach of poetry:

> Anyway, language has to be given ample space for pictural, musical and kinetic values. It has to be disconnected from established meanings and be adapted to the technological atmosphere. Let us not forget that, without integrating technical means, poetry will experience serious difficulties in maintaining itself on a universal and a democratic level.[5]

It is not difficult to imagine De Vree's enthusiasm if he could have witnessed the ongoing technological innovations of the internet and the social media!

Gerhard Rühm

When Gerhard Rühm moved to (West) Berlin, he abandoned a specifically national and reactionary climate in Vienna and pursued his literary career in an international progressively oriented exile. Furthermore, he also left behind dialect poetry to refine new and strict forms of concrete poetry and to try new possibilities in the field of prose work. The following prose works — all of them collected in the Rowohlt volume *windows* (1968, *fenster*) — can be considered paradigmatic in this respect: 'description of a tree' (1964, 'beschreibung eines baumes'), 'sylvia's ball gown' (1966, 'sylvias ballkleid') and 'the folded watch' (1966, 'die gefaltete uhr'). Examples of concrete works include poems collected in *Gesammelte Gedichte und visuelle Texte* (1970a) such as 'europe' (1963, 'europa'; 169–70), 'sonnet' (1965, 'sonett'; 174), 'flower piece' (1969, 'blumenstück'; 180) and the constellation 'Weg weg' (1964: 223), which refers to Konrad Bayer's death and which will be looked at more closely here.

The word sequence *weg* clearly manifests the tension between the economy of the material and formal composition process on the one hand and complex layers of meaning on the other. In this respect, Rühm's poem can be seen as a stroke of luck, in its independent adaption and its attempt at semantically exhausting a static form type. The poet arranges the sequence in such a way that the movements counter-rotate:

WEG
WEG
WEG
WEG
regen
WEG
WEG
WEG
regen
regen
WEG
WEG
regen
regen
regen
WEG
regen
regen
regen
regen

10.10.1964 (© Gerhard Rühm)[6]

'WEG' (printed in upper case) and 'regen' (in lower case) increase or decrease reversely and proportionally in a ratio of 4:3:2:1. The word material is ambiguous: 'WEG' can be read as 'der Weg' [the way or road] or 'weg' [off, gone, away]; regen can be interpreted as 'sich regen' [to move] or 'der Regen' [the rain]. The text provokes the reader by the appearance of a textual column in which the words are not organized next to each other, but below one another. The textual coherence is strengthened by the fourfold repetition of 'WEG' at the beginning and 'regen' at the end. If one reads the word sequence in the common reading direction (top down), the capital letters 'WEG' seem to suggest a structured and prescribed life cycle which has to gradually challenge a self-reliant life. On the other hand, when reading from bottom to top, the reader gets the impression of an animated life on its way or rather being guided, a dynamics which is suggested by the powerful demonstration of capitalization.

More alternatives emerge if one interprets 'weg' as 'weg von' [off, away from] and 'regen' as 'Regen bzw. es regnet' [rain or it rains]. From the perspective of a speech-score, the use of upper and lower case could indicate loudness as well. If one reads top down, the repulsion, for instance, then appears as a condition for creativity and freedom. Moreover, various semantic associations are evoked by the signature at the bottom — Konrad Bayer's date of death — which functions graphically as the column's base. Thus, Rühm's poem realizes both an autobiographical and a poetological perspective, since Bayer commissioned his life for the unleashing of poetry. If the reader analyzes the mutual permutation procedure in its significance and likewise uses the accordance of 'weg', then yet another reading mode emerges, which argues that exemption from adjustments leads to uninhibited creativity, but also to losing the path and directly facing death.

In the common reading direction, the word sequence reaches its climax in death. Therefore, it seems reasonable to posit that the fourfold occurrence of 'regen' also transfers the image of rain to the symbolic level of grief and desolation. Multiple correlation of the text results from several factors. On the one hand, it follows from the absence of a subject (contrary to the presence of an object) and from the isolation of unreflected words. On the other hand, it results from the accordance and vertical arrangement of the body of the text, which suggests the image of a textual column and leads the view (contrary to the usual reading direction) from bottom to top. Through the reader, the signature provides a frame of reference for a deeper meaning.

Rühm's 'Weg weg' also calls to mind August Stramm's poem 'Urdeath' ('Urtod'), in which the sequence of words shapes the life process within the interaction of space and time by means of an ascending and descending vitality curve. At that moment, Rühm was already familiar with word sequences, among others from the work of Franz Richard Behrens, which he discovered and promoted. In 'Weg weg' the textualization method focuses on an explicitly formal and serial basis, turning the creative poet into some kind of artistic technician. The individual consciousness remains hidden behind the structure of the material. Rühm's radical reductionism thus demonstrates several central ideas of concrete writing:

a) the construction of a semantic field of tension based on isolated word material;
b) a semantization of the field;
c) a functional use of printing organization and page margins;
d) the release of typography in view of the overall structure;
e) the dissolution of the closed text in order to activate and to sensitize the reader

(see Fisch 2010: 274).

Rühm soon turned these experiments with concrete poems into a comprehensive conceptualization of visual poetry, which also integrated graphic and other non-linguistic elements into the composition. Transitions and intermediate stages in this evolution can be observed in his text images, for instance the handwritten additions to a typographic text (as in 'my life' ('mein leben'), a typocollage from 1964 or in 'n icht s' from 1963 (see Figure 1.1)) or instances of photographic material (as in the case of 'lauren and' ('lauren und' — see Figure 1.2)), a photo collage from 1960, or 'Epitaph for Marilyn Monroe' ('Epitaph auf Marilyn Monroe'), a journal collage from 1962 (see Figure 1.3). This multiple use of materials and media related Rühm's works to diverse forms of art. In that way, he consciously and repeatedly succeeded in reaching the limits of the performing arts. However, not only the visually transmitted material is concrete and/or radical, but first and foremost the acoustic dimension. For Rühm, as a musician of the avant-garde, the phonetic aspects of language were always of primordial interest (see Rühm 2013: 881–903).

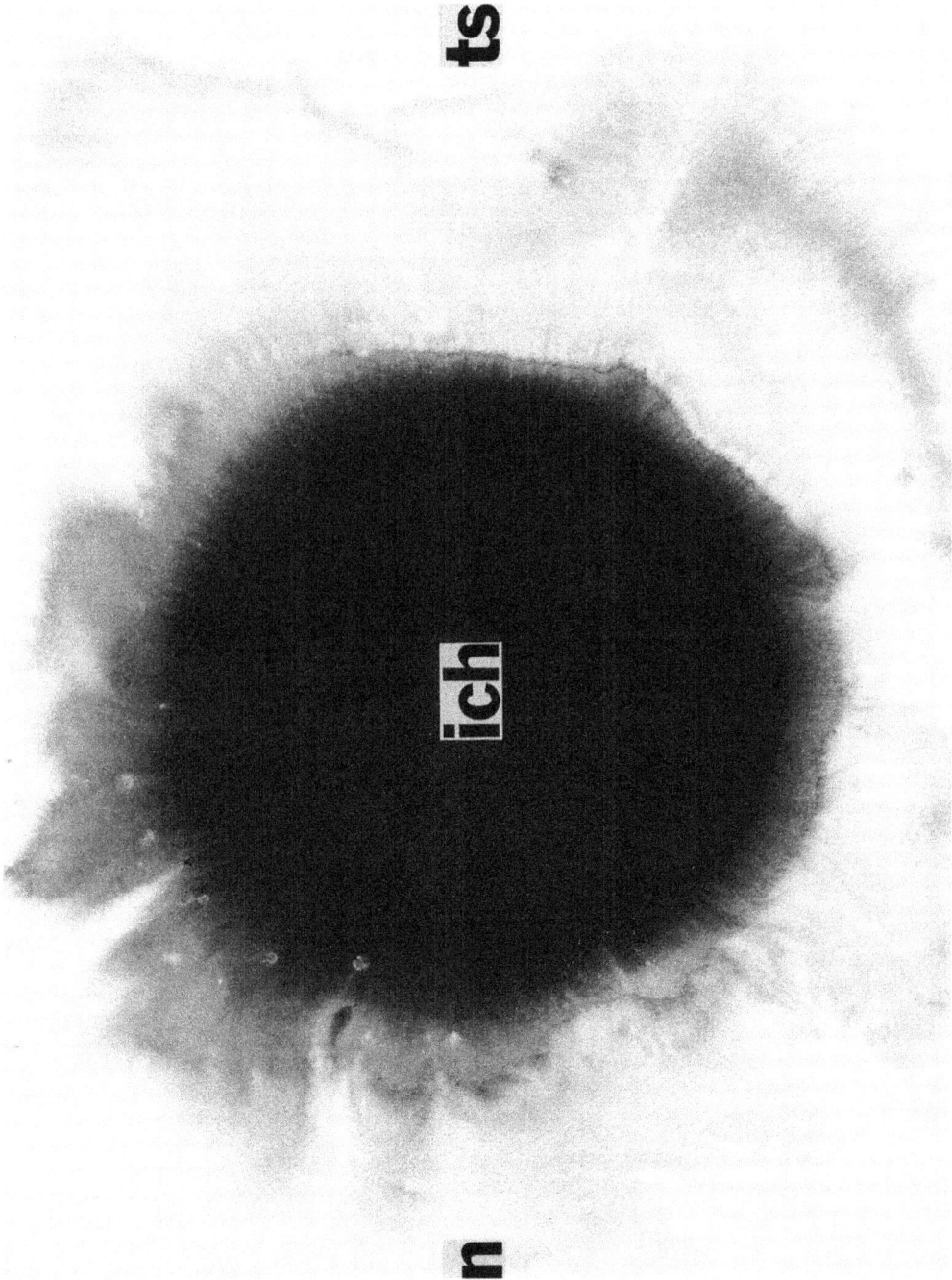

FIG. 1.1. Gerhard Rühm, 'n ich ts' (2006, II.I: 696, © Gerhard Rühm).

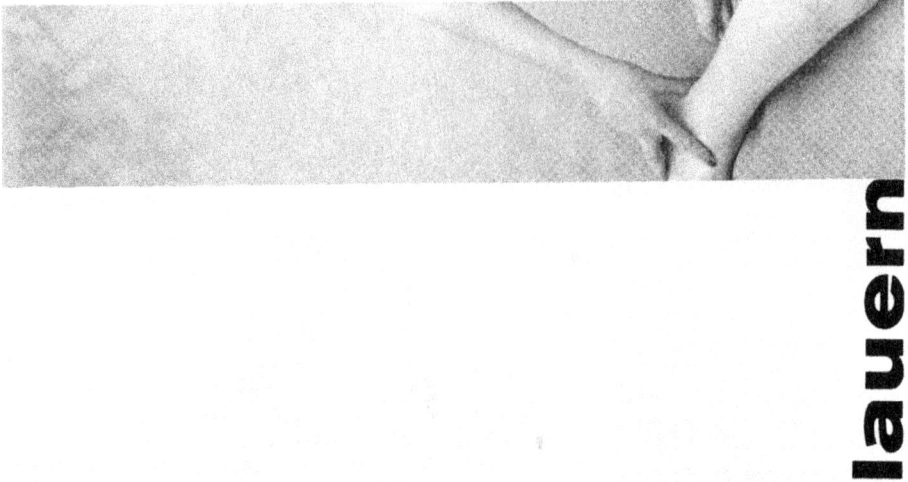

FIG. 1.2. Gerhard Rühm, 'lauren und' (2006, II.I: 254, © Gerhard Rühm)

Gerhard Rühm's theoretical texts can be roughly classified in three periods. In the period from 1957 to 1962, three texts are of crucial importance: 'on the experiment in modern poetry' (1957, 'über das experiment in der modernen dichtung'), 'shaping words — shaping sounds' '1958, 'wortgestaltung — lautgestaltung'), 'principles of the new theatre' [1962a, 'grundlagen des neuen theaters'). For the timespan from 1965 to 1968, there are three significant texts: 'the new notion of text' (1965, 'der neue textbegriff'), 'preface'('1967: 7–36, vorwort), and 'poetry today' (1968b, 'lyrik heute'). In the years 1970 to 1977, the following new theoretical texts may be considered important: 'on my auditory texts' (1970, 'zu meinen auditiven texten'), 'a possible extension of concrete poetry' (1972, 'mögliche erweiterung der konkreten poesie'), and 'auditory poetry' (1977, 'auditive poesie'). In fact, more than sixty theoretical essays were written in the period between 1956 and 2004 (Fisch 2010: 367–70). More specifically, Rühm was at that time particularly interested in transgressing existing generic boundaries and in the development of new genres. Concrete and visual poetry became, in theory as well as in practice, central issues in many discussions (Fisch 2008).

Rühm introduced the generic category of 'auditory poetry' as an analogy to the notion of visual poetry in 1977 (Fisch 2009). In this new genre, the characteristics of 'speech sound and articulation, concept and acoustic, voice characteristics and auditory parameters, expressionistic gesture and intonation schemes are of

Fɪɢ. 1.3. Gerhard Rühm, 'Epitaph auf Marilyn Monroe'
(2006, II.I: 279, © Gerhard Rühm)

particular importance' (Lentz 2000: 133),[7] as they are experienced immediately by the audience. These aspects were also highlighted in Rühm's performances (often in a duet with Monika Lichtenfeld). Hence, a representational and an expressive dimension of the text have to be distinguished in the case of visual and auditory poetry, because in its representation the text benefits from a presentation of a conceivable world, and as an expression it provides information about the writer's characteristics.

In his discussions with Michael Lentz, Rühm profitably and informatively formulated the basics of these 'qualities of differences' [Differenzqualitäten] and the generic relevance of his 'poetological studded terms' [poetologisch besetzten Begriff]. He stated:

> under the umbrella term "auditory text", i contrast spoken texts, i.e. live texts, which are intended for the actual performance, with mere audio tape texts, which are set down to the most minute detail. in this respect, not any kind of margin exists any longer for the interpreter since his voice was tape-recorded, however, now only managed as material. that is, after a strict score (mostly on graph paper), it was processed with the studio's technical possibilities. (quoted in Lentz 2000: 1121)[8]

Rühm's auditory poetry originated in 1952 through his friendship with pianist Hans Kann, who later became a professor at the Vienna University of Music and Dramatic Arts from 1977 to 1995, and coincided with the emergence of the *musique concrète* in France. However, at that time French concrete musicians such as Pierre Henry and Pierre Schaeffer were unknown to both Viennese. Gerhard Rühm stated:

> from today's point of view, i would say that in the meantime the possibilities of mere oral recitation are explored to a large extent. this of course does not mean that there is nothing remarkable left to create. in a broader sense, i differentiate even more consistently between absolute oral and sound recitation. (Lentz 2000: 1126)[9]

It was typical for various manifestations of concrete art, concrete poetry, concrete music, etc. that they emerged internationally from the outset and that they have continued to exist next to each other. Most of its representatives got to know each other, in person or via their work, only at a later stage. Rühm never knew Paul de Vree in person; yet, it cannot be ruled out that they attended certain festivals at the same time. Hence, Gerhard Rühm only knows Paul de Vree because he read his texts (Lentz 2000: 771–92; 1121–30). The title of de Vree's central poetry collection, *Zimprovisations* (1968, *Zimprovisaties*), contrasts with Rühm's work *windows*, which dates from the same year. As a matter of fact, Rühm sets this concept against improvisation especially with reference to print products. Occasionally, improvisation and spontaneity could occur at the Wiener Gruppe performances, which were related to concrete performance practices that often had uncertain realizations.

Next to his concrete poems and various forms of concrete art and concrete music, Rühm 'created a form of visual music as a counterpart to visual poetry' (Lentz 2000:

1130).[10] Thus, the writer stated: 'i do not only commit myself — in making art — to one option' (1129).[11] Rühm characterized his own oeuvre as follows: 'radical thinking, thinking things through the end, has always attracted me because only imaginary endpoints truly motivate' (1124).[12]

Whereas it could be argued that the single sound functions in the composer Anton Webern's (1883–1945) music as an elementary unit, one can refer — in the words of Michael Lentz (2000: 771, 792) — to Rühm's spoken texts as 'reduction models' or 'sound poetry of reduction'. However, the idea of authenticity remained of crucial importance to Rühm and his work. He intended not to write 'simulated, but rather authentic' because he worked 'with the concrete material language' (Lentz 2000: 1128).[13] Rühm observed:

> concrete poetry just simply denotes composing poetry, which works with the concrete material language. in the field of language, this work is possible in two ways: on the one hand, the material — in spoken language — is the voice, and on the other hand, the material — in written language — is the handwriting, typewriters type or block letter. usually, one can indisputably determine what a visual and what an auditory text is. (Lentz 2000: 1128)[14]

Terminological clarity matters to the writer, while many artists still use the term *concrete poetry* rather loosely. Rühm said: 'i think that one truly has to differentiate between the comprehension of visual poetry per se and visual concrete poetry' (Lentz 2000: 1129).[15] Indeed, his many poetological texts fully demonstrate that Rühm is not only a practitioner but also an important theoretician of poetry.

After World War II, the scepticism towards language and the desire for its radical change — emerging from the damage of language under the threat of Nazism as well as from its violation by modern civilization — undoubtedly found their most radical realization in diverse ways of experimental writing, and unquestionably their momentous expression in the field of concrete poetry (see Rühm 2005, I.II: 1175–76). Consequently, representatives of experimental lyrical poetry could take up partially pre-war traditions as writers of traditional hermeneutic poetry did. In fact the labels *concrete*, *experimental*, and *avant-garde* often got mixed up. For the most part, they were used temporarily and served as keywords for an approximate comprehension.

Rühm's work certainly belongs to traditions of the literary avant-garde in general, rather than to the specific developments of the neo-avant-garde in the 1960s. He did not search primarily for answers to contemporary avant-garde questions. His artistic intention was in this respect mostly experimental and conceptual. He considered new artistic possibilities in the idea of reduction and regarded the emphasis on material as a new resulting potential (see Fisch 2016: 95–147). The writer himself preferred the term *conceptual* in order to distance himself from experiments in the natural sciences. What is more, he fundamentally questioned the notion of *experiment*. He was also favourable to Oswald Wiener's approach: 'art was experimental because the varied impact on others and especially on myself could have been the subject of observations which could allow for hypothesis regarding underlying mechanisms' (Fetz and Matt 1998: 23).[16]

Many readers and recipients still regard genre transgressions by experimentally working poets as a provocation. Consequently, they often contest the mere idea that poetical creations of experimental writing — concrete poetry in particular — can be seen as genuine poems at all. By contrast, Ernst Jandl (1999: 46–47) pleaded in 1969 for a more open perspective on the category *poem*: 'One can margin the term of poem through aesthetic taste and previous manifestations of the poem in general [...]; one can also keep it open at any time in favour of the unpredictability of the ever-changing poem.'[17] According to Ernst Jandl, it was unacceptable to approach experimental poetry with traditional expectations. The reader should unconditionally be open to experimental ways of writing or at least recall their specific tradition.

Most experimental post-war poets referred to their own poetic compositions as concrete poetry. This concept of experimental poetry — which Eugen Gomringer described as 'a well-known concept which is obliged to nothing at all' — was emphatically rejected by some poets despite their use of the term 'concrete poetry' which was problematized by internal contradictions. Therefore, Gomringer (1991: 6) said: 'Who wants to accept that you should not also work experimentally.'[18] Even Jandl, although he himself used the term 'experimental poetry' and spoke of 'the modern experimental world poetry' in 1966, considered its peculiarity as concrete only when 'it realizes possibilities within language and creates subjects out of language' (1999: 12).[19]

Generally speaking, concrete poetry manifested itself through a diversified range of methodological poetic options between the poles of reduction and genre transgression. Reduction can entail destruction of syntax, subversion of semantics, concentration on fundamental linguistic structures, poetic calculation, release from image and metaphor, disclosure of rhyme, meter, line, and so forth. Transgressing genres can result in visualization of the text (ideogram), modification of text images (typogram), typographic dissolution of textual contexts (pictogram), acoustic alteration and interpretation (sound poem), internal textual correspondences (palindrome), and so on.

Linguistic surface contexts can be destroyed both in the case of reduction and genre transgression, whenever language turns into its own subject by means of written, visual, and acoustic signs. The conventional communicative character of language then resolves and changes in the middle of the process of its own resolution. It constitutes itself in the new creation within unusual contexts. Simultaneously, also the medium of poetry enlarges audiovisually (Fisch 2010: 13–14). Instances of Rühm's creations are labelled as 'concrete poetry' ('konkrete poesie'; Rühm 2005, I.I: 7–121), 'constellations and ideograms' (konstellationen und ideogramme) from 1954 to 1964, 'visual poetry' ('visuelle poesie'; Rühm 2006) and 'visual texts' ('visuelle texte'; Rühm 1962b), 'auditory poetry' ('auditive poesie'; Rühm 2013) and 'prose texts' ('prosatexte'; Rühm 2020).

3. Reception

Paul de Vree

As a prominent spokesman of all kinds of (post-)experimental poetry — and, more broadly speaking, also of numerous neo-avant-garde literary and artistic practices — Paul de Vree was appreciated particularly in his own circles. The main monographs about his work were in fact written by intimate friends and colleagues: Henri Floris Jespers (1977), a lifelong friend and collaborator of *The Round Table*, and the Dutch concrete artist Ton Luiting (1971). His advocates praised his open-mindedness and his eagerness to gain familiarity, both theoretically and practically, with all kinds of innovative approaches to language and image. Moreover, De Vree had a formidable network, within the Belgian context but especially abroad. In fact, his creations have been selected for anthologies of visual poetry all over the world.

Reviews of particular poetry books tried to articulate De Vree's importance mostly by situating his work within the context of the neo-avant-garde, often taking recourse to the author's own essayist terminology. In his earlier years (till the end of the 1960s), especially the German context of concrete poetry was foregrounded, using also ideas from international scholars such as Siegfried Schmidt, Klaus Peter Dencker, and Max Bense. His audiopoems, on the other hand, were mainly associated with French poet Henri Chopin. However, when De Vree started to criticize the very principles of concrete poetry and opted for a more engaged position, his attention shifted towards the Italian scene. Apart from the positive reviews in most neo-avant-garde periodicals, however, De Vree's visual realizations were mostly neglected in more traditional literary circles.

Gerhard Rühm

Before 1967 and his first publication with an established publishing company (Rowohlt), Gerhard Rühm had already released more than 200 individual publications. His edition of the volume about the Wiener Gruppe (1967) and the following works *windows* (1968a) and *collected poems and visual texts* (1970, *gesammelte gedichte und visuelle texte*) collected individual texts from the past fifteen years of his productivity. When the writer was at the culmination of his career, he received his first literary award, the Austrian Honorary Award For Literature in 1976, when he was already 46 years old. One year later, he was honoured with the Karl-Szuka-Prize, which Rühm would receive again, almost four decades later, in 2015.

The fact that Rowohlt was interested in Rühm's work went back to the publisher's growing interest in all kinds of experimental texts. Among those were such writers as Friedrich Achleitner (1970), Konrad Bayer (1966), Elfriede Jelinek (1970), Friederike Mayröcker (1966; 1968; 1971), and Oswald Wiener (1969). Their works illustrate the broad range of conceptual writings printed by a publishing house commonly perceived as rather middle-class.

Rowohlt intended not only to promote a singular writer (in this case Gerhard Rühm) but rather to situate him in a flourishing environment of experimental working writers. In the end, seven quite distinct titles were released: *windows* (1968a), *collected poems and visual texts* (1970a), *the frogs and other texts* (1971, *die frösche und andere texte*), *message for the future. collected texts for speaking* (1988, *botschaft an die zukunft. gesammelte sprechtexte*), *travel nerves: theatrical events in five parts* (1989a, *reisefieber: theatralische ereignisse in fünf teilen*), *sex, anyway: chansons, romances, poems* (1990, *geschlechterdings: chansons, romanzen, gedichte*) and *text in space: a utopian novel* (1993, *textall: ein utopischer roman*).

4. Literary Practice

Paul de Vree

The poetical convictions sketched above bring us, finally, to Paul de Vree as a poet with his own preoccupations and his own merits. Regarding De Vree's literary production, the mid-1960s constitute once again a crucial period in his career, both quantitatively and qualitatively. Several publications confirm De Vree's longstanding literary career as a kind of artistic continuum; yet, at the same time, they focus on his modernist orientation and his unremitting avant-garde posture as well. A typical example of this double strategy is the small anthology which De Vree compiled himself in 1965 for the prestigious and canonizing series *The Poetic Heritage of the Low Countries* [Poëtisch Erfdeel der Nederlanden]. De Vree's booklet is already number 39 in the series. The anthology stresses both his canonized position and his impressive poetic career (also a decisive factor for the literary evaluation in those days and for the selection in this particular series as well). To this end, De Vree selects both some of his earliest and a number of his most recent poems. In fact, the anthology opens with some poems from his second poetry volume *The White Blowing* (1936a, *Het blanke waaien*) and it concludes with a few recent texts from his collection *Zimprovisations* (1936b, *Zimprovisaties*), which was published simultaneously with the anthology. Yet, this stress on a continuous oeuvre is supplemented by a sketch of permanent evolution and innovation. In fact, in the booklet De Vree divides his own career as a poet into three distinct periods, the last of which is assumed to begin in 1953, with the start of the periodical *The Round Table*. As a consequence, the rather traditional character of his early poetry, both thematically and formally, is contrasted with the modernist 'rupture', which is considered to be fundamental for his more recent work. In this respect, the booklet demonstrates not only a chronological overview but also a kind of teleological artistic project which culminates in the practice of *concrete poetry*.

As a matter of fact, although this avant-garde posture is at that time a still ongoing process, the final poems of the anthology clearly demonstrate De Vree's fascination with what can be called *sound* and *image*. Yet, because of the typographic limitations of the series, this explicitly neo-avant-garde move remains still rather allusive; on the whole, the visual dimension of his recent texts remains subsidiary to the use of written language. Perhaps the strongest indication of this orientation is the very title of the anthology, *h.eros.hima* (1965a), which defies all traditional clichés of romantic or generic titles. The reference to the traumatic events of the atomic bomb dropped in the Japanese city of Hiroshima contrasts with the romantic nature of most poetry (even that of the early poems in this book), which is supposed to deal with Eros. Even more symptomatically, the specific spelling alludes to De Vree's fascination with lettrism and, more in general, the possibilities of the visual sign. Both the strange typography and the contrast between war and love, Thanatos and Eros, constitute a direct echo of De Vree's earlier poetry volume, which had a similar title: *Pl.acid.amore* (1963).

This conscious attempt to radically expand the possibilities of the traditional literary medium is demonstrated more outspokenly in De Vree's next poetry books, *Explositives* (1966, *Explositieven*) and especially *Zimprovisations* (1968a). *Explositives* experiments with typography and the traditional poetic conventions by disseminating combinations of letters across the page, thus creating lettrist constellations which resemble graphs. The texts — which De Vree himself called 'mechanical poems' — were created by means of a simple type writer, by typing a few letters and subsequently extracting and re-entering the page into the machine in order to get the specific spatial effects. At first sight, the mere form of these letter constellations — chosen randomly and often hesitating between centripetal and centrifugal movements — constitutes its exclusive meaning, since the reader cannot recognize any existing words. Yet, a closer look — which is confirmed by the table of contents of *Explositives* — reveals that quite a number of these poems were originally created on the basis of an original word or word sequence — for instance 'love' (see Figure 1.4) or 'april in paris' (see Figure 1.5; also the title of a

FIG. 1.4. Paul de Vree, 'love' (1968a: 77, © erven Paul de Vree).

FIG. 1.5. Paul de Vree, 'april in paris' (1968a: 81, © erven Paul de Vree).

famous jazz composition by Charlie Parker which provided the inspiration for a famous poem by the Flemish experimental poet Hugo Claus).

Zimprovisations, on the other hand, definitely functions as a much more ambitious and much more comprehensive project. In this major book, which incorporates some texts from *Explositieven* as well, De Vree reflects on his own drastic evolution and anticipates, so to speak, his own future. This double movement, backwards and forwards into time, turns *Zimprovisations* into a crucial and very fascinating collection. The title itself is a non-existing word, a portmanteau word which brings together on the one hand the component 'zin' (referring to both 'sentence', the syntactic structure, and 'meaning', the semantic dimension of language), and on the other hand the notion of 'improvisations' ('improvisaties'). Hence, the very idea of intentionality, the conscious desire to communicate meaningfully, is linked to a kind of spontaneous, organic impulse or, to put it differently, written language is associated with the ways in which jazz musicians vary upon general schemes in order to realize a kind of 'constrained creativity' of their own.

Moreover, the use of the plural form in the title underlines De Vree's ambition to present to the public a very large variety of avant-garde texts, which could be subsumed under the general label of *concrete poetry*. More specifically, the texts in this volume are organized in six sections which obviously present different types of poetic experimentation: 'audio-visual poems', 'concrete poems', 'typograms', 'visual poems', 'explositives' and finally even 'texts' as such. Consequently, the overall book can be read in different ways: as a kind of musical or visual composition, consisting of several episodes (musical movements) or visual series, as an encyclopaedic catalogue, or even as a kind of narrative, which might then be linked to successive stages in De Vree's own poetic career.

The first section, entitled 'audio-visual poems', explores the multiple possibilities of visual language to evoke a kind of complex soundscape. Various typographical means (from the use of specific fonts to the spatial organization of the text) suggest auditory dimensions, such as changes in speed, intonation, tone or intensity. As a matter of fact, several texts can nowadays be listened to on UbuWeb in order to get a better idea of De Vree's use of sound technology.

The next sections of *Zimprovisations* investigate primarily the complex graphic and spatial dimensions of the poetic text. In a number of cases, the written message still prevails. Yet, some elements are clearly meant to intensify and to deconstruct the common use of language as a communication medium, which conveys meanings in an entirely transparent manner. To this end, firstly, the traditional poetic form is dispersed and destroyed in several ways, for instance by scattering the lines across the page, by suggesting repetitions and variations typographically, by using different fonts and type sizes. Secondly, and even more importantly, De Vree expands the idea of a national and natural language by exploiting multilingualism (a practice which in some respects resembles the ideas of the Wiener Gruppe), thus generating multiple effects. He demonstrates the absence of fixed boundaries in the case of literary language and turns the ideology of particular national languages into an international melting pot. At the same time, the poet also produces all kinds of magical and incantatory effects of sound, thereby experimenting with the idea of a unique 'literary language' (see e.g. the poem 'kids' — Figure 1.6). The same dynamics of linguistic destruction and creation is to be found in numerous other neo-avant-garde manifestations in the same period.

In other poems, however, the traditional conception of poetry is almost entirely abandoned in favour of a graphic constellation. Some texts tie in with the international practice of concrete poetry, using geometric graphs or pictures which may be seen as iconic representations of the meaning of the printed words. For instance, a wall consisting of solely the phrase 'een steen' [a brick/stone] — playing also on the partial homophony of the indefinite determiner 'een' and the noun 'steen' — is rather self-evident and by no means innovative, at least not from an international perspective (De Vree 1968a: 22). Other texts, however, already fully explore the complex attraction of the visual image, which even prevails over the linguistic message, although especially the interaction between both media seems at stake. The poem 'Eros' (see Figure 1.7), for instance, combines the concept of 'eros' with a labyrinth-like graph, which is explicitly linked to Greek mythology (suggested by the proper names Knossos, Tauros, Icaros, and Daidalos). Thus, a multi-layered artwork is constructed.

```
                    kids

        ki    kiki    ki    kiki    kidsss
        ki    kiki    ki    kiki    kidsss
                                    kidsss

                           i    like    kidsss
    here   ki    there    ki

                           kiddekidkidkidsss

    for their whywhy- ki
    what forfor- ki
    pourquoioioi-ki
    warumumum-      ki
    for thi-thi-things i    never can tell
                            never can tell
                                      well
                      i    never can tell
                            nevet can tell
                                      well
        ki    kiki    ki    kiki    kidsss
        ki    kiki    ki    kiki    kidsss
         i           i
                           like      kidsss

        kids kiddekid   kiddekid   kidkids
        kids kiddekid   kiddekid   kidkids
        kids kiddekid   kiddekid   kidkids
        kids kiddekid   kiddekid   kidkidsss
                                   kisses
                                   kisses
                                   kisses
```

FIG. 1.6. Paul de Vree, 'kids' (1979: 276, © erven Paul de Vree)

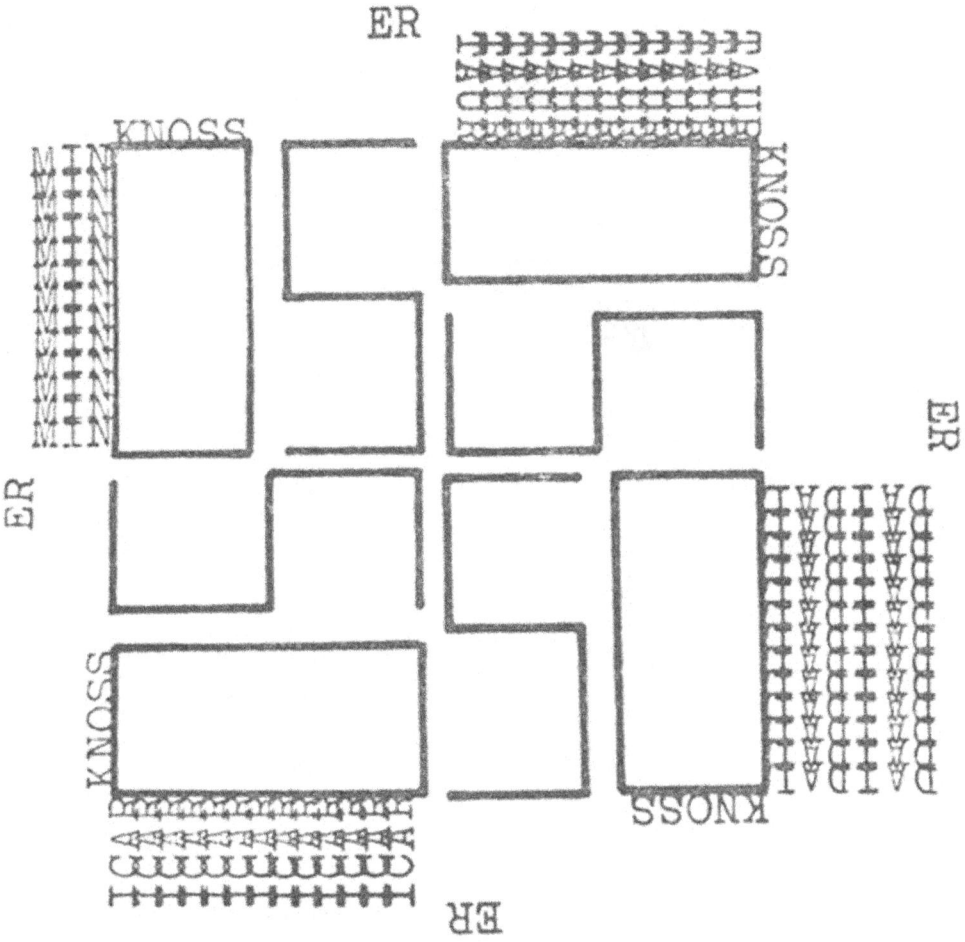

FIG. 1.7. Paul de Vree, 'Eros' (1968a: 59, © erven Paul de Vree).

FIG. 1.8. Paul de Vree, 'Revolutie' (1968a: 73, © erven Paul de Vree).

Finally, some texts already point at De Vree's further evolution in which the dimension of art and visuality will become more and more important. The most famous example is his classic poem 'Revolution' (see Figure 1.8), which is based on the permutation of the letters.

The circle refers to the etymological meaning of the Latin verb *revolvere* [turning], but also to the pessimistic (circular) outcome of most revolutions. In addition, the relative disintegration of the letters alludes to the radical process of dislocation, with which revolutions confront humanity. In short, by means of its graphic composition, this poem literally demonstrates how revolutions lead to drastic changes, and yet, in the end, most things remain recognizable.

The tension between revolutionary idealism and critical engagement on the one hand and relative pessimism on the other hand will become a dominant theme in De Vree's future career as a visual poet. Instead of his former explicit political and ideological 'neutrality' — without any doubt a reminiscence of his traumatic political involvement during the wartime period — , De Vree now

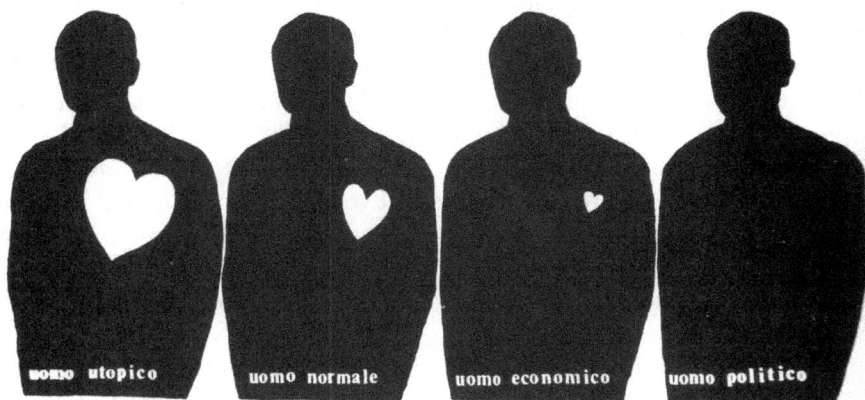

FIG. 1.9. Paul de Vree, 'Uomo' (1981: 17, © erven Paul de Vree).

advocates the full responsibility of writers and artists in a rapidly changing society. More specifically, he starts to criticize the artistic autonomy of (German) concrete poetry as being sterile and irresponsible and turns towards the Italian communist *poesia visiva*. Consequently, his later works demonstrate a prominence of the visual image as such, resulting in ingenious collages on the basis of photographic images, propaganda and advertisements (see e.g. 'Uomo', Figure 1.9).

Thus, the final shift in De Vree's career demonstrates once again his endless search for artistic fluidity and permanent experimentation, in an era which contests both the so-called modern autonomy of literature and the linguistic medium (a national language) literature used to be associated with.

Gerhard Rühm

Gerhard Rühm rejected all conventional literary decorum because he was convinced that all traditional genres — all epic narrative, lyric, and dramatic ways of writing, in short: every form of literary fiction — were completely outdated. Therefore, he developed new poetic methods which should guarantee that spaces of linguistic and aesthetic communication could be expanded and that the subject was reflected upon in the actual writing process. In 1982, he summarized these ideas as follows:

> as the overall artistic development stands now, it is illusory to ask whether we deal with poetry or rather music or graphic, with (mobile) plastics or (theatrical) action. we cannot determine the productions solely based on the range of material or expression. in fact, our interest concentrates on the issue of expression and mediation in general, the expansion of material and consciousness. (2)[20]

In its essence, Gerhard Rühm's work may be characterized as original. Yet, he was inspired by various Sturm-Expressionists and Dadaists. Texts by Franz Richard Behrens, Kurt Schwitters, August Stramm, Rudolf Blümner, Otto Nebel, and

Lothar Schreyer can indeed be seen as partial sources at the beginning of his career. Albert Soergel's *Contemporary Poetry and Poets: German Literature of the Previous Decades* (1911, *Dichtung und Dichter der Zeit: Eine Schilderung der deutschen Literatur der letzten Jahrzehnte* and his *Under the Spell of Expressionism* (1925, *Im Banne des Expressionismus*), Gottfried Benn's anthology *Poetry of the Expressionist Decade: From the Precursors to Dada* (1955, *Lyrik des expressionistischen Jahrzehnts: Von den Wegbereitern bis zum Dada*), and Carola Giedion-Welcker's *Anthology of the Eccentrics* (1965, *Anthologie der Abseitigen*) were also theoretical sources. Furthermore, it is equally important to mention French avant-garde poets such as Guillaume Apollinaire, Charles Baudelaire, and Stéphane Mallarmé, as well as English writers such as Samuel Beckett, James Joyce und Gertrude Stein, who also illustrate fundamental elements of Rühm's literary genealogy.

Expressionism, including its further developments and its diverse literary, musical, and artistic manifestations, was of crucial importance for Rühm. However, according to the writer's conception, a direct influence is hardly noticeable since poetry rather creates its own particular reality. Yet, Rühm also assumed that nothing stands on its own. Hence, he emphasized that loneliness does not actually exist. Loneliness illustrates rather a kind of fiction, based on a misunderstanding of the human communication system. Experiencing loneliness, standing alone in a room without a partner to communicate with, implies neglecting to observe images on the wall, the tree outside the window, or the dog running past outside. Indeed, it is possible to communicate with virtually anything. Unfortunately, humans have forgotten how to communicate:

> Gerhard Rühm's works illustrate possibilities of interpretation and communication in research of communication and perception mechanisms as well as sensibility for distinct sensual perception, in investigation of genre transgressions of passed on possibilities of expression and capacities of understanding. What you can unfold of your potential is in each case up to the recipient. (Fisch 2010: 61)[21]

In his seminal text 'Lyric Poetry and Society' (1957, 'Rede über Lyrik und Gesellschaft'), Adorno pointed out that (the theory of) poetry of the modern era faced problems which were unknown to ancient writers and theoreticians. These contemporary issues resulted from the alienation of the individual in society, reflected in the conception of poetry as restoring immediacy and therefore realizing the immediate expression of poetic subjectivity (see also Fisch 2016: 67–93):

> Nowadays, I assume that the prerequisite of that term 'poetry' — the individual expression, so to speak — appears to be profoundly shaken in a stage of crisis for the individual and, at diverse positions, it pushes the collective undercurrent of poetry upward. First of all, it pushes upward as a mere ferment of the individual expression. Later, perhaps, it does so as an anticipation of a certain condition positively surpassing absolute individuality. (Adorno 1974: 59)[22]

In his preface to the anthology of the Wiener Gruppe, Rühm (1967: 9) wrote: 'In our opinion, they represent the found, original tradition which our aspirations organically joined. Where should it continue, when it should not continue analogously at the endpoints?' Although in the early 1970s Rühm conceded that the

Dadaists' works had been based merely on 'the smashing and shaking' (1967: 10) of elements, he also highlighted their constructive efforts, which were convincingly present in Franz Richard Behrens's 'Blooming Blood' ('Blutblüte') and in Kurt Schwitters's 'Consistent Poetry' ('Konsequente Dichtung').[23]

During his Viennese period, Rühm performed his 'most compressed, a kind of "webernesque" poetic words that often cover only a few [...] sounds' (1967: 10).[24] These performances created his first explosive sound poems, which were exceedingly welcomed by Hans Carl Artmann, the inventor of a characteristically extended poetry. Additional expressive sound poems (among others, sound poems in the Viennese dialect) were recited at events that were organized by the literary cabaret of the Wiener Gruppe. In fact, the sound poems of Rühm's solo performances were often considered the highlight of the concert programme. Whenever Rühm discussed theoretical issues, he was aware of the historical manifestation of this special genre, which he has continued to practice till the present day: 'Creating sound poetry does by no means signify an end of poetic development, but rather it illustrates one of its most exciting and promising consequences. The discovery of sound poetry has only just started' (1967: 11).[25]

In Rühm's opinion, this project implied reducing poetry to a conglomerate of material and other enriching possibilities and options. In this context, he stated,

> that — at the turn of the century — a growing tendency towards the material aspect of language began to emerge and eventually was consciously manifested, and that writers started to treat the poetic material — words, syllables, sounds — similarly autonomously from purely artistic points of view (1968b: 22)[26]

Not only the isolated word, the single letter and paper have to be taken into account as 'essential materials' for writing poetry, but above all 'the single phonetic sound' (Rühm 1968b: 23).[27] As a consequence, language was not regarded as a superficial signifier; the activities of the Wiener Gruppe no longer concentrated on its practical value and its narrative use. Quite on the contrary, the verbal, visual and vocal material of language should function as a productive starting point, since poets should not create in a superficially thematic way, but rather 'substantially' (1967: 32).

Moreover, this implied that the individual material elements of language and its elementary relations should be valorized. Such intense considerations with regard to the form and the structure of language, its expressive possibilities and boundaries as well as its diverse procedures — through which language manifests itself as an autonomous reality — were seen as basic premises for a radical linguistic criticism. In other words, language should be dismantled as a formal structure demonstrating a normative and manipulative character. This materialization of language demonstrated a fierce rejection of a hierarchically structured linguistic world as well as of conventionalized, syntactic, and semantic-linguistic complex dependencies. Not only literature, sentences and words, syllables and letters were treated as material, but even linguistic sounds as such. For the same reason, Rühm favoured the use of lower-case letters. He stated: 'Language expresses itself by means of acoustic signs (sounds) and visual signs (scripture). Therefore, language operates with two completely distinct media.' (1965: 9).[28]

Like music, language manifests a sign system that can be completely detached from conceptuality, because the sign character of musical notation differs substantially from common linguistic signs. Significant forces — as well as sounds and letters — refer to something that remains absent. In the case of musical notation, they refer to non-present actions, since they indicate commands or instructions for actions which have to be performed by individual interpreters. Music is available mainly as a potential to concretize in the course of each interpretation.

Rühm presented in some of his creations his own musical notation, by dissolving notation elements from their original rehearsal contexts, subsequently transferring them to other contexts and eventually transforming their very essence of being. For instance, in the spoken text 'piece of music for one speaker' (1979, 'musikstück für einen sprecher'), the poet isolated the common international indications for sound volume, speed, and expression — the Italian musical expressions, so to speak — from their original musical context. Sonorous Italian terms were thus deprived of their original pragmatic function and used instead as linguistic-musical material for the so-called musical piece (Rühm 2013, III.I.: 117–30).

Moreover, Rühm felt the need to examine the reality of media not only as far as their communicative function is concerned, but also by treating their specific character as a means of expression. This consideration led to the 'material-related distinction between sounding and visual texts' (Rühm 1965: 10).[29] As a poetic consequence of this focus on the material aspect of the characters, Rühm, on the one hand, set typefaces and, on the other hand, devised sound compositions. In 1968, Rühm explained this strategy in detail:

These characters must not merely exist (as formative unnoticed medium for the purpose of a message), but they can even be set as a means of expression. signs have their own reality regardless of their communicative function: you are able to see or listen to them. if you completely remove them from the intention (only by means of their own material laws), typefaces or sound compositions arise. (1968b: 23)[30]

Thus, Rühm reached the conclusion that he would no longer accommodate acoustic texts or auditory texts to writing. Instead, he distinguished acoustic poetry (poetry for listening) from phonetic poetry (non-conceptual poetry) and he considered both as auditory poetry. Due to the fact that auditory texts can only be listened to, they were broadcast on the radio or distributed as audio tapes. 'The spoken word is', the author stated (1962a: 11), 'an entity of sounds (vowels) and noises (consonants) and furthermore, it signifies a conception', which was subsequently reduced in his sound compositions.[31]

Rühm characterized the material principles of spoken language — which served as a basis for the differentation of the 'speaker's intonation' (Rühm 1962a: 11) — as follows:

a) standard speaking voice (starting point),
b) speaking (roughly or precisely) on a specified tone pitch or (and) rhythmically fixed
c) singing voice[32]

Correspondingly, the following can be fixed or indicated:

a) tone pitch;

b) sound volume (stages from whispering to shouting, continual swelling and subsiding of the sound volume over listed distances);

c) tone length (duration of tolerating vowels and sonorous consonants;

d) speed (stages of temporarily fixed division of words, syllables or sounds up to summarizing greater passages in the course of one breath in which case rapid speaking speed was forced to become faster or slower over listed distances);

e) tone color (man, woman, child, harsh, soft, hoarse, falsetto, etc.);

f) expression. (Rühm 1962a: 12)[33]

Rühm always considered the possibility of changing voices via tape manipulations. The sound poem 'hymn to lesbians' (1956, 'hymne an lesbierinnen') made use of these in a radiophonic version which dated from twenty years later.[34] In the following quotation, the high awareness of the author with respect to the specific design potential becomes obvious:

> at
> at
> dat
> dat d
> d
> d
> u o ai
> i
> it
> it
> dit
> dit o
> o
> o
> u
> ui u
> ut
> ut
> dut ut d
> d d d d
> diu
> dju
> dj
> dj u
> dj o
> dj o a
> dj i
> dji
> j
> j
> jt
> jt
> .
>
> uk e

uk e
r
bup pu e
r
bup
r
rk
ä
blm
ä
blm
p blm
u rk
u rk
kr
blm
kr
blm
kr blm u
i h

.

in
in
in e
n
e
n n
in e n
en
en
ep
b ep
nb
np

bb
b

(Rühm 2013: 24–25, © Gerhard Rühm)

Gerhard Rühm integrated various musical parameters (which he knew very well as a composer and a pianist), such as speed, tone colour, pitch and sound volume into the overall composition of this sound poem. In his tone poems, Rühm experimented with the transfer of linguistic characters onto musical parameters. For example, in 'the life of chopin — for piano' (1982, 'das leben chopins — für clavier'), a biographical text was transformed into music by associating each letter of the alphabet to a specific sound on the keyboard. Each letter sounded in its own height; syllables formed connections. Rühm was particularly fascinated by the expressive content of speech sounds (Fisch 2010: 133). These musical parameters were directly expressive, because they articulated the emotional state of the articulating person.

Thus, according to the writer, the communicative character of the vocal gestures existed in their specific musical expression.

Rühm's phonetic poetry was also motivated emotionally, because the 'strong emotional participation in speaking blurs the border between sign and meaning [...]; the phonetic material stimulates expression, all the way to emotional identification with the wording' (Rühm 1989b: 130).[35] The author referred to speech that supports the emotional content of a combination of sounds as 'vocal gestures', which he considered meaningful, because 'they tell us something about the person and emotional state of the speaker.' (1989b: 130).[36] This immensely broad field of expression became of great importance, since Rühm attempted to take into account 'a specific expression of the human voice in different psychological moods and states of mind'. In his opinion, 'the match between construction — that is, truly conscious artistic work — and unconscious impulses' (Fisch 2010: 133), or linguistic gesture, articulated the aesthetic value of sound poetry.[37]

In short, Rühm's works are ultimately based on a deliberate attempt to break down normative and manipulative systems of conventional language and to stimulate a growing awareness — by means of the aesthetic dimension — for the perception of speech and pre-conceptual, extra-linguistic (even musical) forms of communication. At the same time, the musical version of speech sounds symbolized for him a transformation of 'what was limited nationally and defined ambiguously, and yet was subtly differentiated into the process.' Hence, it marked the 'transformation of the merely representative in presentation' (Rühm 1967: 130).[38] The musicalization of language provided for Rühm the actual aesthetic act by which linguistic signs are turned into direct sounds, which express what is actually meant.

5. Conclusion

This chapter has demonstrated the productivity of various forms of visual, auditory and concrete poetry during the 1960s. This neo-avant-garde dimension may even be considered the most innovative and international movement during that period. Its innovative potential is not restricted to the process of artistic creation, it is also realized in numerous essays and poetological statements. Yet, it remains difficult to speak of a homogeneous movement, with writers from different national traditions working together on the basis of shared principles and practices.

In fact, our confrontation of Gerhard Rühm and Paul de Vree has shown how, despite some obvious similarities, both writers experiment with the various layers of language and with multiple other media in their own way. For Rühm, these experiments can be seen as his 'natural' biotope, resulting in an impressive oeuvre which aims at new generic constellations, and the use of new media for poetry. In this respect, Rühm's lifelong career can be seen as a broad catalogue of what 'concrete poetry' can embody. In the case of De Vree, such experiments are the result of an evolution, which led the poet to abandon his former traditional premises in order to search for new ideas and new forms to express those in an optimal way. At the end of the 1960s, both authors have fully found their artistic destination.

Rühm opts for a broad realization of diverse kinds of literature, always looking for the border of traditional media and genres. De Vree, on the other hand, opts for an explicit political and societal involvement.

Yet, both writers remain attached very closely to the historical avant-garde. In fact, one could even state that this awareness of historical connections even dominates the connections with contemporary art and literature. In this respect, Rühm as well as De Vree may be considered as the real heirs of the avant-garde spirit.

Works Cited

ACHLEITNER, FRIEDRICH. 1970. *prosa, konstellationen, montagen, dialektgedichte, studien* (Reinbek bei Hamburg: Rowohlt)

ADORNO, THEODOR W., and ROLF TIEDEMANN. 1974. *Noten zur Literatur* (Frankfurt a/M: Suhrkamp)

BAYER, KONRAD. 1969 [1966]. *der sechste sinn: Roman*, ed. by Gerhard Rühm, expanded edn (Reinbek bei Hamburg: Rowohlt)

——. 1977 [1968]. *Das Gesamtwerk*, ed. by Gerhard Rühm (Reinbek bei Hamburg: Rowohlt)

——. 1992. *Theatertexte*, ed. by Gerhard Rühm (Frankfurt a/M: Verlag der Autoren)

——. 1996. *Sämtliche Werke*, ed. by Gerhard Rühm (Stuttgart: Klett-Cotta)

BENN, GOTTFRIED (ed.). 1995. *Lyrik des expressionistischen Jahrzehnts: Von den Wegbereitern bis zum Dada* (Wiesbaden: Limes)

BREICHA, OTTO. 1992. *Miteinander, Zueinander, Gegeneinander: Gemeinschaftsarbeiten österreichischer Künstler und ihrer Freunde nach 1950 bis in die achtziger Jahre* (Klagenfurt: Ritter)

DE VREE, PAUL. 1933. *Over den roman* (Langemark: Vonksteen)

——. 1936A. *Het blanke waaien* (Mechelen: De Bladen voor de Poëzie)

——. 1936B. *Hedendaagsche romanciers en novellisten* (Mechelen: De Eenhoorn)

——. 1938. *Een kringloop* (Antwerp: De Nederlandsche Boekhandel)

——. 1941. *Zang in de Landouw* (Antwerp: Die Poorte)

——. 1963. *Pl.acid.amore* (Antwerp: Ontwikkeling)

——. 1965A. *h.eros.hima* (Hasselt: Heideland)

——. 1965B. *Vlaamse avant-garde (1921–1964)* (Lier: De Bladen voor de Poëzie)

——. 1966. *Explositieven* (Antwerp: De Tafelronde)

——. 1968A. *Zimprovisaties* (Antwerp: De Tafelronde)

——. 1968B. *Onder experimenteel vuur: Transit documenta: Vade mecum voor de Vlaamse experimentele poëzie 1953–1967* (Bruges and Antwerp: De Galge)

——. 1968C. *Poëzie in fusie* (Lier: De Bladen voor de Poëzie)

——. 1979. *Verzamelde gedichten* (Bruges and Nijmegen: Gottmer/Orion)

——. 1981. *Paul de Vree* (Hasselt: Provinciaal Museum)

FETZ, WOLFGANG, and GERALD MATT (eds). 1998. *Die Wiener Gruppe* (Vienna: Kunsthalle Wien)

FISCH, MICHAEL. 2005. *Gerhard Rühm — Ein Leben im Werk 1954–2004: Ein chronologisches Verzeichnis seiner Arbeiten* (Bielefeld: Aisthesis)

——. 2008. 'Textkritische Überlegungen zu einer Ausgabe der Gesammelten Werke von Gerhard Rühm aus Anlass des ersten Bandes mit Gedichten', *Beihefte zu editio*, 29: 425–40

——. 2009. 'Die Landschaft ist die Sprache: Über Bedingungen und Möglichkeiten einer Ausgabe der Gesammelten Werke von Gerhard Rühm', in: *Beihefte zu editio*, 28: 153–60

———. 2010. *Ich und Jetzt: Theoretische Grundlagen zum Verständnis des Werkes von Gerhard Rühm und praktische Bedingungen zur Ausgabe seiner Gesammelten Werke* (Bielefeld: transcript)

———. 2015. *Es kenne mich die Welt, auf dass sie mir verzeihe: Aufsätze zu Adelbert von Chamisso (1781–1838), Paul Ernst (1866–1933) und Hubert Fichte (1935–1986)* (Berlin: Weidler)

———. 2016. *Wer wusste je das Leben recht zu fassen: Aufsätze zu Johann Wolfgang von Goethe (1749–1832), Sigmund Freud (1856–1939) und Paul Celan (1920–1970)* (Berlin: Weidler)

———. 2020. *Wer die Schönheit angeschaut mit Augen: Aufsätze zu Gotthold Ephraim Lessing (1729–1781), August von Platen (1796–1835) und Ernst Jünger (1895–1998)* (Berlin: Weidler)

GIEDION-WELCKER, CAROLA (ed.). 1965. *Anthologie der Abseitigen* (Zürich: Schifferli)

———. 2020. *Wer die Schönheit angeschaut mit Augen: Aufsätze zu Gotthold Ephraim Lessing (1729–1781), August von Platen (1796–1835) und Ernst Jünger (1895–1998)* (Berlin: Weidler)

GOMRINGER, EUGEN (ed.). 1991. *Konkrete Poesie: Deutschsprachige Autoren* (Stuttgart: Reclam)

HANDKE, PETER. 2007. *Meine Ortstafeln. Meine Zeittafeln. 1967–2007* (Frankfurt a/M: Suhrkamp)

———. 2015. *Tage und Werk. Begleitschreiben* (Frankfurt a/M: Suhrkamp)

HAUER, JOSEF MATTHIAS. 1920. *Vom Wesen des Musikalischen: Ein Lehrbuch der atonalen Musik* (Leipzig: Waldheim-Eberle)

JANDL, ERNST, and KLAUS SIBLEWSKI. 1999. *Autor in Gesellschaft: Aufsätze und Reden* (Munich: Luchterhand)

JELINEK, ELFRIEDE. 1970. *wir sind lockvögel baby!* (Reinbek bei Hamburg: Rowohlt)

JESPERS, HENRI-FLORIS. 1977. *Paul de Vree* (Antwerp: De Nederlandsche Boekhandel)

LENTZ, MICHAEL. 2000. *Lautpoesie und Lautmusik nach 1945: Eine kritisch-dokumentarische Bestandsaufnahme*, 2 vols (Vienna: Selene)

LICHTENFELD, MONIKA. 1964. *Untersuchungen zur Theorie der Zwölftontechnik bei Josef Matthias Hauer* (Regensburg: Bosse)

LUITING, TON. 1971. *Paul de Vree* (Bruges: Orion/Desclée De Brouwer)

MAYRÖCKER, FRIEDERIKE. 1966. *Tod durch Musen: Poetische Texte*, afterword by Eugen Gomringer (Reinbek bei Hamburg: Rowohlt)

———. 1968. *Minimonsters Traumlexikon: Texte in Prosa*, afterword by Max Bense (Reinbek bei Hamburg: Rowohlt)

———. 1971. *Fantom Fan* (Reinbek bei Hamburg: Rowohlt)

RÜHM, GERHARD. 1957. 'über das experiment in der modernen dichtung', in *Neue Wege: Kulturzeitschrift junger Menschen* 123: 10

———. 1958. 'wortgestaltung — lautgestaltung', in *Programmblatt der Galerie Würthle in Wien vom 20. bis 30. Mai 1958*

———. 1962A. 'grundlagen des neuen theaters', *Der Aufbau*, 4–5: 5–8

———. 1962B. *visuelle texte* (Ulm: studio f)

———. 1965. 'der neue textbegriff', *diskus*, 2: 9

——— (ed.). 1967. *Die Wiener Gruppe. Achleitner, Artmann, Bayer, Rühm, Wiener: Texte, Gemeinschaftsarbeiten, Aktionen* (Reinbek bei Hamburg: Rowohlt)

———. 1968A. *fenster. texte* (Reinbek bei Hamburg: Rowohlt)

———. 1968B. 'lyrik heute' in *Kolloquium Poesie 1968: Dokumentation*, ed. by Peter Weiermair (Innsbruck: Allerheiligenpresse), pp. 7–11

———. 1970A. *Gesammelte Gedichte und visuelle Texte* (Reinbek bei Hamburg: Rowohlt)

———. 1970B. 'zu meinen auditiven texten', in *Neues Hörspiel. Essays, Analysen, Gespräche*, ed. by Klaus Schöning (Frankfurt a/M: Suhrkamp), pp. 46–57

———. 1971. *die frösche und andere texte* (Reinbek bei Hamburg: Rowohlt)

———. 1972. 'mögliche erweiterung der konkreten poesie', in *Konkrete Poesie: Akten des Kolloquiums in Lille vom 4. bis 6. Mai 1972*, pp. 105–06

———. 1977. 'auditive poesie', in *kontextsound*, ed. by Michael Gibbs (Amsterdam: Stedelijk Museum), n.p.

—— (ed.). 1981. *Konrad Bayer Symposium Wien 1979* (Linz: Edition Neue Texte)

——. 1982. *Schriftzeichnungen 1956–1977* (Hannover: Zweitschrift)

——. 1983. 'Josef Matthias Hauer: Die andere Zwölftonmusik', *Falter: Wiener Programmzeitschrift*, 5: 9

—— (ed). 1985. *Die Wiener Gruppe: Achleitner, Artmann, Bayer, Rühm, Wiener. Texte, Gemeinschaftsarbeiten, Aktionen* (Reinbek bei Hamburg: Rowohlt)

——. 1988. *botschaft an die zukunft: gesammelte sprechtexte* (Reinbek bei Hamburg: Rowohlt)

——. 1989A. *reisefieber: theatralische ereignisse in fünf teilen* (Reinbek bei Hamburg: Rowohlt)

——. 1989B. 'Wiener Vorlesungen zur Literatur, zur Geschichte der Lautdichtung, der Wortkünstler Kurt Schwitters, Dichter und Dichtung des Sturms, Musiksprache und Bildmusik, intermediale Aspekte meiner Arbeit', *Wespennest*, 74: 107–34

——. 1990. *geschlechterdings: chansons, romanzen, gedichte* (Reinbek bei Hamburg: Rowohlt)

——. 1993. *textall: ein utopischer roman* (Reinbek bei Hamburg: Rowohlt)

——. 1996. *Visuelle Poesie: Arbeiten aus vier Jahrzehnten* (Innsbruck: Haymon)

——. 2005–10. *Gesammelte Werke*, ed. by Michael Fisch in 10 vols — vol. I.I and I.II: *gedichte* (2005); vol. II.I: *visuelle poesie* (2006); vol II.II: *visuelle musik* (2006); vol. III.I: *auditive musik* (2013); vol. III.II: *radiophone poesie* (2016); vol. IV.I: *prosatexte* (2020); vol. IV.II: *bildgeschichten* (2019); vol. V: *theaterstücke* (2010). Not yet published are vols VI.I and VI.II: *tondichtungen, klavierstücke*; vol. VII: *melodramen, lieder, chansons*; vol. VIII.I and VIII.II: *bildnerische arbeiten*; vol. IX: *theoretische schriften*; and vol. X: *nachträge* (Berlin: Matthes und Seitz)

SOERGEL, ALBERT. 1911. *Dichtung und Dichter der Zeit: Eine Schilderung der deutschen Literatur der letzten Jahrzehnte* (Leipzig: Voigtländer)

——. 1925. *Im Banne des Expressionismus* (Leipzig: Voigtländer)

WIENER, OSWALD. 1969. *Die Verbesserung von Mitteleuropa* (Reinbek bei Hamburg: Rowohlt)

Notes to Chapter 1

1. 'Gerhard Rühm suchte sein Heil in Versuchen, aus der graphischen Anordnung von Wörtern zu neuen Bildern zu kommen, wobei er freilich eine konventionelle Grundhaltung nicht mehr verbergen konnte.'

2. 'Es wird nämlich verkannt, dass die Literatur mit der Sprache gemacht wird, und nicht mit den Dingen, die mit der Sprache beschrieben werden.'

3. 'Ich erwarte von der Literatur ein Zerbrechen aller endgültig scheinenden Weltbilder.'

4. 'der freundliche kontakt zwischen den ehemaligen gruppenmitgliedern ist nach dem tod bayers keineswegs abgebrochen, er intensivierte sich sogar in berlin zeitweise wieder zu engerer zusammenarbeit in einer neuen, lockeren gruppierung, die nun vor allem dieter roth und günter brus mit einschloss.'

5. 'Het tijdperk van Gutenberg loopt ten einde. [...] Alleszins zal men de taal de ruimte moeten geven voor pikturale, muzikale en kinetische waarden, haar ontkoppelen van de afgesproken betekenis, haar aanpassen aan het technisch levensgevoel, want, laat ons niet vergeten, zonder het integreren van de mechanische middelen zal zich de poëzie op universeel en demokratisch vlak mettertijd moeilijk handhaven.'

6. Rühm wrote this poem as early as 1964, but it was not published until 1970. The date in the final line refers to the death of Konrad Bayer. In the edition of the collected works, a revised version of the text is to be found, with slight visual alterations as well (2005, I.I: 111).

7. 'Sprachklang und Artikulation, Konzept und Akustik, Stimmmerkmale und auditive Parameter, Ausdrucksgestus und Intonationsschemata von besonderer Bedeutung.'

8. 'unter dem sammelbegriff auditive texte stelle ich den sprechtexten, die zum vortrag bestimmt, also live-texte sind, die reinen tonbandtexte gegenüber, die bis ins kleinste detail genau fixiert sind. hier gibt es für einen interpreten insofern keinen spielraum mehr, als seine stimme zwar auf band aufgenommen, dann aber nur noch als material behandelt, das heisst nach einer strengen partitur (meist auf millimeterpapier) mit den technischen möglichkeiten des studios verarbeitet wird.'

9. 'vom heutigen standpunkt aus gesehen, würde ich sagen, dass die möglichkeiten der reinen lautdichtung inzwischen weitgehend erkundet sind, was natürlich nicht bedeutet, dass da nichts bemerkenswertes mehr zu machen wäre. ich unterscheide zwischen absoluter lautdichtung und klangdichtung im weiteren sinne noch viel konsequenter'.

10. 'als pendant zur visuellen poesie eine form der visuellen musik entwickelt'

11. 'ich lege mich nicht auf nur eine möglichkeit, kunst zu machen, fest.'

12. 'radikales denken, zu-ende-denken, hat mich immer angezogen, denn nur scheinbare endpunkte führen wirklich weiter'

13. 'eben nicht simuliert, sondern authentisch' [...] 'mit dem konkreten material sprache'

14. 'konkrete poesie heißt ganz einfach eine dichtung, die mit dem konkreten material sprache arbeitet. In der sprache ist das auf zweierlei weise möglich: zum einen, in gesprochener sprache, ist das material die stimme, zum anderen, in geschriebener sprache, ist das material die handschrift, die schreibmaschinentype oder der druckbuchstabe. in der regel lässt sich eindeutig bestimmen, was ein visueller und was ein auditiver text ist.'

15. 'ich meine, man muss klar abgrenzen, was man unter visueller poesie schlechthin und visueller konkreter poesie versteht.'

16. 'Die Kunst war experimentell, weil die variierte Wirkung auf andere und vor allem auf mich selbst der Gegen- stand von Beobachtungen sein konnte, die Hypothesen über die zugrunde liegenden Mechanismen ermöglichen würden.'

17. 'Man kann den Begriff Gedicht durch Geschmacksurteile begrenzen, und durch die bisherigen Erscheinungsformen des Gedichts [...]; man kann ihn auch offen halten, jederzeit, für die Unvorhersehbarkeit des immer neuen Gedichts.'

18. 'wer möchte es auf sich ruhen lassen, nicht auch experimentell zu arbeiten.'

19. 'sie möglichkeiten innerhalb von sprache verwirklicht und gegenstände aus sprache erzeugt'

20. 'beim gegenwärtigen stand der gesamtkünstlerischen entwicklung ist es illusorisch zu fragen, ob es sich noch um dichtung oder schon musik oder grafik, um (mobile) plastik oder (theatralische) aktion handelt. die produktionen lassen sich nicht mehr auf einen material-, ausdrucksbereich festlegen. das interesse gilt vielmehr dem problem des ausdrucks und der vermittlung überhaupt, der material- und bewusstseinserweiterung.'

21. 'In der Erforschung von Kommunikations- und Wahrnehmungsmechanismen wie auch in der Sensibilisierung für differenziertere sinnliche Wahrnehmung, in der Erkundung von Grenzbereichen tradierter Ausdrucksmöglichkeiten und Verstehenskapazitäten stellen Gerhard Rühms Arbeiten Interpretations- und Kommunikationsangebote dar. Was sie von ihrem Potenzial entfalten können, liegt jeweils am Rezipienten selbst'.

22. 'Heute, da die Voraussetzung jenes Begriffs von Lyrik, von dem ich ausgehe, der individuelle Ausdruck, in der Krise des Individuums bis ins Innerste erschüttert scheint, drängt an den verschiedenen Stellen der kollektive Unterstrom der Lyrik nach oben, erst als bloßes Ferment des individuellen Ausdrucks selbst, dann aber doch auch vielleicht als Vorwegnahme eines Zustandes, der über bloße Individualität positiv hinausgeht.'

23. 'für uns repräsentierten sie die aufgefundene, eigentliche tradition, der sich unsere bestrebungen organisch anschlossen. wo soll es weitergehen, wenn nicht sinngemäß bei den endpunkten'

24. 'das Zertrümmern und Durcheinanderrütteln'

25. 'die lautdichtung ist für mich nicht das ende einer poetischen entwicklung, sondern eine ihrer aufregendsten und viel versprechendsten konsequenzen. ihre eigentliche entdeckung hat eben erst begonnen.'

26. 'dass um die jahrhundertwende sich eine zunehmende hinwendung zum materialen aspekt der sprache abzuzeichnen begann und sich schliesslich bewusst manifestierte' [...] 'man begann das dichterische material — wörter, silben, laute — ebenso autonom, sozusagen nach rein künstlerischen gesichtspunkten zu behandeln.'

27. 'der laut ist eben ein ganz wesentlicher materialaspekt der gesprochenen sprache.'

28. 'sprache äußert sich mittels akustischen zeichen (laute) und mittels optischen zeichen (schrift). sie bedient sich also zweier voneinander völlig verschiedener medien.'

29. 'materialbedingten unterscheidung zwischen ertönenden und sichtbaren texten'

30. 'diese zeichen müssen nicht bloß (als gestalt unbeachtetes mittel zum zweck einer mitteilung)

sein, sondern können selbst als ausdrucksmittel gesetzt werden. zeichen haben unabhängig von ihrer mitteilungsfunktion eine eigene realität: man sieht sie oder hört sie. löst man sie von begriffsinhalten völlig los (ausschliesslich ihren eigenen materialien gesetzmässigkeiten folgend), entstehen schriftbilder oder lautkompositionen'.

31. 'ein gebilde aus klängen (vokale) und geräuschen (konsonanten) und bedeutet darüber hinaus einen begriff'

32. 'a) normale sprechstimme (ausgangsbasis), b) sprechen auf (ungefähr oder genau) bestimmter tonhöhe oder (und) rhythmisch fixiert, c) gesangsstimme.'

33. 'a) tönhohe; b) lautstärke (stufen von flüstern bis schreien, kontinuierliches an- und abschwellen der lautstärke über angegebene strecken); c) tonlänge (dauer des aushaltens der vokale und klingenden konsonanten); d) tempo (stufen von zeitlich fixierter trennung der worte, silben oder laute bis zur zusammenfassung größerer passagen unter einem atem, wodurch rasche sprechtempi erzwungen werden, kontinuierliches schneller oder langsamer werden über angegebene strecken); e) klangfarbe (mann, frau, kind, rauh, weich, heiser, fistelnd usw.); f) ausdruck.'

34. In fact, this sound poem, written in 1956, was performed for the first time in Café Gepler in Berlin on 13 March 1966. It was produced and broadcast by the Hessische Rundfunk (radio) on 3 April 1975.

35. 'starke emotionale beteiligung am sprechen die grenze zwischen zeichen und bedeutung verwischt [...] das phonetische material reizt zur ausdrucksgebung bis hin zur emotionalen identifikation mit dem wortlaut'

36. 'sie sagen etwas über person und gestimmtheit des sprechers aus.'

37. 'das Spiel zwischen Konstruktion, also ganz bewusster künstlerischer Arbeit und unbewussten Impulsen'

38. '[...] des national begrenzten, des definierten ins vieldeutige und zugleich feiner differenzierte, ins prozessuale' [...] 'verwandlung des bloß repräsentierenden in präsentation'

CHAPTER 2

❖

The Winding Roads of the Abstract and the Concrete: Helmut Heißenbüttel and Mark Insingel

Lars Bernaerts (Ghent University) &
Johanna Bohley (Friedrich-Schiller-Universität Jena)

When, at the end of the 1960s, the Flemish author Mark Insingel (born 1935) submitted the manuscripts of two experimental works — one book of prose, one book of poetry — his publisher mentioned the work of the German writer Helmut Heißenbüttel (1921–1996), an author he believed Insingel would definitely be interested in. A few weeks later, Insingel received a 'package of thin, white, album-shaped books' (Insingel 2004b: 145),[1] Heißenbüttel's *Textbücher 1–6* (1960–1967). Insingel describes the discovery of Heißenbüttel's work as an invaluable moment (Insingel 2014). His enthusiastic response was no surprise to anyone — like his publisher — who was familiar with the work of both writers. The two authors, who eventually met in Amsterdam following an invitation from the Dutch author Sybren Polet, have a lot in common: an avant-gardist attitude, a reputation of being writerly writers, an interest in experimental authors such as Gertrude Stein, an innovative approach to genre, a taste for the abstract, a focus on linguistic materiality and a view of the human subject as a 'bundle of language habits' ('ein Bündel Redegewohnheiten'; Heißenbüttel 1995: 233). Still, their oeuvres follow their own paths and diverge on several points.

This chapter discusses such parallels and divergences in the work and careers of Heißenbüttel and Insingel. The first part of the chapter is devoted to introducing the two authors. In a few lines, we aim to draw a precise portrait of their oeuvre, their poetology, and the reception of their work. In the second part of the chapter, we will consider three fields where the confrontation between the two experimental oeuvres is particularly illuminating: linguistic (and visual) repetition plus variation as an experimental technique; the writers' approach to genre and more generally to the text as a model; literary abstraction and concreteness. In these three domains, which we may characterize in general terms as *technique*, *genre*, and *style*, striking parallels and meaningful differences allow us to shed new light on the neo-avant-garde projects of Heißenbüttel and Insingel in the late 1960s and early 1970s, the period in which their paths as writers cross. Developing their own signature style and poetics in that period both authors revitalize the tradition of the avant-garde rather than simply institutionalising it in their own practice.

1. Context and Background: Separate Lives, Related Views

Heißenbüttel: Biographical Context and Literary Developments[2]

Helmut Heißenbüttel was born on 21 June 1921 in Rüstringen near Wilhelmshaven. He returned from World War II as a war invalid in 1941 and studied architecture, followed by German and art history, in Dresden, Leipzig, and Hamburg. Heißenbüttel is considered a key representative and theoretician of experimental literature and the neo-avant-garde in West Germany, especially for the circle around the philosopher Max Bense called the Stuttgart School [Stuttgarter Schule]. His major works include his *Textbooks (Textbücher)* and *Projects (Projekte,* 1970–1980), among which is his antinovel *D'Alembert's End (D'Alemberts Ende,* 1970).

From 1954 to 1957, he worked as a literary editor and advertising manager at the publishing house Claassen in Hamburg. On 1 April 1957 he became an editorial assistant at the Süddeutsche Rundfunk in Stuttgart, at Alfred Andersch's instigation, and shortly after became the head of the 'radio-essay' editorial department. Until his retirement in 1981, he worked as a radio producer and created an ambitious and varied third radio and culture channel. In this capacity, he promoted young authors and introduced the popular radio programme 'Autoren-Musik'. He also worked as a literary critic in newspapers and magazines. As an active member of Gruppe 47, Heißenbüttel also participated in countless conferences, but did not get involved in the debates. Instead, he used his notes taken during the Gruppe 47 conference in Sigtuna to compile the text 'Group Criticism' ('Gruppenkritik'), which is intended as a rondo and makes an ironic statement about the literature industry.[3]

Heißenbüttel's first poems are only available as typescripts to date. This is the case for the poetry collections *I Will Be a Note in Great Song (Ich werde Ton sein zu großem Gesang,* from the 1940s), *Stations (Stationen,* 1941–1951) and *Results (Resultate,* 1950–1952). The formally more traditional elegies such as 'War' ('Der Krieg') and 'Stations' are characterized by metre and rhyme. His first published poetry collection, *Combinations (Kombinationen,* 1954) was published on recommendation from Hermann Kasack by Bechtle Verlag in Esslingen in 1954, under the editorship of Kurt Leonhard. In this publication, Heißenbüttel emerges as the representative of a linguistically experimental avant-garde literature of post-war modernism in West Germany. The *Topographies (Topographien)* followed in 1956, initially with the working title *Catalogues (Kataloge)* and preceded by a quotation from Walter Benjamin: 'But when shall we actually write books like catalogues?'[4] The six large-format, white *Textbooks 1–6 (Textbücher 1–6),* published by Walter Verlag between 1960 and 1967, continued to propagate this concrete, materialistic concept of his work. Alongside neo-avant-garde publications that were usually isolated and, with the exception of Max Bense's *red series (reihe rot),* less prominent in the public eye, they were considered the prime example of experimental literature in 1960s West Germany. Incidentally, Heißenbüttel's popularity curve always reflected the role played by avant-garde aesthetics in the literary field (Friedrich 2011: 364).[5] The *Textbooks* were republished as paperbacks in two later collections, although not in the original order but in a selection from the *Textbooks* entitled *The Textbook* (*Das Textbuch*), published by Luchterhand and Walter Verlag in 1970 and by Klett-Cotta Verlag in 1980.

Heißenbüttel's activity as a literary critic and theorist was closely entwined with his writing. As a critic, theoretician, and poet, he published his work in numerous journals such as *Akzente*, *Du*, *Die Horen*, *Magnum*, *Merkur*, *Der Monat*, *Jahresring*, *Kritisches Jahrbuch*, *Text und Kritik*, *Texte und Zeichen*, and *Theater heute*. His work was also represented in experimental and political journals including *Alternative*, *Augenblick*, *Diskus*, *Schreibheft*, and the *Streit-Zeit-Schrift*.

From the 1960s onwards, the Stuttgart School around Max Bense at Stuttgart Technical University was committed to designing a literature of the future using methods based on information aesthetics. Heißenbüttel also participated in this project, but developed a more individual, subjective poetology that thus came to oppose the characteristically technical information aesthetics. A genuine connection with the Stuttgart School could be found in Heißenbüttel's preoccupation with Gertrude Stein.

Heißenbüttel's work is in dialogue with the Stuttgart School and his methodological collage texts, with their focus on numbers, can indeed be compared to cybernetic programming. However, he does not occupy the role of an ideologist or champion of information aesthetics in the West German neo-avant-garde, instead maintaining a critical, questioning distance to both the formation of the group and to literature as an object and material. When his adherence to the Stuttgart School is mentioned (see also Döhl et al. 2005), it is thus often qualified to allow for his particular role, as documented in Ludwig Harig's 'Group Exhibition' ('Gruppenaufstellung'):

> As I recall, Helmut Heißenbüttel was a similar figure in the Stuttgart School to Gorgias the sophist in *The School of Athens*, the famous painting by Raphael. The School of Athens as an allegory for the Stuttgart School: while Max Bense, as Plato and Aristotle in one, stands on the highest step, all the other concrete thinkers and poets to the left and right have taken up their positions beside pillars and columns: Döhl and Gomringer, Franz Mon and Ernst Jandl, Manfred Esser and Helmut Mader, and of course there I am myself on the stairs, below Bense, right next to Helmut Heißenbüttel, who is preparing to conduct a Heißenbüttel discourse. (1991: 72)[6]

Heißenbüttel generally conducted this discourse of his in the media, for instance when he appeared on the television programme 'Autor-Scooter'.

He provided introductions to numerous exhibitions of modern art, which he later published along with occasional poems as *Occasional Poems and Blurbs* (*Gelegenheitsgedichte und Klappentexte*, 1973). This unity of literary and critical activity also emerged in certain of his speeches about art, where the catalogue text and *Textbook* text are identical.

His concrete writing methods are based on a profound knowledge of literature. This is clarified by his theoretical works and literary criticism: the book *On Literature* (1995, *Über Literatur*) includes his publications from 1955 until 1964. The collection of essays *On the Modern Tradition* (*Zur Tradition der Moderne: Aufsätze und Anmerkungen 1964–1971*) brings together his essays and notes from 1964 to 1971 and was published by Luchterhand Verlag in 1972. *Of Flying Frogs, Libidinous Epics, Novels of the Fatherland, Speech Bubbles and Catchy Tunes* (*Von fliegenden Fröschen, libidinösen Epen, vaterländischen Romanen, Sprechblasen und Ohrwürmern*) was published by Klett Cotta Verlag in Stuttgart in 1982 as a collection of 13 essays.

Instead of a *Textbook 7*, 1970 saw the publication of *Project No. 1: D'Alembert's End* (*Projekt Nr. 1: D'Alemberts Ende*), with its overarching novelistic structure that unfolds through quotations and collages. It creates a panorama of West Germany in July 1968, containing quotations from newspapers such as *Der Spiegel* and *konkret*, but also mining Goethe's *Elective Affinities* (*Die Wahlverwandtschaften*) for material. Besides the narrative form and self-parody, this almost-novel functions as an intellectual dialogue. The parody is formally structured according to a recurrent 'carousel' structure that circles around itself. Inspirations for this formal text structure without a narrator included Marcel Reich-Ranicki's complaint that he was waiting for a novel that would begin like Goethe's novel, *Elective Affinities*. This inspired Heißenbüttel to transfer *Elective Affinities* to a present-day setting in 1968: 'Eduard — being the name of a radio producer in the prime of life — Eduard had been spending the best hour of a July afternoon (25 July 1968) on the Munich to Hamburg express (arr. Central Station 21:19) and looked with satisfaction at the area between Lüneburg and Harburg' (1970: 11).[7]

The four other *Projects* are more closely involved with the prose experiment, in the sense that they are paratextually aligned to the genres of the fairy tale and novella. Thus the *Projects* range from *Chopping the Cabbage: Thirteen Didactic Poems. Project no. 2* (1974, *Das Durchhauen des Kohlhaupts: Dreizehn Lehrgedichte. Projekt Nr. 2*), *Eichendorff's Downfall and other Fairytales. Project 3/1* (1978, *Eichendorffs Untergang und andere Märchen. Projekt 3/1*) and *If Adolf Hitler Hadn't Won the War: Historic and True Incidents. Project 3/2* (1979, *Wenn Adolf Hitler den Krieg nicht gewonnen hätte: Historische und wahre Begebenheiten. Projekt 3/2*) to *The End of the Alternative:. Simple Stories. Project 3/3* (1980, *Das Ende der Alternative:. Einfache Geschichten. Projekt 3/3*). Fifteen years after *Textbook 6*, Heißenbüttel returned to the idea of textbooks. Writing continued on the 'unclosable' text between poetry and prose, which he correspondingly defined as keeping the issue open. *Textbook 12* did not see the light of day. Helmut Heißenbüttel died on 19 September 1996 in Glückstadt after a series of strokes.

Insingel: Biographical Context and Literary Developments

Like Heißenbüttel, Insingel first published poetry in the 1950s which did not yet show the commitment to experimentation that was characteristic of his later work. Insingel was born as Marcus Donckers in 1935, making his debut as a published poet in 1956. The first two books contain traditional poetry, including conventional genres such as the sonnet and the ballad. The first volume under his pseudonym, which he calls his actual debut, was published in 1963 and is called *Driftwood* (*Drijfhout*). The choice of the name Insingel reflects his quest for a signature style and a personal poetics. In 1966, he published his first book–length work in prose, a collection of stories. From then on, prose and poetry alternate in his oeuvre, and sometimes reflect one another in terms of their theme, form and structure. In *Perpetuum mobile* (1969), *Models* (1970b, *Modellen*) and *Posters* (1974), he presents the concrete and visual poetry with which he has been associated ever since (see Figures 2.1 and 2.2). The novels *Reflections* (1968, *Spiegelingen*) and *A Course of Time* (1970a, *Een tijdsverloop*) from the same period are the counterparts to the poetry of *Perpetuum mobile* and *Models* respectively. By about that time, Heißenbüttel had already published his first six *Textbücher,* which reveal a number of similar preoccupations. Our analysis in the second part of this chapter will be centred on these pivotal works.

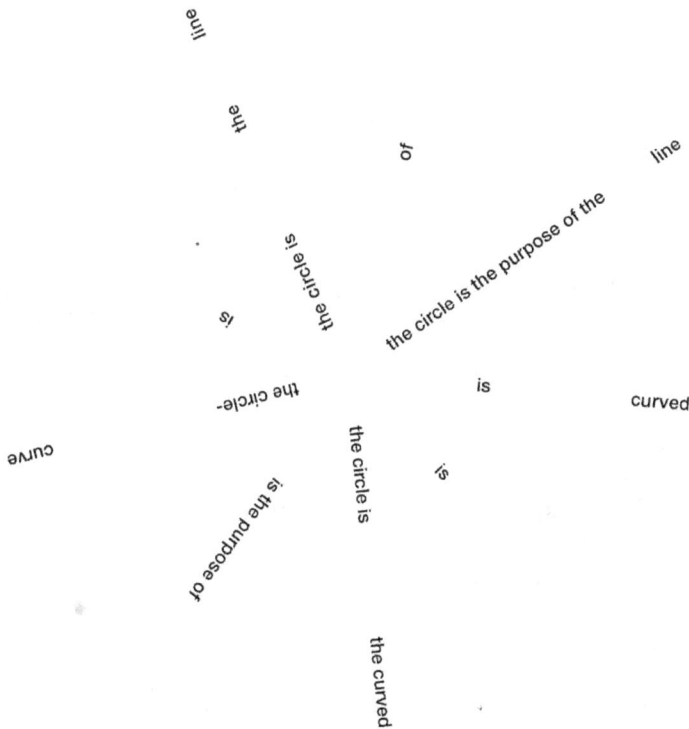

FIG. 2.1. Mark Insingel, 'the circle is the purpose of the line / is curved' (*Perpetuum mobile*, 1969, translation Willem Groenewegen, © Mark Insingel)

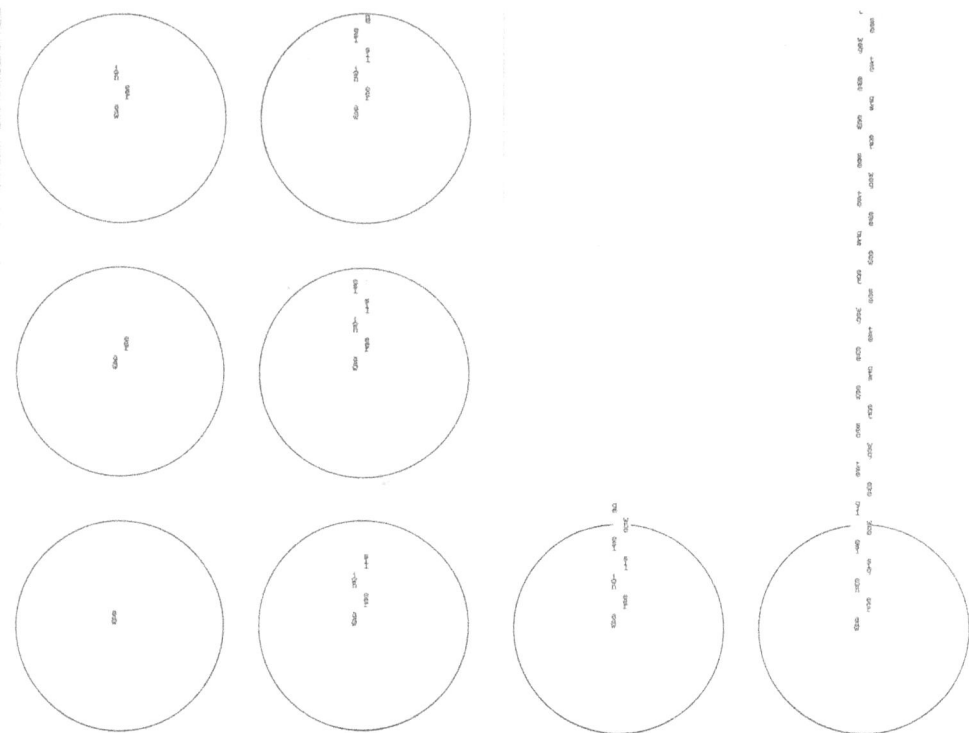

FIG. 2.2. Mark Insingel, 'Where there's a will where there is a way'
('Waar een wil is waar een weg is', Posters, 1974, © Mark Insingel)

Throughout his career, Insingel has published his work in major literary magazines of the Low Countries, especially in those with a progressive profile (e.g., *Raster*,
Revisor, *De Gids*), and also in more marginal, avant-garde periodicals (e.g., *Radar*,
Labris, *De Tafelronde*). He has never been an editor of a literary magazine himself,
unlike the prominent experimental Flemish and Dutch writers of his generation.
Equally in line with his reputation as an isolated poet, he rarely collaborates with
other writers either.[8] Still, he considers writing to be his profession and sole
occupation, and his praxis is geared to that: he is an active member of PEN (and
its treasurer from 1985 to 2001) and the Royal Academy for Dutch Language and
Literature.

In the 1970s he wrote a number of radio plays for the national radio station.
Remaining loyal to his poetics, these radiophonic pieces are among the rare
examples of Dutch-language experimental radio plays in the tradition of the
German 'neues Hörspiel', a new kind of radio drama. The parallel to Heißenbüttel's
literary innovation through radio is clear. Along with the prose text *That is To
Say* (1974, *Dat wil zeggen*), the texts for radio form the aural counterpart of his
visual texts. In the paratext of the blurbs, these two genres are labelled with the
German terms 'Hörtexte', texts to hear, and 'Sehtexte', texts to see. Insingel has also
occasionally written essays on commission, a selection of which are published in

Words are Places (1981, *Woorden zijn oorden*). The essays contain many explicit claims with respect to his poetics, as we will see.

Insingel's work has gained an international dimension through the translation of a number of titles into English and German. Moreover, his work was shown at an international exhibition of concrete poetry at the Stedelijk Museum Amsterdam (1970), which travelled to Antwerp, Stuttgart, Nuremberg, Liverpool, and Oxford. His work has also been represented at several small-scale exhibitions of concrete poetry, for example in the Institut Néerlandais in Paris (1975, curated by Paul De Vree). Furthermore, Insingel participated in poetry events with an international orientation. At Poetry International Rotterdam (1971), he met kindred spirits such as Ernst Jandl and Eugen Gomringer. In the margins of this event, Insingel performed with Jandl at Rotterdam Central Station (Van der Straeten and Van Imschoot 2017).

Though Insingel's literary practice has remained loyal to certain poetological principles throughout his career (see above), the early 1980s represent a transition in his oeuvre. In his continuing literary exploration of human relations and societal pressures, personal affects, which are implicit in the earlier experiments, move to the surface in poetry and novels written after 1980. This development is also apparent in his recent poetry, for example in the love poetry of *Nothing* (*Niets*, 2005) and *Something* (*Iets*, 2007). What remains constant in terms of technique is lexical and metaphorical sparseness and syntactic repetition and variation, for example in the poem 'They defend what they have' ('Ze verdedigen wat ze hebben') from *The Grapes Which Hang Too High* (1994a, *De druiven die te hoog hangen*). These procedures result in a circular structure and in a tension between the abstract and the concrete, as we will discuss in more detail below. What changes, however, is that autobiographical materials and the central psychological motifs of loneliness, shame, existential angst, and social anxiety are not as thoroughly abstracted as they were in earlier texts.

> They defend what they have.
> What do they have?
>
> They have what they think they have.
> What do they think they have?
>
> They defend what they think they have.
> What do they think?
>
> They think they defend.
> What do they think that they defend?
>
> They think they defend what they have.
> What do they have that they defend?
>
> (Insingel 1994a, trans. Willem Groenewegen,
> © Mark Insingel)

Insingel and Heißenbüttel were both born before the war, started publishing their major works in the 1960s, identifying with experimental authors and keeping in touch with them. Still, it would be misleading to construct strong parallels between their lives. In fact, the dividing lines between the two immediately are readily apparent: whereas Heißenbüttel, who is fifteen years older, is active and influential in networks of writers, Insingel insists upon his isolated position. This divergence will partly be confirmed in the discussion of their literary views, which will be our next step. Nonetheless, the next section will also show points of agreement on what really matters here: the nature and workings of literature.

2. Poetology

Heißenbüttel's Poetology

Heißenbüttel's defence of the experimental against Hans Magnus Enzensberger's accusations is well-known. He understood the literary experiment as a public test setting located between the abstract and the concrete:

> Experiment and experimental in the twentieth century really do mean a literature and poetry that try things out without being certain of their results. Their basic conception is as close to Bertolt Brecht's *Experiments* as to the opposition of the concrete and the abstract in visual art. (Heißenbüttel 1983: 3)[9]

The central reference parameter here was the work of Gertrude Stein (Kramer 1993), which Heißenbüttel discovered and read from the mid-1950s onwards. What fascinated him about Stein was the model of a concrete literature that defied traditional authorship and concepts of the work. Disassociating itself from the traditions of narrative literature, it did not claim any intellectual property for itself. Stein herself reduced this perspective to the well-known formula 'who can steal from me' (1928: 105). Heißenbüttel adopted this anti-originality principle, mainly as his own understanding of his method, in which the principle of authorship became increasingly irrelevant. Heißenbüttel often oriented himself in terms of Stein's portraiture and word compositions. In this respect, Stein's 'insistence' style from the period 1906–1908 was what influenced him most to experiment with musical techniques and combinatorial processes.

Inspired by New Music, particularly the compositions of Karlheinz Stockhausen, the 'idea that pauses are part of speech' (Rotermund),[10] moreover presented a fundamental formal and structural principle for the texts. It was only by attributing meaning to pauses and silences that Heißenbüttel could favour a poetology of adding fragments, quotations, minute notations, phenomenological documents, scraps of memory, everyday moments and snapshots. Art forms such as writing and image came closer together, generating an 'open' unity. Thus the poem demonstrated an inconsistent world of language, necessitating skim reading. In parallel to his early *Combinations*, Heißenbüttel was already working on experiments with a paintbrush and stencils that represent fields, combinations, pauses and structures, thus reflecting the poetology of the poems in visual form (see Bohley and Dittrich 2012 for reproductions of some these). These painted works meet the definition in the text *The Water Painter* (1998, *Der Wassermaler*) in their pursuit of a poetics of nothingness through traceless painting on water, representing 'games made of curve wave reflection shadow of traces and traces of traces' (Heißenbüttel 1961: 14).[11]

Through the use of collage and montage processes and concentration on the materiality of language, the border between poetry and prose dissolves. Back in the time of Alfred Andersch's journal *Texte und Zeichen*, Heißenbüttel referred to this undefined, experimental literary genre as 'abstract prose' and later as 'texts'. The texts were accompanied by the creation of painted and, in particular, photographic works focused on shapes, structures and often reflections, thus also giving visual form to the literary experiment.

Poetic experiments with grammar can be found in *Applications* (*Einsätze*) and the *Simple Grammatical Meditations* (*Einfache grammatische Meditationen*), the compositional principles of which are based on statistical processes. As a specific method, they in turn influenced Karlheinz Stockhausen's *Mikrophonie I + II* (Peters 1996: 36).

If Heißenbüttel initially referred to his experimental genres as demonstrations (1960: 51),[12] the term 'text' was agreed upon for prose poetry and was booming because for him it corresponded to the idea of transgression in terms of genre theory (1983: 10). 'The emergence of Heißenbüttel in the 1960s', Hubert Arbogast comments,

> was accompanied by conceptual innovation. With the concept of the text, he removed the border between poetry and prose and focused attention on texture, the consciously produced aspect of the literary construction. His principle was the testing of possibilities. Of possibilities for change. He never definitively committed himself here, doggedly persisting with his enquiry. (1998: 181)[13]

His poem 'Political Grammar' ('Politische Grammatik'), likewise indebted to Gertrude Stein, appeared in *spirale*, one of the first Swiss neo-avant-garde journals, edited by Eugen Gomringer. More because of where it was published than because of the text itself, Heißenbüttel was subsequently considered a concrete poet. His serial language experiment, reduced to lexis and syntactically overstretched (Kramer 1993: 149), reflects the language of German repression and the post-war period in a combinatorial work based on a grammar of speech:

> Oppressors oppress the oppressed. But the oppressed become oppressors. And because the oppressed become oppressors, the oppressed become the oppressive oppressed and the oppressors, oppressed oppressors. Yet oppressed oppressors in turn become oppressors [oppressive oppressed oppressors]. (1961: 38)[14]

Likewise, his *Portraitures* derived from Gertrude Stein's portraits enabled Heißen-büttel to explore the experimental possibilities of images of the self and other. It was precisely in distancing himself from concrete tendencies that he discovered, still early on, a way of integrating autobiographic material and the possibilities of acknowledging autobiography in the experiment. As he had already done with the *Combinations*, he accompanied this exploration with a material counterpart, this time in the form of double photographic portraits: 'I exist (everything I can speak of exists) because I can step outside the circle of this (with the help of) and defy fiction and rhetoric as if not. I speak as if not because the speech I speak speaks as if' (1961: 38).[15]

In his lecture on poetics, 'The Fundamental Concepts of a Poetics in the Twent-ieth Century' (1995: 134–224; 'Grundbegriffe einer Poetik im 20. Jahrhundert'),

Heißenbüttel does not present himself in a naively affirmative fashion as a poet or author. Neither does he make an artificial separation between his experimental authorship and the knowledge of literary theory and poetry he possesses as a critic, radio producer and book reviewer. Instead, his critical, theoretical and artistic activities form a whole: the critic determines the writer, the reader is a philosopher and theoretician and vice versa, while the book reviewer grasps the awareness of literatures and the writer searches for methods. Thus Heißenbüttel's discourse on literature is dominated by the loosening, penetrating and puncturing of an ossified 'presentation formula' of literature and speech. His statements are about experimental topics, such as the questions of whether literature is quantifiable or practicable, and how the sum total of works and literatures can be conceived as a broader, historic epistemological value.

Likewise, his practical poetology at this time was still focused on a 'literature of the future'. Instead of plot, genre and entertainment, this literature was supposed to reflect methodologically upon its material, create new forms of perception, teach critical awareness and demand that its recipients play an active role, a working contribution to the work. In doing so, however, Heißenbüttel does not restrict himself to an anti-poetics, assuming a position of rejection, but rather concentrates on developing questions, approaches and possibilities for a new literature of this kind. Thus he orients this literature between the coordinates of a subjective freedom and the more objective possibility of the appropriate and feasible. In this, the activity of writing is subordinate to the 'commitment to knowledge'. Focusing on insight was, above all, intended to communicate a method. This can be seen in his response in an interview with Klaus Ramm (2006: 133–41):

> RAMM: Where is the specific possibility of knowledge in literature located?
>
> HEISSENBÜTTEL: In the way things are formulated, in the formulation of sentences, and that formulation is dependent upon method. I believe that ideas of a methodological nature already possess a moment of knowledge.[16]

Resulting from this, the first of the '13 Propositions about Poetry' (1967, '13 Sätze über Poesie') establishes language as a central, defining connection that transitorily subordinates itself to the circumstances at hand in a way that enables insight, since 'language is characterized, among other things, by its tendency to be poetry' (Heißenbüttel 1972: 358).[17]

In *Textbook 1*, Heißenbüttel developed his methodological trademark, which Franz Mon called 'non-literary structuring principle based on the number 13',[18] and which he would continue to use until the late *Textbooks*: 'Unnoticed, this prime number that is avoided in social settings conveys remoteness, resistance, repugnance' (2012: 32).[19] *Textbook 1*, moreover, is composed of closed text groups that are traditionally based on the poem. The title and designation 'Textbook' came from a recommendation by Alfred Andersch; the German word also means an opera libretto. *Textbook 2*, which was written before *Textbook 1*, is dominated by grammatical language games, which like *Political Grammar* focus on a kind of parabolic structure — 'Oppressors oppress' — and transform it linguistically. *Textbook 3* to *Textbook 5* continue this process of permutation, a process that

Insingel's poetry frequently performs as well. From *Textbook 5* onwards, stronger political themes determine the texts, which are formed methodically by means of the collage principle. For example, an inventory of language is drawn up by means of sayings and expressions and transferred to a 'hallucinatory' new world of language, as shown in 'Calculation of What Everyone Knew' (1965, 'Kalkulation über was alle gewußt haben'):

> of course everyone did know something, some knew this and others knew that, but no one more than that and somebody should have found out even more by asking around if they could have done but it was difficult because everyone only got to hear this or that here or there [...] and that's how it worked. (10–11)[20]

In conjunction with an autobiographical turn in 1965–66, political and historical, erotic and autobiographical themes determine the texts in *Textbook 6*, dedicated to Wolfgang Koeppen. Along with the now continuous formal organization into blocks of 13, however, the texts themselves are structured according to principles of chance. A well-known, often-discussed text in the collection, 'Germany 1944' ('Deutschland 1944'), consists almost entirely of found texts and text segments in aleatorical combination (Friedrich 2011: 395). The text material reconstructs a reality of the last year of the war by means of speech, expressions, reports, verses, remarks and documents. It is composed of verbal and written quotations from Heinrich Himmler, Adolf Hitler, Joseph Goebbels, Ernst Jünger and Friedrich Georg Jünger, Kunrat von Hammerstein, Gottfried Benn, Josef Weinheber, as well as anonymous authors of Wehrmacht reports and the 'News of the Reich' bulletins.

The quotations from 1944 apply an aesthetics of shock, which — according to Jörn Stückrath's argument (1981: 243) — almost brings back those involved by invoking past horrors. The author recorded some passages himself in the audio version: 'when I write all this down like this, I am gripped again by the monstrosity of these things to the extent that I believe I need to wake from a bad dream'[21] and 'I was standing partly at the window partly in the field to imprint first this and then that impression upon myself like someone working on a long series of recordings' (1967: 30–31).[22] This can also be understood as autopoetic reflection and explanation, through which the combination and montage process primarily arranges images of reality. This reinforces Franz Mon's interpretation that the work develops an experimental theory of memory (1981: 55–59).

Based on the idea that literature has an epistemological function, many texts present themselves as both text and a working poetology. Explicitly poetological texts such as the '13 Propositions about Poetry' show that the poetic text is identical to the theoretical text. In the theoretical works, Heißenbüttel conveys the methods and concept of an 'open literature' mediating between the arts in the consciousness of present-day modernity:

> anyone attempting to make something contemporary and interesting and led by fascination will not be helped at all by clinging to these boundaries [of art]. He needs to get out into the open. He needs an immediate relationship, with concrete methods, with the concrete insight and also with the agreement, the possible and tentative agreement between method and insight. [...] I am

convinced, in any case, that it is this act of leaving things open that decides everything. (1972: 55)[23]

Beginning in 1968, Heißenbüttel engaged in his own acoustic experiments and, to a considerable extent, became a theorising practitioner of the 'new radio play'. He was awarded the Blind Veterans' Radio Play Prize for the audio work *Two or Three Portraits* (*Zwei oder drei Portraits*) in 1971. From the 1970s onwards, with the advent of the *Projects*, his concept of a methodologically understood, experimental literature turned into an 'open literature'. *Projects no. 1 and 2* extended the concept of literature from a material repertoire of language to include acoustic dimensions as well. Thus the central, fundamental innovation of *Project no. 2* mainly lies in the act of bringing the literary and acoustic text together: '[a]ll texts have the possibility to be realised in sound; some are broadcast as radio plays' (1974, blurb).[24] Until 1979, numerous radio plays, also labelled *Projects*, appeared in parallel to the publications, as well as in a productive interaction of audio and visual texts.[25]

Project no. 2, a radio play, takes up the theme of the literary *Project no. 1: D'Alemberts End*. Here nine almost interchangeable voices represent a social class. 'So What Are We Going to Broadcast Then?' (1970; 'Was sollen wir überhaupt senden?') is a parody of public broadcasting officials based on notes of meetings.

A typical West German expression in the post-war period had to do with what would have happened if the Nazis had won World War II. The radio play *If Hitler Hadn't Won the War* is a fictive thought experiment exploring how that reality might actually appear, through the example of a nominal member of the party. In this fictional universe, after Hitler won the war in an alliance with Stalin, a totalitarian regime was established across Europe in the form of a 'Confederation of European People's Republics' (Heißenbüttel 1980a: 8), that got rid of its 'surplus' humans by means of a randomizer and an electronic surveillance system.

A mixture of methods involving word combinations as grammatical micro-structures from 'vocabularly' ('vokabulär') and a process of the long poem from 'Cluster with Imposed Metre' ('Menge mit aufgeprägter Metrik') from *Textbook 6* resulted in *Project No. 1*, an open genre that is both a long text and something akin to a novel. To create the 'Cluster with Imposed Metre' in *Textbook 6*, Heißenbüttel had jotted down things he saw and heard on trips on the tram and underground railway in Hamburg over the course of eight days, which he used as material for the text, in turn giving form to a 'trace' of personal life. To a greater extent than the aforementioned *Project no. 1: D'Alemberts End*, *Project 2: Chopping the Cabbage* reuses the accumulating principle from the *Combinations* (1954). It concentrates on language as material, ranging 'from the advertising text to the philosophical thesis, from the dialogue of a comic to the results of a survey on group sex, from banal rhyming to sentences from linguistic exercises about the Bavarian politician Franz Josef Strauß, from recollected dreams to quotations from world history' (Heißenbüttel 1974: blurb).[26] Fragments of speech, poems, chatter, etc. are mixed and juxtaposed. This is the reason why the *13 Didactic Poems* present themselves as kind of didactic guide to poetry, for example in the sense that rearranging the quotations results in new perspectives on literature.

Conversely, the three *Project 3*s have the structure of a sequence of recounted events, reduced 'simple stories' in the form of concise prose sketches. Once again, they address the demand for new genres — a concern shared by Insingel — and create 'modern fairy-tales' that shed a critical light from the future on the present. Isolated beginnings of storylines contrast with the hackneyed narrative montages and simultaneously demonstrate the end of the New Narrative. Exaggerated anecdotes of private life parody the subjectivity of the 1970s and generate more new anti-genres. These *Projects* are playfully connected by the question as to whether it is possible to renew older literary traditions such as the novel or the historic essay to the present. This results in 'simple stories' based on quotations, to which cut-up methods are applied in such a way that their artificiality, construction and method remain visible.

Textbook 8. 1981–1985 contains three types of text: 'Twoliners over a Year' ('Zweizeiler über ein Jahr'), which brings together couplets over the course of the months, 'Poem Poems' ('Gedichtgedichte') as notes on observations, reading and thoughts and 'Comforting Sayings' ('Trostsprüche'). His material is the observation of landscapes through the seasons, reading experiences and old age. *Textbook 9. 3x13x13 Sentences. 1981–1984* (*Textbuch 9. 3x13x13 Sätze. 1981–1984*) is a declination of 39 models of reality in treatises, announcements and headlines of leading articles. Political phraseology, affluent society, daily life, sexual fantasies, the production of literature and the literature business are its themes. Heißenbüttel glued strips of text out of an edition of *Time* magazine in English onto a few galley proofs of *Textbook 9* and added his own brightly-coloured scribblings in felt tipped pen. *Textbook 10: On the art of love* (1986, *Textbuch 10: Von Liebeskunst*), two thousand years after Ovid's *Ars Amatoria*, is devoted to the love poem, which has dissolved in the postmodern era into 'an impenetrable crisscrossing of sex research data and stories from magazines, handy psychoanalytical categories, drivel about relationships and trivial myths' (Heißenbüttel 1986: blurb).[27]

Each of the 13 lessons, divided in turn into 13 sections or 39 verses, begins with a reference to the writing method. Like basic musical motifs, the name of the author is now mentioned from whom the plot, images and metaphors for the textures of the text blocks are derived. Heißenbüttel added artwork to the early versions and manuscripts of *Textbook 10*, gluing in painted strips of paper, prints, painted-over letters and diagonally cut strips of fabric. *Textbook 11 in Sanitized Language* (1987, *Textbuch 11 in gereinigter Sprache*) consists of combinations of sentences, dream sequences, scraps of memory, poetological notes, moments of insight and images of nature, infused with quotations. The methodological goal is 'to select, break and re-interpret elements of text in the literary tradition' (Heißenbüttel 1987).[28] After the treatises and lessons in *Textbook 9* and *Textbook 10*, Heißenbüttel returns to more visual forms reminiscent of the early poems in *Textbook 11*, using empty space, pauses and silence. As early as *Project 3*, short texts can be found slotted in between aphorisms and anecdotes that are referred to as 'Autumns' ('General Autumn', 'Office Sex Autumn', 'Psychoanalyst Autumn', 'The Autumn of Love', 'The Autumn of Marriage', etc.).[29] The late collection *there's no more to say about it*

(1983, *mehr ist dazu nicht zu sagen*) is a delayed stand-in for the missing *Textbook 7*. At this point the 'Autumns' have become independent and repeat forms of speech and narrative methods from the nineteenth century. *Oedipus Complex Made in Germany* (1981, *Ödipuskomplex made in Germany*) is a collection of occasional poems, elegies and landscapes from 1965 to 1980.

Heißenbüttel took stock of the water painter in 1988. In his late poetics, his earlier search for methods of generating new literature and genres led to the attempt to make the incomprehensible comprehensible with open artistic categories:

> A water painter is someone who does something that doesn't exist. [...] In theory, painting on water means doing something that makes use of inappropriate means. Inappropriate from the perspective of usual and customary activity. Which is to say, painting in order to portray something, in a representational way or not, something that can be looked at, can be taken home and stored as a treasure, even if only a small one, subject to the changes wrought by the years. [...]
>
> To define the water painter clearly, once and for all: it is not this, not a planned activity, not a choreography, not something that can be transmitted in any kind of notation. Without water painting, painting on water, all kinds of water, puddles, the surface of lakes, the meniscus of filled pots, spilled water, bathwater, seawater, the open sea, means extracting oneself from all conditions and reconfiguring oneself from the very beginning. Totally reconfiguring, leaving nothing out, completely. I don't want to make anything. I don't want to produce anything or set anything down, as categories outside which I move. If I move outside of them, I have changed, I am an Other. [...]
>
> I make nothing, produce nothing and set nothing down. But I do not make nothingness, produce nothingness or set nothingness down. Water painting lies in between. [...] It is something into which one leaps, hops, slides, something to which one surrenders oneself. And does not know it. Without the memory of the point at which it happens. That is where the real difficulty is: making comprehensible that which escapes comprehension.
>
> (Heißenbüttel 1998: 165–67)[30]

Insingel's Poetology

Insingel's poetology is more consistent and less elaborated, but the contentions about the role and the preferred form of literature bear considerable resemblance to Heißenbüttel's. Looking back at his career as a poet, Insingel remarks that he sees himself as 'the avant-garde in myself and for myself' (Van der Straeten and Van Imschoot 2015: 40),[31] which is to say that he subscribes to the broad aims of the avant-garde, but does not want to belong to a group or become part of a movement. The statement is representative of Insingel's 'posture' (Meizoz 2007), i.e. the way he positions himself and at the same time is positioned by others.[32] In the case of the quotation, the interviewers and the literary magazine in which the interview has appeared contribute to this positioning.

In the dominant portrayal of his authorship, Insingel emphasizes two components: profound attachment to the avant-garde, and deliberate isolation. Before charting the ramifications of this authorial posture, we should note that it contains a telling contradiction. An author who acknowledges his affinity with a group of artists already mitigates his isolation. What is more, the history of the avant-garde is inextricably linked to the formation of groups (see Poggioli 1968 for a classical account of the avant-garde 'movement'). With this in mind, let us take a closer look at the way Insingel constructs his authorial identity and develops a poetology centred on these ideas.

How does Insingel shape his allegiance to the avant-garde? In his literary work, the avant-garde tendency is mainly formal rather than straightforwardly political. In general terms, his poetry and prose break with conventions of realism, narrative and genre, turning to alternative semiotic strategies (visual, aural, syntactic) to fulfil aesthetic functions. Instead of lexical texture and semantic density, he develops a personal diction of syntactic repetition and variation similar to that of Heißenbüttel's work. In Insingel's prose, the ordering and reordering of textual fragments generates meaning. As in Heißenbüttel's work, these fragments can be speech materials from everyday conversation. Spatial metaphors and metalanguage underline the aesthetic autonomy of the text, as does the central image of the circle. On balance, through his technique and style, Insingel aligns with the avant-garde.

In the peritext and the epitext (Genette 1987) of Insingel's works, this link with the avant-garde is reinforced. The exclusion of his early poetry mentioned above is already part of this strategy. In essays and interviews, Insingel stresses the formally realized autonomy of the work of art and refers to avant-garde and neo-avant-garde artists to support his view. Apart from Helmut Heißenbüttel, recurring names are Paul van Ostaijen, Samuel Beckett,[33] Gertrude Stein, Nathalie Sarraute, Ferdinand Kriwet, and Arno Schmidt. In an interview in 1990, Insingel states that he read a lot of French new novels in the 1950s and 1960s, but 'the German literature of the 1960s had a greater impact on [him]' (Kuypers 1990).[34]

Where he mentions Heißenbüttel's work, Insingel not only suggests similarities in literary practice, he also adopts Heißenbüttel's poetological vocabulary on several occasions. Commenting upon the creative process of literature, he posits in 'Writing in 70' (1969, 'Schrijven in 70'): 'Perhaps I put too much emphasis on the "unrepresentational" ideal for literary creation. However, it does not [...] entail an attitude free of commitment. On the contrary, I am convinced that the work of art only fully acquires its "Erkenntnisfunktion" (Helmut Heißenbüttel) in this ideal' (Insingel 1981 [1969]: 41).[35]

Similarly, when he discusses language as the poet's material, he clarifies: 'it is the enjoyment of the medium's "Erkenntnisfunktion" (Helmut Heißenbüttel); your drives turn you into a visionary' (Insingel 2004a: 192).[36] And in an essay about Maurice Gilliams, the Flemish author whom he considers a direct predecessor, he portrays Gilliams's poetics as follows: 'Yet he does not operate "in" language, he does not handle it "semantically" like, for example, Joyce and Gertrude Stein, and unlike these authors, neither does he exit the "communicative sphere of language" (Heißenbüttel)' (1981 [1968]: 28).[37] These are indications that Heißenbüttel remained an available and desirable point of reference, strongly compatible with his own theory and practice.

Like Paul van Ostaijen, whom he also construes as a predecessor,[38] Insingel considers the autonomy of poetry as primordial. Literature is 'an end in itself' and '[a]vant-garde literature is pre-eminently without function' (Spaninks 1978: 103). This autonomy can — or *should,* from the perspective of the author's poetics — be underlined in the composition. Literature can achieve this by stressing its artificial nature and exploiting literature's basic materials (Insingel 1981: 101): words, sounds and syntactic and visual organisation. In Insingel's view, the result is an aesthetic coherence which cannot be replaced or paraphrased (106), a form of communication in which 'the true battle is fought on the level of form' (107).[39] In other words:

> Art begins where the act of saying becomes more important than the said, where a music of meanings comes into being, which can imply that in the purest form of art the act of saying cancels what is said. [...] [W]hat is said is then inscribed in its totality in the circle, its presence or absence in itself does not play a role. (Insingel 1981: 35)[40]

If the work of art is autonomous thanks to its form, then what is the relationship between the work and reality? The mimetic dimension of Insingel's poetics is less straightforward, possibly even inconsistent. In his view, art does not represent reality but it adapts and re-models reality, resisting dominant ways of thinking, perceiving, and speaking (1981: 113). Still, the conventional world-view is often recognizable in his work, because he imports these dominant discourses, giving them a new context, as Heißenbüttel does. In *That Is to Say,* for example, a military and political discourse is evoked and called into question:

> Has the country been liberated? (Can occupation threaten?)
> Has the country been occupied? (Is liberation approaching?)
> Are the citizens weak? (Do many possess little?)
> Is the army strong? (Do few possess little?)
> Are the people divided?/Is the nation united?
> Is there faith?/Is there doubt?
> (Insingel 1994b [1974]: 62, trans. Theo Hermans 1994)

Defamiliarisation is then realized through the decomposition, recontextualisation and repetition of these language materials, and sometimes by explicit reflection. From these formal procedures, a critical stance emerges. Insingel's texts stage a deep scepticism toward the socialised subject, who replicates doxa and language habits. This scepticism is extended to the world of appearances which arises in capitalism and applies to the external control of desire, the projection of desire, and the creation of illusions (e.g. in advertising). He is particularly critical of the bourgeois subject, who typically adopts the conventional ways of speaking described and tends to accept the world of appearances. For Insingel, there are also personal reasons to take a stand against these reprehensible structures. In that sense, the aesthetically sublimated protest entails an expressive dimension, even though the relationship between literature and the writer's subjectivity is not so much expressive as performative. Literature namely realises the writer's urge to 'become an autonomous human being' and to 'save the self in the deadly air of an authoritarian environment' (Spaninks 1978: 104–05).

```
zolang zal niets veranderen


zolang de meesten die aan het roer staan
zolang de meesten die aan het roer staan en de koers bepa
len
zolang de meesten die aan het roer staan en de koers bepa
len en niet kunnen zien dat de zon in het water schijnt
zolang de meesten die aan het roer staan en de koers bepa
len en niet kunnen zien dat de zon in het water schijnt e
n tegen de klippen opvaren
zolang de meesten die aan het roer staan en de koers bepa
len en niet kunnen zien dat de zon in het water schijnt e
n tegen de klippen opvaren en tussen de klippen door zeil
en
zolang de meesten die aan het roer staan en de koers bepa
len en niet kunnen zien dat de zon in het water schijnt e
n tegen de klippen opvaren en tussen de klippen door zeil
en en het schip dragende houden
zolang de meesten die aan het roer staan en de koers bepa
len en niet kunnen zien dat de zon in het water schijnt e
n tegen de klippen opvaren en tussen de klippen door zeil
en en het schip dragende houden en koers houden
zolang de meesten die de koers bepalen en niet kunnen zie
n dat de zon in het water schijnt en tegen de klippen opv
aren en tussen de klippen door zeilen en het schip dragen
de houden en koers houden
zolang de meesten die niet kunnen zien dat de zon in het
water schijnt en tegen de klippen opvaren en tussen de kl
ippen door zeilen en het schip dragende houden en koers h
ouden
zolang de meesten die tegen de klippen opvaren en tussen
de klippen door zeilen en het schip dragende houden en ko
ers houden
zolang de meesten die tussen de klippen door zeilen en he
t schip dragende houden en koers houden
zolang de meesten die het schip dragende houden en koers
houden
zolang de meesten die koers houden
```

FIG. 2.3a. Mark Insingel, 'zolang zal niets veranderen' ('meanwhile [for that long] nothing will change'), and 'de stabilisering van de vooruitgang' ('the stabilization of progress') (Insingel 1990 [1974]: 94-95, © Mark Insingel)

de stabilisering van de vooruitgang
van de ontwikkeling van de wetensc
happen van de mens van de stabilise
ring van de vooruitgang van de ontw
ikkeling van de mens van de wetensc
happen van de stabilisering van de
vooruitgang van de mens van de ontw
ikkeling van de wetenschappen van d
e stabilisering van de mens van de
vooruitgang van de ontwikkeling van
de wetenschappen van de stabiliser
ing van de vooruitgang van de ontwi
kkeling van de wetenschappen van de
stabilisering van de vooruitgang v
an de wetenschappen van de ontwikke
ling van de stabilisering van de we
tenschappen van de vooruitgang van
de ontwikkeling van de stabiliserin
g van de vooruitgang van de ontwikk
eling van de stabilisering van de o
ntwikkeling van de vooruitgang van
de stabilisering van de vooruitgang
van de stabilisering

de mens van de vooruitgang van de o
ntwikkeling van de wetenschappen va
n de stabilisering van de mens van
de vooruitgang van de ontwikkeling
van de stabilisering van de wetensc
happen van de mens van de vooruitga
ng van de stabilisering van de ontw
ikkeling van de wetenschappen van d
e mens van de stabilisering van de
vooruitgang van de ontwikkeling van
de wetenschappen van de mens van d
e vooruitgang van de ontwikkeling v
an de wetenschappen van de mens van
de vooruitgang van de wetenschappe
n van de ontwikkeling van de mens v
an de wetenschappen van de vooruitg
ang van de ontwikkeling van de mens
van de vooruitgang van de ontwikke
ling van de mens van de ontwikkelin
g van de vooruitgang van de mens va
n de vooruitgang van de mens

FIG. 2.3b. Mark Insingel, 'zolang zal niets veranderen' ('meanwhile [for that long] nothing will change'), and 'de stabilisering van de vooruitgang' ('the stabilization of progress') (Insingel 1990 [1974]: 94-95, © Mark Insingel)

In this respect, Insingel's work is less detached from reality than some of his explicit poetological claims suggest. 'As a *human being*', Insingel writes at the end of the 1960s, 'I can be (socially and politically) committed and I have many means to action at my disposal, but as an *artist* I have none' (1981 [1969]: 35).[41] If we take the effect of formal procedures into consideration, however, this claim needs to be adjusted. Whether or not Insingel's work propels people towards social and political action, his comments upon contemporary society's uses of language are critical and committed. His book of concrete poetry *Posters* (1974), for example, has political, activist undertones (see Figure 2.3 for two examples). We can explain the ambiguity by looking at the pragmatic dimension of his poetology. Although explicit contentions about the reader are rare, the implication of Insingel's claims is that literature should challenge and defamiliarize the reader. On balance, however, the means are more important than the ends as far as the reader's response is concerned. Or to rephrase it from Insingel's point of view: the formal structure of the work is a goal in itself and the defamiliarisation and concomitant commitment are secondary effects. In this approach to literature, Insingel is related to Paul van Ostaijen, Samuel Beckett ... and Helmut Heißenbüttel.

The list of artistic points of reference does not stop with literary writers. Insingel develops and illustrates his views by mentioning abstract art, minimalist painting and minimalist music, including work by Piet Mondriaan (Roggeman 1975: 35; Insingel 2004b: 155), Iannis Xenakis (Insingel 1981: 101), and Steve Reich (Insingel 2004b: 155). In a strict sense, Insingel is not active in other art forms — though his concrete poetry can be interpreted as visual art — but he constructs a fundamental link between artistic projects across avant-garde practices, an idea which is very much in line with avant-garde thought (we might think, for example, of the many art forms, media, and materials in *De Stijl* or Dada).

Does Insingel's view on literature develop throughout his career? Even though his literary practice has evolved, the rudiments of his poetology, as sketched in the previous paragraphs, have remained the same. Still, he has dealt with the paradoxes of the avant-garde in different ways at different stages, as Geert Buelens notes (2001: 930). While adhering to the avant-garde in the majority of his explicit claims (mainly interviews and essays), he occasionally expresses scepticism toward the notion. In a 1984 interview, he rejects the term 'because the avant-garde implies a belief in progress' (Flamend 1984: 6)[42] to which he cannot subscribe. All in all, however, it is striking how stable the belief in the avant-garde remains in Insingel's theoretical positioning.

In our discussion of Heißenbüttel's and Insingel's views, it has become apparent that the two authors adhere to a similar ambiguous principle of experimental and autonomous literature. They both suggest that literature can generate new knowledge through experimental procedures ('demonstrations', in Heißenbüttel's terms). Both authors are drawn to the idea that calculated combinations of linguistic signs are a valuable alternative to a romantic poetics of original creation. What is ambiguous about these views is the fact that they do integrate language materials from the outside world and that their seemingly cold abstraction can still provide support for subjective expression. In the following paragraphs, we will examine how critics and scholars have responded and contributed to these views. How are Heißenbüttel and Insingel portrayed in contemporary criticism and extant scholarship, and how are they positioned in literary history?

3. Reception

Helmut Heißenbüttel

When Karl Riha describes Helmut Heißenbüttel as the representative of an 'innovative poetics of the modern' (1997: 552), it is clear from this that Heißenbüttel's work is subject to a reception that is limited to the experimental to an almost stereotypical degree. As a consequence of institutionalizing him as a representative of neo-avant-garde literature, literary historiography usually attributes an 'experimental literature that holds itself supreme' (Barner 1994: 605)[43] to Heißenbüttel, along with Jürgen Becker and Ror Wolf. Thus the fortunes of the literary experiment can be deduced from his person and the reception of his work.

In his overview of Heißenbüttel research, Hans-Edwin Friedrich states that the reception of Heißenbüttel's work mainly concentrates on his *Textbooks* and his lectures in Frankfurt in 1963: as such, he considers Heißenbüttel's lectures on poetics entitled 'The Fundamental Concepts of a Poetics in the Twentieth Century' ('Grundbegriffe einer Poetik im 20. Jahrhundert', Heißenbüttel 1995: 134–224) 'the most highly elaborated contributions to modern literary theory' (Friedrich 2011: 363). The perception of his work is apparently reduced to *Textbook*, *Project 1* and *On Literature*, with the further development of his avant-garde work hardly coming into the picture (see Combrink 2011 as an exception to this rule). The highest concentration of research is in the 1970s. Indeed, this was the period when Heißenbüttel, through Rosmarie Waldrop's translations, also received considerable attention in the English-speaking world.

The methodological and playful approach in Heißenbüttel's work was established as a reference parameter by later experimental tendencies in which this approach was even more pronounced. The interpretations that arose among the poets of the later Bielefeld Colloquium for New Poetry [Bielefelder Kolloquium Neue Poesie] mainly concentrated on the category of participation, activation of the reader, which was claimed to be a central category of understanding for Heißenbüttel's texts. This was, according to Siegfried J. Schmidt, intended to restore aesthetic distance, so that 'the recipient experienced and confirmed him/herself as a creator' (1970: 32).

Ulf Stolterfoht, a member of a more recent generation of experimental poets, received the Peter Huchel Prize in 2008 for his collection *wood smoke over heslach* (*holzrauch über heslach*), whose title is a quotation from Heißenbüttel. This demonstrates that modern experimental poetry has a strong preference for Heißenbüttel's work, and also tries to overcome this influence in finding new figures in understanding language as a protagonist. The quotation comes from Heißenbüttel's long poem in 13 blocks, 'Poem of the Exercise in Dying' ('Gedicht von der Übung zu sterben') in *Textbook 3*:

Wood smoke over Heslach February sun dazzles noise on the
railway embankment shouting echo steps model landscape ageing
grid text diagonally considered emphatically thoughtfully carelessly
(1962: 37)[44]

The experimental intention of the text was to gather impressions in the period from
February 1961 to February 1962 and then combine, compile and arrange them using
a bricolage technique. As shown in the still-life image of a *wood smoke over heslach*,
the collected notes bring together ideas, verbal reductions, expressions, images
of the time from reading newspapers, poetic metaphors, song lyrics, impressions
and conversations from trams and underground trains, involving quotations from
literary, ordinary and external sources that are extracted from their old contexts
and put into new ones. Among these personal impressions and collections are also
reading notes documenting the reading biography of the literary theorist and critic,
likewise 'gathering' reading experiences.

Mark Insingel

Mark Insingel's profile as an isolated avant-gardist catches on in the reception
of his work. Early critics had mixed feelings about his conventional poetry and
the first titles presented under the name of Insingel are sometimes described as
immature. Once Insingel developed his signature style, several critics responded
very positively. In particular, the works published in the late 1960s and the 1970s
attracted the attention of a number of critics. Most of them were charmed by his
persistence with an experimental poetics. Some, however, consider his formal
procedures 'sterile' (Faes 1970: 75) or merely computational (Brems 1972). One
critic even calls his work epigonic (De Haes 1975). The labels 'sterile', 'mechanical',
and 'computational' regularly pop up in criticism of Insingel from the early 1970s
until the early 2000s. In turn, they are associated with familiar concepts of aesthetic
criticism, namely 'minimalism' and 'constructivism'. The latter terms, however, are
frequently used in a positive rather than a negative judgment of Insingel's literary
practice, as well as suggesting a connection between Insingel's literary project and
developments in the arts. Applied to Insingel's work, constructivism frames the
use of circles and skeletal grammatical structures as a form of aesthetic abstraction
and decomposition. The term 'minimalism' highlights the restrictions that reduce
the work to elementary forms, which are repeated and varied to generate aesthetic
effects.

Progressive critics and scholars of innovative literature (Beekman, Bousset,
De Vree, and Wesselo) soon discovered and promoted the original work of
Insingel. Paul de Vree, an active promoter of experimental poetry, commended
(1971) Insingel's novel *A Course of Time* as a 'surprisingly clever and progressive
work which brings Insingel close to the vanguard of our experimental writers'.[45]
Tellingly, many of the positive reactions come from fellow writers, including Lidy
van Marissing (1971), Pol Hoste (1981, 1982), Jan H. Mysjkin (1983), and Kees 't Hart
(2004). In other words, Insingel is a writer's writer and a writer of writerly texts. It
is somewhat ironic in that respect that one critic classifies his work as unreadable

(Kars 1975: 77). Indeed, one could say, his work is not readable but it is writeable. The reader of his work shifts to the position of the writer because of the work's unconventional, challenging nature. In Roland Barthes' words, which are very apt in this context, the model of the writerly text is 'productive' and not 'representational':

> the writerly text is *ourselves writing*, before the infinite play of the world (the world as function) is traversed, intersected, stopped, plasticized by some singular system (Ideology, Genre, Criticism) which reduces the plurality of entrances, the opening of networks, the infinity of languages. [...] The writerly is the novelistic without the novel, poetry without the poem, the essay without the dissertation, writing without style, production without product, structuration without structure[46] (1974: 4–5).

The quotation is all the more pertinent as Barthes suggests a kind of dissolution of *genre*, an 'evaporation' we could say, revealing the bare essentials of art and the creative process: the novelistic without the novel, poetry without the poem, production without a product. We will come back to the issue of genre later on. Needless to say, the applicability of Barthes's concept is not coincidental, and neither is the appearance of terms such as 'computational' in 1970s criticism. Insingel's poetics has an affinity with structuralist thought in which such terms and concepts are cultivated and it was in the 1960s and 1970s that this discourse was adopted by innovative writers.

In 2004, the Dutch novelist and critic Kees 't Hart (2004) summarized Insingel's reputation (at the same time contributing to it) and offered a correction that came into vogue around that time:

> Over the last forty years, Insingel has built a reputation as someone who makes rather "sterile" and "laboured" literature: he is thought to write "concrete" poetry and prose, to be a follower of constructivism in general and an advocate of "abstract" and "theoretical" literature. I have never believed a word of it. His work is to be considered as an unabashed, very personal and stubborn fit of rage about the effect of societal structures on human relations, in particular those in which he himself has to function.[47]

Interestingly, 't Hart's characterisation of Insingel is not only compatible with developments in the poet's work but also with the discursive evolution of literary criticism. Readers and critics have become more receptive to the psychological and autobiographical motifs in the work (see e.g. Vandevoorde 1996 on *Eenzaam lichaam*). While Insingel's way of writing has not fundamentally changed, the focus of critics has shifted in that direction.

The 1970s and early 1980s — as a favourable biotope for experimental literature and structuralism (see Wesselo 1983) — offered the right conditions for a relatively great amount of critical attention. In the late 1980s and early 1990s, the work of Insingel was not intensively reviewed or commented upon. In the 2000s, leading critics (such as 't Hart, T. van Deel, and Hans Groenewegen) and academics (Buelens 2001; T'Sjoen 2004; Deckmyn and Vandevoorde 2012) devoted essays to his work, paradoxically 'canonizing' him as a marginal author. This process had already been instigated by academic criticism (e.g. Beekman 1975 and 1990;

Bousset 1990) and through the appearance of Insingel in Sybren Polet's milestone anthology *Ander proza* (1978). Because of its literal as well as metaphorical visibility, his concrete poetry has a special status in its reception. Insingel's visual poems are well-known and recognised by a wide audience.[48] Summarizing the sixty years of reception of Insingel's work, we can say that the dominant image is that of the avant-garde writer's writer who operates in the margins but who appeals to a broad audience with his concrete poetry. As in the case of Heißenbüttel, the 1960s and early 1970s are often considered to be the breeding ground for Insingel's poetics and authorship. Since this period also represents a surge in the neo-avant-garde and a time of literary kinship for Heißenbüttel and Insingel, the experimental literature of the late 1960s and early 1970s will be the focus of the next segment of this chapter.

4. Literary practice: Repetitive Experiments as Objective Abstraction? Heißenbüttel alongside Insingel

'This is the model. The model is always the same. The model is what always remains the same.' (Heißenbüttel 1980b: 85)[49]

The main site of telling convergence and meaningful divergence between Helmut Heißenbüttel and Mark Insingel are the literary works themselves. The core examples for the comparative analysis are taken from their literary production at the end of the 1960s and the early 1970s. Not only is this focus understandable given the general aims of the present volume, it is also intrinsically motivated. For it is in this particular stretch of time that Heißenbüttel's and Insingel's ways of writing show strong affinities, in which we differentiate three levels, namely technique, genre and style. First, on the level of technique, both authors invest a lot of creative and intellectual energy in linguistic repetition and variation. Second, both their works are distinctive because they go beyond traditional generic distinctions. Third, characteristic of their work is the tension between literary abstraction and concreteness, which goes hand in hand with a tension between objectivity and subjectivity.

Helmut Heißenbüttel

Heißenbüttel's processes of repetition and variation are primarily intended to question the limits and possibilities of the poem. The focus is always on a specific visual form. As a block or concrete design, the poems clearly distinguish themselves from poems in verse. A further difficulty is the extremely reduced language, essentially constructed out of a linguistic micro-unit, which tends towards inauthenticity, mainly because of its deliberate lack of clear propositions. Repetitions and permutations turn these phrases and basic patterns, usually taken from everyday language, into a cluster, which makes them visually striking even though their proposition remains unclear. As is the case in 'Political Grammar', this way of constructing series is dominant in most of the texts: ongoing repetitions, usually dozens of times or more, render a linguistic and propositionally reduced micro-unit visible without, however, clarifying it. Often the phrase is presented through paradoxes, ironically or humorously, as a phrase. There is wide scope for interpretation of this idiosyncratic form. It may refer to banality, affirmation, redundancy, aggression, violence or even the stupidity of expressions. Ironic aspects are also a factor, or at least do not fail to make an appearance. The focus on the materiality of language and understanding language as a material highlights the artificiality of the texts and the fact of their production time and again. A distance is thus created that makes it possible to recognize the method-based nature of the texts. The act of demonstrating the presence of linguistic material creates an interface for thinking and an awareness that the texts are also situated in a conceptual tradition:

> Heißenbüttel's montages are not only attempts to give worn-out words a new weight, but even to make pre-formulated sentences and phrases astonishing, to give them a new meaning free of their original context, reject habitual associations and to provoke thought rather than blind parroting, precisely by dint of this transformation of the preconceived. It takes a long time even to start to understand these "compositions". (Wiegenstein 1970: 203)[50]

The texts take a variety of forms, from the simpler collages of words or phrases in *Textbooks 1–3* to a few instances of 'Speech Words' ('Sprech-Wörter'), with their stronger visual compositions, in *Textbook 4*. Then again, there are somewhat more complex, less visual, but materially legible arrangements that emerge in texts ordered according to aleatoric principles, such as 'Germany 1944'. The arrangement of the collage material follows a mathematical, numerical code here that determines the text according to a method. Its combinational principle can be traced through a few originals in the Heißenbüttel archive at the Academy of Arts. For example, individual verses are numbered by hand on a few of the typewritten originals.[51] It is a similar story with the compositions, the texts constructed entirely from found materials using a cut-up method. We find further patterns of repetition in 'Final Solution' ('Endlösung') or 'Calculation of What Everyone Knew' ('Kalkulation über was alle gewußt haben') from *Textbook 5*, which are based on expressions to do with the discussion of the Holocaust. In speech without a subject, they develop lines of argument that appear to be causal because they are logical. Although these lines are heavily intertwined, no propositions are developed, because the same argument is constantly repeated and reconfirmed in a circular structure that returns it to its beginning — a procedure we have described as the signature of Insingel as well. If the text with no way out thus demonstrates an absence of understanding, it does demand that the reader break open this circular structure. Such approaches clarify a specific form of *Erinnerungsliteratur* — the literature of coming to terms with the Nazi past — within the neo-avant-garde, in which the demonstrative aspect in the open form is oriented towards a political consciousness besides and beyond an aesthetic awareness.

Striking among the examples of visual literature are the list-like configurations of Speech-Words with their visual narratives in *Textbook 4*.[52] The best-known example is a list structure invented by Heißenbüttel himself for an example text that is also cited in the *Frankfurt Lectures*. When it was printed in the literary magazine

Akzente in the 1950s, it was received with a storm of indignant letters to the editor (Heißenbüttel 1995: 135):

I	man	on	I	bench	
I	cookie	in	I	hand	
			I	hand	
		in	I	hand	and
I	man				and
I	cookie				and
				hand	
		in		hand	and
		on	I	bench	
I	cookie				and
	crumbs				

(Heißenbüttel 1964: 15, © Erben Helmut Heißenbüttel)

As Rosmarie Waldrop (1969: 134) notes in her essay on Heißenbüttel, the specificity of the individual word is highlighted here, although its meaning is not as prominent as its typographic positioning — Waldrop compares the latter to an orchestral arrangement. The key model for these arrangements and permutations is most likely found in musical compositions. Furthermore, Waldrop identifies what is ultimately a persistent failure on the part of the reader when s/he attempts to interpret the sentences and underpin them with meaning (134). The most striking thing about this visual composition is the highly controlled configuration, similar to Insingel's poetic experiments around that time, with its clear axes and divides that construct and thus restrict its spatial form. The lists permit a vertical reading as well as a horizontal one, which in addition to the experiments with expressions and the grammar of speech portrays a somewhat restricted pattern of speech. Nonetheless, the focus is on the spatial arrangement; the second voice in the empty spaces functions mainly as a variation for a kind of instigator.

That the texts function as models that take literary genres to their limits and thus extend them is clear from the frequently occurring examinations of the novel in the context of the neo-avant-garde. This entails the critical investigation of a literary genre in terms of its narrative patterns and the confrontation with an opposing, anti-literary version:

I
I am a story.
II
I am a story of someone.
III
Someone of whom I am a story is the story that I am. I am someone who is a story.
IV
I don't tell. I'm told. While I'm being told the tale to be told is telling.
[...]
XVIII
I am someone who is the only true and real story. I am the only true and real story of someone.

XIX
The truth and reality of the story that I am is this story.
XX
There.
XXI
Irreversibly there.
(Heißenbüttel 1961: 26–27)

Like a definition of the anti-programmatic novel, the text ends in the utopia of a future, exemplary narrative model that has completely liberated itself from fictional contexts. Here, too, we find an almost imperceptible concurrence of the poetic and poetological text. The poetological basis for this model drawn from the novel builds upon an understanding of literature oriented towards methods, as Heißenbüttel explains in the *Frankfurt Lectures*:

> as a writer I am looking for the methods that can express my experience, the things that provoke me in the world in which I live [...]. [... A]s a writer, I would like to make a few suggestions that give food for thought and are intended to loosen, penetrate and puncture a formula for the presentation of literature that is already perhaps all too ossified. (1995: 135)[53]

The 'methods' he refers to here are precisely those of a literature emphasizing its own production. This results in a cognitive effect: a reading schooled in comprehension and interpretation is extended to include the seeing and hearing of structures. Thus the text represents a model, directing the focus of observation solely towards the methodological design. A possible objective of these open, questioning forms is therefore that these processes also attempt to convey a new repertoire for literature. Furthermore, they are exercises in a changed way of reading, which sensitises the reader to methods of permutation, visual form and repetition.

A frequently employed, tried and tested method of pinpointing the neo-avant-garde is by understanding it through its defining relationship to a traditional literature. It is striking, not least because of his affinity with poetic statements and his poetry lectures, created in parallel to the *Textbooks* in the 1960s and no less famous, that Heißenbüttel's openly neo-avant-garde discourse is directed at literary traditions and consistently builds upon certain developments against that background, in an entirely positivistic sense. Heißenbüttel locates an early concept of the concrete right back in the Baroque. Naturalism, however, is closer to his own experiments, particularly Arno Holz's poem 'Kurfürstendamm Villa' ('Kurfürstendammvilla') from his collection *Phantasus*, in which the words are used for their concrete aspect and the poem has already turned into a 'catalogue of vocabulary' (Heißenbüttel 1969: 98). To continue this development, Heißenbüttel devotes himself in his textual artefacts to the dissolution of subjectivity and metaphorical writing focused on meaning. This predestines the text to an interdisciplinary, hybrid form that fluctuates between the arts. Accordingly, his concrete poetry is understood as open literature precisely to avoid being considered within a doctrinaire concept of concrete poetry in the 1950s (Heißenbüttel, 1969: 51).

The abandonment of formal subjectivity (e.g. first-person narration) had not been fully realised in the 1960s, but rather took the form of an ambiguous subjectivity whose speakers or speech could not be precisely located. However, this approaches the concept of a reality composed of a plurality of worlds:

> This multiple subjectivity adopts a perspective based on several viewpoints at once. The simultaneity of the viewpoints corresponds to the hallucinatory method of literature, which explains the common ground between linguistic and technical processes through the realm of language. (Heißenbüttel 1995: 224)[54]

This conception is appropriate to the substantial and formal aspects of abstract arts. Above all it represents in a very consequent and convincing way a literary analogy to the abstract and the concrete in the arts. With its focus on techniques of language it explores one essential aspect of literature and constitutes an alternative draft to common literature. Heißenbüttels and Insingels reduction of language produced a series of artefacts which constituted multifaceted exercises to change consciousness and perception.

Mark Insingel

In a confrontational reading, one can see how Heißenbüttel's reproduction and recapitulation and Insingel's technique of repetition and variation chime together well. Just as Heißenbüttel, Insingel also weaves doxa and commonplaces into his texts. Some of Heißenbüttel's *Textbooks* texts clearly share with Insingel's poetry a preoccupation with abstract patterns of folk logic and with the syntactic form of language. The second poem in *Textbook 1* is an excellent example. We can read it in dialogue with two poems from *Models*:

> das Sagbare sagen
> das Erfahrbare erfahren
> das Entscheidbare entscheiden
> das Erreichbare erreichen
> das Wiederholbare wiederholen
> das Beendbare beenden
>
> das nicht Sagbare
> das nicht Erfahrbare
> das nicht Entscheidbare
> das nicht Erreichbare
> das nicht Wiederholbare
> das nicht Beendbare
>
> das nicht Beendbare nicht beenden
>
> (Heißenbüttel 1960: 6 and 1980b: 7,
> © Erben Helmut Heißenbüttel)

mag	[may/ is allowed to]
kan	[can/ is able to/ is possible]
is	[is]
mag niet	[may not/ is not allowed to]
kan	
is	

mag
kan niet
is

mag
kan
is niet

mag
kan niet
is niet

mag niet
kan niet
is

mag niet
kan
is niet

mag niet
kan niet
is niet
(Insingel 1970b: 22, © Mark Insingel)

denken   zeggen
kunnen   durven
denken te kunnen   zeggen te durven
kunnen denken   durven zeggen
        denken te kunnen zeggen
        zeggen te durven denken
        (denken te durven zeggen
        zeggen te kunnen denken)
denken te durven   zeggen te kunnen
durven denken   kunnen zeggen
denken te zeggen   zeggen te denken
kunnen durven   durven kunnen
                kunnen

FIG. 2.4. Mark Insingel, Poem from Models (Insingel 1970b: 27).
Translation: 'think / say | be able to / dare to | think you're able to / say you dare to |
be able to think / dare to say | [...]', © Mark Insingel)

Much can be said about the meaningful differences between the compositions and interpretive options, for example if we read Heißenbüttel's poem as a metapoetical text portraying literature as the domain of possibilities and impossibilities. The apparent difference between the poems immediately exemplifies why the poet Insingel of the 1970s can appropriately be called minimalist. In Insingel's poems, we are left with a bare minimum of grammatical combinations and verbs with abstract meanings though clearly linked to human dispositions and basic relations between a subject and a group or society (e.g. having the courage ['durven'] implies the possibility of fear, and being allowed to ['mag'] implies an authority that allows as well as someone who accepts this authority).

Let us focus on the technique of repetition and variation. Both authors exploit and sometimes seemingly exhaust syntactic and morphological options.[55] The quoted poems repeat the same basic words and then apply negation or modality. In Heißenbüttel's text the suffix '–bar' indicates possibilities. The first stanza has a tautological, circular effect in that it suggests the possibility of realising an activity which already has the potential of being realised. The second stanza shifts the attention to impossibilities. The third stanza introduces a new combination based on repetition and could be seen as the start of another series but also as the end of the poem, something to which the line alludes. Not only the stems of verbs are repeated (all of them three times except 'beend'), but mainly the article 'das' and the adverb 'nicht' and the suffix 'bar'. Still, the poem is full of variation, each verse is different. It shows the constructivism, abstraction and apparent objectivity we can also find in Insingel's poems: there is no personalised lyrical persona, apostrophe or addressee.

A lot of Insingel's poetry also hinges on linguistic procedures such as negation, modality, word order, and basic communicative functions. Often, repetition and variation take the shape of sequences in which grammatical combinations are juxtaposed. The word order is altered or verses are gradually — line by line — expanded and then shortened again. Every combination and each juxtaposition creates and adds new meanings.

> the father is first, the son is further
> the father is son first
> further the son is father
> the father and the son are son and father
>
> first the father is further
> the son is further first
> first is further
> first the father is first
>
> (Insingel 1970b: 5, trans. Willem Groenewegen,
> © Mark Insingel)

The poems of *Models* start with a premise and end with a premise that could be the start of the same poem. Beginning and end are often variations of each other. In other words, the end mirrors the beginning. This structure is characteristic of Insingel's work on several levels. It is a formal realisation of the idea that the human subject is caught in circles of social relations and relations of power.

The nature of repetition and variation and of the circular movement is not just grammatical, lexical, and semantic, but also phonological, auditory, spatial, and visual. Consider the following poem (Figure 2.5, 'from you to me [there] is a distance | from me | to | you is love'):

```
van jou tot mij is een afstand
van          mij
         tot
      jou              is                         liefde
                       is een afstand
van jou tot mij is
van.         mij
         tot
      jou              is een afstand van liefde
                       van mij tot jou
                       is
   een afstand            van           jou
                                   tot
                              mij
                       is
               liefde is
   een afstand            van mij tot jou
                       is van           jou
                                   tot
                              mij
                       is
   een afstand van liefde
```

FIG. 2.5. Mark Insingel, 'van jou tot mij is' (Insingel 2004c: 53, © Mark Insingel)

This version is not the actual poem published in *Perpetuum mobile* (see Figure 2.6). It is, according to Insingel himself (2004c: 52–54), one of the stages in the genesis of the poem. Insingel not only visualizes the 'distance of love' in the final version, but also the inescapable circularity of intimate relationships and the linguistic concreteness of such relationships:

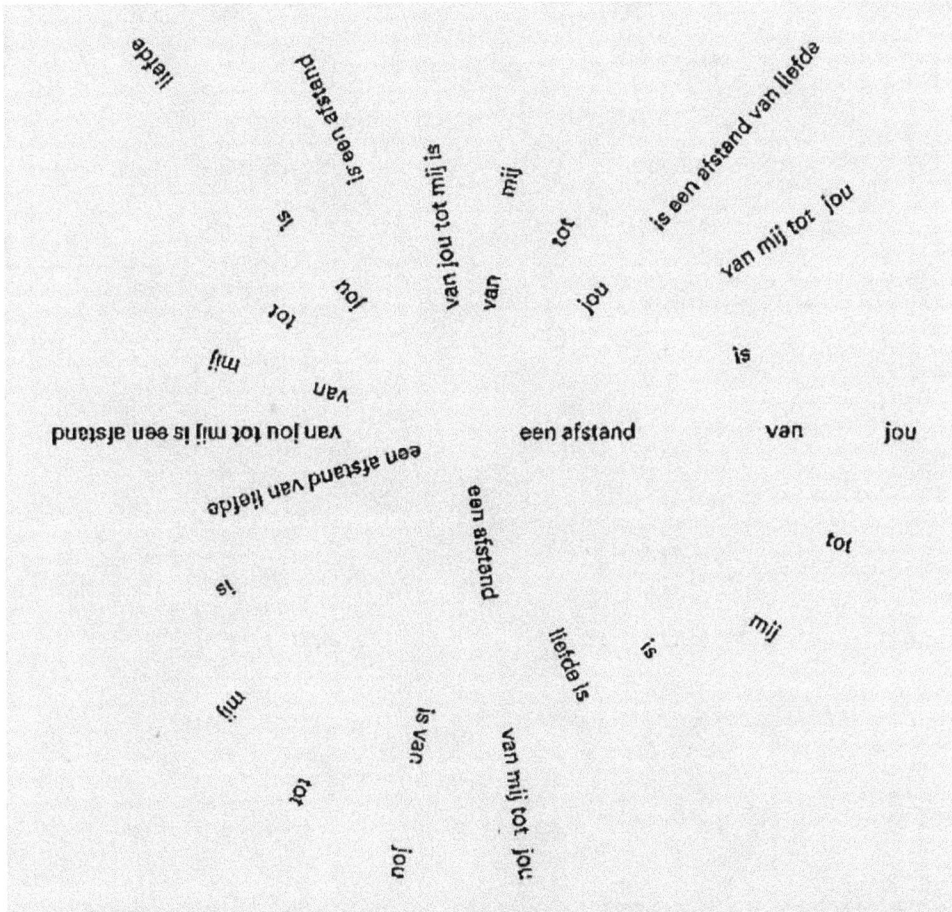

FIG. 2.6. Mark Insingel, 'van jou tot mij is' (Insingel 1990 [1969]: 20, © Mark Insingel)

In *Perpetuum mobile,* Insingel has published several poems of this type. If we confront it with Heißenbüttel, then his 'Speech Words'[56] ('Sprech-Wörter') from *Textbook 4* (1962–1963) are particularly interesting. A representative example is 'from there to' (see Figure 2.7).

In a confrontational reading, the 'poems' (texts) of 'Speech Words' undoubtedly take centre stage even though they are a rarity in Heißenbüttel's work. The principles of vertical ordering and word repetition generate auditory rhythm and visual patterns. Like Insingel's repetitive and permutational poems, these 'Speech Words' are analogous to minimalist music. Think of compositions by the American

```
                    von   da   nach
                          da
                    von   da   nach  rechts
                    von   da   nach
links               von   da   nach  oben    oder
unten                                         oder

                                      rechts
                                      oben    oder
links
unten                                         oder
                    von
links               von               rechts
                          nach  rechts
                    von
links                     nach
links               von
links                           oben
                          da    nach
                          nach
                          da                  oder
                          da
unten
```

FIG. 2.7. Helmut Heißenbüttel, 'von da nach' (1980b: 137, © Erben Heißenbüttel)

composer Steve Reich such as *Clapping Music* (1972) or *Music for Pieces of Wood* (1973) also from the early 1970s, with their gradual rhythmic shifts in the form of polyrhythms. With every perceived minor alteration, the musical experience further develops while the building blocks (tone, sound) remain limited and unsophisticated. In Insingel's and Heißenbüttel's poems, we are similarly dealing with simple words but multiple meanings through permutational combinations and the addition of a spatial, visual or vertical reading which reinforces the rhythm.

It is this kind of visually ordered texts with open slots that Insingel decided to 'complete' by putting them in a circular form. This is Insingel's technique of repetition and variation. Several kinds of parallel constructions (parallel syntax, anaphora, epistrophe, asyndeton, chiasmus), word repetition, as well as visual and rhythmic patterns combined with the principle of circularity achieve particular aesthetic and interpretive effects.

If we want to bring Heißenbüttel's handling of genre in dialogue with that of Insingel, the mediality of Insingel's work is an interesting point of departure. Since the techniques of repetition and variation are realised not only on the level of syntax, but also by means of visual presentation and aural effects, Insingel's texts can be read as hybrid media, similar examples of which we have encountered in Heißenbüttel's *Textbooks*. More accurately, however, they are not so much hybrid in terms of medium, but they emphasize the inherently multimodal nature of poetry and iconicity by exploiting the visual and aural dimensions. Yet, hybridity is a relevant concept in regard to the way Insingel handles traditional literary genres, the epic and the lyric, but also poetry and prose. The poetry of *Perpetuum mobile, Models* and *Posters* is not narrative nor does it evoke lyrical moments of heightened, subjective emotion. It moves away from subjective as well as objective lyric through its foregrounding of lexical repetition and syntactic variation. As a result, the poetry can resemble argumentative prose or even mathematical reasoning.

In that respect, not unlike the generic openness of Heißenbüttel's *Textbooks*, Insingel's approach to genre involves a deconstruction of conventional boundaries. Yet, considering his work from the long 1960s, the difference with Heißenbüttel's approach immediately surfaces. Whereas Heißenbüttel's works are presented invariably as 'text', Insingel publishes separate works which are two sides of the same coin but are still materially recognizable as poetry versus prose. The visual poetry of *Perpetuum mobile* (1969) and the novel *Reflections* (1968) echo each other, and the same goes for the poetry of *Models* (1970b) and the novel *A Course of Time* (1970a). But if we look more closely at how this mutual resonance is realized, then it becomes clear that the traditional demarcation of genres is nullified. In other words, the genre frames are partly evoked and partly ignored.

What exactly is the nature of the relations between poetry and prose in Insingel's work of the late 1960s? It is adequate to say that the question of genre is trumped by other structural principles. Let us consider the examples of *Perpetuum mobile* and *Reflections*. The self-referential visual poetry of *Perpetuum mobile* explores such themes as the autonomy of language and the circularity and tautology of reason, for example in verses such as 'the rounding | of a round thing | makes the thing

| round' (1990: 18), which seems to turn around a centre like a circle.[57] What is foregrounded in this poetry is not the metaphorical potential or lexical variety of language, but the objective concreteness of linguistic signs, including their visual arrangement. In other words, it belongs in the specific experimental genre of concrete poetry, a genre in which 'different elements are taken from different systems and incorporated into a completely new experience', as Victoria Pineda puts it (1995: 380).[58] In that, it distances itself from the prototype of lyrical poetry.

As a whole, the volume displays the same circularity as many of the individual poems. The first and the last poem are each other's counterpart. In a characteristic fashion (see above), the last poem is a formal variation of the first one (see Figure 2.8).

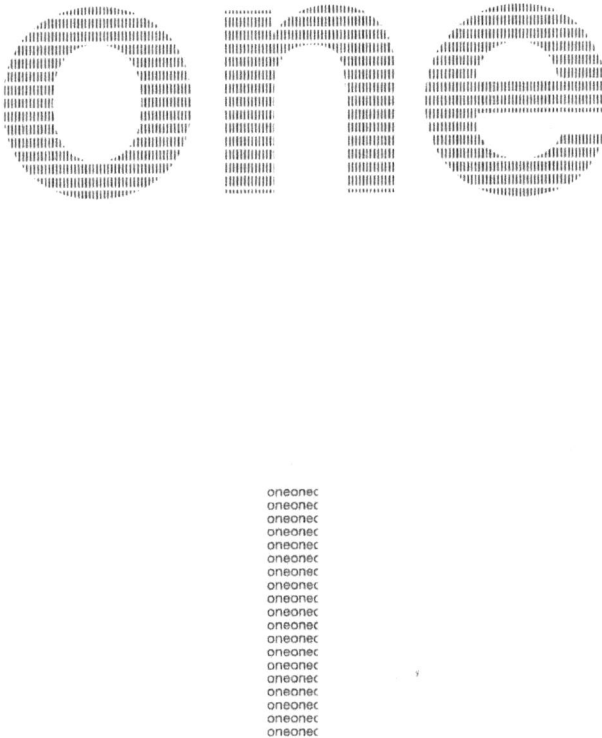

FIG. 2.8. Mark Insingel, 'one' and 'I' (1990 [1969]: 9 and 51, translation Willem Groenewegen, © Mark Insingel)

The same goes for the second and the one but last poem, the third and the second but last one. As a result, the book stresses in its form the autonomy of literary language and the idea that the subject (the 'I') is trapped in anonymous group-entity ('one'), which means the 'I' reproduces ways of thinking and speaking of a group that itself consists of many selves who in turn are governed by the dominant logic of 'one' — etcetera, etcetera, in circles.

In the novel *Reflections* we can notice that the narrative is equally circular and the prose is infused with lyrical procedures. The narrative structure is concentric instead of linear, in the sense that the novel does not read from the beginning of a story to the end of a story but from the circumference to the centre and back to the circumference. In other words: the narrative structure is that of a reflection. At the centre there is a mirror, so to speak, which reflects the first half of the novel into the second half. The settings in the first and the last part of the novel are identical and the scenes are similar. In the first part of the novel the anonymous male protagonist is a child who enjoys the company of his grandfather and who disapproves of his parents. In the middle part, the male protagonist is an adult in relationship with a woman, whom he follows through the city and with whom he walks in its labyrinthine avenues. In the last part of the novel the main character is a child again, looking for his grandfather.

On the level of style, the prose gains a lyrical flavour through devices that slow down the pace of reading, in particular parentheses and apo koinou (an asyndetical blend of two clauses through a lexical word which has two syntactical functions, one in each of the blended clauses), as we can see in this representative example:

> a lady (woman) stands opposite a gentleman (man) stands opposite a lady lets him in, the door is closed, net-curtains hang in front of the windows, blackbirds hop around on the lawn round the house stands in a garden adjoining other gardens in which are houses (1971: 37)

Clearly, the prose of *Reflections* is not the narrative prose one could expect in a novel. The novel is characterized by a level of 'poetic artifice' (Forrest-Thomson 1978), or 'poetic function' as Roman Jakobson calls it, that is a defining feature of poetry according to some, even though the novel does not deploy the 'segmentivity' that is the defining feature of poetry according to others (DuPlessis 1996; McHale 2009).

In the book with the programmatic title *Models,* the generic hybridity takes more clearly a Heißenbüttel-like shape, as the volume ends with three texts — entitled 'argument (1)' ('betoog 1'), 'argument (2)' ('betoog 2') and 'story' ('verhaal') — which are presented in a form associated with prose, namely without line-breaks or enjambments in the familiar sense and with a lot more (but not exclusively) grammatical clauses than the preceding poems. In keeping with the objective of 'lyricization', however, the pace of reading is slowed down by parentheses and *Schlangensätze* [protracted sentences] as in *Reflections*.

As the literary texts and the authors' own comments show, both Heißenbüttel and Insingel develop an idiosyncratic and critical but constructive approach to genre. Rather than putting energy in breaking down the boundaries between genres, their works advocate generic openness and deploy alternative principles of framing. Finally, in both cases the idiosyncratic perspective of genres is intertwined with tensions between the abstract (as in literary abstraction) and the concrete (as in the concreteness of concrete poetry), between objectivity and subjectivity.

As does Heißenbüttel's, Insingel's oeuvre too buries subjectivity into objective structures. The concrete characters and situations of traditional fiction are partly replaced by abstract figures and patterns. In *Reflections* the intricacies of this style become very tangible. The novel foregrounds a tension between abstraction and concreteness, and between objectivity and subjectivity. The narrator of *Reflections* describes abstract configurations and movements of characters and objects in the fictional world. He does this in a seemingly objective way. Gradually, however, this objectivity turns out to be impossible, much like in Robbe-Grillet's novel *Jealousy* (1957, *La jalousie*). The internal conflict between the objective and the subjective is visible in the second-person narration, in the questions and in the frequent parentheses as in the earlier example ('The door opens (is opened), a lady (woman) stands opposite a gentleman (man) stands opposite a lady lets him in'). In brackets, the narrator puts forward alternative ways of understanding a situation. In most cases, these parentheses offer either the conventional, accepted interpretation or the objective visual information, depending on what precedes. In the example, 'the door opens' is the objective visual information, and 'the door is opened' is the conventional interpretation. We can say that, paradoxically, the narration — objective as it is — makes the reader very aware of the subjective nature of perception, understanding that they are already interpreting whilst perceiving.

In aiming to be as objective as a camera eye, the narrator resorts to abstraction. He reduces settings and other spatial frames to their geometrical composition, and he reduces the interactions of characters in locations to their essentials as well. As in certain forms of painterly abstraction, with which the text can clearly be associated, the spatial frames are combinations of circles, lines, and colours. The narrator objectively describes configurations and movements of characters and objects in the fictional world. At least, he tries to. Since perception is always interpretation, this objectivity is impossible. Moreover, the narrator objectively juxtaposes the textual actual world and alternative possible worlds such as dreams and fantasies, which are in fact very subjective. In sum, Insingel's style, which oscillates between abstraction and concreteness, reminds readers of the way subjectivity is inscribed in language and how at the same time this language can gain a seemingly autonomous status in literature.

5. Conclusion

What emerges from the confrontation between Heißenbüttel and Insingel, is the image of strong divergences in career paths and literary activities and a remarkable convergence in their views on literature and in the way they shaped these views in literary texts. These points of contact are most manifest in the 1960s and 1970s. In that period, both authors developed a methodical approach to literature, in which speech and language are exploited as a reservoir of materials that can be selected, reduced, and combined. Inspired by writers such as Paul van Ostaijen and Gertrude Stein they opt for a concrete and often repetitive quasi-prosaic poetry that trades on auditive and visual effects. In Insingel's work, visual and circular principles are more dominant than in Heißenbüttel's work, but both of them create abstract and minimalist textures in the 1960s instead of plot-driven narratives and psychological portrayals. In that way, they resist narrativisation, psychologisation, and other hegemonic forms of meaning-making. In both Heißenbüttel's and Insingel's work, the aesthetic potential of literature therefore inheres in the winding roads of the abstract and the concrete.

Works Cited

ARBOGAST, HUBERT. 1998. *Zur Auswahl und Anordnung von 'Das Sagbare sagen': Eine Auswahl aus dem Werk* (Stuttgart: Klett-Cotta)

BARNER, WILFRIED, ALEXANDER VON BORMANN, MANFRED DURZAK, and ANNE HARTMANN (eds). 1994. *Geschichte der deutschen Literatur von den Anfängen bis zur Gegenwart*, 12 vols (Munich: Beck), XII: *Geschichte der deutschen Literatur von 1945 bis zur Gegenwart*

BARTHES, ROLAND. 1970. *S/Z* (Paris: Seuil)

——. 1974. *S/Z*, trans. by Richard Miller (New York: Hill and Wang)

BEEKMAN, KLAUS. 1975. 'Experimentele teksten omstreeks '70', *Spektator*, 4.9–10: 529–40

——. 1990. 'Mark Insingel', in *Kritisch lexicon van de moderne Nederlandstalige literatuur*, ed. by Ad Zuiderent, Hugo Brems and Tom van Deel (Alphen aan den Rijn: Samsom), pp. 1–10, A1, B1–B3

BOHLEY, JOHANNA, and LUTZ DITTRICH (eds). 2012. *Helmut Heißenbüttel: Literatur für alle*, booklet accompanying the exhibition in the LiteraturHaus Berlin, Literaturhaus Stuttgart and the Staats- und Universitätsbibliothek Hamburg 2012–13 (Berlin: Literaturhaus Berlin)

BOUSSET, HUGO. 1990. 'Mark Insingel: territorium van woorden', in *Grenzen verleggen: De Vlaamse prozaliteratuur 1970–1986*, 2 vols (Antwerp: Houtekiet), II: *Profielen*, pp. 133–39

BREMS, HUGO. 1972. 'Mark Insingel: Was is (niet)', in *De brekende sleutel* (Antwerp: De Nederlandsche Boekhandel), pp. 121–27

BUELENS, GEERT. 2004. *Van Ostaijen tot heden: Zijn invloed op de Vlaamse poëzie* (Nijmegen: Vantilt)

COMBRINK, THOMAS. 2011. *Sammler und Erfinder: Zu Leben und Werk Helmut Heißenbüttels. Mit einem Nachwort von Alexander Kluge* (Göttingen: Wallstein)

DECKMYN, JEROEN, and HANS VANDEVOORDE. 2012. 'Het dagboek als rollenspel: Insingel en het "nieuwe journaal"', *Interférences littéraires/Literaire interferenties*, 9: 85–96

DE VREE, PAUL. 1971. 'Mark Insingel of de linguïstische wetmatigheid', *Periscoop*, 21.6: 3

DÖHL, REINHARD, JOHANNES AUER, and FRIEDRICH W. BLOCK (eds). 2005. *Als Stuttgart Schule machte* <http://www.stuttgarter-schule.de> [accessed 30 May 2019]

DUPLESSIS, RACHEL BLAU. 1996. 'Manifests', *Diacritics*, 26.3–4: 31–53

FAES, GUST. 1970. 'Poëzie in Vlaanderen', *Heibel*, 6.3–4: 73–75

FLAMEND, JAN. 1984. 'Gesprek met Mark Insingel bij het verschijnen van *Een meisje nam de tram*', *Het Belang van Limburg*, 23 January 1984

FORREST-THOMSON, VERONICA. 1978. *Poetic Artifice: A Theory of Twentieth-Century Poetry* (New York: St. Martin's Press)

FRIEDRICH, HANS-EDWIN. 2011. 'Zum Stand der Heißenbüttel-Forschung', in *Reden über die Schwierigkeiten der Rede: Das Werk Helmut Heißenbüttels*, ed. by Hans-Edwin Friedrich and Sven Hanuschek (= *neoAvantgarden* 1) (Munich: edition text + kritik), pp. 363–406

GENETTE, GÉRARD. 1987. *Seuils* (Paris: Seuil)

HARIG, LUDWIG. 1991. '"Ich bin eine Geschichte von jemand": Helmut Heißenbüttel als Erzähler', in *Schrift écriture geschrieben gelesen: Für Helmut Heißenbüttel zum siebzigsten Geburtstag*, ed. by Christina Weiß (Stuttgart: Klett-Cotta), pp. 70–76

HEISSENBÜTTEL, HELMUT. 1954. *Kombinationen* (Eßlingen: Bechtle)

——. 1956. *Topographien* (Eßlingen: Bechtle)

——. 1960. 'Bruchstück III (kurzer Erläuterungstext)', *magnum*, 31 [Lyriker unserer Zeit]: p. 51

——. 1960. *Textbuch 1* (Olten: Walter Verlag)

——. 1961. *Textbuch 2* (Olten: Walter Verlag)

——. 1962. *Textbuch 3* (Olten: Walter Verlag)

——. 1964. *Textbuch 4* (Olten: Walter Verlag)

——. 1965. *Textbuch 5: 3x13 mehr oder weniger Geschichten* (Olten: Walter Verlag)

——. 1967. *Textbuch 6* (Olten: Walter Verlag)

——. 1969. 'Was ist das Konkrete an einem Gedicht?', in *Was ist das Konkrete an einem Gedicht? Zwei Ansätze* (Itzehoe: Hansen & Hansen), pp. 47–119

——. 1970. *Projekt Nr. 1: D'Alemberts Ende* (Neuwied and Berlin: Luchterhand)

——. 1972. *Zur Tradition der Moderne: Aufsätze und Anmerkungen 1964–1971* (Neuwied: Luchterhand)

——. 1974. *Das Durchhauen des Kohlhaupts: Dreizehn Lehrgedichte. Projekt Nr. 2* (Neuwied: Luchterhand)

——. 1980A. *Wenn Adolf Hitler den Krieg nicht gewonnen hätte: Historische Novellen und wahre Begebenheiten. Projekt 3/2* (Stuttgart: Klett-Cotta)

——. 1980B. *Textbücher* (Stuttgart: Klett-Cotta)

——. 1981. 'Unterdrückte Sprechwörter 1962', in *Helmut Heißenbüttel: Text + Kritik*, ed. by Heinz Ludwig Arnold, *Zeitschrift für Literatur* 69–70: 34–37

——. 1981. *Textbuch 8. 1981–1985* (Stuttgart: Klett-Cotta)

——. 1981. *Textbuch 9. 3 x 13 x 13 Sätze. 1981–1984* (Stuttgart: Klett-Cotta)

——. 1981. *Ödipuskomplex. Made in Germany* Gelegenheitsgedichte, Totentage, Landschaften 1965–1980. (Stuttgart: Klett-Cotta)

——. 1983. 'Text oder Gedicht? Anmerkungen zur theoretischen und praktischen Aktualität dieser Frage — eine Abschweifung', in *Textsorten und literarische Gattungen: Dokumentation des Germanistentages in Hamburg vom 1.–4. April 1979* (Berlin: Erich Schmidt Verlag), pp. 3–24

——. 1983. *mehr ist dazu nicht zu sagen. neue herbste* (Stuttgart: Klett-Cotta)

——. 1986. *Textbuch 10: Von Liebeskunst* (Stuttgart: Klett-Cotta)

——. 1987. *Textbuch 11 in gereinigter Sprache* (Stuttgart: Klett-Cotta)

——. 1995. *Über Literatur* (Stuttgart: Klett-Cotta)

——. 1998. 'Wassermaler: 35 Jahre danach', in *Das Sagbare sagen* (Stuttgart: Klett-Cotta), 165–67

HOSTE, POL. 1981. 'De Vlaamse literatuur is op al lang aangelegde autosnelwegen gaan rijden', *De Nieuwe*, 29 October 1981

——. 1982. 'De intimiteit tussen de arbeider en zijn materiaal', *Provinciale Zeeuwse Courant*, 20 February 1982

INSINGEL, MARK. 1963. *Drijfhout* (Colibrant: Drongen)

——. 1968. *Spiegelingen* (Amsterdam: Meulenhoff)

——. 1970A. *Een tijdsverloop* (Amsterdam: Meulenhoff)

——. 1970B. *Modellen* (Amsterdam: Meulenhoff)

——. 1971. *Reflections*, trans. by Adrienne Dixon (London: Calder and Boyars)

——. 1974. *Dat wil zeggen* (The Hague: Nijgh en Van Ditmar)

——. 1977. *A Course of Time*, trans. by Adrienne Dixon (New York: Red Dust)

——. 1981. *Woorden zijn oorden* (Haarlem: In de Knipscheer)

——. 1990. *In elkanders armen*, collected poems 1969–1990: *Perpetuum mobile, Modellen, Posters, Het is zo niet zo is het, Jij noemt stom wat taal is* (Amsterdam: In de Knipscheer)

——. 1994A. *De druiven die te hoog hangen* (Amsterdam: In de Knipscheer)

——. 1994B. 'That Is to Say', trans. by Theo Hermans, *Review of Contemporary Fiction*, 14.2: 56–76

——. 1998. '"Ich will nackt sein und anfangen": Über den Radikalismus Paul van Ostaijens', in *Paul van Ostaijen, die Avantgarde und Berlin*, ed. by Lut Missinne and Loek Geeraedts, Niederlande-Studien, Kleinere Schriften, IV (Münster), pp. 91–111

——. 2004A. 'Met eigen woorden', in Yves T'Sjoen, *Stem en tegenstem: Over poëzie en poëtica* (Amsterdam: Atlas), pp. 191–97

——. 2004B. 'Het gedicht als constellatie — mijn persoonlijk verhaal over de zogenaamde concrete en visuele poëzie', *Verslagen & Mededelingen van de Koninklijke Maatschappij der Nederlandse Taal- en Letterkunde*, 114.2: 141–56

——. 2004C. 'Hoe ik het doe', *Freespace Nieuwzuid*, 15.4: 50–63

——. 2010. *Iets & Niets* (Ghent: PoëzieCentrum)

——. (to Lars Bernaerts). 2014. Private correspondence (24 November 2014)

KARS, THEO. 1975. 'Vivisectie op de lezer', in *Parels voor de zwijnen* (Amsterdam: Loeb), pp. 77–81

KRAMER, ANDREAS. 1993. *Gertrude Stein und die deutsche Avantgarde* (Eggingen: Klaus Isele)

KUYPERS, JEROEN. 1990. 'Mark Insingel vat sociale taak als schrijver serieus op: "ik blijf strijden tegen taalvervalsing"', *Het Binnenhof*, 20 July 1990

LAMPAERT, JAN. 2016. *Visualisering netwerk neo-avant-gardetijdschriften*, Research Report for the Center for the Study of Experimental Literature (Ghent)

MCHALE, BRIAN. 2009. 'Beginning to Think About Narrative in Poetry', *Narrative*, 17.1: 11–30

MEIZOZ, JÉRÔME. 2007. *Postures littéraires : Mises en scène modernes de l'auteur* (Geneva: Slatkine érudition)

MON, FRANZ. 1981. '"eine Art von Erinnerung hatte sich erhalten": Zu "Deutschland 1944" von Helmut Heißenbüttel', in *Helmut Heißenbüttel*, ed. by Heinz Ludwig Arnold (Munich: edition text + kritik), pp. 55–59

——. 2012. 'Entwurf neuer Realitätszusammenhänge', in *Helmut Heißenbüttel: Literatur für alle*, edi by Johanna Bohley and Lutz Dittrich (Berlin: Literaturhaus Berlin), pp. 32–34

MYSJKIN, JAN H. 1983. 'Een alternatieve stationsroman', *De Morgen*, 27 October 1983

OTTENHOF, HUMPHREY. 2005. *De letter te lijf: Beeldvorming van concrete en visuele poëzie in Nederland en Vlaanderen* (Zevenaar: DWZ/MAW)

PETERS, GÜNTER. 1996. 'Die ringmodulierte Meditation: Helmut Heißenbüttels *Einfache grammatische Meditationen* in Karlheinz Stockhausens *Mikrophonie II*', in *Autoren-Musik: Sprache im Grenzbereich der Künste*, Musik-Konzepte: Die Reihe über Komponisten, vol. LXXXI, ed. by Heinz-Klaus Metzger, Rainer Riehn, and Günter Peters (Munich: edition text + kritik), pp. 16–40

PINEDA, VICTORIA. 1995. 'Speaking About Genre: The Case of Concrete Poetry', *New Literary History*, 26.2: 379–95

POGGIOLI, RENATO. 1967. *The Theory of the Avant-garde* (Cambridge: Belknap Press)

POLET, SYBREN. 1978. *Ander proza: Bloemlezing uit het Nederlandse experimenterende proza van Theo Van Doesburg tot heden (1975)* (Amsterdam: De Bezige Bij)

RAMM, KLAUS. 2006. '"...wenn man methodisch sich weiterbewegt...": Klaus Ramm in conversation with Helmut Heißenbüttel', in *Selbstaussagen im Konjunktiv. Helmut Heißenbüttel: eine Hommage*, ed. by Thomas Combrink and Norbert Wehr, *Schreibheft: Zeitschrift für Literatur*, 67: 133–41

RAMON, RENAAT. 2014. *Vorm & visie: Geschiedenis van de concrete en visuele poëzie in Nederland en Vlaanderen* (Ghent: PoëzieCentrum)

RIHA, KARL. 1997. 'Experimentelle Literatur', in *Deutsche Literatur zwischen 1945 und 1995: Eine Sozialgeschichte*, ed. by Horst A. Glaser (Bern: Haupt), pp. 535–55

ROGGEMAN, WILLEM M. 1975. 'Mark Insingel', in *Beroepsgeheim: Gesprekken met schrijvers 1* (The Hague: Nijgh & Van Ditmar), pp. 25–35

ROTERMUND, HERMANN [N.D.]. 'Helmut Heißenbüttel im Gespräch mit Hermann Rotermund: Wahrscheinlich ist es in den Wind geredet' <http://www.stuttgarter-schule.de/interview_hh2.htm> [accessed 30 May 2019]

SCHMIDT, SIEGFRIED J. 1970. *Ästhetische Prozesse: Ein Beitrag zur Konzeption einer nach-konkreten Kunst* (= *schriften zur konkreten kunst*, III, ed. by Siegfried. J. Schmidt), (Karlsruhe: Sema Verlag), pp. 11–33

SPANINKS, PIERRE. 1978. 'Licht uit, spot aan: Vijf avant-gardisten over experimentele literatuur', in *Experimenteel-dubbelnummer*, special issue of *Van*, 1.7–8: 99–118

STEIN, GERTRUDE. 1928. *Useful Knowledge* (New York: Payson & Clarke)

STÜCKRATH, JÖRN. 1981. 'Helmut Heißenbüttels "Deutschland 1944"': Deutung und Theorie einer Zitatmontage', in *Literarische Collagen: Texte, Quellen, Theorie*, ed. by Volker Hage (Stuttgart: Reclam), pp. 233–57

'T HART, KEES. 2004. 'Woedende pracht', *De Standaard*, 23 September 2004

T'SJOEN, YVES. 2004. 'Verwijlen bij circulaire taallichamen: Over de autonomistische kunstopvatting van de dichter Mark Insingel', in *Onderstroom: De vergankelijkheid van het schrijverschap*, ed. by Yves T'Sjoen and Ludo Stynen (Ghent: Academia Press), pp. 77–88

VANDEVOORDE, HANS. 1996. '*Eenzaam lichaam* van Mark Insingel: Een intieme en vooral confronterende spiegel', *Knack*, 17 November 1996

VAN DER STRAETEN, BART, and TOM VAN IMSCHOOT. 2015. '"Ik was de avant-garde in mezelf en voor mezelf": Een gesprek met Mark Insingel', *Poëziekrant*, 39.4: 38–41

——. 2017. 'De lijst als lyricisering: Een gesprek met Mark Insingel', in *Legendes van de literatuur*, ed. by Lars Bernaerts, Bart Van der Straeten, Tom Van Imschoot, and Hans Vandevoorde (Ghent: Academia Press), pp. 17–21

VAN MARISSING, LIDY. 1971. 'Vlaming Mark Insingel: sprinter of dichter? De literatuur in het tijdperk van de audio-visuele media', *De Volkskrant*, 9 January 1971

WALDROP, ROSMARIE. 1969. 'Helmut Heißenbüttel, Poet of Contexts', *Germanic Review*, 44:2: 132–42

WESSELO, J.J. 1983. 'Het territorium van Mark Insingel', in *Vlaamse wegen: Het vernieuwende proza in Vlaanderen tussen 1960 & 1980* (Antwerp: Manteau), pp. 119–35

WIEGENSTEIN, ROLAND H. 1970. 'Kritik', in *Grenzverschiebung: Neue Tendenzen in der deutschen Literatur der 6oer Jahre*, ed. by Renate Matthaei (Cologne: Kiepenheuer & Witsch), pp. 203–04

Notes to Chapter 2

1. 'een pak met dunne, witte, albumvormige boeken'
2. The translations of the Heißenbüttel sections in this chapter and of the literary quotations from Heißenbüttel's work are Helen White's, unless indicated otherwise.
3. 'Walter Mannzen doesn't know if Günter Grass knows if Brecht could know what Grass knows and Unseld might know what Brecht knew and Grass knows whether Brecht could know if Unseld knows what Grass doesn't know but he's not telling either' ('Walter Mannzen weiß nicht ob Günter Graß weiß ob Brecht wissen konnte was Graß weiß und Unseld wissen kann was Brecht wußte und Graß weiß ob Brecht wissen konnte ob Unseld weiß was Graß nicht weiß aber er sagts auch nicht' (Heißenbüttel 1965: 48)).
4. 'Wann aber wird man soweit sein, Bücher wie Kataloge zu schreiben?'
5. 'Heißenbüttels Popularitätskurve [zeigte] an, welche Rolle die avantgardistische Ästhetik im literarischen Feld einnahm.'

6. 'In meiner Erinnerung steht Helmut Heißenbüttel in der Stuttgarter Schule wie Gorgias, der Sophist, in der Schule von Athen, jenem bekanntem Gemälde von Raffael. Die Schule von Athen als Sinnbild der Stuttgarter Schule: Während Max Bense, Plato und Aristoteles in einer Gestalt, auf höchster Treppenstufe steht, haben alle anderen konkreten Denker und Poeten links und rechts, an Pfeilern und Säulen Position bezogen: Döhl und Gomringer, Franz Mon und Ernst Jandl, Manfred Esser und Helmut Mader, und ich selbst stehe ja auch auf der Treppe, unterhalb von Bense, unmittelbar neben Helmut Heißenbüttel, der sich anschickt, einen Heißenbüttel-Diskurs zu führen.'

7. 'Eduard — so nennen wir einen Rundfunkredakteur im besten Mannesalter — Eduard hatte im D-Zug München — Hamburg (Ankunft Hauptbahnhof 21.19) die schönsten Stunden eines Julinachmittags (25.7.1968) zugebracht und betrachtete mit Vergnügen die Gegend zwischen Lüneburg und Harburg.'

8. In a visual mapping of the neo-avant-garde networks in the 1960s (Lampaert 2016) it becomes clear that Insingel has a limited number of strong connections (e.g. membership of institutions and participation in events) in the network, unlike other neo-avant-garde authors.

9. 'Experiment und experimentell im 20. Jahrhundert meinen gerade eine Literatur und Poesie, die ausprobiert, ohne sich ihrer Ergebnisse sicher zu sein. Ihr Grundverständnis steht den *Versuchen* Bertolt Brechts ebenso nahe wie der Opposition des Konkreten gegen das Abstrakte in der bildenden Kunst.'

10. '[die] Idee, daß die Pausen mitsprechen'

11. 'Spiele aus Kurve Welle Reflex Schatten aus Spuren und Spuren von Spuren'

12. 'I am ever more inclined to define these things neither as poems nor as texts, but as demonstrations. Demonstration, in the double sense of the word, seems to me to be that which is necessary. More would be presumptuous, less might be beautiful "poésie pure", dishonest. I think such demonstrations are capable of admitting everything, the subjective as well as the general and the political!' — 'Ich neige immer mehr dazu, diese Dinge weder als Gedichte noch als Texte zu bezeichnen, sondern als Demonstrationen. Demonstration im Doppelsinn dieses Wortes scheint mir das zu sein, was notwendig ist. Mehr wäre vermessen, weniger, etwa schöne "poésie pure", unredlich. Ich denke, daß solche Demonstrationen fähig sind, alles aufzunehmen, sowohl das Subjektive wie das Allgemeine, das Politische!'

13. 'Das Auftreten Heißenbüttels in den sechziger Jahren war von einer konzeptuellen Neuerung begleitet. Mit dem Begriff des Textes hob er die Grenzen zwischen Poesie und Prosa auf und schärfte den Blick für die Textur, für das bewußt Verfertigte des literarischen Gebildes. Sein Prinzip war die Erprobung von Möglichkeiten. Von Möglichkeiten des Veränderns. Endgültig festgelegt hat er sich dabei nie, er fragte beharrlich weiter.'

14. 'Verfolger verfolgen die Verfolgten. Verfolgte aber werden Verfolger. Und weil Verfolgte Verfolger werden werden aus Verfolgten verfolgende Verfolgte und aus Verfolgern verfolgte Verfolger. Aus verfolgten Verfolgern aber werden wiederum Verfolger [verfolgende verfolgte Verfolger].'

15. 'Es gibt mich (es gibt alles wovon ich reden kann) weil ich aus dem Zirkel dieses (mit Hilfe von) heraustrete und mich über die Fiktion hinwegsetze und rede als ob nicht. Ich rede als ob nicht weil die Rede die ich rede als ob redet.'

16. 'Ramm: Wo steckt da die spezifische Erkenntnismöglichkeit für die Literatur? Heißenbüttel: Im Formulieren, in der Ausformulierung der Sätze, und die Ausformulierung hängt ab vom Methodischen. Ich glaube, daß Einfälle methodischer Art schon ein Erkenntnismoment haben.'

17. 'Sprache ist unter anderem dadurch gekennzeichnet, daß sie die Tendenz hat, Poesie zu sein.'

18. 'auf der Zahl 13 beruhendes, nichtliterarisches Strukturprinzip'

19. 'Unbesehen vermittelt diese im gesellschaftlichen Ambiente gemiedene Primzahl Abseitiges, Widerständiges, Widerwärtiges.'

20. 'natürlich haben alle was gewußt der eine dies und der andere das aber niemand mehr als das und es hätte schon jemand sich noch mehr zusammenfragen müssen wenn er das gekonnt hätte aber das war schwer weil jeder immer nur an der oder der Stelle dies oder das zu hören kriegte [...] und so hat das funktioniert.'

21. 'wie ich das alles so hinschreibe erfaßt mich wieder dermaßen die Ungeheuerlichkeit dieser Dinge dass ich meine ich müsse aus einem bösen Traum erwachen'

22. 'ich stand teils am Fenster teils auf der Wiese um mir bald diesen bald jenen Eindruck einzuprägen wie jemand der mit einer großen Reihe von Aufnahmen beschäftigt ist'

23. 'wer sich bemüht, aktuell und interessant und der Faszination folgend etwas zu machen, erfährt keine Hilfe, wenn er sich an diese Abgrenzungen [der Kunst] hält. Er muß ins Freie. Er muß sich unmittelbar verhalten, zur konkreten Methode, zur konkreten Einsicht wie zur Übereinkunft, zur möglichen und auszuprobierenden Übereinkunft zwischen Methode und Einsicht. [...] Ich bin dabei allerdings überzeugt, daß es dies Offenlassen ist, das alles entscheidet.'

24. 'Alle Texte haben die Möglichkeit der akustischen Realisation; einige wurden als Hörspiel gesendet.'

25. Examples of texts and radio plays from *Project 2: Chopping the Cabbage* are: 'Max Immediately Before Going to Sleep, Sequence in 0+2 Measures', 'So What Are We Going to Broadcast Then, 2 Sequences in 21 Measures each', 'Marlowe's End Analysis and Synthesis of a Dialogue', 'Nipples and all or a Short Introduction to Psychoanalysis', 'News Barrier', and 'My Name is Ludwig Wittgenstein' ('Max unmittelbar vorm Einschlafen Ablauf in 0+21 Takten', 'was sollen wir überhaupt senden 2 Abläufe in je 21 Takten', 'Marlowes Ende Analyse und Synthese eines Dialogs', 'Warzen und alles oder eine kleine Einführung in die Psychoanalyse', 'Nachrichtensperre', and 'mein Name ist Ludwig Wittgenstein').

26. 'vom Werbetext bis zur philosophischen These, vom Dialog eines Comics bis zu den Ergebnissen einer Untersuchung über Gruppensex, von banalen Reimereien bis zu linguistischen Übungssätzen über Franz Josef Strauß, von Traumprotokollen bis zu Zitaten der Weltgeschichte'

27. 'in ein undurchschaubares Überkreuz aus Sexualforschungsdaten und Illustriertenstories, aus handlichen psychoanalytischen Kategorien, Partnerschaftsgefasel und Trivialmythen'

28. 'Textelemente der literarischen Tradition auszuwählen, zu brechen und umzuinterpretieren'

29. 'Generalsherbst', 'Bürosexherbst', 'Psychoanalytikerherbst', 'Herbst der Liebe', 'Eheherbst'

30. 'Ein Wassermaler ist jemand, der etwas tut, was es nicht gibt. [...] Auf Wasser malen bedeutet im Prinzip, etwas tun, das sich ungeeigneter Mittel bedient. Ungeeignet vom Standpunkt der üblichen und gebräuchlichen Tätigkeit. Was heißt: malen, um etwas darzustellen, abbildhaft oder nicht abbildhaft, etwas, das betrachtet werden kann, als, wenn auch einer kleinen, über Jahre währenden Veränderung unterworfen, Schatz nach Hause mitgenommen werden und aufbewahrt werden kann. [...] Um den Wassermaler eindeutig und ein für alle Mal zu definieren: es ist dies nicht, kein Geplantes, keine Choreographie, kein in eine Art Notenschrift Übertragbares. Sondern Wassermalen, auf Wasser malen, alle Arten von Wasser, Regenpfützen, Seeflächen, Wasserspiegel vollgelaufener Töpfe, übergelaufenes Wasser, Wasser in einer Badewanne, Meerwasser, das offene Meer, bedeutet, sich herauszunehmen aus allen Bedingungen und von Anfang an neu einzustellen. Ganz und gar einzustellen, ohne Rest, vollkommen. Ich will nichts machen. Ich will nichts festlegen, herstellen als Kategorien, außerhalb derer ich mich bewege. Indem ich mich außerhalb bewege, bin ich verändert, ein Anderer. [...] Ich mache nichts, lege nichts fest und stelle nichts her. Aber ich mache nicht Nichts, lege nicht Nichts fest und stelle nicht Nichts her. Wassermalen liegt dazwischen. [...] Es ist eine Sache, in die man hineinspringt, hineinhüpft, hineingleitet, sich hineinbegibt. Und weiß es nicht. Ohne die Erinnerung an den Punkt, an dem es geschieht. Darin besteht die eigentliche Schwierigkeit: begreiflich zu machen, was sich dem Begreifen entzieht.'

31. 'Ik was de avant-garde in mezelf en voor mezelf.'

32. Meizoz focuses on self-positioning. Needless to say, the image of an author is always also mediated by others and by external factors in discursive contexts.

33. Also in the privileged peritext of the motto in *Reflections* (1968, *Spiegelingen*) and *Something & Nothing* (2010, *Iets & Niets*).

34. 'de Duitse literatuur van de jaren zestig maakte meer indruk op me'

35. 'Ik leg misschien te zeer de nadruk op het "voorstellingloze" ideaal voor de literaire creatie. Dit duidt nochtans [...] niet op een vrijblijvende houding. Integendeel, ik ben ervan overtuigd dat het kunstwerk eerst in dit ideaal ten volle zijn "Erkenntnisfunktion" (Helmut Heissenbüttel) verkrijgt.'

36. 'het is het genot aan de "Erkenntnisfunktion" (Helmut Heissenbüttel) van het medium, je drift maakt een ziener van je'

37. 'Hij werkt echter niet "in" de taal, hij gaat er niet "semantisch" mee om zoals b.v. Joyce en Gertrude Stein, en evenmin treedt hij, zoals deze laatsten, "aus der Kommunikationssphäre der Sprache" (Heissenbüttel).'

38. Since Paul van Ostaijen is the most prominent figure in the Flemish avant-garde, Insingel's explicit and elaborate response (see Insingel 1998) to Van Ostaijen's work can also shed light on Insingel's own views. Van Ostaijen is a well-suited lens to examine the nature of 'Insingel's' neo-avant-garde. In his monumental study of Van Ostaijen's influence on Flemish poetry, Geert Buelens has traced Insingel's indebtedness to Van Ostaijen from his debut until 1978. Buelens (2001: 936) points out that the similarities between the two poets' views on literature are fundamental, even though Insingel draws upon the dominant theoretical discourse of his own time — structuralism — to voice them.

39. 'De ware strijd wordt gevoerd op het vlak van de vorm.'

40. 'Kunst begint nu daar waar de mededeling belangrijker wordt dan het medegedeelde, waar er een muziek van betekenissen ontstaat, waaruit kan volgen dat in de zuiverste vorm van kunst de mededeling het medegedeelde volkomen uitschakelt. [...] [H]et is alleen in zijn totaliteit in de cirkelstructuur ingeschreven, zijn aan- of afwezigheid speelt op zich zelf geen rol.'

41. 'Als *mens* kan ik (politiek en sociaal) geëngageerd zijn, beschik ik over heel wat actiemiddelen, als *kunstenaar* over geen enkel.'

42. 'met die term ben ik helemaal niet gelukkig, omdat de avant-garde een vooruitgangsdenken impliceert'

43. 'sich experimentell verabsolutierende Literatur'

44. 'Holzrauch über Heslach blendet Februarsonne Geräusch am | Bahndamm Zuruf Echoschritt Musterlandschaft veraltet | Gittertext quer überlegt nachdrücklich nachdenklich nachlässig [...]'

45. 'Een verrassend knap en progressief werk dat Insingel dicht bij de spits brengt van onze vernieuwende prozaschrijvers'

46. 'le texte scriptible, c'est *nous en train d'écrire*, avant que le jeu infini du monde (le monde comme jeu) ne soit traversé, coupé, arrêté, plastifié par quelque système singulier (Idéologie, Genre, Critique) qui en rabatte sur la pluralité des entrées [...]. Le scriptible, c'est le romanesque sans le roman, la poésie sans le poème, l'essai sans la dissertation, l'écriture sans le style, la production sans le produit, la structuration sans la structure' (Barthes 1970: 11)

47. 'Insingel heeft de laatste veertig jaar in ons taalgebied een reputatie opgebouwd van een maker van nogal "steriele" en "bedachte" literatuur, hij zou "concrete" poëzie en proza schrijven, een navolger zijn van het constructivisme en in het algemeen een voorstander van "abstracte" en "theoretische" literatuur. Ik heb daar nooit een bal van geloofd. Zijn werk is op te vatten als een ongegeneerde, zeer persoonlijke en hardnekkige woedebui over de uitwerking van maatschappelijke structuren op menselijke verhoudingen, in het bijzonder die waar hij zelf binnen moet functioneren.'

48. For a more general overview of visual and concrete poetry in the Low Countries, we refer to Ottenhof 2005 and Ramon 2014.

49. 'Dies ist das Schema. Das Schema ist immer dasselbe. Das Schema ist das was immer dasselbe bleibt.'

50. 'Die Montagen Heißenbüttels sind Versuche, nicht nur verbrauchten Worten neues Gewicht zu geben, sondern sogar vorformulierte Sätze und Satzteile überraschend zu machen, sie gelöst aus ihrem ursprünglichen Zusammenhang einem anderen Sinn zu übergeben, gewohnte Assoziationen abzuweisen und nicht Nach-Denken, sondern Denken zu provozieren, gerade vermöge der Umwandlung von Vorgeprägtem. Man braucht lange, bis man diese "Zusammensetzungen" auch nur einigermaßen versteht.'

51. For example, at the Berlin Academy of Arts, Reinhard Döhl estate. 2560, Helmut Heißenbüttel.

52. Heißenbüttel 1964. These are supplemented by a later publication in the *Zeitschrift für Literatur*: Heißenbüttel 1981.

53. 'als Schriftsteller suche ich etwa nach den Methoden, die meine Erfahrung, meine Irritation in der Welt, in der ich lebe, ausdrücken können [...]. [... A]ls Schriftsteller möchte ich ein paar Vorschläge machen, die zum Nachdenken anregen und ein vielleicht schon allzusehr erstarrtes Vorstellungsschema auflockern, durchbrechen, durchlöchern sollen.'

54. 'Diese multiple Subjektivität steht in einer auf mehrere Punkte zugleich bezogenen Perspektive. Die Simultaneität der Bezugspunkte hat ihre Entsprechung in der halluzinatorischen Methode der Literatur, die über den sprachlichen Bereich die Gemeinsamkeit zwischen sprachlichen und technischen Verfahren begründet.'

55. Another Heißenbüttel example is 'the future of socialism' (1980b: 230–32; 'die Zukunft des Sozialismus'). Consider the first verses of the four stanzas: 'no-one possesses something', 'no-one possesses nothing', 'everyone possesses everything', 'everyone possesses nothing' ('niemand besitzt was', 'niemand besitzt nichts', 'alle besitzen alles', 'alle besitzen nichts').

56. The original title is a pun on the German word for a 'saying', a 'proverb' [Sprichwort].

57. 'de ronding / van een rond ding / maakt het ding / rond'. Together with the remaining two verses, these lines are put around a circle.

58. To suggest that this is less prototypical poetry and thus puts the genre attribution under pressure, however, would be tantamount to missing an important point. What defines poetry, as Rachel Blau DuPlessis (1996) and Brian McHale (2009) argue, is segmentivity. The kind of concrete poetry Insingel writes exploits and extends the means for segmentivity.

CHAPTER 3

❖

Hybrid Hydra-Heads:
Friederike Mayröcker versus
Lucienne Stassaert

Inge Arteel (Vrije Universiteit Brussel) &
Jeroen Dera (Radboud University)

In this chapter we present Friederike Mayröcker and Lucienne Stassaert, both of whom are considered to be the main women writers with a distinct profile in their respective experimental contexts during the 1960s. This chapter wants to explore how, if at all, this shared exceptional gender related status is reflected in their self-positioning and poetics. What was their relationship with their respective male dominated artistic environments like? How did their artistic practice take shape? As we will show, both authors share(d) a preference for *Einzelgängertum* [going it alone] and volatility in their literary self-positioning, with a similar evolution towards less explicit experimentalism around 1970. Their concrete literary practice of the late 1960s, however, diverges greatly. Related though they are regarding their position in the literary field, their texts demonstrate that this does not lead up to a uniform gendered poetics. Biographically too, differences come to the fore, especially concerning the generations they belong to, as well as the national and institutional context they grew up in, as the following paragraphs will make clear.

1. Background

Mayröcker

Born in Vienna on 20 December 1924, Friederike Mayröcker's young adult years were profoundly marked by World War II, the last three years of which she had to work as a *Luftwaffenhelferin* [air force assistant]. Though the war years and their impact remain in an explicit sense largely absent from her work, indirect signals can easily be identified, such as how Mayröcker as a youngster tried to safeguard a world of her own amidst the national socialist climate, a place 'behind a glass wall', as she herself called it (Mayröcker 2001c: 127).[1] The passionate study of English and French, both language and literature, and the interest in classical music (with some preliminary piano lessons) coincided with her early wartime writing endeavours and have continued to influence her writing ever since.

Born in a family of limited financial means, Mayröcker had to earn her own living, and in 1946 she took on a job as an English teacher at several Viennese secondary schools, a bread-and-butter job she would fulfil for 23 years. This background of economic austerity provided a common ground with her longtime companion, Ernst Jandl. Moreover, it distinguished both of them from the members of the Wiener Gruppe [Vienna Group], who could afford not having to work for a living and — paradoxically — promoted this as an anti-bourgeois attitude.

1946 also marks the beginning of Mayröcker's writing career: her first poem was published in the Viennese periodical *Plan*. In 1947, *Plan* published 5 more poems, and 3 others were included in the anthology *The Collection: Young Poetry from Austria* (*Die Sammlung: Junge Lyrik aus Österreich*). *Plan*, edited by Otto Basil, was a small-scale, short-lived platform (1946–1948) that sought to connect new Austrian literature with the historical avant-garde (especially French surrealism), all ties to which had been severed by the Nazi regime. But in this first post-war decade Mayröcker reached out to both sides of the polarized Austrian cultural climate (cf. the introduction to this volume): to the leading figure of the conservative establishment, Hans Weigel, who in 1952 published her first longer prose text in his anthology *Voices of the Present* (*Stimmen der Gegenwart*), as well as to the neo-avant-gardists of the Wiener Gruppe and authors surrounding this group, with whom a few joint public reading sessions were organized. Mayröcker's acquaintance with Andreas Okopenko, who was first linked with the journal *neue wege* [New Roads] and then founded the more radical *publikationen einer wiener gruppe junger autoren* [Publications by a Group of Young Viennese Writers], provided an opportunity to publish on a more regular basis. Eventually, an anthology of this first decade of writings, entitled *Larifari: A Confused Book* (*Larifari: Ein konfuses Buch*; 'larifari' means 'humbug'), was published in 1956 with the Viennese Bergland Verlag.

Leading Austrian experimental journals and literary figures became even more important as instigators and institutional intermediaries for Mayröcker's literature during the 1960s and 1970s. Mayröcker was a regular contributor to trend-setting journals such as *manuskripte*, *protokolle* and *neue texte*. Especially Otto Breicha and his *protokolle* provided her with a platform for writing and publishing new texts.

At the 1954 *Innsbruck Weeks of Young Culture* (*Innsbrucker Jugendkulturwochen*), Mayröcker met Ernst Jandl, an English teacher like herself, who was just about to make his first steps in the neo-avant-garde scene. The date marks the beginning of an intense and lifelong partnership between the two poets, though they differed greatly in their poetics and posture, and ended only with Jandl's death in 2000. Whereas Mayröcker facilitated Jandl's acquaintance with the Wiener Gruppe in the 1950s, Jandl would prove to play a decisive role as a *Vermittler* or agent of Mayröcker's work in Germany in the 1960s: while visiting West-German publishers in 1963, Jandl promoted Mayröcker's poems to Max Bense of the Stuttgarter Schule. In the series *rot text*, edited by Bense and Elisabeth Walter, Mayröcker published a selection of eight so-called long poems, entitled *metaphorical* (1964, *metaphorisch*).

As for many other innovative Austrian authors, the German institutional context would become increasingly important in the following years. Rowohlt and Luchterhand Verlag, both dedicated to new Austrian literature, provided Mayröcker with publication opportunities: an anthology with poems spanning a period over 20 years was published by Rowohlt in 1966, *Death by Muses: Poetic Texts* (*Tod durch Musen: Poetische Texte*), followed by two prose anthologies, *Mini-Monster's Dream Lexicon: Texts in Prose* (1968, *Minimonsters Traumlexikon: Texte in Prosa*), and *Phantom Phan* (1971, *Fantom Fan*). Luchterhand published the next volume, *Aria on Feet of Clay: Metaphysical Theatre* (1972, *Arie auf tönernen Füßen: Metaphysisches Theater*), as well as *with each clouded peak: story* (1973, *je ein umwölkter gipfel: erzählung*). Mainly due to political reasons — Mayröcker did not agree with the explicit leftist orientation of Luchterhand Verlag — Mayröcker in 1975 left Luchterhand for Suhrkamp, where she has stayed ever since. Her motives for moving are also reflected in her poetics: in contrast to her fellow authors, Mayröcker never defined her poetics out of a resistance against Austrian restorative cultural politics. Similarly, she cannot be said to have shared the explicit anti-establishment sentiment characteristic of Lucienne Stassaert, as we will argue below.

Next to poems, 'poetic texts', and 'texts in prose', Mayröcker in the late 1960s started to write radio plays. This move was in tune with the growing popularity of the radiophonic medium at the time. Between 1967 and 1977 she wrote 18 radio plays as sole author, and 4 more together with Ernst Jandl. Most of the texts were commissioned by one of the then prominent radio studios committed to radio plays and acoustic art (e.g. at the *Westdeutscher Rundfunk*, the *Südwestfunk*, and the *Bayerischer Rundfunk*), that provided the opportunity to experiment with the new medium of stereophony and, on a more mundane level, to earn more money than with printed publications.

Quitting her teaching job in 1969 (as did Jandl in the same year) eventually allowed Mayröcker to concentrate fully on her activities as a writer. This turning point in her career provided the momentum, which she maintains until this very day, for her impressive literary output, resulting in numerous volumes of both poetry and prose. It also facilitated the creation of a stronger artistic network in the following decades, with long lecture tours abroad (to the US, the Soviet Union, France, and Italy), longer stays in Berlin (in 1973 and 1993), and regular attendances at initiatives such as the yearly *Bielefelder Colloquium Neue Poesie*. Collaborative projects increased as well, especially literary dialogues with painters and, to a lesser extent, film makers, next to a continuing interest in the medium of the radio play.

Stassaert

Lucienne Stassaert is considerably younger than Mayröcker. An only child in a family of barbers, she was born on 10 February 1936. In her teenage years — between 1951 and 1953 — she studied the piano at a private school. Despite (or maybe because of) her father's expectations, the young Stassaert did not wish to concentrate exclusively on a career in music. In the early 1960s, she started to combine playing the piano with exploring the field of the visual and literary arts. A catalyst in this respect might have been her marriage to the visual artist Wybrand Ganzevoort, a painter and sculptor, in 1960, with whom she had two daughters (Régine in 1961 and Anouk in 1963). Their relationship lasted until 1994.

Stassaert's first publications date back to 1961 and appeared in neo-avant-garde journals like *Nul*, which was distributed on a very small scale by the forgotten author Dirk Claus. *Nul* was one of the many representatives of the so-called 'stencilled revolution' in Flemish literary history — a hausse of limited editions and cheaply produced little magazines, edited by a young generation that revolted against the literary establishment and its corporate conservatism that blocked literary innovation. Such an anti-establishment sentiment, which is an important thematic thread in both Stassaert's poetology and her literary practice, is also manifest in the little magazine that is closely connected to the way Stassaert is mainly framed in literary history, viz. the neo-avant-garde journal *Labris*.

Labris existed between 1962 and 1973 and strived explicitly for the autonomy of poetry. Hence, *Labris*-poems were typically characterized by procedures like typographical experiment, ungrammatical phrasing (e.g. apo koinou, anacoluthon) or labyrinthine writing. Due to the high density of such alienating techniques, *Labris* has frequently been compared to the traditions of surrealism — more specifically the French ideal of *poésie maudite* — and the American Beat Generation (e.g. Van der Bent 2007; Wilmots 2008). Important influences are, amongst others, Alfred Jarry, Comte de Lautréamont, Antonin Artaud, and Jack Kerouac.

Stassaert was one of the recurring authors in *Labris* between 1964 and 1967. Thus, in a 1967 interview by Hugo Neefs (1967: 45), she explicitly stated that it was inevitable that she was conceived as a typical *Labris*-writer, although she did not appreciate the concrete poetry of editor Leon Van Essche. This rejection of Van Essche's work indicates that the typical neo-avant-gardist tension between abstraction and concreteness (cf. the introduction to this volume) is not of particular interest to the early Stassaert. More importantly, though, it shows that Stassaert did not want to blindly conform to the poetic preoccupations of the magazine she was primarily affiliated to. Neither was she comfortable with being associated with a single magazine. Hence, she refused to join the editorial board of *Labris*, for being — as she vividly remembers in her collection of memoirs *Souvenirs* — 'a bit uneasy with the fact that the freedom [she] had achieved had to make way for a new discipline' (2014: 138).[2] Such an emphasis on 'freedom' instead of 'discipline' might be considered typical for the posture of a bohemian poet, an ideal that Stassaert openly admired. This marks an ambivalent similarity with Mayröcker, who equally did not want to align herself with a strict poetics but did not embrace the bohemian posture.

Stassaert's ambiguous attitude towards *Labris* is further underscored by her decision not to publish her literary debut under the auspices of the journal. Instead, *Stories of the Noblewoman with the Spade* (1964, *Verhalen van de jonkvrouw met de spade*) appeared as an independent publication with a limited volume of just 34 copies (2008: 76). Paratextually, this collection of short stories is a typical heir of the stencilled revolution — it was published on thin and almost translucent paper, containing typewritten prose without page numbers. The experimentalism of this work, on which we will elaborate later, implicitly connects it to the *Labris*-poetics. Stassaert's ambivalent affinity with this little magazine is also apparent in her collaboration with editor Max Kazan (pseudonym of Jef Bierkens), with whom she published the highly experimental — and also stencilled — text *Bongo Blossom Blood* (*Bongobloesembloed*) in 1966. Stassaert, whose lyricized prose accompanied Kazan's surrealist poetry, appeared on the front page as 'Lulu Stassaert', possibly referring to the sexually complex Lulu-figure in Frank Wedekind's plays *Earth Spirit* (1895, *Erdgeist*) and *Pandora's Box* (1904, *Die Büchse der Pandora*).

At the end of the 1960s, the vibrant experimentalism of *Stories of the Noblewoman with the Spade* and *Bongo Blossom Blood* is replaced by a more sober style, possibly in accordance with Stassaert's grief about her father's death in 1965. Compared to her earlier work, which can be characterized as highly diffuse prose, the poems in *Fossil* (1969, *Fossiel*) are extremely dense, while the 1970 novella *The Woodworm* (*De houtworm*) might still be a polyphonic text, but one with less experimental features than the debut stories. Retrospectively, then, *Fossil* and *The Woodworm* can be considered as heralds of Stassaert's literary evolution into a communicative author whose work does not flinch from using experimental devices. This evolution reminds one of the changes in Mayröcker's poetics around 1971. In that year she retrospectively situates her turn towards less experimental narrative prose (see below), a turn she partly explains by pointing to her new career as a freelance author.

Stassaert's development towards a more communicative way of writing, which is also reflected through her turn towards (semi-)official publishers, becomes even more apparent in the 1970s. In the collection of poetry *In the Clock of the Machine a Human Ticks* (1973, *In de klok van de machine tikt een mens*) and the novel *A Small Sea Anemone* (1975, *Een kleine zeeanemoon*), Stassaert combines experimental writing techniques with an explicit and impossible-to-miss critique of capitalism. Her determined social criticism of the 1970s is, in turn, nuanced in the 1980s — one of the stories in *Daylight Saving Time* (1984, *Het zomeruur*), for instance, caricatures the naïve hopes of the prototypical social poet who thinks their verses are capable of changing the world. Accordingly, in this phase of her career, Stassaert starts to focus more on fellow artists — most notably Edvard Munch, Emily Dickinson, and Sylvia Plath, many of whose works Stasseart translated.

As this concise sketch shows, Lucienne Stassaert consistently reinvents and reshapes her literary persona. In her case, there is no essence to grasp: neither does she confine herself to one art form or institutional constellation, nor does her literary work consist of variations on a (set of) basic scheme(s). More or less the same goes for Friederike Mayröcker. As a consequence, this confrontation between Mayröcker and Stassaert can only deal with some of the many aspects of the multifaceted authors. We take a closer look at the early Stassaert of the 1960s, shifting between the extravagant neo-avant-gardism of her debut stories and the soberness of the poems in *Fossil*. In Mayröcker's case, we focus on her so-called 'prose texts' of the late 1960s, that perpetuate the experimental make-up of the Wiener Gruppe in a strikingly anarchic way, while also preparing her for her longer, more expansive and narrative prose of the years to come.

2. Poetology

Mayröcker

When considering the beginnings of her writing, Mayröcker draws on the religious image of the chosen one. The poem 'The Calling' ('Der Aufruf', written in 1961 or 1962) reconstructs the moment in which the lyrical I realizes its vocation as a poet: 'suddenly called out by my name', the lyrical I steps out of its hitherto protected life and heads for 'an outlandish moving target : | without any choice | but with an impatient heart' (2007: 18).[3] In retrospect, Mayröcker has situated the moment of that calling as early as 1939, coinciding with the outbreak of the war. That as a youngster Mayröcker wrote her first poem when suddenly being confronted with a burning bush in the backyard of a dilapidated house is one of the more persistent biblical images in the constant reworking of her private mythology.

There are hardly any poetological comments of the author dating back to the 1960s. In later years, interviews and concise texts on her poetics (usually published in literary journals) do pop up regularly. In a short but highly illuminating untitled text published in 1970 Mayröcker writes (2001a: 9), reflecting on the texts that were to be published in the volume *Aria on Feet of Clay* (1972): 'The theories and principles that accompany my work find themselves in a state of permanent movement, constantly changing its pace but without any point of fixation, as this would disturb the working process itself.' Whenever a fixed stance crystallizes, it is dissolved again or its contradictions are demonstrated, resulting in 'a confusion of voices, never a choir'. Theories come and go 'as part of the writing process but not as a comment on the texts in order to lend them more meaning', 'schemes are quoted and simultaneously rendered absurd.'[4] In this poetics of constant flux and mutation the idea of text production is presented as a protean energy, constantly changing shapes, tipping over sense and meaning into nonsense and meaninglessness, and considering all kinds of texts, also theoretical ones, as material, not as explanatory frames. This profound agility seems to never solidify into a recognizable form. The author seems to suggest that this is the price to be paid for resisting monopolization by a certain poetics: one's own shapelessness. Such a resistance against a fixed shape is also highly characteristic of Stassaert's early prose, which is replete with chameleonic and kaleidoscopic features.

In 1972, Mayröcker wrote a two-page programmatic text with the telling title 'DADA'. Compared to the 1970 text, this one is of a more systematic and concrete referential nature. In eleven points the author enumerates authors, artists, and aesthetic programmes that she feels an affinity with. It is a highly diverse and diachronic list ranging from Hölderlin to her contemporary Arno Schmidt, but it also mentions many surrealist painters (Max Ernst, Magritte), and places particular emphasis on the historical avant-garde of Surrealism and Dadaism. Without any anxiety of influence or *Berührungsangst* [haphephobia] Mayröcker here constructs her own intermedial network as an experimental writer, strikingly enough without mentioning her fellow Austrians — who did share her fascination for Surrealism and Dadaism. Moreover, from the very start the urge for self-positioning — already relativized through the network constellation — is ironically undermined. The first sentence reads: '1 if after a probing self-analysis I try to understand myself correctly, I find myself at times wedged between the two monsters Dadaism and Surrealism and in a kind of double relationship with them' (2001a: 335). It is hard to miss the irony about the urge for one's own aesthetic 'self-analysis' in this rather pathetically and hyperbolically formulated revelation. And in the following entries, trying to clearly pinpoint one's own position is indeed met with profound scepticism: '2 but at times the utmost contradictory hybrids have arisen', '4 [...] my doubts, my reservations in all directions, from all perspectives' (335–36). The text follows a kind of dialectical 'yes, but...' structure, continuously vacillating between opposite positions: '7 so, a playful attitude? [...] 8 withdrawal: though playfulness often provides the first impulse, I don't want to advocate it' (336).[5]

What Mayröcker claims in these two texts, then, is the construction of an idiosyncratic network of influences and inspirations, in a way that both acknowledges and dissolves the authority of each and every quoted author or artist, while at the same time establishing new, possibly contradictory correspondences between them. These texts point to a view on authorship as shamelessly re-appropriating pre-existing material — in later utterances on her poetics, Mayröcker calls her authorship 'parasitic'. Mayröcker's resulting 'own' voice does not hide its infusion with foreign material; indeed, it shows how a derivative voice, having dismissed the illusion of sovereign and pure authenticity, might even be the liveliest one. Later on in her writing career, Mayröcker explicitly links this view to the philosophy of Jacques Derrida. His texts — e.g. 'La parole soufflée' and *The Post Card* — reverberate through her work as endlessly re-appropriated intertexts.[6]

The 'DADA' text contains some more statements on the adaptation of Surrealist and Dadaist techniques. *Écriture automatique* is rejected because of its 'trifling randomness' ('leichtfertige Willkür', Mayröcker 2001a: 336), *collage* on the other hand is favoured as it allows for the systematic and disciplined handling of the material to be combined with the subjective associations of a 'private language' ('Privatsprache'). In later decades, subjectivity gains ever more importance in Mayröcker's work, not in the profound sense of the cryptic expression of inner emotional life but on a performative, cognitive and embodied level. Both in her longer prose works — in which without exception an I-narrator speaks — as well as in her poetry, Mayröcker explores how the thoughts and perceptions of a singular mind and body are transposed into the literary, aesthetic realm, and thereby depersonalized. These later works of Mayröcker could thus be termed experimental life writing: the transposition of a living being — itself infused with foreign material — into an aesthetic corpus.

But already in the 1960s, Mayröcker raised cognitive questions of subjectivity and consciousness — themes that also occupied Stassaert. They coincided with important genre discussions of the time, namely on the so-called 'long poems' and the 'new radioplay'. Mayröcker had been experimenting with long poems since the beginning of the 1960s, that is, some years before Walter Höllerer in 1965 created a polemic with his 'Theses on the long poem' ('Thesen zum langen

Gedicht'). Höllerer put forward a lengthier poetic form as a means to criticize hermetic modernist poetry and to produce a more readable and realistic poetic form for the expression of inner life. Mayröcker, however, opted for the long poem as her own variation of concrete poetry (*Konkrete Poesie*), in which she lets the words sprawl over several pages, filling it with intertextual and intermedial references and elaborating on traditional metaphors (Kühn 2002b). She thereby not only diverged from Höllerer's view but also from the norms of her fellow concrete poets, who adhered to the stylistic principles of subtraction and condensation. Mayröcker defines her long poems as 'excerpts of the totality of my *consciousness of the world*' (Beyer 1992: 31),[7] thereby making the relation with her own experience of the world explicit; the word 'excerpt' [Ausschnitt], however, already indicates that rather than realistic expression, a Dadaistic manipulation of experienced reality is presented. Indeed, nearly all long poems are entitled 'Text with ...', indicating their primarily (meta)textual character that presents itself as a discussion 'with', not as a text 'about' concrete phenomena of (textual) reality.

Questions concerning the poetic rendering of consciousness and subjectivity are also at the centre of her radio plays. Here, 'poetic' shifts in the direction of 'acoustic' or even 'musical'. Whereas the radio plays Mayröcker wrote with Jandl experimented with the relatively new technique of stereophony to express ideological and discursive critique — and are thus quite compatible with the standards of the so-called 'new radio play' (cf. the introduction to this volume) — her own radio texts written since the late 1960s tended to focus on the acoustic representation of streams of consciousness, experimenting with stereophony as a means to open up a radiophonic space of simultaneous cognitive processes. As Mayröcker put it in one of her then rare public statements — the speech she and Jandl gave in 1969 when accepting the award *Hörspielpreis der Kriegsblinden* for their joint radio play *Five Man Humanity* (*Fünf Mann Menschen*) — she expected from the radio play an 'acoustic satisfaction [...] close to the one induced by music' (Pauler 1999: 94).[8]

Though she herself has called her radio plays a 'side track' in her work, the genre has clearly shaped her longer prose texts: dialogical structures, a simultaneity of voices, the text as echo chamber of previously spoken, heard or read language, the tension between lasting memories and elusive presentism, or, on the very basic level of text production, word generation through the sound play of alliteration and assonance — these are all techniques and structures that link Mayröcker's radio texts to her prose work. Another characteristic of those longer and later prose texts is their search for ways of unconventional story-telling, by reworking conventions of (autobiographical) narrativity such as the use of a confessional I-narrator, schemata of childhood memories and love relationships, everyday anecdotes, letters, conversations with friends and the suggestion of homely intimacy. The experimental character remains fairly dominant: the micronarrative elements do not develop into a full story. The constant metatextual allusion and reflection on how to transform experienced reality into literature, however, guarantees the coherence of this deregulating writing practice.

Stassaert

As discussed before, Lucienne Stassaert too is a hydra-headed author, whose literary work deliberately resists labels and compartmentalization. This becomes even clearer from her early-career poetology, which is characterized by constantly oscillating between 'open/communicative' and 'hermetic/experimental' poetics. In Stassaert's recent statements about her poetics, this seeming undecidability is no longer manifest — in a 2011 interview, for instance, she resolutely argues that she has written only two experimental texts: *Stories of the Noblewoman with the Spade* and *Bongo Blossom Blood* (De Coux 2011: 47), indicating that her other works have a demonstrably different orientation. Over three decades earlier, though, Stassaert deeply problematized the possibility of making such a clear-cut division between 'open' and 'experimental' writing. In a 1976 interview by the poet Daniël Billiet, she even described the choice between 'a simple or a more experimental manner of writing' as 'a tantalization'.[9] In this interview, she also stated that every time she tried to move beyond experimentalism, she felt tempted to return to this mode of writing again.

When presenting the opposition between 'simple' and 'experimental' writing as a 'choice', Stassaert too seems to divide literature into compartments. Typical for the poetic framework of her oeuvre, though, is that the construction and articulation of binary oppositions usually coincides with the deconstruction of such schemes (cf. Jespers 1999). The antithetic relationship between 'communicative' and 'experimental' literature, for instance, does not hold for Stassaert's early work, in which hermetic and clear passages are frequently mixed up. This characteristic seems to be connected to Stassaert's attitude towards the content-versus-form dichotomy, which she does not (want to) reject. According to the early Stassaert, content is 'primordial' over style (Roggeman 1975: 285), indicating that her experimental style should be seen as a means of expression, rather than as an attempt to push language to its limits.

At this point, it is important to ask what is actually expressed in Stassaert's early work. The answer is, at least initially, quite simple: Stassaert's literary texts might be read as an obsessive expression of mortal fear. The impenetrable awareness of the concept and presence of mortality, which is even reinforced by the death of the author's father, invites us to read Stassaert's writing in the 1960s as a mode of introspection which deals with both the conscious and unconscious preoccupations of the author. Such an expressive poetics, though, conflicts with the experimentalist and even autonomist orientation of these texts, which consistently obscure the author's expressions through literary devices like ungrammaticality and dense metaphor. In doing so, Stassaert again seems to merge two seemingly opposed poetological positions.

Obviously, we might conceive Stassaert's approach psychoanalytically, deciphering her neo-avant-gardist language as an expression of the author's unconscious anxieties, which can only be represented in the unusual grammar of a fragmented literary work. However, the interrelation of an expressive and experimental poetics can also be interpreted along the line of mystical poetry (e.g. Hadewijch, St John of the Cross), in which the mystic's verbal expressions of the encounter between poetry and divinity are concealed in cryptic language. Stassaert also underlines her interest in mysticism by interweaving the concept of death with the semantic field of the erotic, thus using erotic language and metaphors in order to bridge the gap between heaven and earth. As the author expressed in one of her interviews: 'Eros and Thanatos are invincible and unavoidable twins' (De Coux 2011: 47).[10] The quote is a striking example of Stassaert's attitude towards thinking in compartments: on the one hand, she stages the binary opposition between life and death through two archetypal figures; on the other hand, she deconstructs this opposition by presenting these archetypes as twins rather than as antagonists.

By positioning her work in a female mystical discourse, Stassaert implicitly draws attention to the issue of gender. As Hugo Bousset (1980: 440) has put it, one of the structural dilemmas in Stassaert's work is the desire to write like a man, despite the constant awareness of being a woman. Perhaps this tension is felt even more keenly in the case of neo-avant-garde literature: axioms such as originality and innovation are not only associated with masculinity rather than femininity; but the Flemish neo-avant-garde literary network of the 1960s was a male bastion as well. The same can be said about the early Austrian literary neo-avant-garde, especially when talking about the Wiener Gruppe. Unlike Stassaert, Mayröcker has never commented on the gender question during that period and even in later decades only reluctantly addressed the issue. Her later prose texts, though, present several parodic variations on a gendered love relationship or friendship between a male and a female voice that often turns into a poetic contest (cf. Arteel 2012: 38–45). Moreover, as will be shown, some of her experimental texts can very well be said to broach the issue of gender blindness of her fellow authors.

An important text with regard to gender is an extensive essay that Stassaert published in the literary journal *De Vlaamse Gids*, addressing a question (formulated by the magazine's editors) that is almost misogynist: 'Why do women writers usually write bad texts?' (Daniël Robberechts in Stassaert 1972: 4).[11] Interestingly, Stassaert does not problematize this question, in which an opinion is presented as a fact. Instead, she defends the claim that women writers are the subalterns of their male colleagues, combining anthropological, sociological, and literary insights in her argumentation. Stassaert argues that even in primitive societies, women have never been allowed to take their part in ritual processes — they can be the *object* of such rituals, but the act of initiation is the privilege of men (5). As a consequence, male writers have a tradition going back centuries to position themselves in, while female authors are working in a so-called 'no-man's-land' (NB the Dutch word *niemandsland* does not contain the gender ambiguity of 'no-man's') with only a few remarkable exceptions to the rule as predecessors. In another essay (1975: 205), Stassaert captures this inequality strikingly: 'This consistently recurring difference: Adam with his phallic pencil and Eva with tiny dots on her breasts.'[12]

As opposed to the binary oppositions mentioned before — 'open/hermetic', 'expressive/experimental', 'life/death' — the inequality of gender roles is an antithetic relationship Stassaert does not deconstruct, at least not in her early years. She even confirms the stereotypical view on female authorship, arguing that the exclusion of women from cultural rituals has led to a so-called 'thematic dependency' (1972: 6, 'thematische afhankelijkheid') of female literature. Because women have been denied access to social and intellectual development in the past, Stassaert claims, they can only rely on (the semantic field of) emotions in their writing. The consequence is that most women writers are incapable of thinking outside the box, especially regarding the theme of love, while the prevalence of expression and emotion also leads to the marginalization of literary form and technique. In this respect, Stassaert even reproaches her fellow female authors for their 'neglect' of the technical-formal aspects of texts (8).

Partly because of this problem, Stassaert urges herself and her colleagues to embrace the concept of total writing in a Rimbaudian sense, that is: a mode of writing in which both content and form strive for perfection and overwhelming originality. Stassaert claims that until now, no female author has ever attempted such total writing, implying that she herself is amongst the first to step outside this gendered box. The Rimbaudian concept also resonates in the 1967 interview in *Labris*, though: here, Stassaert argues that literature is about 'saying it all [...] IN SPITE OF your attempts to keep on working until you crack up' (Neefs 1967: 43).[13] In this case, however, there is no reflection on the formal component of 'total writing', for the axiom of 'saying it all' connects more to content than to form.

Stassaert's account of the gender relations within the literary field shows that her literary practice is explicitly related to hegemonic societal structures in the 1960s and 1970s. As we have noted before, Stassaert's literary production in the 1970s might also be considered as an articulation of an explicit critique on society, particularly concerning the hegemonic position of capitalism. In the *early* neo-avant-garde phase of her career, however, this ideological orientation is less manifest — in 1967, Stassaert's response to the question whether her work contained a specific vision on society, was even a simple and short 'no' (Neefs 1967: 43). Yet, this does not mean that she believed that artists should hide away in their ivory towers: in her view, writers can give an impetus to change society by showing the gap between illusion and reality. Thus, by frustrating the conventions of representation and narrative, literature is able to unmask the illusory certainties of societal structures. As such, Stassaert's experimentalism is not only a vehicle of the literary expression of personal obsessions, but also an implicit way of criticizing dominant hegemonies and hierarchies (especially regarding social class).

In conclusion, Stassaert's poetics can be summarized in four points: a) she does not wish to conform to binary oppositions and compartmentalization; b) she strives to unmask so-called societal and ideological realities as illusions; c) she desires to practice 'total writing', by pushing both content and form to its limits, thus moving beyond the stereotype of female sentimentalism; d) she combines this experimental orientation with the personal expression of particular obsessions, especially concerning death. This most certainly is an ambitious poetics, but — not unexpectedly — the hydra-headed Stassaert did not hesitate to ironically mock her own ideals. Referring to the seeming infeasibility of her project, she defined herself as 'a failed mystic, cemented in the ground' (Neefs 1967: 44).[14] The poetical qualification that seems to remain, then, is that of Stassaert's hybridity.

3. Reception

Mayröcker

With her first journal publications of the late forties, Mayröcker had drawn the attention of the inner circle of experimentally oriented poets. Her writings were met with acclaim, but also with a certain perplexity. The stylistically heterogeneous character of these early writings, with their refusal to take sides, might have played a role in that reaction, as well as the fact that she was one of the very few female writers in Vienna at the time (cf. the introduction to this volume). Indeed, though Andreas Okopenko in 1963 — in what probably is the first lengthy article on Mayröcker — acclaimed the analytical experimental approach that made her language 'concrete in the very details' (in Schmidt 1984: 31), he deplored its emotionality, or, in his own words, its 'sentimentality' (in Schmidt 1984: 29). More striking, however, is his bewilderment regarding Mayröcker's posture as an author, which did not seem to fit with what was expected from female artists: 'Friederike Mayröcker is a woman for whom writing has been a necessity from the start, and for many years even — to my abhorrence — her only fulfilment in life' (in Schmidt 1984: 34).[15] He also felt at a loss at the sheer 'cruel' ('grausam') quantity of her literary output, with its poetology of constantly rewriting and recycling previous material. As early as 1963 he rightly predicted the impossibility of ever archiving her estate ('Nachlass') — which still presents a challenge to scholars interested in genetic criticism of Mayröcker's work.

Several other neo-avant-garde contemporaries too have portrayed and commented on Mayröcker's work of these first decades. The young Peter Weibel (born 1944), who at the time collaborated with the Wiener Gruppe, was one of the first to take the literary aspects of Mayröcker's texts seriously. In 1966 he pointed out the musical quality of Mayröcker's poetry in particular, and her recycling and collaging of traditional, mainly baroque metaphors. Contrary to Okopenko, Weibel identifies the tension between exploring 'progressive' literary techniques and drawing on old, 'regressive' semantics (e.g. lyrical 'Urbilder' concerning nature, or emotional and existential topoi of love and death) as inherent to the poetry of many neo-avant-gardists, even as a demonstration of 'the legendary spirit of the time' (in Schmidt 1984: 39).[16]

One could take Weibel's reflections as a starting point to move beyond the dichotomy of progressive versus regressive (and form versus content) and read Mayröcker's poetry as fusing experimental calculation with transgressive pathos. A rich historical continuum opens up here; we could think of Goethe's *Sturm und Drang* poetry and the early Romantics, up to the lyrical expressionism of Else Lasker-Schüler. With her recent poetry collection *Scardanelli* (2009), a dialogical interaction with the late Hölderlin, Mayröcker explicitly situates herself in such a continuum. Apart from some essays (most recently in Lughofer 2017) and two dissertations (le Née 2013; Reumkens 2013) Mayröcker's extensive lyrical oeuvre largely remains academically unexplored territory. This situation contrasts sharply with the vivid reception of her poetry by fellow poets of several generations, ranging from Elke Erb (1938) over Thomas Kling (1957–2005), Ulrike Draesner (1962) and Marcel Beyer (1965), to younger ones like Mikael Vogel (1975) as well as slam poets Markus Köhle (1975) and Mieze Medusa (1975).

In several short essays Ernst Jandl has written about the work of his companion. In the tentatively formulated 'First fragmentary approach for a text on Friederike Mayröcker's poem "Winter-Nightingale"' (1975, 'Erster fragmentarischer Ansatz zu einem Text über Friederike Mayröckers Gedicht "Winter-Nachtigall"') Jandl seems to take up Weibel's reflections and comments on how Mayröcker puts conventional lyrical requisites to new use, thereby 'making them new and fresh just as Gertrude Stein's rose' (in Schmidt 1984: 49).[17] 'A new poetic space' ('Ein neuer poetischer Raum', 1974) deals with the prose volume *Mini-Monster's Dream Lexicon* (1968). Jandl analyses the reworking of conventions and models of what he calls 'prose genres' (talks, radio plays, protocols etc.) and the thwarting of the expectations raised by those conventions. Jandl concludes that Mayröcker's prose, in reflecting on and stretching its own possibilities, resolutely breaks new poetic ground.

Just as Mayröcker's poetry in general is underrepresented in scholarship, so are the prose texts of the 1960s and 1970s.[18] It is only with the much more explicit turn to the conventions and models of autobiographical life writing since the late 1970s that the scholarly reception of her work has really started. The first Mayröcker symposium, held in 1978 in Vienna, also seems to have laid the groundwork for her being awarded the *Großer Österreichischer Staatspreis* in 1982. With the second Viennese conference, organized on occasion of her seventieth birthday in 1994, Mayröcker scholarship really gained momentum, though for several years it remained largely restricted to her prose of recent decades, that has been studied from cognitive-constructivist, genetic, narratological, intermedial, and poststructuralist perspectives. More recent edited volumes tend to cover all genres and also older texts (Kühn 2002a; Strohmaier 2009). Only one monograph so far has dealt with Mayröcker's radio plays (Pauler 2010). Honorary doctorates of the University of Bielefeld (in 2001, the same year that she was awarded the prestigious *Georg-Büchner-Preis*) and Innsbruck (2015) testify to Mayröcker's academic and artistic canonization, although the impression of belatedness is never far away. After all, Mayröcker had to turn 90 to get her Austrian honorary doctorate.

Mayröcker's work has enjoyed a remarkably consistent and favourable reception in the media. With advanced age, her mediatized appearance seems to grow ever more iconic: the self-fashioning of the corporeal author with the never changing masquerade of black hair and attire; her quiet, monotonous but insisting reading voice — Mayröcker has been a frequent guest at public readings and has recorded several of her texts on cd — ; and reports of her apartment fully overgrown with textual materials — pictures of her private space have made it into several journals and newspapers. What shows up, then, is the paradoxical image of a writerly existence both mysterious and transparent.

Stassaert

In 2014, Lucienne Stassaert published a wide variety of memoirs under the title of *Souvenirs: Notes Through the Course of Time* (*Souvenirs: Aantekeningen in de loop van de tijd*). In some of these texts, she reflects on her early years in the literary field, particularly concerning her position in the history and network of *Labris*. Condemning the fact that critics of her work keep mentioning (the poetics of) this magazine as decisive for her literary style, Stassaert sighs: 'To me, it is a punishment that my contributions to *Labris* have led me to be labelled this way' (2014: 34).[19] This label especially hurts the author because her colleague and friend Marcel van Maele did — at least in her eyes — not get the same treatment, although he too evolved in a totally different direction than neo-avant-gardism.

As such, the notion of gender might also be at stake in the reception history of Stassaert's oeuvre. In this respect, it is striking that Hugo Neefs, in his review of *Stories of the Noblewoman with the Spade* in *Labris*, explicitly remarked on the specific feminine character of this prose. To some extent, his comments seem to prelude Stassaert's own critical examination of female authors' inclination toward emotional writing. 'Female poetry', Neefs claims (1965: 76), emphasizing that this concept differs from 'poetry written by a woman', 'quickly degenerates into pornography or into sentimental rubbish, [but] in Stassaert's work, it becomes a dramatic, primal power loaded with tension.'[20] As discussed in the previous paragraph, it is this explosive or even cosmic pathos, manifest in both content and form, that lies at the heart of Stassaert's view of total writing.

According to Neefs, his colleague's vehement passion proved her artistic abilities. He was one of the few who noticed Stassaert's early prose, though, undoubtedly because of their respective positions in the *Labris* network. Given the fact that *Stories of the Noblewoman with the Spade* appeared in an edition of just 34 copies, this limited critical reception can hardly be a surprise. In this context, it is more remarkable that Stassaert's debut stories also gained attention in the Dutch national newspaper *Algemeen Handelsblad*, in which the Flemish critic Jan Walravens regularly wrote a feature on Flemish literature. In most cases, these contributions were published earlier in the newspaper *Het Laatste Nieuws*, Walravens' forum for literary criticism in Flanders. The fact that Stassaert's niche-market debut stories were reviewed in two nationwide media, is primarily due to the literary profile of the critic: between 1949 and 1955, Walravens was one of the front men of *Tijd en mens*, a little magazine that played a significant role in the innovation of Flemish literature after World War II. In line with his experimentalist poetics, Walravens (1965) praised Stassaert's deviations from common syntactic and semantic patterns, which culminated in a laudatory comparison of *Stories of the Noblewoman with the Spade* with the works of the painter René Magritte: 'This is nothing less than an attempt at transferring a Magrittean surrealism to the possibilities of her own language.'[21]

On the other side of the spectrum, the Flemish author Robin Hannelore criticized Stassaert's unconventional mode of writing for being 'lettrist, mannerist and a "vocabularist" affectation' (1965: 63).[22] In a review of *Fossil* in the literary magazine *Heibel*, of which Hannelore was one of the instigators, he did not hesitate to make clear that this poetry irritated him: 'I'd rather hear the jabbering of Chinese or Zulu people' (1965: 63).[23] As befits the satirical nature of literary criticism in *Heibel*, Hannelore concluded his review with a parody of Stassaert's poetic style, producing joking phrases such as 'Lucienne Stassaert dregs-corn-flower poetess', 'Language dainty in bonbon shop Flanders' and 'Using darning needles on the backside of pain paper' (64).[24]

One can wonder whether Hannelore's criticism of *Fossil* does justice to the condensed nature of Stassaert's debut poems, since *Fossil* is far less rooted in mannerism than, for instance, *Stories of the Noblewoman with the Spade*. In the reception history of Stassaert's oeuvre, however, this notion of 'mannerism' frequently recurs. Joris Gerits has even argued that the author's 'mannerist handling of language', along with her bohemian attitude and her obsessive themes, is the main reason why her work fails to attract a large group of readers (1988: 254).[25] The fact that this quote dates from 1988 — that is: during a more communicative and less experimental phase of Stassaert's career — is indicative of the persistent image of Stassaert as a 'difficult' author.

An interesting account of this problem is to be found in Erik Spinoy's review of Stassaert's collection of poems *Molting* (*Rui*, 1987). Spinoy ascertained that this collection is illustrative for the poet's development towards a more sober and terse style, but he also posited that Stassaert's 'cure from mannerist writing'[26] (1987: 69) was illusory: to him, these poems were still all about sound, rhythm, and music, and certainly were *not* about content or the creation of meaning. Since our contribution to the reception history of Stassaert's work primarily focuses on her work in the 1960s, we do not seek to put this image of the mannerist poet to the test. Yet, our account of Stassaert's early literary practice will show that even in the experimentalist phase of her career, the notions of 'content' and 'meaning' are never discarded.

4. Literary practice

Mayröcker

Both from Mayröcker's own early programmatic texts as well as from her contemporary reception it has become clear that she took great care to position herself in between trends and traditions and that her contemporaries did indeed consider her to be an *Einzelgänger*. In what follows we will take a closer look at some trends in Mayröcker's prose texts of the late 1960s, and we will try to get a more analytical grasp of their self-proclaimed shapelessness. We will also examine the possible differences and similarities between Mayröcker and other protagonists of the Austrian neo-avant-garde of the time.

The texts selected for this chapter were published in *Phantom Phan* (1971) and *Aria on Feet of Clay* (1972). Together with the preceding volume *Mini-Monster's Dream Lexicon* (1968), these anthologies testify to Mayröcker's high productivity of short texts at the end of the 1960s, to her international orientation and intense reception of other languages and of both 'high' and 'low' culture, and to the new and increasing opportunities for publication. Whereas Ernst Jandl subsumed Mayröcker's texts of that period under the overall label 'prose texts', the 'prose' of these three volumes is of a strikingly hybrid nature, intermingling intra-literary transgressions (resulting in prose poems, or the lyricalization of prose) with intermedial ones, such as the profound theatrical and metatheatrical quality of many texts.

Theatrical Sketches: Hybrid Genres, Hybrid Voices

Probably the most striking and also quantitatively dominant commonality of Mayröcker's texts of the late 1960s is indeed their quality as theatrical sketches. Though some of them still adhere to certain generic drama conventions (characters are named, they each speak a part, and there are some stage directions), mostly these conventions are blown up in a Dada-like gesture. Rather than fragmentary drama texts, then, these sketches present highly theatricalized dramaturgical scenes that deal with the (im)possibility of speaking or singing on stage. The sketch entitled 'comic strip, an opera' (1970, 'comicstrip, eine Oper') is exemplary in this respect. The character named maria callas (sic) is unable to sing, partly because 'the agility of her mouth section has suffered greatly' (Mayröcker 2001b: 189)[27], partly because the stage is taken over by several choirs who fight each other by sneezing and coughing, by loudly screaming phonetic sounds (both 'voiced', 'stimmhaft', and 'unvoiced', 'stimmlos'), or with instrumental noise (2001b: 190):

> and makes noise with small drums, timbals, trombones,
> violins, children's trumpets etc.
> until noise monstrous —
> maria callas keeps her ears shut[28]

Towards the end of the text, this rather hilarious staging of the failed performance of an iconic opera diva takes a turn that in an ironic gesture seems to address the performance practices of the Wiener Gruppe. Written in 1970, more than a decade after the two infamous Literary Cabarets of the Gruppe, it is hard not to read the text as ironizing the self-adopted aggressive and provocative poses of their members, including the intimidating terrorist-like posture they embraced as a gesture of ultimate freedom. Mayröcker (2001b: 190–91) writes:

> from the trapdoor — at the far right —
> the statue of liberty arises with a grenade in her
> pumping fist
> all automatically throw themselves to the ground[29]

After the explosion the stage is empty, and snoopy (sic), maria callas's voiceless and crying companion, wanders about, 'looking around | as if he is looking for something..' (2001b: 191).[30] Indeed, the opera diva has effectively been removed from the stage.

With the violent elimination of the female diva, the terror-like attack has a clearly gendered outcome. In other sketches too the hindrance of the female artist is staged. The sketch entitled 'Aria on Feet of Clay' (1969) develops a triangular relation between a female opera singer, her male companion on the piano and the female prompter. The text performs a total loss of vocal and musical mastery and the impossibility of playing or singing together. Ex negativo it more specifically builds on the stereotyped expectations that surround the gendered image of the opera diva: both hysteric eccentricity and a perfectly natural mastery of the voice are part of this image. The text demonstrates how these expectations obscure the highly unnatural, hierarchical and gendered conditions of disciplined training and artistic production.

Several theatrical sketches also share a remarkable generic feature, which could be summed up as the independence [Autonomisierung] of the side text. Indeed, both texts referred to above wholly consist of so-called 'disdascalia' or stage directions. The scenes that they present are not staged directly, in a showing mode, but indirectly, through the telling mode of the stage directions. The fact that a narratorial voice can make itself heard through stage directions, however hidden and implicit it might be, is not uncommon in modern drama. Here, however, this voice has completely replaced the dramatic dialogue. Indeed, rather descriptive passages alternate with clear directives for the implied director and interpretative judgments, or, even more strikingly, fragmentary internal focalizations of the character described, as in the beginning of 'Aria on Feet of Clay': '(heartbreakingly she wants to go | disguised as liverpool)' (2001b: 191).[31] This hybrid narratorial voice does lend the stage directions a narrative quality; though no full, coherent story line is developed, clear micronarrative events are related: the battle of the choirs as well as the bomb attack leading to the disappearance of maria callas in the snoopy text, the female singer's extremely corporeal, pantomimic performance to compensate for her lost voice in the Aria text.

The fact that the stage directions do not amount to full-fledged narratives, is largely due to lyrical denarrativization — which brings us, next to the narrative qualities of the dramatic stage directions, to another striking intraliterary quality: the lyricalization of the prose text. At intervals the snoopy text is typographically laid out as a poem, with e.g. a single word exposed on a line (Mayröcker 2001b: 189):

> as soon as the tidal wave has subsided
> snoopy
> maria callas
> appear
> and smile[32]

Other lines contain elliptical, grammatically incorrect parts of sentences: 'shakes mane of hair', 'until noise monstrous — '.[33] The externally focalized characterization of maria callas, 'the agility of her mouth section has suffered greatly', is, with small variations, repeated three times throughout the short text.

The 'Aria' text is stylistically even more lyrical. Grammatically incorrect sentences abound, images and metaphors are accumulated, parts of sentences dissolve into intertextual wordplay, e.g. with the names of Hanswurst figures from eighteenth-century century Viennese folk comedies that parodied the courtly opera: he 'disturbs him with fuchsmundi mirlifax'.[34] A representative example is found in the following lines (Mayröcker 2001b: 192):

> while the *singer* remains in her horizontal position
> the *accompanying pianist* calls the little owl calls
> the counterpoint to order deals the mitten
> a soft nose punch fastens an accolade
> to the point[35]

These lines consist of a syntactical structure with four paralleled main clauses ('ruft', 'ruft', 'versetzt', 'fixiert'), the regular structure of which is disturbed by their irregular distribution along the verse lines and the omission of punctuation. The lyrical quality is furthermore enhanced by the accumulation of surreal imagery that constantly shifts between metaphorical and literal usage, and implies the graphic sphere of (musical) notation: the musical principle of the counterpoint ('Kontrapunkt') becomes the point ('Punkt') as punctuation mark, the corporeal act of the nose punch ('Nasenstüber'), which metaphorically also stands for a reprimand, becomes the punctuation mark curly bracket, or, in terms of musical notation, the accolade ('Nasenklammer'). Along the way the counterpoint is also narrativized, as it becomes a living character in this theatrical scene.

To sum up the formal characteristics of these theatrical sketches of the late 1960s, their extreme intermingling of generic conventions comes to the fore: inscribing themselves in conventions of dramatic writing, they adopt and at the same time undermine techniques of narrativization, while on top of that confusing both the dramatic and the narratorial characteristics with a profound lyricalization of the text. In an anarchic Dada gesture this intermingling blows up any definite generic identification. This can be seen as exemplifying Mayröcker's endeavour to paradoxically find her own voice in a protean process of non-recognisable forms.

Strikingly enough, the micronarratives that both texts under scrutiny present, reflect on this same (im)possibility of finding one's own voice: the female singer is violently removed from the stage (in the snoopy text) or really struggles to find her own voice (in the 'Aria' text). In their meta-dramatic reflection on the medium of the opera these texts align well with the preoccupations of the Wiener Gruppe. In both text and performance its members practiced an artistic disruption of the conventions of courtly opera, of its culturally authoritative status, its setting as an agonistic vocal arena, and its rhythmical structure based on entering and leaving the stage (on *Auftritte* and *Abtritte*; see Vogel 2008). The exemplary figure personifying this disruption is the Hanswurst (Schmidt-Dengler 1994), a character explicitly devised, as early as the seventeenth century, to parody the high style of courtly opera. Both Mayröcker and the Wiener Gruppe thus inscribe their experiments in a long-lived Viennese tradition. In the two selected Mayröcker texts the Hanswurst figure is either represented by a character of contemporary popular comics culture (the voiceless, pantomimic snoopy) or conjured up via intertextual signals that open up a continuum of cultural memory ('fuchsmundi mirlifax', names that in the diegesis of the text are used to 'disturb him', 'him' being the harmonic composition principle of the counterpoint).

What distinguishes these texts from similar ones of the Wiener Gruppe, is the introduction (and deconstruction) of creative female characters (quite absent as artists in the texts of the Gruppe), as well as the parodic approach to actions and attitudes of the neo-avant-garde of the late 1950s and early 1960s (the Gruppe itself was of course not devoid of self-irony either). Stylistically an extreme anarchic intermingling of generic conventions and a constant insertion of intertextual and intermedial signals come to the fore, lending these texts an outspoken unrecognizable genericity and a hermeneutically 'unreadable' quality.

Didactic Sketches: Mastering and Losing One's Voice

Next to the dramatic sketches, the second striking feature we want to point out here is the didactic character of many texts of the late 1960s that are presented as taken from text books, conversation lexicons, instruction manuals, etc. Their imperative gesture is nearly always adopted to instruct the addressee in aesthetic matters. The text 'Pick me up, my wing' (1969, 'Pick mich auf, mein Flügel...') cites in its title a mystic image of inspirational elevation; the subtitle, 'Instructions for poetic behaviour' ('Anleitungen zu poetischem Verhalten'), informs the reader in a more down to earth manner about the learning process that can bring about this poetic posture. The text itself immediately parodies the seriousness of its instructive character, as the guidelines are obviously meant to alleviate the stress and pain of the addressee's visit to the dentist with a walk through Vienna:

> At night in May go slowly down the Strudlhof stairs after a painful dental treatment, look in all the grassy cracks, bird steps, reservations, pause at the bust of Gido Hasen, throw lots of glances at the kloppen & daken of the Salvation Army [...] fly from the bottom of the stairs to Tokyo with country horse beurre (as butter) .. pick me up, my wing. (Mayröcker 2001b: 94)[36]

During a highly surreal (and multilingual) guided city tour, the speaking voice not only points out the details of the urban landscape but also reminds the addressee, towards the end of the above quotation, of the transgressive inspirational elevation. After these introductory lines, with their constant shift between a Dadaist presentation of found objects and phrases, and cryptic Surrealist imagery, the text resorts to a stricter prescriptive voice: for the length of two pages imperative commands are accumulated, insistently calling to the addressee. Repetitive and clear though the syntactical structure is — and with a high degree of rhythmical lyricalization through the endless series of paralleled imperative exclamations, which give the text an emphatic, chanting quality — , the content is not. Invocations of nonsensical anarchic behaviour reminiscent of Dadaist happenings alternate with appeals for the activation of dreamlike surreal fantasies and follies. Metalinguistic and metatextual utterances gradually dominate the nonsensical make up. The addressee — who, quite paradoxically, until the very end is addressed in the formal 'Sie' mode — is explicitly asked to experiment with language, to play with words in order to liberate them from their grammatical rules and referential framing:

> Let the words yowl out!
> Say boingg-boingg a few times!
> Forget the whole language!
> Put syllables on ice!
> Warm your feet with declinations!

> Inflate the grammar!
> Throw yourself at daily conversations!
> Jeopardize set square and compasses!
> Disturb the language a bit more!
> Push her against the wall until she screams!
> Go down in the elevator with her!
> Let her fly by! (Mayröcker 2001b: 97)[37]

What's more, even the background of the dentist visit turns out to be meaningful, as the mouth is put forward as the organ that can produce this autonomous language play. The character of the dentist, as someone who, often painfully, repairs damage to the oral cavity, is contrasted with the 'Kieferzertrümmer', the 'jaw smasher', an imaginary machine that can or should violently loosen speech and speech organs from conventional utterances: 'Help building the jaw smasher! [...] Dream about the construction of the jaw smasher!' (Mayröcker 2001b: 95–96)[38]

This didactic text thus can be read as offering lessons in a poetics between the 'two monsters' Dadaism and Surrealism. It performs the paradox that even anarchic poetic behaviour obviously does presuppose repeated listening, learning and training. This paradox is taken up as well in the text 'PNEUMA or the domestication of the actor' (1970, 'PNEUMA oder die Domestikation des Schauspielers'), which connects the teaching mode with the profession of the actor. Again, the title mentions a highly poetic, inspirational concept: the Greek *pneuma*, breath, refers to the creative power of a person and was a keyword in seventeenth-century theories of acting (Jürs-Munby 2007: 132). The *pneumatic* inspiration of the actor was considered both a privilege and a danger, though: as it could easily become uncontrollable, it was met, from the eighteenth century onward, with the need for domestication. The second part of Mayröcker's title, a blunt non-poetic educational statement, indicates exactly that.

A long list of paratactically ordered sentences, this text too is of a high rhythmical lyricality, as it is fully constructed along an anaphoric principle: every sentence starts with the imperative clause 'Stellen Sie sich vor' followed by a subclause. The instructive sentences allude to the actors' training method to extemporize on certain given fictitious characters or situations in order to trigger the actor's empathetic imagination and bring to perfection the role-playing techniques. In a metatheatrical sense, on the contrary, to extemporize is linked with the act of stepping out of one's role, of trespassing against the conventions of illusionist, bourgeois drama. This too demands perfection. The seemingly abrupt improvisational gesture of the extemporizer is only a mask for the mastery of the situation and his or her own skills. Again, as in Mayröcker's dramatic sketches above, the Viennese tradition of the Hanswurst is cited, as extemporizing was crucial to his role as a 'trained' (Jürs-Munby 2007: 132) violator of 'the [bourgeois] disciplined art of acting' (129).

The repetitive anaphoric structure of the instructions suggests the speech of a depersonalized, maybe choric voice with an inescapably insisting quality. Indeed, this insistence is confirmed at the very end of the text (Mayröcker 2001b: 223), when a kind of stage direction concludes:

(It is recommended that the director speaks this suggestive text
on tape and has it played
before and during rehearsals
nonstop, on
full blast)[39]

Again the successful instructive quality is in many ways subverted. The concluding direction transposes the instructions into an omnipresent deafening soundscape. Efficient guidance is also thwarted by the sheer amount of highly divergent instructions. Some clear guidelines can be singled out, e.g. 'Imagine someone spitting pumpkin seeds at you!' Others, however, present images not unlike Dadaist collages — e.g. 'Imagine you have to share your place to live with giant lobelia's moss phlox and dryadic underwear ..' — or surrealist micronarrative scenes, e.g. 'Imagine someone breathes you in an anachronistic way (like the unicorn next-door) on the billboard namely while the swan ('swan') on the turntable with fork & knife simulates SSSSSSSSSSSSSSSSSSSs! ——' (Mayröcker 2001b: 221–22).[40]

The domestication of the actor, then — as well as, it should be added, of the reader/audience — can hardly be identified as the aim of this text. Though it pretends to guide the imagination of the addressee, the actual prescriptions rather leave him or her at a loss. This gives the text an iconoclastic quality, as it replaces coherent, identifiable 'Vorstellungen' or imaginings with an accumulation of centrifugal fragmentary images. Moreover, the text exposes how these fragments are assigned to the addressee in a heteronomous way, from the outside, and not dug out by delving into an inner self. Rather than presenting a pedagogical truth about actors' training, the text sets free an anarchic energy while at the same time questioning its very intelligibility and communicability. What, then, is the kind of mastery this anarchic energy demands, from actors and audience alike?

As was the case with the transgressing of generic conventions in the theatrical sketches, Mayröcker continues an important preoccupation of the Wiener Gruppe with these pseudo-didactic texts. Its members explored the appellative, instructive character of the voice, with both its authoritarian and subversive potentials, in sound poetry, performance, and scenic fragments alike (Fetz 2008; Steinlechner 2008). The narrators of these texts frequently adopt the pose of a (unsuccessful) language teacher or lexicographer. Questions regarding both the de- and prescriptive character of language, and the communication and intelligibility of speech acts are at the core of many experiments. Probably the best know is Konrad Bayer's 'kasperl am elektrischen stuhl' (1957), in which the illiterate Hanswurst character, assuming the active part of an author, disrupts all efficient communication (Schmidt-Dengler 1994). These Gruppe texts predate Mayröcker's by many years, though, and seem to be more concerned, albeit in a (self-)ironic way, with analysing from a clear philosophical and ideological perspective the seemingly natural mechanisms of language acquisition, as well as their (mis)use in the National-Socialist climate (Steinlechner 2008).

Prose Poems: The (Im-)Possibility to Tell a Story

The third and last category within the so-called prose texts of the late 1960s we want to present here, are short pieces that experiment with the (im)possibility of telling a story — a theme also apparent in Stassaert's oeuvre. They could be termed prose poems when we define this subgenre as short autonomous texts without versification, with a high self-referential quality, and structurally generated by repetition and variation, parallelism, and contrast (Bernaerts, Vandevoorde, and Vervaeck 2013). A representative example is 'Bad tidings or the 19 stage entries' (1969, 'Hiobs-Post oder die 19 auftritte'). The text consists of 19 lines of one sentence each, which function rather like 19 abbreviated paragraphs than as 19 verse lines. Each line or sentence looks as if it's the beginning of a story, using the classical narrative disposition 'when ...' plus past tense (Schmidt-Dengler 2001: 601).[41] In this repetitive, paralleled and largely anaphoric structure, each line syntactically varies the limited elements of the sentence, namely 'this one' who 'talks', and 'another one' who 'enters' and 'says' or 'speaks'. While each line is, apart from the comma rules, grammatically correct, the syntactical variation renders ambivalent the referentiality of the two figures: do the sentences present various scenarios with the same two figures, or is there an accumulative effect, with ever more figures taking the place of the previous ones?

> when this one was still talking another one entered and spoke
> when this one spoke another one entered and said
> this one was still talking when another one entered and spoke
> (Mayröcker 2001b: 199)[42]

The telling never really takes off and each of the lines modifies a micronarrative structure with a highly theatrical dimension: the interruption of a person telling a story by another one entering and taking over the floor. We do not know whether the 'other one' really comes to bring a 'Hiobspost' or bad tidings, as the title suggests. Indeed, as in the previous texts, even in this prose poem no real content, no — in a quite literal sense — subject matter, let alone an inward perspective, is transmitted. Instead the formal structure of a speech act in 19 scenes or 'stage entries' (the '19 auftritte' of the subtitle) is described. This prose poem, not unlike the dramatic sketches and the instructive texts that considered the (im)possibility of finding and mastering one's own voice, thus reflects on the (im)possibility of taking the floor and telling a story of one's own.

The text does not only consist of 19 sentences, though. It concludes with a '*post scriptum*' that voices a narrator's comment or annotation, but in the form of a poem, a short epic poem telling us, with dense surreal images and agrammatical syntax, that '.. once he was water pipe and | crocodile nice sweet and happy', whereas 'now he is splinter in the flesh of the world | a | terrifying display of worms | [...] | and ready to die ..' (Mayröcker 2001b: 199–200).[43] Formally, the poem transgresses the characterization of the text as a prose poem, or rather: it adds the fragment of an epic poem to the above prose poem, turning the text into a generic hybrid. Content wise, the attached epic poem might well contain the bad tidings the main prose poem leaves out, even referring quite literally to the shifting destiny of the biblical Job, the Hiob of the poem's title (see Schmidt-Dengler 2001: 602). Reading the prose poem from the perspective of the concluding epic poem with its biblical reference, one might consider it not only to comment on the modalities of storytelling but also on those of listening. The prose poem then conjures up a plethora of competing messenger voices that do not listen to each other and whose simultaneous talk makes it impossible for the audience as well to hear and understand *a*, let alone *the* message. The epic poem on the other hand, displaced to the margins, suggests expressing the essence of the message.

The basic theatrical structure of entering a place or stage to tell or perform a story, and the disruptions this might cause, is a micronarrative element that regularly pops up in early writings of the Wiener Gruppe as well. Again Konrad Bayer can be referred to, for instance with his early untitled text (*c.* 1953) 'when the messengers entered the garden' ('als die herolde den garten betraten') or the later (*c.* 1962) very short prose texts 'when the young giantess comes into the city' ('wenn die junge riesin in die stadt kommt') or 'when he opened the door' ('als er die tür öffnete'). Bayer's story 'when the admiral came back' ('als der admiral zurückkehrte', *c.* 1962) opens with the following sentence: 'when the admiral came back after he had decided seven battles on the high seas in his favour, his country house awaited him in a completely changed state' (Bayer 1996: 421).[44] These opening lines, echoing the parable-like tone of Kafka's short prose, read as the dark fairy tale background to Mayröcker's later prose text 'first time the construction worker came to the house' (1972; Mayröcker 1998: 13–16), which negotiates the modalities of 'unconventional storytelling' (see above) at greater length and with more explicit narrative elements than in her prose poems under scrutiny here. Indeed, prose poems like 'Bad tidings' show that the break with 'experimental writing' that Mayröcker in an interview in 1983 situates around 1971, was a gradual rather than a radical one, as she herself seems to indicate in the following statement:

> In 1971 I was suddenly fed up with so called experimental prose writing [...] It didn't appeal to me anymore. It was boring, in a sense. Of course that doesn't mean that I left out montage techniques etc. altogether. I stuck to that but I went from a purely experimental writing to a kind of narrational writing, though in interviews I have always declined to label my writing as storytelling. I would still decline to do this today. I don't want to write stories in any usual sense but I want to approach a totally unconventional, unorthodox narrational writing, if one can call it like that. (Schmidt 1984: 264, 267–68)[45]

Stassaert

In order to analyze the early neo-avant-gardist work of Lucienne Stassaert adequately, we first need to address her perspective on literary genres. As mentioned before, the author herself classified her early prose works *Stories of the Noblewoman with the Spade* and *Bongo Blossom Blood* as the only exponents of her experimental period, implying that the poetry collection *Fossil* marks a new phase in her oeuvre. This deviation seems to be related to Stassaert's shifting views on the connection between poetry and prose. In her *Labris*-period, she did not consider the distinction between these two genres to be absolute. Retrospectively, she even described the first years of her career as a period in which 'poetry was infiltrated in everything I did' (Billiet 1976).[46] As Lars Bernaerts and Sven Vitse have pointed out, then, the early Stassaert is one of the experimental authors in the Low Countries whose prose is representative of the process of 'lyricization', in the sense that traditional narrative devices are undermined by lyrical processes like reasoning by association, word merging and versification (Bernaerts 2013: 63; Vitse 2013: 84–86).

At the end of the 1960s, however, Stassaert started to realize that there is an absolute difference between prose and poetry. In 1967, she already indicated that her poetry was more 'static' than her prose (Neefs 1967: 42), hinting at an opposition between *condensation* (poetry) and *dispersion* (prose). Nine years later, the difference had become even more pronounced: after the self-proclaimed failure of the novel *A Small Sea Anemone* (1975, *Een kleine zeeanemoon*), condemned by the author because she thought her language had been too complex to effectively convey her message, Stassaert posited the dogma that prose should never be complicated. From now on, the so-called 'testing' of words was allowed in nothing but poetry (Billiet 1976).

Taking note of the importance of this genre problem in Stassaert's oeuvre — especially regarding the early work — this account of her literary practice confronts the neo-avant-gardist debut stories in *Stories of the Noblewoman with the Spade* with the hermetic, yet more traditional poems in *Fossil*.

Stories of the Noblewoman with the Spade

In several respects, Stassaert's debut stories are a striking example of the author's resistance against compartmentalization. Her defiance against subjecting literary expression to traditional schemes is first and foremost apparent from the radical deconstruction of typical genre conventions. By explicitly marking the prose texts in her debut as 'stories' ('verhalen'), Stassaert activates the generic expectations of her readers, but the assumptions that come with the term 'story' are ultimately not met. In the first place, the mode of narration in *Stories of the Noblewoman with the Spade* does not correspond to traditional storytelling, in which a number of events are presented by a narrator, whether or not in a (plot-driven) logical-chronological order. In Stassaert's 'stories', it is hardly possible to determine 'events', which radically undermines the possibility of reconstructing the relationship between *fabula* and *syuzhet*.

The stories' narrative style is reminiscent of the Surrealist technique of *écriture automatique*. Often converging with the focalizing subject, the narrator presents a series of associations that are, as noted before, in some way connected to her emotions. We would like to characterize Stassaert's mode of narration as 'lyrical-eruptive writing': rather than constructing a *syuzhet* that can (whether or not easily) be decoded into a *fabula*, she composes her experimental stories by phonetic-rhythmical improvisation. A quote from *Stories of the Noblewoman with the Spade* may elucidate this point:

> she strolls
> breath of forest women tears open
> secret veins in her skin, a water creases
> her shoes hammer the road shut, mul-
> tiply ani-ina-vagina-nina, summer-
> ly sultrily cedars her skin, wind shy
> smells climbing clammily up and down
> (Stassaert 1964: n.p.)[47]

The phrase 'mul- / tiply ani-ina-vagina-nina' is the most obvious example of Stassaert's lyrical-eruptive narrative style, but the eruption is also manifest in the semantic chain unfolding itself in 'forest women', 'veins' and 'cedars'. The lyrical design of this fragment is also apparent in the ambiguity of Stassaert's sentences — the sequence 'a water creases / her shoes hammer the road shut', for instance, contains an apo koinou that is stressed by the enjambment after 'creases'. Along with the highly metaphoric character of Stassaert's language, these devices enforce the impression that the 'stories' in *Stories of the Noblewoman with the Spade* are actually close to poetry.

Stassaert's lyrical-eruptive narrative style results into a second mismatch between readers' expectations — as activated by the concept of 'stories' — and her performance of the genre. The absence of events limits the space of protagonists to perform actions, which further deconstructs the canonical narrative scheme, as captured in for instance Greimas' famous actantial model. Because Stassaert erases epic elements from her stories, the characters in *Stories of the Noblewoman with the Spade* tend to merge with the impressions they embody. According to Erik Spinoy, the protagonists in Stassaert's early prosaic works are 'surrounded by a cloud of delusions' (1986: 289),[48] which frustrates the reader's capability to sketch their homogeneous psychological portraits. In her lyrical-eruptive prose, Stassaert rather gives voice to a disfigured consciousness and its ruptured expressions. To her, subjects are essentially polyvalent, which is irreconcilable with a literary universe that stays within the boundaries of logical-chronological narration and the framework of a protagonist with a coherent psychology. Not surprisingly, then, the strolling woman in the fragment above is depicted as tree-like: her persona can be defined in terms of constant ramification.

The polyvalence of the narrator-subject resembles Stassaert's literary style, which can be considered as a third device that deconstructs the traditional scheme of telling stories. Stassaert's sentences are often ungrammatical, especially with regard to verb placement, but above all, they form a chain of sometimes bizarre metaphors, oxymorons and neologisms, underlining the lyrical characteristics of this prose.

To further elaborate on these three aberrations from traditional prose, we will have a closer look on the title story of *Stories of the Noblewoman with the Spade*. The following is a typical excerpt from the story:

> I've already dug for a couple of years, the building will
> appear in the mist someday like the stone
> of wisdom strong. let me laugh. laugh. laugh
> and the old Pieter Breughel and his tower

and the parties and the songs of the old trou-
badours
this all together me-forming life with the
inertness of an undeciphered hieroglyph.
sometimes I then speak French if things get too hard
for them [...]
(Stassaert 1964: n.p.)[49]

Clearly, Stassaert's narrator is not concerned with telling a story with a logical-chronological coherence. The order of these lines, with their versification, seems to be based on association rather than emplotment or reasoning. This impression is enforced by the fact that many textual elements do not have an explicit referent. It is, for instance, not clear what 'building' is mentioned here, nor can we identify the 'them'-figures in the final line. Similarly, it is hard to grasp the identity of the protagonist of Stassaert's story. As implied by the phrase 'this all together me-forming life', the narrator's subject is polyvalent in the sense that it is built out of totally different building stones — from the mist to Breughel, from laughing to speaking French (the latter of which might be connected to Belgium's division into Dutch-, French-, and German-speaking communities). Finally, the poly-interpretability of this fragment is enhanced by Stassaert's writing style. To use the phrase 'this all together me-forming life' as an example again: this sequence can be identified as an apo koinou, since it is unclear whether or not we should consider 'life' as a part of a constituent that also contains 'me-forming'.

Stassaert's lyrical-eruptive mode of writing may complicate the possibility to provide an overarching interpretation of the *Stories of the Noblewoman with the Spade*, but it certainly does not result in meaningless gibberish. The first lines of the title story are indicative of one of the core aspects of Stassaert's self-presentation, namely her revolt against demarcations and against compartmentalization. The unstable identity of Stassaert's narrator is exemplary for this position. She is not only polyvalent in the sense that her persona is a multilayered amalgam of all kinds of elements, but she also goes through a continuous process of metaphoric metamorphosis — amongst many things, the 'I' figure takes the shape of a horse, a mummified cat, and a goldfish.

The story intimates that this constant reshaping is not a hindrance, but something to be desired. At its beginning, the narrator identifies herself with a horse because of its lack of freedom: 'I cannot bear the fatality of being always four times legs always two times eyes and I burst' (Stassaert 1964: n.p.).[50] Here, the act of bursting is explicitly related to the incapability of reshaping. Moreover, the necessity of escaping a unilateral existence is connected to Stassaert's revolt against servility. The horse metaphor might be denoted as a symbol of this servility, or even servitude, for the 'I' figure states that she hates 'the cart that zealous people hitch me to' (Stassaert 1964: n.p.).[51] We might interpret the ongoing metamorphosis in this story, then, as an attempt of the implied author Stassaert to free herself from such shackles through the act of writing — a real horse is not capable of destroying the cart, but equine personifications actually are.

By means of metamorphosis, the noblewoman with the spade is able to consolidate a fluid position in her literary universe, ensuring that she will not be caged. Such an 'uncaged' position means that the noble woman, interpreted as the archetypal appearance of Stassaert's protagonists, can free herself from hegemonic patterns and constellations. We might, for instance, think of hegemonic gender positions here: by describing Adam as a 'mother's milk-sucking paradoxist' (1964: n.p.),[52] Stassaert inverts the culturally rooted hierarchy in which a man stands at the beginning of creation. In line with her thematic obsessions, however, there is one particular chain she cannot get rid of, as is expressed in the following lines:

> [from time to time] the ten thousand doubles in me change position and
> become horse cat or birds:
> horses in the black meadow
> cats in the hookers street
> birds in the cold wind[53]

Through the phrase 'the thousand doubles', the passage underlines the polyvalence of the narrator's identity and her ability to reshape herself. The act of metamorphosing is not able to halt the ongoing process of deceasing, though (compare Snoek 1993: 412). Whether we are human, cat, horse or bird: the meadows stay black; the wind stays cold; the cities stay dark. At some point in the story, the narrator tries to counter this pessimism by urging herself to cheer up a bit, using the cliché that 'it is time that I start seeing the sun' (Stassaert 1964: n.p.).[54] Ultimately, though, she fails to overcome her mortal fear, which is — as we have noted before — an important thread in Stassaert's early work. In *Stories of the Noblewoman with the Spade*, this preoccupation with death is best illustrated by the noble woman's view on love, which she describes as 'the mass grave love love love'[55] — a word cluster echoed in Stassaert's designation of Eros and Thanatos as 'invincable and unavoidable twins' (De Coux 2011: 47). Given this glaring awareness of the indestructibility of death and, at the same time, the destructive powers of love, it is no wonder that the ongoing metamorphosis in this story finally results in the surrealist metaphor of a fish-woman who is caught by an angling rod: 'the golden fish ME | floundering' (Stassaert 1964: n.p.).[56]

As this example shows, we should not only interpret Stassaert's neo-avant-gardist experimentalism as a mode of resistance against absolute demarcations and conventions. The deviation from traditional storytelling is also an iconic attempt to counter the ultimate of all linear forces: the indelible line between birth and death. Underlining the definiteness of its temporality, Stassaert represents death as 'an hour driven in nails' that cannot be pried out, not even by using the scattering nature of literary language. Literature, however, is at least able to create the illusion of crossing spatial and temporal boundaries, which undeniably offers consolation.

In this respect, it is important to address the meaning of the 'noblewoman with the spade' as a metaphor. Like the cats, the birds and the floundering fish, the noblewoman is one of the many shapes taken by Stassaert's narrator. Unlike these animals, the noblewoman signifies the presence of the late medieval period in the narrative present. She is depicted digging in the soil of history, preserving almost rotten entities by perpetuating them in the literary text: 'I dig up old mists almost wine-worthy brown yeasts pink worms wood worm on a clammy coffin rising shadows' (Stassaert 1964: n.p.).[57] The medieval noblewoman might be seen as such a rising shadow herself. As such, she is a vehicle of Stassaert's revolt against linear time and, by implication, death.

This preoccupation with literature as an area of preservation is manifest in the majority of Stassaert's works. In *Stories of the Noblewoman with the Spade*, it is underlined by numerous references to antique cultures that may have disappeared, but that are still existent through the relics they have left behind. To speak with the extensive quote we used to discuss Stassaert's narrative style: these relics are 'undeciphered hieroglyphs', just like the references to Egyptian and Greek mythology and the recurring mummy motif, which most notably marks the theme of preservation. It is this issue of conservation that most evidently links *Stories of the Noblewoman with the Spade* to *Fossil*, Stassaert's first collection of poems.

Fossil

Characteristic of Stassaert's first poems is their short length — they rarely exceed eight lines — and their extreme density, which accounts for the most prominent difference with her early prose. Thematically, though, *Fossil* and *Stories of the Noblewoman with the Spade* share a revolt against death. In the *Fossil* poems, a lyrical 'I' figure mourns the decease of her lyrical 'you', who might be interpreted as Stassaert's father. Evoking a mystical reading of her poetry, Stassaert describes this 'you' figure as sexually potent, thus underlining the power of erotic language as a means of bridging the seemingly infinite gap between heaven and earth. In this respect, the following poem is exemplary:

> although your shaky leafs never autumn
> this pine tree pelvis of your gothic
> once sweeter winged flesh
> nonetheless your voice is
> smothered in peak silence
> how livid is the rose
> retching in her prime
> too late
> dreamt to nothing
> (Stassaert 1969: n.p., © Lucienne Stassaert)[58]

In this poem, Stassaert draws a literary universe in which the semantic field of sexuality is prominent. The central line — 'smothered in peak silence' — is surrounded by sexually connoted metaphors: the first four lines contain the phallic symbols 'pine tree pelvis' and 'winged flesh', whereas the livid rose in the final four lines has the connotation of a vagina. In spite of the death of the lyrical 'you', his erotic powers seem to be alive, for the 'shaky leafs' of the pine tree do not 'autumn'. His feminine counterpart, on the other hand, is 'retching', which is a typical example of Stassaert's ambiguity: on the one hand, this verb suggests she is past her 'prime'; on the other, the image of a retching rose might refer — just like the noun 'prime' — to an orgasm. The prevalence of such erotic symbols, which paradoxically underlines the persistence of the corporal, conflicts with the disappearance of the mourned figure's singularity. There may be some erotic powers left, at least as long as the rose is not 'dreamt to nothing', but his voice has not been preserved. This maintenance of (poetic) voice is one the central motifs of *Fossil*. Indicative in this respect is the following poem:

> subtropical in the flake-light
> unharmed my body of glass grinds to powder
> in marsh gas of the afterpains
> still a smoking hieroglyph
> words like pearls in the pitch
> (Stassaert 1969: n.p., © Lucienne Stassaert)[59]

In this poem, the 'I' figure quite literally connects her fear of losing voice to the existence of linguistic signs, that might function as a means of conservation. Destruction is master of the universe Stassaert sketches here. Her 'body of glass', which symbolically marks the fragility of the corporal, is grinding to powder while *appearing* unharmed — a situation which might be connected to Heidegger's concept of the *Sein-zum-Tode* [being-toward-death], which postulates that human beings are always heading towards death. In Stassaert's poem, even the surroundings of the narrator's glass body are exposed to the destruction: instead of a solid beam of light, the dense poetical universe contains 'flake-light'. Despite the lurking dangers exposed to the lyrical 'I' figure, though, there are elements in this poem that actually *can* stand the heat caused by the exploding marsh gas. While the corporal elements of the lyrical subject are (necessarily) about to fade, both the hieroglyph and the words on the page stay intact as vivid traces from artistic activity.

Hence, Stassaert celebrates the stubbornness of literary language. This is subtly underlined by the ungrammaticality of the second line of the poem — in Dutch, the verb for 'grinds to powder' ('verpulvert') is placed in an incorrect sentence position. Along with the thematic focus on prevalence and the revolt against a linear conception of time and space, such syntactic ambiguity connects *Fossil* to *Stories of the Noblewoman with the Spade*. However, as presaged by Stassaert's reflections on the differences between poetry and prose, the differences between these works seem to prevail. Where the experimental *Stories of the Noblewoman with the Spade* are highly dispersed, the poems in *Fossil* are extremely compressed. This clenched nature is, of course, mirrored in the title of the collection: Stassaert's poems are themselves compressed like a fossil. At the same time, the title hints at an underlying poetics in which poetry is a vital literary genre that allows us to preserve a singular voice that refuses to be caged into a fully comprehensible compartment. As such, at the core of Lucienne Stassaert's literary work in the 1960s is not so much the language experiment itself, but the highly human desire of escaping 'the mass grave love love love'.

5. Conclusion

In this chapter we dealt with the confrontation between two female authors, both of them the main women writers in their respective experimental environment of the long 1960s. Differences in generation and context have led to different institutional careers and national reception. Along with the striking popularity and canonization that the poets of the Vienna neo-avant-garde experienced in the previous decades, Mayröcker too, though with some more delay, has gradually been recognized as a leading Austrian poet. With Stassaert on the other hand, the prevalent label of hermetic poetess seems to have firmly situated her at the margins of the Dutch speaking cultural field.

Though the respective prose texts and poems analyzed here are quite different as well, some poetic similarities do come to the fore: both authors deliberately wanted to break with conventions of narrative writing and promoted a poetics that could not be pinned down to one poetic programme, distancing themselves from the more group-oriented programmes of their male contemporaries. Ambiguity and volatility run through their respective oeuvres. Nevertheless, the question of and quest for one's own voice also links both authors, at least in their work of the late 1960s. Stassaert seems to be more concerned with unearthing and preserving subconscious traces of an authentic aesthetic voice that predates any female stereotyping. Mayröcker for her part seems to situate her own voice in highly anarchic, decentred collages of contemporary generic and aesthetic discourses, touching on the gender question in a parodic way.

Works Cited

ARTEEL, INGE. 2012. *Friederike Mayröcker* (Hannover: Wehrhahn)

BAYER, KONRAD. 1996. *Sämtliche Werke*, ed. by Gerhard Rühm (Vienna: ÖBV)

BERNAERTS, LARS. 2013. 'De hausse van het experiment: Lyricisering in de jaren zestig', *Revue Belge de Philologie et d'Histoire*, 90.3: 57–78

——, HANS VANDEVOORDE, and BART VERVAECK. 2013. 'Inleiding: Generaties en lyricise-ring van het experimentele proza', *Revue Belge de Philologie et d'Histoire*, 90.3: 551–60

BEYER, MARCEL. 1992. *Friederike Mayröcker: Eine Bibliographie 1946–1990* (Frankfurt a/M: Peter Lang)

BILLIET, DANIËL. 1976. '*ik geloof niet dat er voor mij redding bestaat buiten het woord*: Poëziekrant sprak met Lucienne Stassaert', *Poëziekrant*, 1.2: 6

BOUSSET, HUGO. 1980. 'Hermafroditisch schrijven', *Nieuw Vlaams Tijdschrift*, 33.3: 439–42

DE COUX, ANNELEEN. 2011. 'Hier vecht een vogel voor zijn opvlucht', *Poëziekrant*, 35.8: 44–53

EDER, THOMAS, and KLAUS KASTBERGER (eds). 2000. *Schluß mit dem Abendland! Der lange Atem der österreichischen Avantgarde* (Vienna: Paul Zsolnay)

——, and JULIANE VOGEL (eds). 2008. *verschiedene sätze treten auf: Die Wiener Gruppe in Aktion* (Vienna: Paul Zsolnay)

FETZ, BERNHARD. 2008. '"ihre stimme klingt manchmal als wären es sie"': Zur Vielstimmigkeit der Wiener Gruppe', in *verschiedene sätze treten auf*, ed. by Thomas Eder and Juliane Vogel, pp. 119–32

FOSTER, HAL. 1996. *The Return of the Real: The Avant-Garde at the End of the Century* (Cambridge: MIT Press)

GERITS, JORIS. 1988. 'Stassaert, Lucienne', in *Geboekstaafd: Vlaamse prozaschrijvers na 1945*, ed. by Marcel Janssens, Marita de Sterck, and Luc Lannoy (Leuven: Davidfonds), pp. 251–54

HANNELORE, ROBIN. 1965. 'In het akwarium van de poëzie', *Heibel*, 5.2–3: 63–64

HÖLLERER, WALTER. 1965. 'Thesen zum langen Gedicht', *Akzente*, 12: 128–30

JESPERS, HENRI-FLORIS. 1999. *Lucienne Stassaerts orakeltaal: Van 'De verhalen van de jonkvrouw met de spade' tot 'Bongobloesembloed'* (Antwerp: Jef Meert)

JÜRS-MUNBY, KAREN. 2007. 'Hanswurst and Herr Ich: Subjection and Abjection in Enlightenment Censotship of the Comic Figure', *New Theatre Quarterly*, 23.2: 124–35

KÜHN, RENATE (ed.). 2002a. *Friederike Mayröcker oder 'das Innere des Sehens': Studien zu Lyrik, Hörspiel und Prosa* (Bielefeld: Aisthesis)

——. 2002B. 'Herme(neu)tik: Zur ersten Sequenz von Friederike Mayröckers "langem Gedicht"' *Text mit den langen Bäumen des Webstuhls*', in *Friederike Mayröcker oder 'das Innere des Sehens'*, ed. by Renate Kühn, pp. 41–104

LE NÉE, AURÉLIE. 2013. *La poésie de Friederike Mayröcker: Une 'œuvre ouverte'* (Bern: Peter Lang)

LUGHOFER, JOHANN GEORG (ed.). 2017. *Friederike Mayröcker: Interpretationen, Kommentare, Didaktisierungen* (Vienna: Praesens)

MAYRÖCKER, FRIEDERIKE. 1998. *with each clouded peak*, trans. by Rosmarie Waldrop and Harriett Watts (Los Angeles: Sun & Moon Press)

——. 2001A. *Magische Blätter I–V* (Frankfurt a/M: Suhrkamp)

——. 2001B. *Gesammelte Prosa I, 1949–1977*, ed. by Marcel Beyer (Frankfurt a/M: Suhrkamp)

——. 2001C. *Gesammelte Prosa III, 1987–1991*, ed. by Klaus Kastberger (Frankfurt a/M: Suhrkamp)

——. 2004. *Gesammelte Gedichte 1939–2003*, ed. by Marcel Beyer (Frankfurt a/M: Suhrkamp)

——. 2007. *Raving Language: Selected Poems 1946–2006*, trans. by Richard Dove (Manchester: Carcanet)

NEEFS, HUGO. 1965. 'Notisie 21', *Labris*, 3.3: 73–76

——. 1967. 'Hugo Neefs interviewt Lucienne Stassaert', *Labris*, 5.4: 43–46

PAULER, MONIKA. 1999. 'Die Erfindung der Trennung in Friederike Mayröckers Hörspiel *dein Wort ist meines Fuszes Leuchte*', in *Friederike Mayröcker*, ed. by Gerhard Melzer and Stefan Schwar (Graz: Droschl), pp. 91–125

——. 2010. *Bewußtseinsstimmen: Friederike Mayröckers auditive Texte* (Berlin: LIT)

PUFF-TROJAN, ANDREAS. 2012. 'Eine Unmenge "kommunizierender Gefäße"': Zu Friederike Mayröckers Lyrik und (autobiographischer) Prosa im Verhältnis zu André Bretons "Licht des Bildes"', in*'Einzelteilchen aller Menschengehirne': Subjekt und Subjektivität in Friederike Mayröckers (Spät-)Werk*, ed. by Françoise Lartillot, Aurélie Le Née, and Alfred Pfabigan (Bielefeld: Aisthesis), pp. 85–95

REUMKENS, NOËL. 2013. *Kunst, Künstler, Kontext und Konzept: Intermediale und andersartige Bezugsnahmen auf Visuell-Künstlerisches in der Lyrik Mayröckers, Klings, Grünbeins und Draesners* (Würzburg: Königshausen & Neumann)

ROGGEMAN, WILLEM M. 1975. 'Lucienne Stassaert', in *Beroepsgeheim: Gesprekken met schrijvers 1* (The Hague: Nijgh & Van Ditmar), pp. 277–303

SCHMIDT, SIEGFRIED J. (ed.). 1984. *Friederike Mayröcker* (Frankfurt a/M: Suhrkamp)

SCHMIDT-DENGLER, WENDELIN. 1994. 'Die Einsamkeit Kasperls als Langstreckenlaufer: Ein Versuch zu H.C. Artmanns und Konrad Bayers Dramen', in *verLOCKERUNGEN: Österreichische Avantgarde im 20. Jahrhundert*, ed by Wendelin Schmidt-Dengler (Vienna: Praesens), pp. 75–93

——. 2001. 'Demontagen, Variationen und Übergänge', in *Friederike Mayröcker: Gesammelte Prosa I, 1949–1977*, ed. by Marcel Beyer, pp. 595–605

SNOEK, KEES. 1993. 'De tastzin van een blinde passagier: De poëzie van Lucienne Stassaert', *Ons erfdeel*, 36.3: 411–18

SPINOY, ERIK. 1986. 'Lucienne Stassaert of de verwoording van een visie', *Dietsche Warande & Belfort*, 131.4: 289–94

——. 1987. 'Vlaams dichterschap', *Dietsche Warande & Belfort*, 132.5: 69–71

STASSAERT, LUCIENNE. 1964. *Verhalen van de jonkvrouw met de spade* (Antwerp: n.p.)

——. 1969. *Fossiel* (Bruges: Desclée de Brouwer)

——. 1972. 'Waarom schrijven vrouwen gewoonlijk slecht?', *De Vlaamse Gids*, 56.11: 4–11

——. 1975. 'Ik weet zeer goed dat ook mannelijke auteurs zich gediskrimineerd voelen', *yang* 11.62–64: 205–06

——. 2008. 'Over debuteren. Van "Verhalen van de jonkvrouw met de spade" (1964) naar "De hunkerbunker van Moe Poezeloes" (2008) of: een debuut met verstrekkende misverstanden', *Deus ex machina*, 32.126: 76–78

——. 2014. *Souvenirs: Aantekeningen in de loop van de tijd* (Leuven: Uitgeverij P)

STEINLECHNER, GISELA. 2008. 'kämme mich, — etwas behutsam: Aus der Lehrmittelkammer der Wiener Gruppe', in *verschiedene sätze treten auf*, ed. by Thomas Eder and Juliane Vogel, pp. 174–91

STROHMAIER, ALEXANDRA (ed.). 2009. *Buchstabendelirien: Zur Literatur Friederike Mayröckers* (Bielefeld: Aisthesis)

VAN DER BENT, JAAP. '"Kerouac en zo": Vlaanderen, de Beat Generation en het tijdschrift *Labris*', in *Van Hugo Claus tot hoelahoep: Vlaanderen in beweging*, ed by Kevin Absillis and Katrien Jacobs (Antwerp: Garant), pp. 221–33

VITSE, SVEN. 2013. '"Klankmuziek & poëzie plus anti-poëzie ineen": Lyricisering in de jaren zeventig', *Revue Belge de Philologie et d'Histoire*, 90.3: 79–103

VOGEL, JULIANE. 2008. 'Auftritte, Vortritte, Rücktritte: Konrad Bayers theatrale Anthropologie', in *verschiedene sätze treten auf*, ed. by Thomas Eder and Juliane Vogel, pp. 29–38

WALRAVENS, JAN. 1965. 'Het laboratorium van Lucienne Stassaert', *Algemeen Handelsblad*, 13 March 1965

WILMOTS, LIES. 2008. 'All that jazz: het tijdschrift *Labris*', *Zuurvrij*, 15: 74–85

Notes to Chapter 3

1. 'die Kriegsjahre welche mich gleichermaßen beschädigt wie verschont hatten, habe ich wie hinter einer gläsernen Wand verbracht'. Except for the poem 'the calling' (see below) all Mayröcker translations are by Inge Arteel.

2. 'Ik was [...] een beetje onwennig dat de vrijheid die ik stilaan had veroverd, voortaan zou moeten wijken voor een nieuwe discipline.'

3. 'plötzlich aufgerufen bei meinem Namen | [...] | auf ein fremdes bewegtes Ziel gesetzt : | ohne Wahl | aber mit ungeduldigem Herzen' (Mayröcker 2004: 93)

4. 'Die meine Arbeit begleitenden Theorien und Ansichten befinden sich in einem Zustand permanenter Bewegung, die zwar ihr Tempo ändert, sich aber an keinem Punkt fixieren läßt, weil dadurch die Arbeit selbst gestört würde. [...] wie diese Punkte [...] ein Durcheinander von Stimmen ergeben, nie einen Chor. [...] Immerfort kommen und gehen Theorien zur eigenen Arbeit, als Teil des Arbeitsprozesses, aber nicht als Aussagen über die Texte, diesen zusätzlich Gewicht zu verleihen. [...] Formen [werden] zitiert und gleichzeitig ad absurdum geführt.'

5. '1 wenn ich nach bohrender Selbstbefragung mich recht verstehen will, sehe ich mich zuzeiten eingekeilt zwischen den beiden Monstren Dadaismus und Surrealismus und in einer Art Doppelbeziehung zu ihnen stehend [...] 2 aber auch die widersprüchlichsten Kreuzungen sind schon entstanden [...] 4 ich habe des öfteren [...] meine Zweifel angemeldet, auf meine Vorbehalte nach allen Seiten hin, von allen Blickpunkten aus, verwiesen [...] 7 spielhaftes Anliegen also? [...] 8 Rückzug : obwohl Spielerisches mir oft zum ersten Antrieb hilft, möchte ich ihm nicht das Wort reden'

6. Mayröcker's references to the historical avant-garde remind us of Hal Foster's genealogy of the second neo-avant-garde and its deconstructive 'move away from grand *oppositions* to subtle *displacements*' (Foster 1996: 25).

7. 'einen Ausschnitt aus der Gesamtheit meines *Bewusztseins von der Welt*' (emphasis Beyer)

8. 'es muss akustisch befriedigen [...] etwas, das in der Nähe musikalischen Genusses liegt'

9. 'Want het is een tantaluskwelling geweest: de keuze tussen een eenvoudige of een meer experimentele zegging.'

10. 'Eros en Thanatos vormen een onoverwinnelijke en onvermijdelijke tweeling.'

11. 'Waarom schrijven vrouwen gewoonlijk slecht?'

12. 'Dat stelselmatig wederkerend onderscheid: Adam met de phalluspen en Eva met de puntjes op de borst ...'

13. 'alles te zeggen [...] ONDANKS de relativiteit van je pogingen door te werken tot je barst'

14. 'een mislukte mystieker, in de grond gemetseld'

15. 'konkret bis ins Detail', 'Sentiment', 'Friederike Mayröcker ist eine Frau, der das Schreiben schon früh dringlich, lange Zeit hin — zu meinem Entsetzen — sogar einziger Lebenssinn war'

16. 'Der Progression in den künstlerischen Mitteln wirkt eine Regression im künstlerischen Material entgegen. [...] Dieses Dilemma ist bezeichnend für die Autoren von Max Bense bis zu H.C. Artmann und für den legendären "Geist der Zeit".'

17. 'neu und unverbraucht wie die "Rose" der Gertrude Stein'.

18. Strikingly, Peter Weibel's early reading of Mayröcker within a neo-avant-garde context has hardly been perpetuated in Mayröcker scholarship. Mayröcker is for instance conspicuously absent in *Schluß mit dem Abendland!*, an edited volume on Austrian neo-avant-garde (Eder and Kastberger 2000). Apart from brief mentions in passing in several essays, the only more extensive analysis in a neo-avant-garde context is Andreas Puff-Trojan's (2012) reading of Mayröcker with Breton.

19. 'Ik ervaar het als een straf dat mijn medewerking aan Labris zo'n stempel op mij heeft gedrukt'.

20. 'Waar vrouwelijke liriek (d.i. niet noodzakelijk de liriek geschreven door een vrouw) snel ontaardt in pornografie of in een sentimenteel gewauwel, wordt ze bij Stassaert een geladen dramatise oerkracht.'

21. 'Hier wordt niets minder gepoogd dan de overbrenging van een Margritteaans [sic] surrealisme naar de eigen mogelijkheden van de taal.'

22. 'lettristische, maniëristische en 'vocabularistische' aanstellerij'

23. 'ik hoor nog liever een Chinees of een Zoeloe tateren'

24. 'Lucienne Stassaert droesemkollebloemdichteres', 'Taalversnapering in bonbonnière Vlaanderen', 'Met stopnaald op achterwerk van pijnpapier'

25. 'maniëristische taalhantering'

26. 'genezing van het gemaniëreerde schrijven'

27. 'bei maria callas hat die Beweglichkeit der mundpartie | sichtlich gelitten — '.

28. 'und lärmt mit kleinen Trommeln, Pauken, Posaunen, | Violinen, Kindertrompeten etc. | bis lärm monströs — | maria callas hält sich die ohren zu'

29. 'aus der versenkung — extrem rechts — | steigt die freiheitsstatue mit einer Handgranate in der | schwingenden faust / alles wirft sich automatisch zu boden'

30. 'umherblickend | als ob er etwas suche..'

31. '(herzzerbrechend möchte sie weg / als liverpool verkleidet)'

32. 'sobald sich die flutwelle gelegt hat | erscheinen | snoopy | maria callas | und lächeln'

33. 'schüttelt mähne', 'bis lärm monströs — '

34. Fuchsmundi is the main character in a collection of comical scenic sketches probably written by the Austrian actor and author Joseph Anton Stranitzky (1676–1726), who regularly performed as a Hanswurst figure. The collection also contains 'politische Nasenstüber', political reprimands. Stranitzky's successor as Hanswurst performer was the Viennese Gottfried Prehauser (1699–1769), who was the creator of the comic character called Mirlifax.

35. 'während die *Sängerin* in ihrer horizontalen Lage verharrt |/ ruft ihr *Begleiter auf dem Klavier* das Käuzchen an ruft | den Kontrapunkt zur Ordnung versetzt dem fäustling | einen weichen Nasenstüber fixiert dem Punkt eine | Nasenklammer' (emphasis and double blank Mayröcker)

36. 'Gehn Sie abends im Mai nach schmerzhafter Zahnbehandelung über die Strudlhofstiege langsam abwärts, sehn Sie in alle Grasspalten, Vogeltritte, Reservationen, bleiben Sie an der Büste von Gido Hasen stehn, werfen Sie viele Blicke in die kloppen & daken der Heilsarmee [...] fliegen Sie von der Fußstelle der Stiege gegen Tokyo mit Landpferd beurre (wie butter) .. pick mich auf, mein flügel.'

37. 'Lassen Sie die Wörter aufjaulen! | Machen Sie öfters mal boingg-boingg! | Vergessen Sie die ganze Sprache! | Legen Sie Silben aufs Eis! | Wärmen Sie sich an die Deklinationen die Füße! | Überhöhen Sie die Grammatik! | Fliegen Sie aufs alltägliche Gespräch! | Setzen Sie Winkelmaß und Zirkel aufs spiel! | Stören Sie die Sprache ein wenig mehr! | Drücken Sie sie gegen die Wand bis sie schreit! | Fahren Sie mit ihr im Lift abwärts! / Lassen Sie sie vorüberfliegen!'

38. 'Baun Sie mit am Kieferzertrümmerer! [...] Träumen Sie von der Konstruktion des Kieferzertrümmerers!'

39. '(Dem Regisseur wird emp- | fohlen diesen Suggestiv-Text | auf Band zu sprechen und ihn | *vor und während der Proben* | ohne Unterbrechung, in größ- | ter Lautstärke abspielen zu las- | sen.)'

40. 'Stellen Sie sich vor jemand spuckte Kürbiskerne gegen Sie!'; 'Stellen Sie sich vor Sie müßten Ihren Wohnplatz mit riesigen Lobelien Polsterflox und dryadischer Unterwäsche teilen ..'; 'Stellen Sie sich vor jemand hauchte Sie anachronistisch (wie's einhorn von nebenan) auf die Plakatwand nämlich während der schwan ('schwan') auf dem plattenteller mit gabel & messer simuliert SSSSSSSSSSSSSSSSSSSs. ——' (double blank in the original)

41. A more idiomatic translation of the German 'als' in this text would certainly be 'while' or 'as', but in the frame of this article I keep to 'when', in order to preserve the reference to the story-like character.

42. 'als dieser noch redete kam ein anderer und sprach | als dieser sprach kam ein anderer und verkündete | noch redete dieser als ein anderer eintrat und sprach'

43. '.. war er früher Wasserpfeife und | Krokodil schön sanft und fröhlich | [...] | so ist er jetzt Span im Fleisch der Welt | ein | schreckliches Schaugebilde von Würmern | [...] und bereit zum Tode ..'

44. 'als der admiral zurückkehrte, nachdem er sieben schlachten auf offener see zu seinen gunsten entschieden hatte, fand er sein landhaus in einem völlig veränderten zustand wieder'

45. '1971 hatte ich plötzlich genug vom sogenannten experimentellen Prosaschreiben. [...] Es hat mir einfach keinen Spaß mehr gemacht. Ich habe es irgendwie als langweilig empfunden. Das heißt natürlich nicht, daß ich nicht auch in den Büchern danach noch mit Montage-Techniken usw. gearbeitet habe. Das habe ich alles beibehalten, nur bin ich vom rein Experimentellen mehr hingegangen zu einer Erzählhaltung, obwohl ich mich eigentlich in Interviews immer dagegen gesträubt habe, meine Arbeit als Erzählung zu bezeichnen. Das würde ich auch heute noch sagen. Ich will nicht in einem üblichen Sinne erzählen, sondern mich an ein ganz unkonventionelles, unorthodoxes Erzählverhalten annähern, wenn man so sagen kann.'

46. 'de poëzie was in alles geïnfiltreerd'

47. 'zij wandelt | adem van bosvrouwen trekt in haar vel | geheime nerven open, een water plooit | haar schoenen hameren de weg dicht, ver- | menigvuldigen ani-ina-vagina-nina, door- | zomerd luw cedert haar huid, windschuwe | reuken klimmend klam op en neer'

48. 'omgeven door een wolk van hersenspinsels'

49. 'ik graaf al een paar jaar, het gebouw zal | eens in de mist verschijnen als de wijsheid- | steen stevig. laat mij lachen. lachen. lachen | en de oude Pieter Breughel en zijn toren | en de feesten en gezangen van de oude trou- | badours | dit alles samen mij-vormend leven met de | traagheid van een te ontcijferen hieroglief | soms spreek ik dan frans als het hun te moeilijk | wordt [...]'

50. 'de fataliteit van het altijd viermaal poot altijd tweemaal oog zijn kan ik niet verdragen en ik barst'

51. 'de kar waarmee ijverige mensen mij dan bespannen haat ik'

52. 'op de moedermelk zuigende paradoxer'

53. 'zo van tijd tot tijd [...] wisselen de tienduizend dubbelgangers in mij zich om en worden paard kat of vogels. | paarden in de zwarte wei | katten in de hoerenstraat | vogels in de koude wind'

54. 'het is tijd dat ik de zon begin te zien'
55. 'het massagraf liefde liefde liefde'
56. 'de gouden vis IK | spartelend'
57. 'graaf ik oude misten op, bijna-wijn geworden bruine gisten roze wormen houtworm op een klamme kist rijzende schimmen'
58. 'al najaart nooit je sidderloof / het pijnboombekken van je goties / eertijds zoeter vledervlees / is desondanks je stem / in spitsrust uitgedoofd / hoe driftig is de roos / kokhalzend in haar bloei / te laat / te niet gedroomd'.
59. 'subtropies in het schilferlicht | heelhuids mijn glaslichaam verpulvert | in brongas van de napijn | nog een rokend hieroglief | woorden als parels in het pek'

CHAPTER 4

❖

Vogelaar and Wiener —
the Minds of Artistic Agitation

Thomas Eder (Universität Wien) &
Sven Vitse (Utrecht University)

In his book *Writing Back* (1987, *Terugschrijven*), a collection of essays from the 1980s, Dutch neo-avant-garde writer Jacq F. Vogelaar mentions his Austrian colleague Oswald Wiener twice. In both cases, the name appears in an enumeration. The essay concluding the book lists Wiener among canonical literary innovators such as Mallarmé, Butor, and Borges. These writers, according to Vogelaar, are 'perhaps mainly interesting because of their impossible assignments'.[1] Their conception of literature he likens to his own, which he characterizes as 'combining existing meanings in order to process them — analyse and multiply them', resulting in 'a new collection of texts' (1987: 327).[2]

The second mention, in an essay reflecting upon the art of the 1960s, teams Wiener up with fellow German-language experimentalists Arno Schmidt and Hans G. Helms. All of these, Vogelaar claims, have tried to explore the possibilities for literary experimentation that were opened up by the works of James Joyce. The mention is interesting for one particular reason: when asked in 1969 about contemporary writers he admires or considers kindred spirits, Vogelaar mentions Schmidt and Helms, but not Wiener. This might suggest that at the time Vogelaar was not yet familiar with Wiener's work.

Some ten years after this 1969 interview the Dutch literary magazine *Raster* presented a special issue on the Wiener Gruppe [Vienna Group], including an excerpt from Oswald Wiener's seminal *the improvement of central europe* (1969, *die verbesserung von mitteleuropa, roman*). Although Vogelaar was a founding editor of the journal and was a prolific critic and translator himself, the issue was edited and introduced by Hans Bakx, who also translated all Wiener Gruppe excerpts. Vogelaar's absence is all the more surprising since Bakx's characterization of the Wiener Gruppe poetics seems almost identical to Vogelaar's own conception of literature, as he repeatedly formulated it in the late 1960s and early 1970s. In his introduction Bakx compares the writings and activities of the Wiener Gruppe to the so-called 'generation of 60' in Dutch literature, a group of neo-Dadaist poets who published in the literary journal *Barbarber*. However, Bakx (1979: 19) discerns a crucial difference between the Viennese and the Dutch poets:

the Wiener Gruppe took up a much more extreme and fundamental position: stressing the trivial did not serve to pleasantly surprise the reader, but to debunk and destroy the reality to which those trivialities belonged. The point of impact was language: "language is usually described as social consciousness, even as the memory of mankind. To take this insipid joke literally: then a revolt against language is a revolt against society...", as Oswald Wiener formulates it in *die verbesserung von mitteleuropa*[3]

The 'more extreme and fundamental position' attributed to Oswald Wiener in this quotation suggests a close affinity between Wiener's poetology — at least, in Bakx's perception — and Vogelaar's.

We are quite sure, however, that Oswald Wiener was not familiar with Jacq Firmin Vogelaar nor his work. Wiener has not mentioned Vogelaar in any of his writings. In a personal conversation Wiener denied ever having noticed him. Despite this lack of direct acquaintance there are many indirect signs of hinting at a closer *indirect* relationship on which we will elaborate in this chapter.

The indirect relationship might stem from what Wiener himself once described as special kinds of thoughts or attitudes hovering in the air. This seems aligned with C.G. Jung (without Wiener's being aware of him in the 1960s), who distinguished a fourth category (beyond space, time, and causality) which should permit a scientific explanation of phenomena of synchronicity (Jung 1952). Wiener, for example, frequently stated in his writings and in conversations that the artists of the Wiener Gruppe had quite a few things in common with the Surrealists, without being aware of it or even knowing their writings in detail (at this time they were not able to read French fluently and some seminal books had not yet been translated).

The same seems true for the extent to which Vogelaar was familiar with Oswald Wiener and the works of the Wiener Gruppe in the long 1960s. As stated above, Vogelaar mentioned Wiener in the 1980s, situating him in the company of experimental poets like Arno Schmidt and H.G. Helms. Interestingly, this comparison of Wiener's and Schmidt's work on the grounds of their being experimental poets, differs from Wiener's own view, as we will demonstrate in our discussion of Wiener's poetological development.

The asymmetrical relationship between Vogelaar and Wiener invites a closer comparison between these two writers, as they seem, nevertheless, to occupy similar positions in Dutch and Austrian post-war literature respectively: at the spearhead of both formal experimentation and poetological reflection.

We will refer to Vogelaar and Wiener as neo-avant-gardists without, however, uncritically endorsing Peter Bürger's assessment that 'the neo-avant-garde institutionalizes the *avant-garde as art* and thus negates genuinely avant-gardiste intentions' (1984: 58). In an editorial conversation in the afore-mentioned journal *Raster*, Vogelaar and like-minded writers and critics such as Sybren Polet, J. Bernlef and H.C. ten Berge voiced their concerns about the institutionalization of avant-garde practices in post-war literature. In neo-avant-gardism they distinguished between artists satisfied with renewing literature on the level of technique and content — an imputed position similar to Bürger's view of the neo-avant-garde — and artists who 'challenge art as institution and aim to fit aesthetic means for social change' (*Raster* editors 1978: 12). Quite clearly at this point in his career Vogelaar is not yet prepared to concede the latter ambition and settle for the former.

With regard to Oswald Wiener's relation and contribution to the neo-avant-garde, Thomas Raab, an Austrian writer and theorist working nowadays in conjunction with Wiener, states (2008) that the era of the avant-garde in Western societies was irrevocably coming to an end in 1970: 'avant-garde' was a typically western phenomenon with specific historical conditions, the interaction of which was only possible between 1850 and 1970. From 1970 onwards, an economic and demographic class of uneducated heirs developed in Western societies. The avant-garde thus lost the possibility of referring to an art-historical horizon or educational background (as was still possible in the bourgeoisie and the *épater le bourgeois* before it), rendering their provocations void. The Romantic-Anarchic utopia no longer has a general social counterpart, but is restricted to the respective subculture.

We are especially interested in what Raab calls the 'belief' of all avant-garde in 'art as a more comprehensive means of cognition in relation to the sciences' (2008: 11). This belief is based on the (early) Romantic 'counter-assertion of the arts' against the formal findings of the natural sciences and their 'technical-social implementation', which are advancing into increasingly intimate areas (2008: 18). The romantic-utopian belief in art as a means of cognition finds different implementations in the various phases of the avant-garde: the classical (first) avant-garde (Paris from 1860 onwards) revolted against 'representational realism'; the historical avant-garde (1900–1920) were characterized by 'trying around with sign constellations'; the neo-avant-gardes (1950–1970), finally, elaborated and perfected 'detail innovations of the historical avant-gardes' (in post-Nazi Germany and Austria actually rediscovered). The neo-avant-garde theoretically argues 'against the scientific world view' (Raab 2008: 46).

Wiener's development mirrors that of the post-war avant-garde. This development addresses the Romantic notion that the artist or the writer could oppose science with his work. In the course of the twentieth century, Thomas Raab claims, the 'effort to oppose to the scientific worldview with an equally consistent "non-mechanistic" artistic method has gotten insurmountably large' (2008: 46). Wiener's ironic attitude is turned against his own writings, even against the nucleus of romantic art of the avant-gardes, he became a 'renegade scientist' (2008: 47).

1. Background

Jacq Firmin Vogelaar

Jacq Firmin Vogelaar (a pseudonym for Frans Broers) was born on 3 September 1944 in Tilburg, a mid-sized town in the southern part of the Netherlands. In 1962 he enrolled at the University of Nijmegen to study Dutch language and literature, and philosophy. Three years later he continued his study of philosophy at the University of Amsterdam. By the time Vogelaar arrived in the Dutch capital, the student and artists protest movement was well on its way, and as a young writer and intellectual with a keen awareness of political and ideological conflict, Vogelaar was soon to join their ranks.

While the Provo-movement, with its playful happenings and telegenic disruptions of public events, has left an indelible mark on the Dutch cultural memory of the 1960s, Vogelaar's political commitment led him to pursue a more cerebral and academic course. In the late 1960s he became involved in the Amsterdam branch of the so-called Critical University [Kritische Universiteit] and he participated in the Critical Library [Kritische Bibliotheek], a joint initiative by three Dutch publishing houses (De Bezige Bij, Meulenhoff, and Van Gennep) to publish books on critical theory and leftist politics. In this context, Vogelaar edited a volume on materialist and Marxist literary and cultural theory, *Art as Critique* (*Kunst als kritiek*), which appeared in 1972 and presented translated essays by critical theorists such as Theodor W. Adorno, Walter Benjamin, Lucien Goldmann, and Pierre Macherey. In this period, from 1971 till 1975, he also held teaching positions at the universities of Delft and Amsterdam, and at the Academy of Fine Arts in Arnhem.

At that time, moreover, Vogelaar had already published a series of literary works. Especially in the first five years of his career as a writer his literary production was impressive. Having already published a number of poems in the literary journal *Merlyn*, Vogelaar published his first book, *Ground Floor, and of Glass* (*Parterre, en van glas*), a collection of poetry, in 1965 — his second book of poetry would appear over three decades later. Between 1965 and 1968 four prose works were published, in which the narrative composition became progressively more fragmented and technically challenging, a tendency which culminated in *It Has No Name* (*Het heeft geen naam*), also from 1968, for which he was awarded the Lucy B. and C.W. van der Hoogt prize for fiction.

In Vogelaar's next prose book, *Kaleidofragments* (1970, *Kaleidiafragmenten*), narrative development was completely abandoned, giving way to a non-linear, non-narrative montage of short texts exploring and deconstructing various types of language use. With this work, Vogelaar's literary development entered its second phase, in which disassembling, as the writer put it himself, took precedence over narrative construction. In 1978 Vogelaar presented the results of a near-decade of experimentation in *Riddles of the Bull* (*Raadsels van het rund*), a monumental text which was followed in 1980 by the equally ambitious book *All the Meat* (*Alle vlees*).

In the late 1960s Vogelaar started diversifying his activities, working as a literary critic for the Dutch newspapers *Het Parool* (1967–1968) and *De Volkskrant* (1969). In 1971 he began contributing literary reviews to the Dutch weekly *De Groene Amsterdammer*, a magazine devoted to left-wing political and cultural commentary. In these reviews the critic set out to castigate what he considered to be a post-revolutionary return to anecdotal realism in the literature of the early 1970s. The same year saw him taking up a position as editorial secretary for *Te Elfder Ure*, a formerly catholic magazine which published in-depth articles on politics and culture and had gravitated towards Marxist theory in the 1960s.

Interestingly, this is also the period in which Vogelaar's critical rhetoric takes on a resolutely Marxist character. This change in rhetoric coincides with Vogelaar's growing concern about theoretical debates within Marxist aesthetics, which typically rehearse the early twentieth-century Brecht-Lukács debate over modernism, socialist realism and the opposition between formalist and realist approaches to literature (see *New Left Review* 1974; Kiralyfalvi 1985). In various articles, in *De Groene Amsterdammer* and *Te Elfder Ure* in the early 1970s Vogelaar consistently sides with those rejecting the imperatives of socialist realism in favour of formal innovation (Vitse 2015). His firm commitment to Marxist aesthetics in these years, moreover, inspired Vogelaar to collaborate with Dutch composer Louis Andriessen, who shared his aspiration to revolutionize art both on a formal and a political level (Adlington 2013: 283–306).

Vogelaar would continue contributing to *De Groene Amsterdammer* until the end of his life. Selections of his literary criticism were collected in the volumes *Confrontations* (1974, *Konfrontaties*) and *Orientations* (1983, *Oriëntaties*), and many of the essays in *Writing Back* (1987, *Terugschrijven*) were based on his writings on modern literature (on Joyce, Kafka and Musil, among many others) in this magazine.

Another lifelong commitment was his work as an editor of the literary journal *Raster*, which he pursued for more than thirty years, from 1977 until the demise of the journal in 2009. When Vogelaar joined the editorial board in 1977 the journal already had a history of ten years. It was founded in 1967 by the Dutch writer and translator H.C. ten Berge, who kept the journal going as sole editor until 1973. Vogelaar only published a few essays in this first edition of *Raster*, yet in hindsight his contributions proved to be vital to the journal's image in literary history. From 1973 till 1976 the name *Raster* was used for a series of book publications, but it was not until 1977 that the journal was revived with a new editorial board. In *Raster* Vogelaar and his fellow-editors introduced the state of the art in poststructuralist and neo-Marxist theory to the Dutch reading public, alongside a panoply of innovative — modernist, avant-garde and postmodern — literature from the Western world.

Apart from his work as a writer, a critic and an editor, Vogelaar was an avid and accomplished translator, from the English, the German and the French. He translated extensively for the journal *Raster* — e.g. essays by Roland Barthes in 1981 — and completed several translations of literary works, by Carl Einstein, Gustav Herling, and Daniel Kehlmann, among many others. For his literary achievements he was awarded the Frans Erens prize in 1995 and the Constantijn Huygens prize in 2006. Jacq Firmin Vogelaar died on 9 December 2013.

Oswald Wiener

Oswald Wiener was born on 5 October 1935 in Vienna. Starting out as a jazz musician (playing the cornet as an autodidact) at the age of 16–17, Wiener got in contact with the Viennese jazz scene. Jazz player Walter Terharen introduced him to Konrad Bayer (1932–1964), a poet and jazz musician playing the banjo. Terharen, Bayer and others formed the jazz group 'real jazzband' ('wirkliche jazzband'). Bayer convinced Wiener to accompany him to the so-called *Strohkoffer*, located in the basement of the American Bar (built by Adolf Loos) where the 'art-club' had its venue. The art-club was an association of Viennese artists of the avant-gardes, presided by Albert Paris Gütersloh (1887–1973) and with contacts to international artists and philosophers (e.g. Jean Cocteau, who visited the art-club in 1962). Here, Wiener met Hans Carl Artmann (1921–2000) and Gerhard Rühm (born 1930), with whom he participated in 'poetic acts'. These were processions and gatherings, e.g. one entitled 'IN MEMORIAM TO A CRUCIFIED GLOVE' on 9 January 1954, in H.C. Artmann's 'franciscan catacombes club', 10 Ballgasse, Vienna 1; or on 5 February, when 'the party of st simeon, quasi una fantasmagoria' ('das fest des hl. simeon, quasi una fantasmagoria') took place.

When Friedrich Achleitner (born 1930) had joined them in 1955, the five poets regularly met to discuss their works and aesthetic issues in general. This was a very productive period of literary experimentation. In the years 1955 to 1959 Oswald Wiener dominated the theoretical orientation of the avant-garde formation, which later came to be known under the label 'Wiener Gruppe'. The poets arranged verbal montages, be it by chance or on the basis of mathematical and geometrical principles (e.g. by golden section): the so-called 'inventionism' (Adrian 1980). These algorithmic works (e.g., Bayer and Wiener's collaborative text 'the bird is singing: a poetic machine consisting of 571 parts' — 'der vogel singt: eine dichtungsmaschine in 571 bestandteilen' (1996)) reflected on automatic generation of poetic texts, slightly before others used computers for generating poems (e.g. Theo Lutz).

Wiener produced (cf. Weibel 1997: 629–57) concrete texts ('beast beast beast' ['tier tier tier'] and 'brightbrightbrightbright' ['buntbuntbuntbunt'], as well as scenic texts ('sorrow' ['die sorge'], 'joy ['die freude'], 'the red continent' ['der rote erdteil'], 'snot — a viennese play in dialect' [rotz — eine wiener dialektstück'], 'man — a picturebook' ['der mensch — ein bilderbuch'], etc.) so-called 'constellations' ('konstellationen'), 'montages' ('the day — a rigid montage' ['der tag — eine rigide montage']), chansons, experimental prose, and the famous (and later lost) 'cool manifesto' (see below). First and foremost Wiener was interested in theoretical aspects, being one of the first persons in Austria outside of academia to notice Ludwig Wittgenstein's work (first his *Tractatus Logico-Philosophicus*, later his *Philosophical Investigations*). Philosophy of language and linguistic skepticism were Wiener's core fields of interest during these days, mixing critique of language with political aspects. In this period Wiener basically relied on his studies of epistemology, solipsism, and anarchism (Fritz Mauthner, Max Stirner, and M.A. Bakunin).

Wiener brought this theoretical background to the conception and implementation of two literary happenings of the Wiener Gruppe in 1958 and 1959, the so-called 'literary cabarets' (referring to Dada's 'Cabaret Voltaire' as well as Helmut Qualtinger's cabarets of this time). The two cabarets may be seen as happenings, carried out slightly before the endeavors of the Living Theatre, Allan Kaprow's happenings, and the Independent Group.

Wiener destroyed his (mostly concrete) writings of this phase in 1959 and veered into a bourgeois existence (as head of the Austrian branch of the Italian office equipment manufacturer Olivetti) from which he was 'cured' by former co-member of the Wiener Gruppe Konrad Bayer, who called Wiener back to arts and literature around 1962. Wiener subsequently started writing his novel *the improvement of central europe* (2013 [1969], *die verbesserung von mitteleuropa, roman*). Around 1965 Wiener got in contact with the artists of the Viennese actionism, taking part in many of the important happenings: *actions concert für al hansen* — 29 October 1966, *ZOCK exercizes* — 17 April 1967, *ZOCKfest* 21 April 1967. An early manifesto of ZOCK, authored by Wiener and Otto Muehl had been read out on New Year's Eve 1967 in Wiener's apartment in the Judengasse (in Vienna's district 1), a hot spot for the Austrian avant-gardes of these days. As a consequence of taking part in the infamous happening 'Art and Revolution' ('Kunst und Revolution'), 8 June 1968, at the University of Vienna, Wiener and Brus were prosecuted by Austrian authorities and had to leave Vienna for exile in West-Berlin (cf. Eder 2000a).

In West Berlin Wiener opened several artists' cafés and restaurants (*Matala, Axwax, Exil*) and was one of the leading figures of intellectuals and avant-garde artists. Besides, he studied mathematics at the Technical University Berlin (from 1980 on, in Vienna in the 1950s he had studied mathematics, law, music, and African languages). In 1986 he left Berlin for Canada, where he lived, inter alia, as a cafetier in Dawson City, Yukon Territories until 2013.

Living half of the year in Europe he taught as a professor of literary aesthetics at the Kunstakademie Düsseldorf (1992–2004). In Canada he addressed questions of artificial intelligence (Wiener 1990) and turned completely away from philosophy of language and art (exceptions: his novel *Not Again* [*Nicht schon wieder*], written under the pseudonym Evo Präkogler 1990, and his after-dinner speech *Bouvard and Pécuchet in the Realm of the Senses* [1998c, *Bouvard und Pécuchet im Reich der Sinne*]). In his work from then on Wiener was basically interested in epistemological questions on the basis of Alan M. Turing's theory (cf. Wiener 1996; Wiener et al. 1998). Since 2013 he lives in the south-east of Styria, pursuing his scientific work in the field of automata theory, cognitive studies and psychology of thinking, reintroducing the hitherto scientifically abandoned method of introspection.

For his literary achievement Wiener was awarded the Prize for Literature of the City of Vienna (1987), the Grand Austrian State Prize (1989), and the 'manuskripte'-Prize of the State of Styria (2006), amongst others. In 1995 he received an honorary doctorate of the University of Klagenfurt (Carinthia).

Comparing the author's respective trajectories reveals the second half of the 1960s as a period of convergence. Both Vogelaar and Wiener engage in the artistic and political activism of the time, although the inspiration for their avant-garde activities differs slightly. While Vogelaar at this point derives his poetology primarily from neo-Marxist aesthetics and seeks an alliance with the Marxist worker's movement, Wiener's poetology in that period is mainly inspired by Dadaism and Anarchism. From the 1970s onwards their professional and literary paths start to diverge, Wiener turning to mathematics and cognitive studies, while Vogelaar continues his lifelong effort to explore and propagate innovative literature. However, in the 1960s they share a strong philosophical interest in language, epistemology, and avant-garde aesthetics, and establish themselves as the prime theoreticians on the literary scene. In the next section we will further discuss their theoretical and poetological positions.

2. Poetology

Jacq Firmin Vogelaar

Vogelaar's views on literature and the relationship between literature and society can be summed up by means of two characteristic quotations. The first one is from 1967, from a series of comments ('Topen', 'Topics') on literature and politics he appended to his novel *Enemy Wanted* (*Vijand gevraagd*). It summarizes Vogelaar's conception of the political effects of innovative fiction:

> a change in looking at people and things [...] not in one direction as is the case in publicity, churches and entertainment, but through examples in which the most important is not what can be recognized, but a changed way of looking, a different (open) view of something, that expands develops and therefore changes what exists. A REVOLUTION OF THE EYE AND THE EAR. (155)[4]

The second quotation is from 1972, from Vogelaar's introduction to *Art as Critique* (*Kunst als kritiek*), the volume of materialist literary theory mentioned above: 'If one blames a materialist theory of art for reducing the aesthetic to economic and social determinants and therefore not appreciating the "singular" of the work of art, one blames the theory for that which one refuses to acknowledge in reality' (14).[5] While the first position is similar to the Russian formalist concept of defamiliarization, the second derives from Marxist cultural theory. Vogelaar's desire to reconcile both positions led him to a broadly neo-Marxist conception of literature, in which the defence of formal innovation could be combined with a materialist view of artistic production. It is this desire which guides Vogelaar's early development as a writer in the late 1960s and early 1970s, the period on which this article focuses.

Vogelaar succinctly expresses his early views on the politics of innovative fiction — views he consistently defended throughout his career, albeit in varying rhetorical guises — in a review he published in 1969 in the Dutch journal *Het Parool*. The review discusses the novel *Death of a Director* (1969, *De dood van een regisseur*) by J. Bernlef, a writer who is renowned mainly for his neo-Dadaist poetry, for his contribution to the literary journal *Barbarber* in the 1960s, and also for joining the editorial board of *Raster* in 1977. In Bernlef's novel Vogelaar recognized the voice of a fellow-traveller, since this work explicitly tackles the notions of fiction and reality, and more specifically the artificially constructed nature of the images and narratives that are presented as reality.

Bernlef's writing conscientiously discloses the process of constructing a seamless image that is then passed off as a truthful depiction of reality. It therefore serves to debunk the conception of art as inspired and original creation, which Vogelaar rejects as ideological. To this 'myth of the 'creative process',[6] Bernlef's novel, according to Vogelaar, opposes the openness of the text, which (in Shklovsky's words) lays bare the devices: 'where and how, with which tinkering measures the semblance is prepared, which afterwards is served as easily digestible consumerist good'[7] (Vogelaar 1969a).

This aesthetic laying bare of the device is politically relevant, in Vogelaar's view, because the same principle can be applied to 'public opinion and political decisions'[8] (1969b). Nevertheless, Vogelaar goes on to criticize Bernlef's novel on account of its implicit politics. Whereas Bernlef questions the notions of fiction and reality on an epistemological and ontological level — how do we depict reality?, does reality exist outside of the imagination? — Vogelaar requires literature to question reality on a social and political level. Besides modes of perception and representation literature should tackle social reality in itself. In this critique the tension between formalist and Marxist tendencies in Vogelaar's poetics is revealed:

> Another question mark hanging over Bernlef's book is that he does question whether something is real rather than imagination, or the other way around, but that actually what exists in this reality or this imagination remains unquestioned. He quotes reality but implicitly condones it by leaving it as it is — everything is useful so everything is interesting, apart from that everything is OK. (1969a)[9]

While the interweaving of literary innovation and radical politics can already be discerned in this review, this conception of literature sits more easily with formalist and modernist literary theory rather than with Marxism. Vogelaar's gradual adoption of a Marxist paradigm can be traced in the paratextual sources accompanying his literary work. In the programmatic appendix to *Enemy Wanted* (*Vijand gevraagd*), quoted above, Vogelaar expresses his worldview in terms of relations of power, relying heavily on military imagery and references to the Cold War. The first 'topic', for instance, refers to the West's obsession with 'defence', 'an imaginary attack', 'an enemy' (Vogelaar 1967: 153).[10] The third criticizes a society which uses 'violence' to uphold the hierarchy 'between the powerful and the powerless' and suggests an alternative kind of violence 'to destroy the oppressors and together with those the oppressed' (153).[11] Vogelaar dismisses the faith in 'words which in themselves do not endanger the existing practices': 'tolerance ends when the radical opponents of the system proceed to action' (155).[12] In its most radical phrases, therefore, the appendix calls for illegal activity: 'Injustice does not disappear by law' (153).[13]

While these remarks may sound vaguely leftist, they are not exactly Marxist in their rhetoric or their analysis of the issues at stake. It is in fact the paratextual message 'to the reader', on the opening page of *It Has No Name* (*Het heeft geen naam*), which introduces Marxist jargon in Vogelaar's conception of literature. This message, which has become somewhat canonical in its own right, urges the reader to '[s]teal this book' and goes on to analyse the value and function of a literary work in terms of 'means of production' and 'use value'. As means of production, literary texts produce ideas and forms of consciousness. In the early 1970s Vogelaar publishes a number of essays in which he explores the Marxist tradition in literary criticism and further develops his own Marxist programme for innovative fiction.

This progressive adoption of a Marxist conceptual framework can also be observed in Vogelaar's scattered remarks on the literary field and the function of the writer and the critic. One of the reviews he wrote in the late 1960s for the journal *Het Parool* is very revealing in this respect. The review is devoted to the experimental novel *Catch as Catch Can* (1968) by the Flemish novelist, poet and essayist Willy Roggeman. Vogelaar complains that this type of literature, '[b]ooks which cannot be read mindlessly because they are more than and different from what we already know',[14] tends to be ignored by literary critics, as the latter choose to conform to 'the business desires of the book trade'[15] (1969b). He differentiates between 'books which require thinking' and books which 'again bawl out what everyone already knows'.[16]

A few years later, in an essay called 'Pro domo', the difference is rather that between 'socialist art and bourgeois art', which according to Vogelaar 'cannot exist peacefully side by side', or between bourgeois artists who ally themselves with the workers' movement and those who refuse to acknowledge that 'a different culture is needed in the same way that different social relations are needed' (Vogelaar 1974: 18).[17]

In an article published in the literary journal *Raster* in 1970 and aptly called 'Topography of a Materialist Theory of Literature', Vogelaar analyses the function of literature and literary criticism as part of a Marxist account of contemporary capitalism. In recent years, he claims, capitalist society has increasingly turned to culture and science, including the humanities, in its constant search for legitimacy and social control. As 'sciences of control', the humanities contribute to 'the adaptation of social relations and structures of consciousness' (Vogelaar 1970: 338).[18] In this context Vogelaar calls for a dialectical materialist criticism, which acknowledges both socioeconomic determinants and the semi-autonomous processing of these determinants in the creative act.

Vogelaar's socioeconomic analysis suggests the emergence of post-industrial capitalism, in which the production of ideas and cultural or linguistic forms has become a dominant productive force in itself. In Marxist terms: these forms no longer merely belong to the superstructure, the sphere of ideology, but have become an integral part of the infrastructure, of the means of production. Vogelaar's literary practices function on these two levels: on the one hand he analyses literature as both ideological reflection and critique of ideology; on the other hand, he analyses literature as a productive force and tries to generate alternative means of production. He deconstructs existing forms of consciousness while at the same time generating alternative forms of consciousness. Both tendencies stimulated radical formal innovation, but also created the deadlock in which Vogelaar found himself in the late 1970s. In the early 1970s, nevertheless, Vogelaar finds in Marxism a consistent paradigm to conceptualize his objections to the functioning of literature, of the writer and the critic, in contemporary Dutch society.

Oswald Wiener

In comparing Vogelaar's and Wiener's poetology and literary practice, we have to bear in mind the significant development in the latter's views in the decades following his involvement with the Wiener Gruppe. In order to clarify Wiener's position in the late 1950s and 1960s this paragraph will examine that trajectory.

Wiener's literary and theoretical work of the time being a member of the Wiener Gruppe may be summarized by two different and conflicting intentions. On the one hand, he aims to augment the aesthetic impact triggered by works of art and as a consequence tries to produce more impactful artworks. On the other hand, he attempts to come to a better understanding of the cognitive and emotive processes at play when artworks are perceived.

As Wiener was a poet at this time he tried to come to grips with language and linguistic artworks. Partly on the basis of language criticism he aimed at abolishing conventionalized language and creating a new, artistic language which might better fit the artist's *Lebensgefühl* [spirit]. As a consequence he drafted a statement (later destroyed) entitled *cool manifesto* (1954), stating that the artist has to abandon emotion and empathy as his first virtue. Wiener describes his *cool manifesto* retrospectively as follows: 'Everybody was responsible for the quality of his experience himself, the sovereign mind had no need for art at all, as the key is not producing art, but understanding. This was my version of Dada'[19] (2015a: 285).

In the first phase of their collaboration, from 1953 onwards, the poets of the Wiener Gruppe had the function of 'scouts' aiming at re-discovering the almost disappeared traces of the historical avant-gardes: August Stramm, Kurt Schwitters, Hans Arp, Otto Nebel (whom Wiener visited in 1955 in Berne), Gertrude Stein, the 'Sturm-Kreis', 'Die Aktion', Franz Richard Behrens, the *Anthology of the Bizarres* (*Anthologie der Abseitigen — poètes à l'ecartes*) by Carola Giedion-Welcker (Giedion-Welcker 1946), the re-discovery of Dadaism, etc. Even the two literary cabarets (1958 and 1959) were a successful attempt to overcome Dada, which led Wiener to the thought that Dada had been carried out by the 'wrong people'. Dada, or so he supposes, should have developed into science, into the direction of understanding the peculiarities of language comprehension and semiotics as a whole. A few years later, Paul Feyerabend (1975) addressed this issue by his notion of epistemological anarchism or philosophical Dadaism.

For Wiener science has always meant (natural) science — in German *Wissenschaft* (science) also comprises humanities and sometimes philosophy. This was the starting point for Wiener's turn to (natural) science, artistic or philosophical research being too elastic for gaining real knowledge and insights. Looking back, Wiener writes:

> The need to 'prove individuality'. Freedom of interpretation (the focus of the freedom of personality) would be grounded in the (at first sight presupposed) fact that epistemological spheres of individuals are incommensurable (Bebuquin); that every collection of stimuli may be rendered meaningful in an unlimited number of ways. The task is now to find empirical arguments for this hypothesis, but the understanding of art is too vague and adaptable for that. This was my starting point for an education in (natural) science. (1998a: 27)[20]

Wiener had realized, in the course of his collaboration with the other members of the Wiener Gruppe, that artistic practices may not serve as valuable insights into the functioning of language and thinking. Before this, Wiener had been convinced that manipulation of linguistic units in experimental poetry may reveal the deeper relation between language and thought. When writing his novel *the improvement of central europe* Wiener clearly refuted this view.

The development in Wiener's poetology is concisely demonstrated in a small book Wiener published in 1979, provocatively entitled *We would like to benefit from the Arno Schmidt Year too* (1979, *Wir möchten auch vom Arno-Schmidt-Jahr profitieren*).

As mentioned in the introduction, Vogelaar's comparison of Wiener's and Schmidt's work on the grounds of their being experimental poets, differs from Wiener's own view. In his book Wiener criticizes Schmidt's *Zettel's Traum* (1977), laying bare the psychoanalytic foundations of Schmidt's poetics. According to Wiener, Schmidt is guilty of a simplification of Freud's theory when he uses it to elaborate his own 'Etym-theory' (see below). Moreover, Wiener calls into question whether Freud's theory is fruitful: Wiener doubts the explanatory power of Freud's distinction of the 'presentation of the *word*' [Wortvorstellung] and the 'presentation of the *thing*' [Sachvorstellung].

Freud's view, quoted and criticized by Wiener, reads as follows: 'the conscious presentation comprises the presentation of the thing plus the presentation of the word belonging to it, while the unconscious presentation is the presentation of the thing alone'[21] (Freud 1957: 215). Not only does Freud fail to explain what a 'presentation of the word' or a 'presentation of the thing' might be like in detail. Moreover, Wiener supposes that Freud's view is inaccurate concerning the supposed relation between the 'presentation of the *word*' [Wortvorstellung] and the 'presentation of the *thing*' [Sachvorstellung]. Basically, Wiener doubts that by examining words one can gain insights into the processes of people using (or dreaming) these words. The analysis of words alone provides by no ways any keys for understanding thought processes and imagery:

> for in order that images may be mapped onto language, it requires not only the words, but mainly a number of conditions which specify that the words in the communication process behave similarly to the mental images [Vorstellungen] in the thought processes; it further requires not only a grammar of phrases and sentences, but an implicit interpretation of the relevant communicative situation, which renders the linguistic instantiations reasonable. it would be too naïve to assume that a word need to be linked with a mental image [Vorstellung] only by association. it can be proven from the everyday experience that the concrete choices of words are generally irrelevant once an interpretive situation is defined: in a strong context, any word may stand for any mental image [Vorstellung]. but that means that a 'presentation of the word' [Wortvorstellung] may not be properly separated from a 'presentation of the thing' [Sachvorstellung] as little as these two from the contexts they are projected onto.[22] (1979: 19, trans. by TE)

It is not only important here that Wiener criticizes Schmidt's 'Etym-theory' as being naïve (Wiener 1979: 24; 'that the sorting=storage of words in the brain *relies on grounds of etym*'[23]) and that Wiener also criticizes Schmidt's assumption that every word actually refers to a taboo referent in the genital sphere; more important is Wiener's stance regarding the role that language and linguistic processes as a whole play for thinking. In 1979, when Wiener wrote his book on Schmidt, the picture was quite different from that of the time when Wiener was an experimental poet (as a member of the Wiener Gruppe — *c.* 1954–1959) and from the situation when he wrote his *the improvement of central europe, a novel* (1962–1969; 2013).

From this brief survey of their theoretical positions in the late 1960s it can be concluded that Vogelaar and Wiener in the beginning of their literary career shared a neo-avant-garde rejection of conventional artistic forms. From the outset, however, Wiener focused on the cognitive and affective processes implied by aesthetic form (and their epistemological basis), whereas Vogelaar was primarily interested in ideological effects (although he also strongly distrusted the exploitation of sentiment in literary language). Both writers, moreover, felt the urge to move beyond purely aesthetic concerns and have recourse to sciences they felt were more 'exact'.

Nevertheless, their scientific preferences differed significantly: while Vogelaar derived his concepts from Marxist economics and cultural theory, Wiener turned towards the natural sciences and, as we will see, the cognitive sciences. A further point of comparison concerns the relationship between language and consciousness. Vogelaar strongly believes that language is informed by late capitalist society's ideological structure and that linguistic and literary representations feed back into social and individual consciousness. Wiener, however, from the 1960s onwards gradually abandons the idea that language use is interwoven with the structure of consciousness and thinking.

3. Reception

Jacq Firmin Vogelaar

As Susanne Janssen (1994) demonstrated in her analysis of post-war Dutch literary criticism there have been significant developments in the critical reception of Vogelaar's literary work. These developments, according to Janssen, mirror the general evolution of experimental fiction's status in Dutch literature. In the first phase of his literary career Vogelaar benefits from the relatively positive and sympathetic attitude among critics towards literary experiment and from the willingness of a number of these critics to follow the course of formal innovation the writer pursues. Vogelaar's early novels, *Anatomy of a Glass-like Body* (*Anatomie van een glasachtig lichaam*) en *Enemy Wanted* (*Vijand gevraagd*) in particular, receive relatively widespread critical attention and enjoy a predominantly enthusiastic response. Moreover, critics are prepared to accept the literary frame of reference constructed by the paratext of both *The Man Coming and Going* (*De komende en gaande man*) and *Anatomy of a Glass-like Body*, which compares Vogelaar to Alain Robbe-Grillet and Samuel Beckett and presents his work as a Dutch offshoot of an international vogue for innovative fiction.

In the following decade, however, the prestige of experimental fiction starts to wane and so does the critical appreciation for Vogelaar's work: '[t]he "experiment", which in the second half of the 1960s received widespread attention in the literary debate [...] is quickly relegated to a marginal position on the literary agenda afterwards' (Janssen 1994: 109). A new generation of literary critics has entered the scene and few among those hold formally innovative fiction in their hearts. When in 1978 Vogelaar publishes his major work of montage fiction, *Riddles of the Bull* (*Raadsels van het rund*), he is confronted with a critical reception that — a few highly appreciative responses from sympathetic critics notwithstanding — ranges from incomprehension to outright hostility. *All the Meat* (*Alle vlees*), the third and final instalment of the *Operations*-series, is welcomed as a major achievement by a limited number of like-minded critics and ignored by most of the others.

Hugo Brems, in his authoritative history of post-war Dutch-language literature, considers the late 1970s as a turning-point in the development of post-war experimental fiction: neo-avant-gardism had fulfilled its 'historical role as purification and as resistance against the traditional conventions of the novel' (2006: 386). Moreover, the publication in 1978 of Sybren Polet's anthology of experimental fiction, *Other Prose* (*Ander proza*), at a time when both critics and novelists were growing weary of radical formal experimentation, in Brems's view confirmed the marginalized position of innovative fiction which it was intended to shatter. Polet's anthology nevertheless sealed the critical view of Vogelaar as primarily an exponent of 'other prose', a label which grouped Vogelaar together with fellow neo-avant-gardists such as Dutch writer and publicist Lidy van Marissing, Flemish prose innovators Daniël Roberechts and C.C. Krijgelmans, and of course poet and novelist Polet himself.

The publication of Vogelaar's collection of essays *Writing Back* (1987, *Terugschrijven*) initiates a brief revival in the critical reception of Vogelaar's work. Critics who were wary of his experimental fiction and his Marxist leanings point out that Vogelaar seems to have moved beyond his political and literary radicalism from the 1970s. When Vogelaar publishes his novel *Death as an Eight-Year-Old Girl* (*De dood als meisje van acht*), arguably the most conventional literary work in his career so far, the novel is greeted with widespread enthusiasm and a sense of wonderment, as if critics to their surprise find that Vogelaar can successfully compose a (fairly) traditional novel. This brief surge of enthusiasm, however, does not generate lasting and widespread critical attention for his writings in the following years. Vogelaar's literary, critical and essayistic production in the last two decades of his career elicits few, although generally benevolent, critical comments and reviews.

Academically Vogelaar is best remembered for his writings in the 1960s and 1970s, both for his neo-Marxist poetological and critical programme and for his politically motivated disruption of narrative and linguistic conventions. Brems considers Vogelaar 'the most remarkable' literary exponent of the left-wing cultural contestation of the late 1960s and specifically focuses on 'the ideas and jargon of materialist literary theory' informing Vogelaar's literary criticism (2006: 270).

In *A Literary History of the Low Countries* (2009) Anne Marie Musschoot (2009: 618) lists the main ingredients of this scholarly view on Vogelaar. Whereas his literary experimentation 'drew upon the French *nouveau roman*', his 'view of society derived from the critical philosophers of the Frankfurt School'. In the course of the 1960s and 1970s Vogelaar 'became further radicalized' as a writer, 'until he no longer created an image of reality at all' but rather 'a critical investigation' of the corrupted language use and mentality of his contemporaries. 'Readers lost interest', Musschoot concludes. Ton Anbeek appears to rank himself among those readers when, in his *Geschiedenis van de Nederlandse literatuur tussen 1885 en 1985*, he asks the rhetorical question whether writers such as Vogelaar should not be considered 'much more naïve than the readers they scorn for liking a compelling story with recognizable characters' (1990: 230).[24]

Additionally, there has been some debate on the question whether or not Vogelaar's literary writings are to be considered as 'postmodern'. When the concept of 'postmodernism' was introduced into the study of Dutch-language literature in the 1980s it was retrospectively applied to a number of post-war neo-avant-garde writers, among which those associated with the critical epithet 'other prose'. Comparing the label 'other prose' with the concept of 'postmodernism' Anthony Mertens (1986: 278) summarily concludes that both refer to a similar trend in innovative fiction. In *Literatuur en moderniteit in Nederland 1840–1990*, Frans Ruiter and Wilbert Smulders characterize Vogelaar's writings as a quest for a 'postmodern kind of avant-gardism' (1996: 327).[25] More recently, however, Bart Vervaeck (2007) and Sven Vitse (2009) have argued that Vogelaar's neo-Marxist critical programme and his neo-avant-garde montage technique are incompatible with the poetics and narrative strategies of postmodern fiction.

Oswald Wiener

Wiener's work has been widely discussed and was regarded as one of the most radical instantiations of literary neo-avant-garde in the German speaking countries. For some theorists it marked a turning point within avant-gardist faith in progress, maybe as the first exemplification of a post-modern work. Despite being attested a unique role, Wiener's work is still awaiting a thorough reception which comprises all of its aspects. Until now, only the 'literary' Wiener has been studied in several dissertations and articles (Kubaczek 1992; Kurz 1992; Eder 2000b; Schiewer 2004; Tabbert 2005; Kastberger 2010; Salgaro 2010). These interpretations focus primarily on language criticism and philosophical aspects in Wiener's so-called experimental writing. In some further regards the critics consider Wiener's *the improvement of central europe, a novel* (especially the 'bio-adapter') as the first instantiations of virtual reality or prefigurations of thought experiments carried out later by analytic philosophers ('The Brain in a Vat Argument'; Putnam 1982).

When addressing Wiener's theoretical work, a dilemma becomes evident which is similar to Wiener's own intellectual dilemma. Finding himself socialized in the field of the arts, Wiener later became a scientist due to the inconsistent tension between his ideology and his talents. But at the same time, colleagues from the cognitive sciences and from psychology tend to underestimate his contributions to a current version of a 'psychology of thinking' [Denkpsychologie]. This may partly have its cause in Wiener's attempt to amalgamate automata theory in the sense of Alan M. Turing and its adaption in Artificial Intelligence (which is said to be too strict for coming to grips with human intelligence) and introspection (which has been condemned by psychologists as being too vague).

In the field of literature and the arts Wiener's work has been very influential, having direct and indirect effects on a number of authors of the neo-avant-garde in the German speaking countries (Reinhard Priessnitz, Franz Josef Czernin, Ferdinand Schmatz, Ulf Stolterfoht, Thomas Kling, Frantisek Lesák, Olaf Nicolai,

Ann Cotton, etc.). Moreover, Wiener has influenced some nowadays important artists and musicians who studied with him in Düsseldorf (Rosa Barba, Klaus Sander, Jan St. Werner — Mouse on Mars; with Barba and Werner Wiener (and his wife, the artist Ingrid Wiener) teamed up for the music band Wichtel und die Wuchteln).

4. Literary practice

Jacq Firmin Vogelaar: A Period of Transition

It remains to be seen whether and to what extent Vogelaar's and Wiener's literary conceptions and practices further diverged after this period of convergence. For Vogelaar, in any case, the late 1960s was a period of transition, in which the writer gradually developed his early poetics and politics into the more strictly Marxist views he held for most of the following decade, and which coincided with the most radical experiments with montage techniques in post-war Dutch literature. In what follows we will take a closer look at that period of transition and at a book Vogelaar published in 1968, *It Has No Name* (*Het heeft geen naam*), which we consider to be a pivotal point in Vogelaar's literary development.

In an interview in 1969 Vogelaar commented on his most recently published work, *It Has No Name*, a collection of three experimental prose pieces which on the back cover is described as nothing more than '3 pieces' ('3 stukken'). Vogelaar explains to an interviewer, the Dutch journalist Lidy van Marissing, who would start publishing experimental novels of her own in the early 1970s, that in this work he moved from constructing to deconstructing: 'Now I try to disassemble; instead of montage it is now de-montage, analysis. The centre has also moved somewhat to language' (Van Marissing 1971: 132).[26] Moreover, in his most recent writing, Vogelaar claims, he has developed a more abstract and less narrative style, in which a theme is explored from various perspectives, and characters tend to be reduced to linguistic features or basic binary distinctions: 'The figures are gradually trimmed to a number of data, for instance their sex.'[27]

Given that *It Has No Name* was already Vogelaar's sixth book and that the author was still only twenty-four, this first phase in his career as a writer had been brief but explosive. With the publication of *It Has No Name*, Vogelaar's literary development had reached a pivotal point: the text displays a transition between Vogelaar's subversion of narrative conventions in his early novels, inspired by the French *nouveau roman*, and the ultimate dissolution of these conventions in his *Operations*-series. As Brems aptly points out, in *Kaleidofragments* (1970, *Kaleidiafragmenten*), the first prose work Vogelaar published after *It Has No Name*, narrative conventions can no longer be said to be subverted, as this 'sample sheet of rhetorical manipulations' (2006: 301) foregoes narrative form altogether. *It Has No Name*, then, is a double-faced work of transition, on the one hand anticipating the dissolution of narrative into montage and on the other hand recapitulating the narrative and thematic concern which Vogelaar consistently returned to in his early novels, namely that of confinement and isolation.

It is from this double perspective, both formal and thematic, that Vogelaar's literary practice will be considered in this paragraph. The analysis will demonstrate that the formal and structural properties of the text can be related to its treatment of the aforementioned themes. A thematic reading of the text will reveal how Vogelaar's formal experimentation interlocks with existential anxieties, explored on the level of narrative and character, which Vogelaar has rarely commented upon in his poetological writings. Indeed, in his critical writings Vogelaar has consistently rejected literature as a vehicle for emotional outpourings or subjectivist expression.

We should not conclude, however, that Vogelaar's literary practice was a purely formal affair, or a purely political intervention. Similar to Oswald Wiener's work in the period of the Wiener Gruppe, which sought to develop a literary language better suited to express the artist's *Lebensgefühl*, Vogelaar's experimental fiction can be read thematically as an expression of socially and culturally constructed existential experience, for which Vogelaar's structural innovations provided the appropriate formal framework. The existential experience conveyed in Vogelaar's literary practice can be summarized as the oppressive experience of closure and the concomitant desire to escape from closed circuits, both in language and society.

In the above-mentioned review of Willy Roggeman's *Catch as Catch Can* Vogelaar goes on to explain why this book matters more to him than any of those which present the reader only with ideas and images he or she is already familiar with. Roggeman's novel is a text which acknowledges that both reality and our perception of it are incomplete, even defective, and therefore can be altered and processed. Because of its fragmentary nature the text allows the reader to intervene actively and productively in its construction. Vogelaar argues:

> It is a book which I have been able to chew on and the reading of which has been a productive activity. If writers acknowledge their consciousness, or rather its insufficiency, this means inevitably that they abandon the fiction of sovereignty and refrain from creating a closed world and from producing a closed work. The defective novel, which presents (can present) nothing but fragments, corresponds to a defective reality which is not complete either, not transparent to consciousness either.[28] (1969b)

In Vogelaar's view, at least in his pre-Marxist phase, reality can never be completely mastered by the human mind. Therefore, any text or image pretending to present a complete or totalizing picture of reality — 'a closed work' suggesting 'a closed world' — should be rejected as ideological. Perhaps it is no surprise, then, that Vogelaar's literary work in this early phase is replete with images of closure: a lack of openness, be it spatially, socially, linguistically or otherwise, which is usually perceived as confining and oppressive.

The first poem Vogelaar published in the journal *Merlyn* already contains some of the motifs that will be explored extensively in the works of fiction that he writes in these early years of his career. The poem is called 'Jonas' and is reminiscent of the biblical character Jonah, a prophet from the Old Testament whose chronicle is most famous for the episode in which Jonah spends two days inside the belly of a whale. As the story goes, Jonah tried to escape God's order to go preach in the city of Nineveh by boarding a ship. When the ship meets heavy weather, Jonah manages to calm the storm by having himself thrown overboard. In the water Jonah is swallowed whole by a whale and prays to God inside the whale for two days, until the animal spits him out. The poem alludes to the image of confinement within another living body, adding the notion of motherhood: 'apart from that I will kill her pitch-dark womb [...] I have to hide somewhere'[29] (Vogelaar 1964: 48). Besides the motif of confinement, the poem presents the motif of persecution and victimization, specifically the medieval custom of sticking feathers to the convict's body: 'in pitch-black feathers I stick on, and so I show myself'[30] (48).

The motifs of confinement and persecution are central to Vogelaar's early fiction and will be revisited in the two novels that Vogelaar writes when he returns to the novel form in the 1990s: *Death as an Eight-Year-Old Girl* (1991, *De dood als meisje van acht*) en *Away from the Pain* (1994, *Weg van de pijn*). The first novel, *Anatomy of a Glass-like Body* (1966, *Anatomie van een glasachtig lichaam*), is a painfully precise dissection of a young woman's isolation in an urban environment which she experiences as ever more threatening. In *Enemy Wanted* (1967, *Vijand gevraagd*), as the title suggests, the protagonist ends up being chased and imprisoned in a small rural village he happens to pass through. The protagonist of Vogelaar's third novel, *Metamorphosis or a Metaphorical Mousetrap* (1968, *Gedaanteverandering of 'n metaforiese muizeval*), finds himself trapped and exploited in an obscure conspiracy involving espionage and murder.

This consistent thematic thread might go easily unnoticed, since Vogelaar himself prefers not to discuss it, strictly focusing instead on the formally innovative nature of his writing and the cultural critique underpinning it. Nevertheless, it might be rewarding to explore *It Has No Name* from this angle. The first part of this experimental triptych, 'The Interior', takes up the image that informed the stories collected in Vogelaar's fiction debut, *The Man Coming and Going*: the image of solitary confinement in a small room. The second piece, as its title 'Closed Circuit' ('Gesloten sirkwie') suggests, presents an exploration of closed circuits on various levels. The third part, 'Capita mortua', consists of two dialogical pieces both of which apply montage technique to intercut and splice textual threads in a polyphonic fabric. Following a brief analysis of the first part of the triptych, this paragraph will examine the second part in more detail in order to illustrate Vogelaar's poetics and politics in the late 1960s.

The Interior

Using the letters of the alphabet instead of numbers to break down the text into 26 paragraphs Vogelaar suggests that the title 'The Interior' might refer to language as well as to the enclosed spaces inhabited by the characters. Given that the paragraphs are arranged from a to z, but that there is no paragraph p and that the final paragraph — printed in capital — is bulleted with a capital A, the composition of this piece would indicate that language is a circular and therefore closed, yet incomplete and inconsistent structure.

This notion of a closed yet incomplete interior structure is visually foregrounded by Vogelaar's idiosyncratic use of typography, specifically his deviation from standard rules of indentation. Vogelaar alternates regular indentation with deviating indentation which begins the first line of a new paragraph at the same distance from the margin as the last line from the previous paragraph ended. Often this type of indentation is in the middle of a sentence, possibly to indicate a hiatus in the character's experience of the situation or to shift the focus from one character to another, as in the following example:

> Bites a nail, rubs through his hair. Keeps still and looks obliquely upwards when the other, who was standing in front of the window with his back turned towards him,
> Turns around, takes a letter opener from the desk, damps it with his breath and then polishes it with his blue sweater.[31] (28)

On two occasions — between paragraphs k and l, and between y and x — about a third of a page is left blank. Near the end of the text — in paragraph w — Vogelaar uses excessive spacing between word groups in an enumeration: 'the damp mirror   the curling photos   the grey cinders'[32] (45). Alternatively, in the same paragraph, spaces between words are either omitted or inserted to evoke the character's agitated and incoherent train of thought: 'the bulgingglasses ofthespectacles — the mo vi   ng door knob'[33] (46). Using various typographic techniques, in addition to orthographic deviations, Vogelaar foregrounds linguistic form and structure, questioning the extent to which consciousness is railed off by the closed circuit of language as well as derailed by its indeterminacies and inconsistencies.

A similar conception underlies the narrative structure, which alternates between a limited number of narrative perspectives without, however, providing an overarching structure in which these can ultimately be integrated. In the first paragraph a heterodiegetic, non-dramatized narrator appears to present an externally focalized male character in a room. The suggestion of a purely objective description, however, is subverted by a subtle hint of subjectivity: 'In another place a rectangular shape vaguely remains [...] or maybe it only appears to be like that'[34] (10). In the second paragraph narrative perspective shifts to a homodiegetic narrator alternating between synchronic and retrospective narration. The interior in which this narrator is confined is psychological rather than spatial: seeking refuge from a constant siege of 'thoughts' — 'a destructive weapon' (11)[35] — this character desperately tries to close off a secure mental space.

From paragraph k onwards two characters start to interact — presumably the man in the room from a and the narrator from b — and alternately present their perspective homodiegetically. The narrator in k mentions his red-eyed mask, whereas the narrator in l mentions visiting a man in a room wearing a red-eyed mask — a man, moreover, whom he calls Ben. Things become really confusing when in paragraph o a heterodiegetic narrator presents two characters in a room and narrative perspective subsequently starts to shift between these characters, both of whom appear to narrate parts of the paragraph, ultimately muddling the narrative structure of the story and the distinction between the characters. Additionally, some scenes suggest that the man in the room is imagining an enemy intruding in his room and attacking him from behind.

While thematically 'The Interior' focuses on motifs such as borders, confinement and intrusion, on the level of narrative structure the text confronts the reader with a puzzle which is both ineluctable and inconclusive.

Closed Circuit

'Closed Circuit' depicts the nightmare of a writer who feels trapped both in language and society; at the same time it reflects the writer's desire to escape it through aesthetic means. In the first place, the concept of the closed circuit implies a conception of language as a closed system of signs referring to one another primarily. According to structuralist linguistics, meaning in language derives from internal relations within a system of signifiers and concepts rather than from objects and situations in reality which language might be used to describe. In the 1960s Vogelaar takes an interest in structuralist linguistics because it provides a theoretical foundation for his views on the relationship between language and human consciousness. He shares this interest with Wiener, although the latter gradually abandons the notion that the structure of language is entangled with that of consciousness.

In the opening pages of the text the unnamed narrator tries to find the right word for an unspecified object which is 'small and pointy with little hairs' (35).[36] He finds himself trapped in a chain of signifiers none of which seems to fit the object he has in mind. When he decides to call it 'a sort of plume' (54),[37] the word 'plume' ('pluim') suggests an alternative word which is phonologically similar but denotes a completely different phenomenon: 'fluff' ('pluisje') (54)? Moreover, the narrator soon realizes that linguistic signs imply connotations as well as denotations and that the connotations 'plume' has for him might not be shared by other language users: 'but that happens if you use the word *plume* to me it means a plume in an air rifle on the fun fair or in the attic but for someone else it just means *plumejustlikethat* the worst explanation that's how it happens' (56).[38] The manner in which the narrator plays with minimal phonological distinctions suggests that in his mind the distinction between language and reality has collapsed. To the question: 'how does a mosquito [mug] disappear so what is stronger than a mosquito' (57)[39], his spontaneous reply derives from the universe and logic of the signifier: 'I'd say a sparrow [mus] only one letter difference but immediately the whole mosquito is gone' (57).[40] He imagines, however, objections to his argument deriving from the logic of the real world: 'but yes you'll say there are also towels with which you could kill such an animal fly swats though not officially intended for mosquitoes' (57).[41] Vogelaar's playful experimentation with language can be seen a literary exploration of the interlocking nature of language and consciousness, similarly to Wiener's manipulation of language during his involvement in the Wiener Gruppe.

In a more philosophical way the concept of the closed circuit signals the ineluctable intertwining of subject and object: the implication of the subject in any description or analysis of the object world, or the impossibility of a purely objective vantage point from which to observe the outside world. One of the most fundamental links interweaving subject and object world is time: the subject describing the outside world is as much involved in the sequence of time as his object. The speaking or writing subject, so the narrator understands, can himself never escape the development of objects in time that he wishes to observe. Moreover, as if paraphrasing Jacques Derrida, the narrator acknowledges that the present moment will always necessarily elude his grasp. In order to compensate for this necessarily subjective perspective the subject would need a second hand, so to speak, as in the famous Escher picture 'Drawing hands', to chart the position of the subject's 'first hand'.

> if I had paper and pen now I could write what there is now ie just now a minute ago and so forth who I am how I felt if I felt anything what I was if I was anything at a certain moment no at any random moment for instance now with me an archimedean point I say in that case I write *point* and mean *I* and try to indicate as precisely as possible what time it is [...] I get it one hand is not enough I would have to write with two hands simultaneously with one hand writing where I am and who approximately here and now with the other pen writing that sitting on the attic trapdoor or by the chink I was busy writing where I was (63)[42]

The image of the closed circuit could also be interpreted as a metaphor for ideology in general and the ideological use of language specifically. The narrator of 'Closed Circuit' dismisses the language that he was taught as a closed circle of meanings which works to limit rather than facilitate the freedom of expression that liberal democracy claims to guarantee. From the very first words the child is taught language merely allows the speaking subject to agree with the views he is fed and to conform to the commands he is given: 'that's how it started they turned my questions into answers' (67).[43] The only alternative to ideological compliance would have been to refuse language altogether: 'if I had from a very early age kept my mouth closed ohno they explained my first scream as yes already then I could not go back anymore' (67).[44]

In the world the narrator presents it is not just language that breeds conformism: culture at large functions as a disciplinary machine subjecting individuals to preconceived notions and expressions as well as to stereotypical binary oppositions. The ideal subject of ideology, so the narrator feels, is 'well-fed respectable of equal denomination belonging to one of the two preformed sexes without destructive aspirations prepared to keep breathing and pay taxes' (76).[45] The key word in this disciplinary society is adaptation, since the ideal subject position it projects is both innocent and ignorant of any desires that might deviate from the cultural and ideological mainstream: 'adaptation leaves nothing to be desired concerning grammar and sense of direction and purchasing power and good breeding and lust and history and time management' (76).[46]

In order to maintain social discipline society does not refrain from subjecting its citizens to hygienic and medical treatment: 'hearingnoseprickkneecapsjoints nothing wrong with as far as we can tell you can walk on have you been disinfected yet have you taken your painkillers ogod' (76).[47] The narrator recalls being subjected to various kinds of abuse and bureaucratic control all of which was devised to sculpt him, both physically and mentally, into an obedient and malleable citizen. He 'was beaten dragged into buildings forced [...] to sign forms [...] forced to open my mouth and show my teeth forced to unlearn my mother tongue to act as an adult' (95).[48] His is a world of soldiers and bureaucrats who exercise permanent and panoptic surveillance and organize space in such a way as to acquire complete control over everyone's movements: 'I continually fell into the trap in the hands of uniforms and civil servants' (96).[49]

On an immaterial level the narrator experiences his world as a linguistic and ideological closed circuit. On a material level, moreover, he perceives his surroundings as a secluded environment in which his movements are either inhibited or circular. The essential characteristic of a house, the narrator claims, is closure, which makes it both a protective and an oppressive atmosphere: 'it is closed in all possible ways not just on the outside but also on the inside' (58).[50] Although his whereabouts remain vague at best throughout the narrative the narrator mentions having lived in a barrel before, situated in the vicinity of a church. The capsular nature of this living space is reflected in a simple word play. Inviting a female character to come live with him, the protagonist reversed the order of the letters of the word 'ton' (barrel), possibly also alluding to the German word 'Not': 'come in my barrel [ton] I asked in the what she asked in the lerrab [not] I therefore repeated' (72).[51]

The narrator eventually seems to have moved in with this woman and after having lived with her for a while he apparently moves to the attic, which again isolates him from his environment. However, in his view the differences between spaces are gradual, similar to the differences between the circles of hell: 'I have simply moved from one circle to another maybe it is already the seventh' (80).[52] In line with the circular nature of hell he feels trapped in a loop of inconsequential movements, where neither motion nor rest seem feasible. Although he realizes that 'one only stays alive if one keeps moving', he sees no point in moving since there is no prospect of progress: 'if you start running you know beforehand that you will return' (74).[53] Discouraged by the impossibility of real movement the narrator eventually resigns to a total standstill, reflecting the existential deadlock in which he finds himself. He settles for the fantasy of movement as a surrogate for actual movement: 'to sit on my arse and consider all the places I could have been' (95).[54]

In the end the only option left for the protagonist was to commit suicide: the narrator suggests that he went up the church tower and jumped. But then again, in this circular world past and present are hard to disentangle and a linear narrative with a beginning, a middle and an end can hardly be reconstructed. On the final pages even the narrator's sex seems to have changed: while earlier he refers to his 'thrusting prick in her torn belly' (84)[55] in the end he mentions 'the sordid lips between my legs' (96).[56] One remark indicates that in the present the narrator has returned from the attic and the tower to the ground floor, but perhaps this merely indicates that he is dead. But even in death a stable vantage point in the present seems forever out of reach: 'whereas everyone always dreams of being able to see afterwards whether and how you are being missed' he 'does not even dare to watch what it is like now I am no longer there' (80)[57]. The circuit remains forever closed.

This brief analysis of *It Has No Name* allows us to find common ground between Vogelaar and Wiener. We conclude that Vogelaar's experimental literary practice derives from a philosophical and theoretical concern with the relationship between language and consciousness as well as from a radical rejection of the ideological structure of late capitalist consumerist society. From a Marxist point of view, infused with notions deriving from structuralist linguistics, Vogelaar conceives his literary practice as part and parcel of a broad artistic and political revolt against bourgeois society and its ideological superstructure. This radical engagement with a revolutionary aesthetics is akin to Wiener's participation in the provocative aesthetics of *Wiener Aktionismus* and to his critique of government power in *The Improvement of Central Europe*, to which we will turn in the next section.

Oswald Wiener: The Improvement of Central Europe

The Improvement of Central Europe, A Novel (ICE) is the foremost *Entwicklungsroman* [coming-of-age novel] of the latter half of the twentieth century in at least two respects. First, it documents the author's intellectual development and led to profound changes in his thinking: '[...] so I sit here and write, wondering what strange changes happened to me in the last few years since the first lines of which I do not understand a word'[58] (Wiener 2013: CXVII). In this regard, it marks a turning point. Second, it is a diagnostic and prophetic text concerning the socio–historical, political, and scientific movements and developments in the Western world since the 1950s.

ICE prefigured Wiener's further development. The aggravation of his cognitive interest may be regarded as a necessary movement of the avant-gardes as such, tracing their way out of art into the (natural) sciences.

The book consists of several loosely connected parts, starting with aphorism-like passages, followed by mock theater plays ('"allah kherim!" epiphanies are saved. report on the feast of concepts' ['"allah kherim!" die erscheinungen sind gerettet. reportage vom fest der begriffe'], 'PURIM. a feast'), 'two studies on sitting' ('zwei studien über das sitzen'), in which Wiener offers epistemological speculations in literary form. The two closing parts are essays on the so called 'bio-adapter' (see below). In the first parts of ICE, Wiener refers to his past period as an experimental poet, labelling some of its sections 'core elements regarding an experimental past' (2013: LXXIII; 'kernstücke zu einer experimentellen vergangenheit') and addressing key questions regarding the relation between language and thought, which renders his aesthetics of this time similar to Vogelaar's interest in linguistics:

> sentences as estimations, creating a norm from which you may differ. [...]
>
> the therapeutic failure of psychoanalysis was that making something conscious consists only of the use of an idiom; the language remained unknown to them, they did not even know that the theories themselves are mere speaking habits, I say this benevolent. and as psychoanalysis, clearly, intended to be political, I

mean official politics, was the impetus therefore narrow-chested — and the approach hopelessly outdated also.[59] (Wiener 2013: LXXIII)

Here, again, Wiener attacks psychoanalysis as a means to generate knowledge and he doubts its potential to gain insights into the functioning of the human mind.

The later sections of ICE (especially the two parts on the 'bio-adapter') are characterized as a persistently self-critical essay, which mirrors the development of Western industrial societies as an amalgam of politics, matters of state, and statistics. One possible interpretation of ICE is: from the beginning of the twentieth century onwards behaviorism has become the predominant mindset (meaning the dominant scientific model and method), the entrenched *Weltanschauung* [world view], leading to the loss of the remnants of individuality. Behaviorism and cybernetics are the main targets of Wiener's novel, especially of its closing parts (the infamous 'bio-adapter'). ICE can hence be understood as an argument 'against the scientific worldview, the de facto power of science' (Raab 2008: 46).

In the first sections, Wiener seems to be in line with Hans Bakx's conviction (see above) that the works of the authors of the Wiener Gruppe are mainly about the impact of language on thought processes as well as on social processes. Wiener's argumentation is critically oriented towards media and communication: 'once again and again and again: it is the language the real, the actual, the only, the tangible, the existing, the benchmark is communication'[60] (2013: CXLII). Communication is characterized as 'this inextricable tangle of language, state and reality'[61] (2013: CXLII).

In this way, Wiener advocated the so-called 'language metaphor' [Sprach-metapher],[62] i.e. the over-estimation of the role of language for thought and mind, for art and for science, which inevitably leads to a behaviorist understanding of human thought: man as being controlled by various external media, especially by language.

Wiener is aware of Chomsky's critique of Skinner's influential book *Verbal Behavior* (1959), which is another point of comparison with Vogelaar's interest in structuralist linguistics. Chomsky criticizes Skinner's behaviorist conception of language which aims at providing 'a way to predict and control verbal behavior by observing and manipulating the physical environment of the speaker' (1959: 26). According to Chomsky, it is only metaphorically possible to apply Skinner's scientific concepts (e.g. reinforcement learning) to linguistic behavior — which renders Skinner's endeavor quite unscientific. This is the case as we simply 'cannot predict verbal behavior in terms of the stimuli in the speaker's environment, since we do not know what the current stimuli are until he responds' (32).

In line with Chomsky's arguments, Wiener opens his infamous notes on the concept of the bio-adapter (a sketch of virtual reality avant-la-lettre) by reflections on linguistics and ontology:

one does not rarely come across statements by modern linguists to the effect that their science should ideally become part of behaviorist psychology. how close they have come to achieving this aim remains undecided; it is however certain that it has long since conformed, in accordance with the positivist renunciation of the concept of consciousness as a subject of research, to behaviorism's fundamental attitude towards language: behavioristic psychology and modern linguistics regard the effectiveness of language as limited to a very narrowly defined field, and language itself as one complex of functions among others in society. [...] these difficulties certainly arise from a conflict between unrevised principles of sensory-data and a view of language which denies that language has any influence on perception at all and dismisses all reflection on whether a number of investigations in the fields of sensory psychology and the nervous system might not perhaps, in the end, turn out to be simple linguistic forms, of which those that nevertheless seem to live in relationship to the scientific dispute on the other side do not correspond to the verification [...]. if language is not a system of representing reality (perhaps it is enough to add the continuation: none except its own), it is nevertheless a self-contained system of natural manifestations, studied without auxiliary sciences, at least without ontology).[63] (2013: CXXXIV–V)

This clearly shows some points of contact with Vogelaar's analysis of the closed circuit of language. Both authors conceive of language as a powerful and world-creating medium with its own rules and limitations, hindering the individual from self-determined experiences. Language is the preferred and illusionary medium of the 'closed circuit' in the above sense. Wiener continues in the 'bio-adapter':

only a linguistics which will have eliminated reality can really enable behaviorist psychology to emerge — not however one which vacillates in this important decision. [...] for, paradoxically enough, it is only a language which is not connected to reality which makes objectivity possible; and the realism of the study, which is often driven to extremes, becomes pure solipsism.

admittedly, this ambivalence of behaviorism already has its critics; they, however, are looking for points of departure which cannot be mine; I do not wish to declare my solidarity with the philosophers of sense: all too many people feel uncomfortable with the methodology of a philosophy which is solely interested in the behavior of objects, which goes so far as to theoretically eliminate the observer, or to be more exact, important features of the observer, from the observation process, and vehemently pursues the formal correspondences, limited to a comparatively meagre vocabulary, so that stimulus and reaction are made to serve even the elucidation of teleology. [...]

criticism of behaviorism is, however, also important for me — although it has to come from the other side. this whole essay is devoted to this subject. [...] a rejection of the whole package (largely tare) always has to begin with a re-examination of language, of language and of the various attitudes towards it. [...] both "eastern" and "western" philosophists have made equal contributions to the development of behaviorism, so that in both the east and the west behaviorism is seen as the only possible and only correct sociological and psychological method [...] cybernetics is propagated with the same fervour as the fulfilment of behaviorism in both the east and the west (for marxism perhaps, as an unacknowledged way out of the "fundamental questions of philosophy"), [...] that the linguistic theory of behaviorism (because it dogmatically carries out linguistic research as a branch of psychology and not, as would seem to be more logical, psychology as a branch of linguistic research), as also that of marxism (because it dogmatically regards language as a part of reality, for as a reflection it is such, and not reality as an insinuation of language: reality as a 'reflection' of language) produces the most pathetic results [...]'.[64] (2013: CXXXVI–VIII)

The relation between language and reality is outlined in the following passages in the bio-adapter:

> trivially enough, language presents itself as a norm, above all in the decisions of society, in sociology and in law (marxism also goes so far as to regard consciousness as being based on human social lies, and that alter all means making language a norm!). the use of language possesses the highly remarkable quality which laing must have had in mind when he wrote that our civilization, suppresses every kind of transcendence: it is a protective wall against the attacks of sensation; language goes right through us, prescribing narrow alleys for the reality of our consciousness, producing identity as name, perhaps hampering possible experience.
>
> whoever therefore does not let his language be regarded as the last principle enters into double danger: he loses himself in the landscape of consciousness, to enter which he is lacking equipment; [...] naturally, from the side of the state that all looks like one single thing whoever cannot cope with the reality outlined by language sets himself against society and he suffers confined.[65] (2013: CXXXVIII–IX)

In a nutshell: language is generally characterized as social consciousness and even as the memory of humanity: 'to take this stale joke literally for once: a revolt against language is a revolt against society'[66] (2013: CXLIV).

This was the starting point. Wiener abandoned the study of language in the course of the bio-adapter and of his work after ICE. The proposed decline of the 'linguistic turn', stating that linguistics and philosophy of language are the *via regia* for scientific inquiry, implies further critique on their towering figure, Ludwig Wittgenstein. Throughout ICE, Wittgenstein is being polemically mentioned and addressed. Tenets of his philosophy are quot ed by Wiener: "someone publishes that definition is the manual for the use of words (wiener? Wittgenstein?)"[67] (2013: CXXIX); "if somebody says that the meaning of a word is its use in language, this is nice and of course well-intentioned"[68] (2013: CXXIX); "to use the words. don't understand a word. "using words" sucks. [untranslatable: German saying, grossly obscene, meaning approx.: after dinner you should smoke or copulate — use a female — use a word]: entertainment is essential. have you noticed?[69] (2013: CXXIV). Or, precisely on the topic of our contribution: ' "That which expresses itself in language, we cannot express by language" [Tractatus 4.121], says the 'dark one' in his post-socratic fragments — does anything express itself in language? let alone the "structure of reality"? is anyone familiar with that?'[70] (2013: XVII). Samples like these show one of the main strategies Wiener uses in ICE: concepts which he classifies as failures are refuted without presenting any positive alternatives.

We think it might be worth considering Wiener's movement from art to renegade science (see above) in the light of Peter Bürger's (2010: 704) central and most critical thesis:

> The question of the post-avant-garde situation of art is, without a doubt, the sketchiest part of my book [Peter Bürger's *Theory of the Avant-Garde*] and the one that — not just from today's perspective — is the most in need of elaboration. On the one hand, the book claims that the 'the social institution that is art proved resistant to the avant-gardiste attack,' on the other it asserts

that because of avant-gardist production art 'means are freely available, i.e., no longer part of a system of stylistic norms' ([Bürger 1984:] 17). What remains unanswered is how we should conceive the connection between these two theses in relation to the post-avant-garde situation of art.

In the same essay, Bürger summarizes: 'in *Theory of the Avant-Garde*, the situation of the post-avant-garde, after the failure of the avant-garde project became obvious, was characterized by two theorems: the continued existence of the autonomous art institution and the free use of artistic material' (2010: 706).

In this respect ICE, paradoxically, proves to be a work of art — as its author uses many different aesthetic means — which at least intends to attack the social institution that is art — as it marks a turning point, the suicide (metaphorically speaking) of an artwork. On the other hand, Wiener's ICE aims at changing the attitudes of its recipients, which puts it close to Bürger's reflections on neo-avant-garde: 'This much is certain: the avant-garde's revival (from the perspective of modern art) of obsolete materials (artistic procedures and techniques) succeeded because the avant-gardes did not aim to create works of art that would last through time but wanted to use their manifestations to change the attitudes of their recipients. This means that they situated their aesthetic practices outside those sanctioned by the institution' (2010: 707).

After ICE

When he wrote ICE, Wiener had abandoned the 'language metaphor' [Sprach-metapher], critically showing why it is flawed, but still lacking any theoretical conception to present alternatives. In the meantime this has changed: Wiener now endorses a very clear-cut version of what he calls *Denkpsychologie* (see below) The turning point are some articles Wiener published in the early 1970s, the first of which is entitled 'subject, semantics, mapping relations' (1970, 'subjekt, sema[n]tik, abbildungsbeziehungen').

From then on Wiener endorses the view that the individual's image of the world is largely independent from its linguistic (or generally: symbolic) representation. Wiener's move away from the idea that words or sentences may be analysed in order to gain insight in the designated objects or state of affairs has far-reaching consequences. In the period 1955–1959, when he worked with other members of the Wiener Gruppe, Wiener of course did not endorse this view, explicitly marginalizing the role of language for the 'understanding of understanding' (1970). Retrospectively, Wiener analyses this change as follows: 'understanding of language seemed a royal road to the understanding of all natural phenomena. as far as I am concerned I wanted to become a writer as language seemed to be the hub for all knowledge and communication'[71] (1987: 46).

Slightly later (1987: 48) Wiener changed his mind and conceived of language as being a 'part of the environment onto which one must project one's own content'.[72] Moreover, he starts being critical about 'literary experiments'. The linguistic means used by experimental poets have been reintegrated into traditional ways of expressing contents. He writes (1998b: 8): 'Unfortunately, what has happened is what we feared. In the attempts to mobilize a new meaningfulness the old meaning has survived. Exactly the sentences, terms and styles that we used provisionally to describe an awakening now refer to something which we tried to overcome; the tool has failed'.[73] This is also why literary experiments after 1945 are said to have failed in their intention to criticize all 'formal theories of communication with the goal to establish a sound theory for an individualistic point of view (with regard to content)'[74] (1998b: 19). This goes hand in hand with Wiener's new orientation towards science (and his disdain for art and literature).

Around the time he rejected the arts and literature (also considering philosophy of language and linguistics as fruitless pursuits), Wiener turned to the then relatively new science of cybernetics. Cybernetics was originally designed for the planning of mechanical systems (e.g. in order to steer lockages) and was then transferred to the field of information theory (e.g. by Max Bense). Criticizing this move and the rise of cybernetics as a science used by governments to increase their power is one of the central aims Wiener pursued in writing (and even more: after having written) ICE. The theory of the Turing machine became Wiener's declared interest from this time on — even when he had to regretfully acknowledge that on the basis of the John-von-Neumann computer it will never be possible to implement human thinking and behavior (reading at this time: Iván Flores's *Computer Logic, Functional Design of Digital Computers* [1960] and Boris A. Trachtenbrot's *Why can automata calculate?* [1959, *Wieso können Automaten rechnen?*]).

His declared ideal became to end ICE by a concluding (short) axiom which would describe human thinking and problem-solving. His awareness of the impossibility to do so is the reason why ICE often veers into literary elaboration: 'style is excuse'.

In the bio-adapter, Wiener expounds the idea that cybernetics supports the power of the state and the government via political organization, medicine and science. Cybernetics is accused of suppressing and devastating the individual through the use of statistics. As a consequence, in the bio-adapter Wiener brought anarchic ideas to the field of cybernetics (e.g. Max Stirner). Especially the sciences (and their orientation on behaviorism) are to be refuted and combatted, as they are becoming more and more akin to 'theories of pointer-deflections'[75] (Wiener 2013: CXXXVI). As a remedy, Wiener focuses on the irreducible fact of 'consciousness', not as a metaphysical category, but as something which has to be explained by a strong psychological theory and — on that basis — implemented to machines. When writing the ICE Wiener had no theoretical instruments to cope with the concept of consciousness — that is why many of the pseudo-theoretical parts of ICE are polemic, scornful, and duplicitous. This is how Wiener's work continued after the completion of ICE (as well as where Wiener's and Vogelaar's literary conceptions and practices started to diverge).

While (negatively and sardonically) addressing ontological questions in ICE, Wiener turned to functional questions in his work after ICE: what does something have to be like so that it equals human phenomenal experiences in the course of its thinking and problem-solving? To what degree is this determined by external factors, by heritage; what is analogy, what is semblance, etc. In this respect the later parts of ICE hark back to parts at the beginning, where Wiener tackled language and linguistic theories (how does language as an external stimulus influence consciousness; is it comparable to visual stimuli that change the organism's orientation, i.e. its readiness for action?). In ICE, the author tends to overexaggerate this point and to situate language in the environment. Against this view, as he later realized, it is important to explain how language and thinking (understanding, knowledge, imagination) interact, what aspects in human communication and even individual (silent) problem-solving may count as linguistically bound, and which aspects belong to core thinking.

Political Aspects

In ICE, Wiener tries to overcome and leave behind art, which may be called a 'niche for expression' within the 'enclave of the politically defeated people', to use a phrase coined by Norbert Elias. By proposing to abandon language and civilization as a whole the individual could return to the natural 'right of the strongest'. Thus, the 'governmental monopoly on the use of force' should be placed back into the hands of the individuals who are suitably talented (Schuh 1981: 34) — this point is clearly different from Vogelaar's Marxist approach. Wiener seems to provocatively refer to individual anarchism, as it has been proposed by thinkers like Stirner or Bakunin, who are irreconcilable with orthodox Marxist ideas:[76]

> and how beautiful the world will be if everybody reserves their filthy tongues for spitting; if an enemy is standing in front of me I will not be obliged to describe him or hate him but instead may kill him or else will be killed. And the enemy wants to screw my wife or devour my flesh or simply break my bones and nothing else, at any rate he does not want to make an impression.
>
> In such instances we are young and powerful and stab out and kill without being applauded. And your language may not cause me cancer, I will die because I am simply killed without rage because I stand in the way and because I am nourishing.[77] (Wiener 2013: LXII)

These chocks are bound to epistemological issues, in contrast to the chocks elicited by the historical avant-gardes which basically aimed at *épater le bourgeois*. Wiener does not aim to establish art as 'the conquest of the obscene as a sphere of permitted utterances', but he states that art which 'is directed against any limitation of cognition, is directed against the state'[78] (1972: 55). As a consequence, morals will be suspended by 'linguistic nominalism' (Schuh 1981: 41). This is true for ICE, but will be relativized in Wiener's later work, as he then denies any type of relation between a string of characters (words and sentences) and any kind of content, unless this relation lies within the individual who connects them in the course of understanding. 'Content' may not be derived from the words used — this is why all forms of 'political correctness' lack their theoretical and empirical basis. The goal is to find the theoretical prerequisites for the fact that character strings may be understood in so many different ways without violating principles of plausibility.

Thus, Wiener concludes for the period when he was a member of the Wiener Gruppe:

> We conceived of language (Whorf) and of the social institutions based on language (as it had to be supposed) as the center for restrictions. the orbit of thought curves back to politics; one has to oppose his own production to the linguistic sovereignty of society, but to avoid getting tricked by it [the production]. This will later be the starting point for progressive conservatives to define 'political correctness'.[79] (1998a: 27)

5. Conclusion

In Wiener's view, as it developed after the completion of ICE, external character strings do not have any structural relationship to the thoughts they evoke or to the thoughts the author intended to communicate by them:

> The meaning of a sign is a model which has been activated (caused to be willing to run) by this sign. If the sign is external I shall label it the name of the structure being called. As a structure, meaning may only be experienced in the course of processing, i.e. step by step over time; meaning may never be present as a whole. It is thus implicated that a name may render a model "willing to run" merely in an indirect way, by laying down the tracks for the expansion of specific components of the structure. This expansion is determined by the task or by availability. This process is carried out by the use of 'Weiser' [pointers, but not in the computational sense], for economic reasons and as introspection shows. In a direct way, at best a name may activate a "Weiser" toward the structure — the name is the name of this "Weiser" (in a narrow sense), and its meaning is the meaning of this "Weiser". (Wiener 2008: 133–34)

This is clearly a refutation of all forms of semiotics. Words, sounds, formal linguistic elements are all mere names for a 'structure' being loaded by them. This is also indicated in Wiener's definition of 'structure' which is formulated in the sphere of automata theory in terms of a Turing machine: '[a] *structure* of a character string is a Turing machine which accepts or generates this character string'[80] (2015b: 100).

This definition, stemming from Wiener's studies on Turing's theory, is the starting point and core foundation of his 'psychology of thinking' [*Denkpsychologie*]. Here, Wiener changes from the didactic and epistemological model of the Turing machine to address questions of lively thinking, using the refined method of introspection during problem solving and during mundane events for his theory. This is the starting point for Wiener's current theory (cf. Eder and Raab 2015), a realistic description of lively thinking on the basis of introspection aiming at implementation.

Quite clearly Wiener's theoretical position has evolved significantly since the late 1960s, and it has diverged widely from Vogelaar's poetics. From the 1980s onwards Vogelaar gradually moved away from Marxist cultural theory — at least so far as terminology and concepts are concerned — and reverted to a less overtly politicized late-modernist poetology. This development was strongly inspired by his reading of canonical modernist fiction and specifically by his commitment to the aesthetics of Samuel Beckett and painter Francis Bacon. In his post-Marxist literary practice he adopted what Anthony Mertens (1991) identified as a 'liminal' poetics, studying literature as the intermediate, 'liminal' zone in between the inarticulate real of matter and experience on the one hand and the ideologically and semantically reductive signification of the real in conventional language on the other.

In the late 1960s, however, it seems that the poetics of Vogelaar and Wiener converged, as both writers to some extent shared their critique of language and society and more specifically of the mutual implication of language, science, and state power. There are no indications that Vogelaar at that time was already familiar with Wiener's work, and neither was Wiener aware of Vogelaar's views. In this phase of their development, nevertheless, both writers would seem to agree on a few basic assumptions: that linguistic forms have the power to influence and shape our modes of perception (a position Wiener would soon, even while writing the ICE, abandon); that in post-war capitalist society immaterial, or in Marxist terms, superstructural forms, be they linguistic, cultural or scientific, can be used and are used to wield power and exert control; and that, therefore, to manipulate language is a political act in its own right.

However, even at this stage Vogelaar and Wiener appear to disagree on the status of reality in relation to language. Although Vogelaar claims that the writer's material is primarily language rather than social reality (1967: 156), he never questions the primacy of material reality in all human activity. While he might have agreed with Wiener's view of 'psychology as a branch of linguistic research' (2013: CXXXVI– VIII), he would never have accepted Wiener's (temporarily held and later fiercely rejected) conception of 'reality as a 'reflection' of language', a suggestion Wiener opposes to Marxism's allegedly dogmatic view of 'language as a part of reality' (2013: CXXXVI– VIII). Wiener's explicit mockery of one of Marxism's fundamental tenets — 'to regard consciousness as being based on human social lives' (2013: CXXXVIII–IX) — suffices to show the clear theoretical divide, even at this point of convergence, between both writers' basic intuitions regarding language and society, and as a consequence, regarding literature.

Works Cited

ADLINGTON, ROBERT. 2013. *Composing Dissent: Avant-Garde Music in 1960s Amsterdam* (Oxford: Oxford University Press)

ADRIAN, MARC. 1980. *inventionen*, postface by Gerhard Rühm (Linz: edition neue texte)

ANBEEK, TON. 1990. *Geschiedenis van de literatuur in Nederland, 1885–1985* (Amsterdam: De Arbeiderspers)

BAKX, HANS W. 1979. 'Over de Wienergruppe', *Raster*, 11: 18–21

BAYER, KONRAD. 1996. 'der vogel singt: eine dichtungsmaschine in 571 bestandteilen', in *Sämtliche Werke*, ed. by Gerhard Rühm (Vienna: ÖBV/Klett-Cotta), pp. 496–519 and pp. 802–04

BREMS, HUGO. 2006. *Altijd weer vogels die nesten beginnen: Geschiedenis van de Nederlandse literatuur 1945–2005* (Amsterdam: Bakker)

BÜRGER, PETER. 1984. *Theory of the Avant-Garde* (Minneapolis: University of Minnesota Press)

———. 2010. 'Avant-Garde and Neo-Avant-Garde: An Attempt to Answer Certain Critics of *Theory of the Avant-Garde*', *New Literary History*, 41: 695–715

CHOMSKY, NOAM. 1959. 'Verbal behavior. By B.F. Skinner (Review)', *Language*, 31.1: 26–58

EDER, THOMAS. 2000A. 'Kunst — Revolution — Erkenntnis: Oswald Wiener und ZOCK', in *Schluß mit dem Abendland! Der lange Atem der österreichischen Avantgarde*, ed by Thomas Eder and Klaus Kastberger (Vienna: Paul), pp. 60–80

———. 2000B. 'Erkenntnis! Der Weg O.W.s aus der Literatur und Kunst.', *manuskripte*, 40.147: 125–29

———, and THOMAS RAAB (eds). 2015. *Selbstbeobachtung: Oswald Wieners Denkpsychologie* (Berlin: Suhrkamp)

[*Raster* editors]. 1978. 'Gesprek over Nederlandse proza en avantgarde', *Raster*, 2: 5–25

FEYERABEND, PAUL. 1975. *Against Method: Outline of an Anarchistic Theory of Knowledge* (London: New Left Books)

FLORES, IVÁN. 1960. *Computer Logic, Functional Design of Digital Computers* (Englewood Cliffs: Prentice-Hall)

FREUD, SIGMUND. 1957. 'Appendix C: Words and Things', in *The Standard Edition of the Complete Psychological Works of Sigmund Freud, Volume XIV (1914–1916): On the History of the Psycho-Analytic Movement, Papers on Metapsychology and Other Works. II–VIII*, ed by James Strachey (London: The Hogarth Press and the Institute of Psycho-analysis), pp. 209–16

FREUD, SIGMUND. 1989. *Studienausgabe*, 10 vols, 8th edn, (Frankfurt a/M: Fischer), III: *Psychologie des Unbewussten*

GIEDION-WELCKER, CAROLA. 1946. *Anthologie der Abseitigen — poètes à l'ecartes* (Bern: Benteli)

JANSSEN, SUSANNE. 1994. *In het licht van de kritiek: Variaties en patronen in de aandacht van de literatuurkritiek voor auteurs en hun werken* (Hilversum: Verloren)

JUNG, CARL GUSTAV. 1952. 'Synchronizität als ein Prinzip akausaler Zusammenhänge', in Carl Gustav Jung und Wolfgang Pauli, *Naturerklärung und Psyche* (Zurich: Rascher), pp. 1–107

KASTBERGER, KLAUS. 2010. 'Oswald Wieners Schreib-Szenen zwischen Literatur und Wissenschaft', *manuskripte*, 50,189–90: 289–96

KIRALYFALVI, BELA. 1985. 'Georg Lukács or Bertolt Brecht?', *British Journal of Aesthetics*, 25.4: 340–48

KUBACZEK, MARTIN. 1992. *Poetik der Auflösung: Oswald Wieners 'Die Verbesserung von Mitteleuropa: Roman'* (Vienna: Braumülller)

KURZ, HORST GÜNTER. 1992. 'Die Transzendierung des Menschen im "Bio-Adapter": Oswald Wieners "Die Verbesserung von Mitteleuropa, Roman"' (unpublished doctoral dissertation, University of Michigan; University Microfilms International, Order Nr. 9307798)

MERTENS, ANTHONY. 1986. 'Experimenteel proza', in *Twee eeuwen literatuurgeschiedenis: Poëticale opvattingen in de Nederlandse literatuur*, ed. by G.J. van Bork and Nico Laan (Groningen: Wolters-Noordhoff)

———. 1991. *Sluiproutes en dwaalwegen* (Amsterdam: Sauternes)

MUSSCHOOT, ANNE MARIE. 2009. 'The Revolution of the Sixties, 1960–1970', in *A Literary History of the Low Countries*, ed. by Theo Hermans (Rochester: Camden House)

[*New Left Review* editors]. 1974. 'Introduction to Brecht on Lukács', *New Left Review*, 83: 25–26 <https://newleftreview.org/issues/I84/articles/nlr-editors-introduction-to-brecht-on-lukacs> [accessed 30 May 2019]

PUTNAM, HILARY. 1982. *Reason, Truth and History* (Cambridge: Cambridge University Press)

RAAB, THOMAS. 2008. *Avantgarde-Routine* (Berlin: Parodos)

RUITER, FRANS, and WILBERT SMULDERS. 1996. *Literatuur en moderniteit in Nederland: 1840–1990* (Amsterdam: De Arbeiderspers)

Salgaro, Massimo. 2010. 'Oswald Wiener: Literatur als Experiment', in *'Ein in der Phantasie durchgeführtes Experiment': Literatur und Wissenschaft nach Neunzehnhundert*, ed. by Raul Calzoni and Massimo Salgaro (Göttingen: Vandenhoeck & Ruprecht), pp. 237–61

Schiewer, Gesine Lenore. 2004. *Poetische Gestaltkonzepte und Automatentheorie: Arno Holz — Robert Musil — Oswald Wiener* (Würzburg: Königshausen & Neumann)

Schmidt, Arno. 1977. *Zettels Traum* (Frankfurt/Main: Fischer)

Schuh, Franz. 1981. 'Protest ohne Protestieren: Zur Widersetzlichkeit von Konrad Bayers Literatur', *protokolle*, 4: 31–43

Tabbert, Thomas T. 2005. *Verschmolzen mit der absoluten Realitätsmaschine: Oswald Wieners 'Die Verbesserung von Mitteleuropa, Roman'* (Hamburg: Artislife Press)

Trachtenbrot, Boris A. [n.d; 1959]. *Wieso können Automaten rechnen*, trans. from Russian by Karl-Heinz Rupp (Cologne: Hoffmann)

Van Marissing, Lidy. 1971. *28 interviews* (Amsterdam: Meulenhoff)

Vervaeck, Bart. 2007. 'De kleine Postmodernsky: Ontwikkelingen in de (verhalen over de) postmoderne roman', in *Achter de verhalen: Over de Nederlandse literatuur van de twintigste eeuw*, ed. by Elke Brems, Hugo Brems, Dirk de Geest, and Eveline Vanfraussen (Leuven: Peeters), pp. 133–67

Vitse, Sven. 2009. 'Montage en netwerk: Ander proza en de postmoderne roman', *Spiegel der letteren*, 51.4: 441–70

——. 2015. 'De utopische methode: De poëticale positionering van J.F. Vogelaar in de jaren zestig en zeventig', in *Het lab van de sixties: Positionering en literair experiment in de jaren zestig,* ed. by Lars Bernaerts, Dirk de Geest, Hans Vandevoorde, and Bart Vervaeck (Ghent: Academia Press), pp. 101–18

Vogelaar, Jacq Firmin. 1964. 'Jonas', *Merlyn*, 2.6: 48

——. 1965. *De komende en gaande man* (Amsterdam: Meulenhoff)

——. 1966. *Anatomie van een glasachtig lichaam* (Amsterdam: Meulenhoff)

——. 1967. *Vijand gevraagd* (Amsterdam: Meulenhoff)

——. 1968. *Het heeft geen naam* (Amsterdam: Meulenhoff)

——. 1969a. 'Verbeelding en de werkelijkheid van een film', *Het Parool*, 15 March 1969

——. 1969b. 'Een roman om op te kauwen', *Het Parool*, 17 May 1969

——. 1970. 'Topografie van een materialistiese literatuurteorie', *Raster*, 4.3: 338–73

—— (ed.). 1972. *Kunst als kritiek* (Amsterdam: De Bezige Bij)

——. 1987. *Terugschrijven* (Amsterdam: De Bezige Bij)

Weibel, Peter (ed.). 1997. *die wiener gruppe — the vienna group: a moment in modernity 1954–1960 / the visual works and the actions* (Vienna: Springer)

Wiener, Oswald. 1969. *die verbesserung von mitteleuropa, roman* (Reinbek bei Hamburg: Rowohlt)

——. 1970. 'subjekt, sema[n]tik, abbildungsbeziehungen: ein pro-memoria', *manuskripte*, 10.29–30: 45–59

——. 1972. 'ein merkwürdiges urteil: auseinandergesetzt und kommentiert von oswald wiener', *Neues Forum*, 19.220: 52–57

——. 1979. *Wir möchten auch vom Arno-Schmidt-Jahr profitieren* (Munich: Matthes & Seitz)

——. 1987. 'Wittgensteins Einfluß auf die Wiener Gruppe', in *die wiener gruppe*, ed by the Walter-Buchebner-Gesellschaft (Vienna: Böhlau), pp. 46–59

——. 1990. *Probleme der Künstlichen Intelligenz*, ed. by Peter Weibel (Berlin: Merve)

——. 1996. *Schriften zur Erkenntnistheorie* (Vienna: Springer)

——. 1998a. 'Bemerkungen zu einigen Tendenzen der "Wiener Gruppe"', in *Die Wiener Gruppe*, ed. by Wolfgang Fetz and Gerald Matt (Vienna: Kunsthalle), pp. 20–28

——. 1998b. 'Einiges über Konrad Bayer', in *Literarische Aufsätze*, ed. by Oswald Wiener Vienna: Löcker), pp. 7–20

——. 1998C. *Bouvard und Pécuchet im Reich der Sinne: Eine Tischrede* (Bern: Gachnang and Springer)

——. 2008. 'Über das "Sehen" im Traum: Dritter Teil', *manuskripte*, 48.181: 132–41

——. 2013 [1969]. *Die verbesserung von mitteleuropa, roman*, ed. by Thomas Eder (Vienna: Jung und Jung)

——. 2015A. 'Anfänge', in *Konrad Bayer: Texte — Bilder — Sounds*, ed. by Thomas Eder and Klaus Kastberger (Vienna: Zsolnay), pp. 278–86

——. 2015B. 'Glossar: figurative', in: *Selbstbeobachtung: Oswald Wieners Denkpsychologie*, ed. by Thomas Eder and Thomas Raab (Berlin: Suhrkamp), pp. 99–141

——, MANUEL BONIK, and ROBERT HÖDICKE. *Eine elementare Einführung in die Theorie der Turing-Maschine* (Vienna: Springer)

Notes to Chapter 4

1. 'misschien vooral interessant zijn vanwege hun onmogelijke opdrachten'. All translations from Dutch to English are by Sven Vitse.
2. 'het combineren van bestaande betekenissen om ze zodoende te verwerken — ontleden en vermenigvuldigen. Resultaat: een nieuwe verzameling van teksten'
3. 'Het ligt voor de hand hier een vergelijking te maken met de Nederlandse "Zestigers", de Barbarber-groep, die ook van mening waren dat er in het leven van alledag veel interessants stak dat onopgemerkt bleef. Het grote verschil met deze oer-Nederlandse stroming is echter dat de Wiener Gruppe een veel extremer en fundamenteler standpunt innam: het accentueren van het banale diende niet om de lezer blij verrast te doen opzien, maar om de werkelijkheid waarvan die banaliteiten deel uitmaakten aan de kaak te stellen — en liefst te vernietigen. Het aangrijpingspunt was daarbij de taal: "de taal wordt gewoonlijk als maatschappelijk bewustzijn, ja als het geheugen van de mensheid omschreven. Om die flauwiteit eens woordelijk te nemen: een opstand tegen de taal is dan een opstand tegen de maatschappij...", zoals Oswald Wiener het formuleert in *die verbesserung von mitteleuropa* (1969), de Summa Theologiae van de Wiener Gruppe, zij het een Summa achteraf.'
4. ''n verandering van het kijken naar mensen en dingen [...] niet in één richting zoals door reklame, kerken en amuzement gebeurt, maar door voorbeelden waarin niet de herkenningstekens het belangrijkste zijn, maar 'n veranderde manier van kijken, 'n andere (open) kijk op iets, die wat is uitbreidt ontwikkelt en daarmee verandert. EEN REVOLUSIE VAN HET OOG EN HET OOR.'
5. 'Als een materialistiese kunsttheorie verweten wordt dat ze al het esthetiese reduceert op ekonomiese en sociale determinaties en zodoende het 'eigenlijke' van het kunstwerk onrecht doet, verwijt men de teorie wat men in de werkelijkheid niet wil erkennen'.
6. 'mythe van het "scheppingsproces"'
7. 'waar en hoe, met welke lapmiddelen de schijn, die later als een slikklaar consumptieartikel wordt opgediend, is klaargestoofd'
8. 'de publieke oordelen en politieke beslissingen'
9. 'Een ander vraagteken dat ik bij het boek van Bernlef zet is dat hij zich wel afvraagt of iets werkelijk is en geen verbeelding, of andersom, maar dat eigenlijk wat in deze werkelijkheid of verbeelding bestaat buiten twijfel blijft. Hij citeert de werkelijkheid maar hecht er zijn onuitgesproken goedkeuring aan door haar te laten wat zij is — alles is bruikbaar dus alles is interessant, verder alles o.k.'
10. 'defensie'; 'een denkbeeldige aanval'; 'een vijand'
11. 'geweld'; 'tussen machthebbers en machtelozen'
12. 'woorden die op zich de bestaande praktijken niet in gevaar brengen'; 'de verdraagzaamheid houdt echter op als de radikale tegenstanders van het sisteem tot handelen overgaan'
13. 'Onrecht verdwijnt niet door recht.'
14. 'Boeken die niet gedachteloos gelezen kunnen worden omdat ze meer en anders zijn dan wat men al kent.'

15. 'de zakelijke wensen van de boekenmarkt'
16. 'boeken, waarvoor denkwerk wordt vereist'; 'nog eens uitgalmen wat iedereen al weet'
17. 'Socialistiese kunst en burgerlijke kunst kunnen niet vreedzaam naast elkaar bestaan'; 'een andere kultuur [is] nodig [...] zoals er andere sociale verhoudingen nodig zijn'
18. 'de zgn. geesteswetenschappen, die als beheersingswetenschappen dienen om de aanpassing van de sociale verhoudingen en bewustzijnsstrukturen te bewerken'
19. 'Jeder war für die Qualität seines Erlebens und Verstehens selbst verantwortlich, der souveräne Geist bedurfte der Kunst nicht, denn nicht aufs Machen, auf das Verstehen kommt es an. Dies war meine Idee von Dada.'
20. 'Das Bedürfnis, "den Individualismus zu beweisen". Freiheit der Interpretation (Brennpunkt der Freiheit der Persönlichkeit) sei schon in der (zunächst vorausgesetzten) Tatsache begründet, daß die Verstehenswelten der Individuen inkommensurabel sind (Bebuquin), daß jeder Kollektion von Reizen auf unendlich viele Weisen Sinn verliehen werden kann. Es gilt nun, empirische Argumente für diese Arbeitshypothese zu finden, aber das Kunstverstehen ist dafür zu geschmeidig. Von hier aus geht es für mich in Richtung naturwissenschaftliche Bildung.'
21. 'die bewußte Vorstellung umfaßt die Sachvorstellung plus der zugehörigen Wortvorstellung, die unbewußte ist die Sachvorstellung allein' (Freud 1989: 300)
22. 'damit aber vorstellungen in die sprache abbildbar werden, bedarf es nicht allein der worte, sondern vor allem einer reihe von bedingungen, welche festlegen, dass sich die worte im kommunikationsprozess so ähnlich verhalten wie die vorstellungen im gedankenablauf; es bedarf weiters nicht bloss einer grammatik der sätze und redeabschnitte, sondern noch einer impliziten interpretation der jeweiligen kommunikativen situation, welche den spracherscheinungen erst sinn gibt. anzunehmen, dass ein wort mit einer vorstellung nur assoziativ verknüpft zu sein brauche, wäre zu naiv. es lässt sich aus der alltäglichen erfahrung belegen, dass die wortwahl im allgemeinen unerheblich ist, sobald eine interpretative situation definiert vorliegt: in einem starken kontext kann jedes wort für jegliche Vorstellung stehen. das heisst aber, dass man eine 'wortvorstellung' von einer 'sachvorstellung' so wenig trennen darf, wie beide Vorstellungen von ihren stets aufeinander projizierten kontexten'
23. 'daß die Sortierung=Lagerung der Worte im Gehirn *ebm auf der Etym-Basis erfolgt*' (emphasis Wiener)
24. 'Het is de vraag of auteurs die van zo'n idealistische veronderstelling uitgaan niet veel naïever zijn dan de door hen gesmade lezers die graag een boeiend verhaal met herkenbare personages volgen.'
25. 'een postmoderne vorm van avant-gardisme'
26. 'Nu probeer ik te demonteren; inplaats van montage is het nu demontage, analyse. Het centrum heeft zich ook wel een beetje verplaatst naar de taal.'
27. 'De figuren zijn steeds meer afgekapt tot enkele gegevens, bijvoorbeeld het geslacht.'
28. 'Het is een boek waar ik op heb kunnen kauwen en waarvan het lezen een produktieve bezigheid is geweest. Als auteurs zich rekenschap geven van hun bewustzijn, of liever van de ontoereikendheid ervan, betekent het onvermijdelijk dat ze de fictie van almacht opgeven en ervan afzien een afgesloten wereld te scheppen en een afgesloten werk af te scheiden. De onvolmaakte roman, die niet meer dan fragmenten geeft (kan geven), beantwoordt aan een onvolmaakte werkelijkheid die evenmin af is, evenmin doorzichtig voor het bewustzijn.'
29. 'daarnaast mol ik ook nog haar stikdonkere baarmoeder,, / moedertje, ik moet me toch ergens verbergen'
30. 'in pikzwarte veren die ik opplak, en zo ik me vertoon'
31. 'Bijt op 'n nagel, vrijft [sic] door z'n haar. Houdt stil en kijkt schuin omhoog als de ander, die met zijn rug naar hem toe voor het raam stond, || zich omkeert, van het buroblad 'n briefopener pakt, die met z'n adem bewasemt en dan aan z'n blauwe trui blinkend veegt'
32. 'de beslagen spiegel   de krullende fotoos   de grijze sintels'
33. 'de zwellendeglazen vandebril — de be wegen   de deur klink'
34. 'Op 'n andere plaats is nog vaag 'n rechthoekige vorm achtergebleven [...] of misschien lijkt dat enkel maar zo'.
35. ''n vernietigend wapen'

36. 'klein en spits met haartjes'
37. "n soort pluim'
38. 'maar dat komt ervan als je 't woord pluimpje in de mond neemt voor mij betekent het 'n pluimpje in 'n windbuks op de kermis of op zolder maar voor iemand anders betekent het gewoon pluimpjezondermeer de slechtste uitleg zo gebeurt het'
39. 'hoe verdwijnt 'n mug wat is dus sterker dan 'n mug'
40. 'ik zou zeggen 'n mus één letter verschil maar meteen is ook de hele mug weg'
41. 'maar ja zul je zeggen je hebt ook nog handdoeken waarmee je zoon beest kapot kunt krijgen vliegenmeppers al zijn die offisieel niet voor muggen bedoeld"
42. 'als ik nu papier en balpen bij me had zou ik op kunnen schrijven wat er is nu dwz zojuist dwz al 'n minuut geleden enzovoort wie ik ben hoe ik voelde of ik iets voelde wat ik was of ik wat was op 'n bepaald moment nee op 'n willekeurig ogenblik bijvoorbeeld nu met mij als archimedies punt ik zeg in dat geval schrijf ik *punt* en bedoel *ik* en probeer zo nauwgezet mogelijk aan te geven welk tijdstip het is [...] ik zie het al een hand is niet genoeg ik zou met twee handen tegelijk moeten schrijven met de ene pen schrijven waar ik ben en wie ongeveer hier en nu met de andere pen schrijven dat ik zittend op het zolderluik of bij de kier bezig was te schrijven waar ik zat'
43. 'daarmee is het begonnen van m'n vragen hebben ze antwoorden gemaakt'
44. 'als ik van kleinsafaan m'n bek had gehouden ochnee m'n eerste schreew hebben ze als ja uitgelegd toen kon ik al niet meer terug'
45. 'doorvoed respektabel van gelijke gezindte horend bij een van de twee voorgevormde geslachten zonder destruktieve aspiraties bereid om te blijven ademen en belasting te betalen'
46. 'aanpassing laat niets te wensen over aan grammatika en richtingsgevoel en koopkracht en wellevendheid en lustgevoel en geschiedenis en tijdsindeling'
47. 'gehoorneuspikknieschijvengevrichten mankeert niets bij ons weten u kunt doorlopen bent u al gedesinfekteerd hebt u al uw pijnstillers ingenomen ogot'
48. 'geslagen werd gebouwen binnengesleurd gedwongen werd [...] formulieren te tekenen [...] gedwongen m'n bek open te doen en m'n tanden te laten zien gedwongen m'n moedertaal af te leren gedwongen me volwassen te gedragen'
49. 'voortdurend tippelde ik weer in de val in handen van uniformen en ambtenaars'
50. 'dat het op alle mogelijke manieren dicht is niet alleen van buiten maar ook inwendig'
51. 'kom in m'n ton vroeg ik in de wat vroeg zij in de not zei ik daarom nog eens'
52. 'ik ben eenvoudigweg van de ene kring in de andere gestapt misschien is het al wel de zevende'
53. "n mens blijft alleen in leven als hij in beweging blijft', 'als je gaat lopen weet je altijd al vantevoren dat je weer terugkomt'
54. 'op m'n gat te gaan zitten en na te gaan waar ik niet allemaal geweest zou kunnen zijn'
55. 'mijn stotende pik in haar gescheurde buikje'
56. 'de ransige lippen tussen m'n benen'
57. 'ik durf niet eens toe te zien hoe het is nu ik er niet meer ben terwijl iedereen er altijd van droomt na afloop te kunnen zien hoe en af je gemist wordt'
58. '[...] so sitze ich jetzt da und schreibe, wundere mich was für sonderbare änderungen mit mir passiert sind in den letzten paar jahren seit den ersten zeilen, von denen ich kein wort mehr verstehe'
59. 'sätze als schätzungen, eine norm bildend von der du dich unterscheiden kannst. [...] das therapeutische versagen der psychoanalyse lag darin, dass das 'bewusstmachen' nur aus der anwendung eines idioms besteht; die sprache blieb ihnen unbekannt, sie sahen nicht einmal, dass die theorien höchstselber nur sprechgewohnheiten sind, ich sage das wohlwollend. und als die psychoanalyse, klarerweise, politik zu werden strebte, ich meine, offizielle politik, war der impetus daher schmalbrüstig — und ausserdem der ansatz hoffnungslos veraltet'
60. 'noch einmal und immer wieder: es ist die sprache das wirkliche, das reale, das einzige, das greifbare, das vorhandene, der masstab ist die kommunikation'
61. 'diesem unentwirrbaren knäuel von sprache, staat und wirklichkeit'
62. 'wir andern aber ergänzen schallend: die worte mitsamt ihrem gebrauch sind untrennbar mit politischer und sozialer organisation verbunden, sind diese organisation, sind jenes a priori über

dessen existenz die blödmänner ihre nerven verbraucht haben, sind eigentlich nur dazu da, damit die dümmeren leute an die wirklichkeit glauben wie früher an das jenseits, wie an das jenseits damit die dümmeren leute ordentlich arbeiten, damit sie einander ähnlicher werden und braver [...]'

63. 'nicht selten findet man von modernen linguisten ausgesprochen, es sei das ideal ihrer wissenschaft, ein teilgebiet der behavioristischen psychologie zu werden. wie nahe sie an dieses ziel herangearbeitet worden, bleibe unentschieden; sicherlich aber ist sie schon lange, im einklang mit den positivistischen verzicht auf den begriff des bewusstseins als forschungsgegenstand, mit der grundhaltung des behaviorismus der sprache gegenüber konform: behavioristische psychologie und moderne linguistik sehen den wirkungsbereich der sprache als sehr eng abgesteckt, sie selber als funktionskomplex unter anderen sozialen auch. [...] sicherlich entstehen diese schwierigkeiten durch die konfrontation der unrevidierten sense-data-prinzipien mit einer sprachauffassung, welche der sprache jeden einfluss auf die 'wahrnehmung' abspricht, und jede überlegung verpönt, ob nicht vielleicht eine anzahl von forschungen auf den sektoren der sinnesphysiologie und des nervensystems am ende blossen sprachgebilden gelte, denen, die doch nur im bezug auf die wissenschaftliche auseinandersetzung scheinbar leben, auf der seite der verifizierung nichts entspricht [...]. wenn sprache kein system der wirklichkeitsabbildung ist (vielleicht genügt schon die festsetzung: keine ausser der eigenen), so ist sie ein geschlossenes system von naturerscheinungen, welches ohne hilfswissenschaften, jedenfalls aber ohne ontologie studiert wird'.

64. 'erst eine sprachwissenschaft, welche die wirklichkeit ausgemerzt haben wird, kann eine behavioristische psychologie wirklich ermöglichen — nicht aber eine, die sich um diese klare entscheidung drückt. [...]denn paradoxer weise ermöglicht erst die sprache ohne wirklichkeitsbezug objektivität; und der aufs äusserste getriebene realismus des studiums wird zum reinen solipsismus. zugegeben, diese zweideutigkeit des behaviorismus hat ihre kritiker schon gefunden; diese suchen jedoch ansatzpunkte, welche die meinen nicht sein können; mit den philosophen des sinns mag ich mich nicht solidarisch erklären: für allzuviele ist die methodik einer philosophie, welche einzig am verhalten von objekten interessiert ist, darin so weit geht, den beobachter, oder vielmehr wichtige eigenschaften des beobachters, aus der beobachtung theoretisch zu eliminieren, und die, auf ein vergleichsweise dürftiges vokabular beschränkt, formale entsprechungen so ungestüm verfolgt, dass reiz und reaktion sogar zur erklärung der teleologie dienen müssen, unbehaglich. aber auch für mich ist eine kritik des behaviorismus wichtig — sie muss jedoch von der anderen seite kommen. dieser ganze essay ist ihr gewidmet. [...] eine ablehnung des ganzen pakets (grösstenteils tara) muss immer neu mit der betrachtung der sprache beginnen, der sprache und der verschiedenen attitüden ihr gegenüber. und da ich, wie mir eben auffällt, nun selber in einen akademischen ton zu verfallen beginne, bitte ich den leser, selbst zu bemerken, dass zur entfaltung des behaviorismus '"östliche" und "westliche" philosophenschaftler gleicherweise beigetragen haben, dass in ost und west der behaviorismus als einzig mögliche und einzig richtige soziologische und psychologische methode angesehen wird [...],dass weiters die kybernetik als erfüllung des behaviorismus im osten wie im westen mit gleicher gier vorangetrieben wird (für den marxismus vielleicht, uneingestandenermassen, als ausweg aus der "grundfrage der philosophie"?), dass [...] die sprachtheorie des behaviorismus) (weil sie dogmatisch die sprachforschung als zweig der psychologie, und nicht, wie es selbstverständlich erscheint, die psychologie als zweig der sprachforschung betreibt) wie jene des marxismus) (weil sie dogmatisch die sprache als bestandteil der wirklichkeit, denn als wiederspiegelung ist sie das, und nicht die wirklichkeit als insinuation der sprache betrachtet: die wirklichkeit als 'wiederspiegelung' der sprache) die kümmerlichsten ergebnisse zeitigt [...].'

65. 'trivialerweise zeigt sich die sprache als norm deshalb vor allem in den entschliessungen der gesellschaft, in der soziologie und im recht (der marxismus geht ja auch so weit, das bewusstsein als beruhend auf den gesellschaftlichen beziehungen der menschen zu betrachten, und das heisst doch die sprache zur norm machen!). der sprachgebrauch hat jene höchst merkwürdige eigenschaft, die laing im auge gehabt haben muss, als er schrieb, unsere zivilisation unterdrücke jede art der transzendenz: er ist ein schutzwall vor den anfechtungen der empfindung; die sprache geht sozusagen mitten durch uns hindurch, der wirklichkeit unseres bewusstseins enge

gassen vorschreibend, als nämlichkeit identität erzeugend, die vielleicht mögliche erfahrung verhindernd. wer also seine sprache nicht als letzte richtschnur gelten lässt, begibt sich in zweifache gefahr: er verliert sich selbst in den landschaften des bewusstseins, die zu betreten ihm jedes rüstzeug fehlt; [...] von der seite des staats sieht das freilich aus wie ein einziges ding — wer mit der von der sprache umrissenen wirklichkeit nicht auskommt, stellt sich dadurch gegen die gesellschaft und wird konfiniert.'

66. 'die sprache wird gemeinhin als gesellschaftliches bewusstsein, ja als gedächtnis der menschheit bezeichnet. diesen kalauer einmal wörtlich genommen: ein aufstand gegen die sprache ist ein aufstand gegen die gesellschaft'

67. 'jemand veröffentlicht, definition sei die gebrauchsanweisung von wörtern (wiener? wittgenstein?)'

68. 'und wenn da einer sagt, die bedeutung eines worts sei sein gebrauch in der sprache, so ist das lieb von ihm, und sicherlich auch gut gemeint!'

69. 'die worte gebrauchen. versteh kein wort. " worte gebrauchen" ist mies. nach dem essen sollst du rauchen, oder eine wort gebrauchen: spass muss sein. habt ihrs gemerkt?'

70. ' "Was sich in der Sprache ausdrückt, können wir nicht durch sie ausdrücken", sagt Der Dunkle in seinen postsokratischen fragmenten. — drückt sich was in der sprache aus? vielleicht gar "die Struktur der Wirklichkeit"? kennt sich einer aus?'

71. 'begreifen von Sprache schien ein neuer königsweg zum begreifen des naturganzen. [...] ich selber jedenfalls wollte schriftsteller werden [...], weil Sprache die nabe aller einsicht und allen umgangs schien'

72. 'Bereits wenig später jedoch habe er "Sprache als einen teil der außenwelt wahr[genommen], auf dessen eigengesetzlichkeit man seine 'inhalte' projizieren muß".'

73. 'Was für die Taktik zu befürchten war, ist weitgehend schon eingetroffen, in den Versuchen, eine 'neue' Sinnhaftigkeit zu mobilisieren, überlebt der alte Sinn. Dieselben Sätze, Ausdrücke und Stile, die wir provisorisch benutzt haben, um einen Aufbruch zu beschreiben, bezeichnen nun wieder das, dessen Überwindung sie einleiten helfen haben sollen, das Werkzeug ist abgeglitten.'

74. 'dem inhaltlichen Gesichtspunkt als dem individualistischen eine argumentierbare Theorie zu verschaffen'

75. ' "welche ja immer mehr zu theorien von zeigerausschlägen" ' werden'

76. 'So betrachtet könnte Wieners politische Intention als der Versuch gesehen werden, Kunst, die in der "Enklave der politisch Besiegten" ' eine "Artikulationsnische" (Norbert Elias) ist, zu transzendieren. Durch Abschaffung von Sprache und Zivilisation könne sich der Einzelne ins Naturrecht des Stärkeren setzen, und das "Gewaltmonopol des Staates" soll "wieder zurückkehren in die Hände der zur Gewalt wirklich begabten Individuen".'

77. 'und wie schön ist erst die welt, wenn jeder seine dreckschleuder dem spucken aufhebt; wenn da der feind steht und ich muss ihn nicht beschreiben und nicht hassen sondern töten oder anders getötet werden. und der feind will meine frau vögeln oder mein fleisch fressen oder einfach meine knochen brechen und nichts weiter, jedenfalls nicht einen eindruck machen. | in solchen sachen sind wir jung und kräftig und stossen zu und töten ohne applaus. und deine sprache kann mir nicht den krebs erregen ich werde sterben weil ich schlicht und ohne zorn getötet werde weil ich im weg stehe und weil ich nahrhaft bin.'

78. 'die eroberung des obszönen als eines gebietes erlaubten ausdruckverhaltens [...] kunst, die sich "gegen jede einschränkung der kognitivität wendet, [wendet sich] gegen den staat" '

79. 'Als Zentrum der Einschränkung machten wir die Sprache aus (Whorf), und die auf sie zurückgehenden (wie anzunehmen war) gesellschaftlichen Institutionen. Die Bahn kurvt zurück in die Politik; der Sprachhoheit der Gesellschaft muß man die eigene Produktion entgegensetzen, aber auch ihr darf man nicht auf den Leim gehen. Von diesem Standpunkt aus [...] werden progressive Konservative das "politisch Korrekte" definieren.'

80. 'Eine *Struktur* einer Zeichenkette ist eine Turing-Maschine, welche die Zeichenkette erzeugt oder akzeptiert.'

CHAPTER 5

❖

From the Document to the Sublime, There Is Only One Step: Boxing with Armando and Alexander Kluge

Jaap Grave (Westfälische Wilhelms-Universität Münster) &
Gunther Martens (Ghent University)

This is a confrontation of the two multifaceted artists Armando and Alexander Kluge, both of whom are prominent figures in post-war culture. In four consecutive rounds, we detail the background, the poetology, the reception, as well as the literary practice of both 'interview authors' in terms of a boxing match.

We begin by describing Armando's position in Dutch and European artistic movements and in the literary neo-avant-garde. Then the notion of the sublime and its preference for the fragmentary are linked to early Romanticism, and we indicate similarities between Armando's poetics and the ideas of Carl Schmitt. Finally, the work that Armando published with Hans Sleutelaar, *The SS Men* (1967, *De SS'ers*), is considered in the context of the 1960s. In a second match, similar questions will be asked of Kluge's work, with a special focus on his literary work published during the 1960s. We situate texts such as *Case Histories* (*Lebensläufe*) and *The Battle* (*Schlachtbeschreibung*) in the context of attempts to confront Germany with its recent past. Kluge's relationship to the avant-garde is profiled through his programmatic contribution to the development of New German Cinema.

In conclusion, we provide a brief overview of the reception of both authors' work and the way in which critics evaluate their oeuvre. Both authors partake in the neo-realist and documentary trends of the 1960's, but increasingly transcend this paradigm in keeping with their diverging ideological tenets.

1. Round One: Background

Armando

Armando is the pseudonym of Herman Dirk van Dodeweerd. Armando was born on 18 September 1929 in Amsterdam and died on 1 July 2018 in Potsdam. He studied art history in the city of his birth before developing into a multifaceted artist: apart from writing poetry and prose, he played the violin as well as drawing, painting, and sculpting. He worked as a journalist and actor, and also made documentaries.[1] Between 1950 and 1970, he was directly involved in the developments in Dutch art and literature, and was part of the international artistic network ZERO.[2] From 1979 until 2010, he lived in Berlin and Potsdam, and most of his work was translated into English between 1984 and 1996 and into German between 1987 and 2005.[3] In the English- and German-speaking world, he is most famous as an artist, and only to a far lesser extent as a writer.

As a visual artist, Armando worked in the Cobra style for a short while until he set up the Hollandse Informele Groep in 1958 (a catch-all term for art without recognisable representation). Among the group's members were also Kees van Bohemen, Jan Hendrikse, Henk Peeters, and Jan Schoonhoven. In 1960, Armando was one of the founders of the Nul-Groep, whose members distanced themselves from expressive painting.[4] The group forms part of the international ZERO movement (nul = 0 = zero). ZERO, an 'international network that existed from 1957 to 1967', was created at the instigation of Heinz Mack and Otto Piene in Düsseldorf. In the catalogue for the exhibition in New York, Berlin, and Amsterdam it is described as 'a nucleus of critical and experimental art in post-war Europe' (Pörschmann and Schavemaker 2015: 15). ZERO included 'heterogeneous artists, who often not only belonged to different generations, but were also affiliated with other movements as well (e.g. Nouveau Réalisme, Azimuth, New Tendencies, Fluxus)' (Pörschmann and Schavemaker 2015: 14). International support is important for the position and status of artists from a relatively small country such as the Netherlands, and these are reinforced if the artists also participate actively in an international network such as ZERO. Exhibitions by artists who were members of ZERO, hailing from the Federal Republic of Germany and the Dutch-speaking world, but also from France, Italy, Japan, South America, and Switzerland, were documented between 1959 and 1965 in the Netherlands and Belgium (Amsterdam, Antwerp, Brussels, The Hague, and Ghent) with further exhibitions in New York, Milan, Bern, and various German cities. As was so often the case after 1945, the names ZERO and Nul refer to a new beginning: 'ZERO consciously distanced itself from the most recent strategies of dealing with the past. It wanted to begin aesthetically and idealistically at point "zero", adopting an optimistic and idealistic attitude to promote change in the direction of a new aesthetic sensitization' ('ZERO' 2018).[5] The question at stake then is to what extent this also applies to Armando's strategy and poetics.

Armando made his debut as a poet in 1954, in the journal *Podium*. He subsequently published work in the Flemish-Dutch journal *Gard Sivik*, which he also edited in 1959. Aside from this, he became the arts editor of the weekly newspaper *Haagse Post* in 1958, where he continued to work until the end of the 1960s. Along with Peeters and Sleutelaar, he also formed the editorial team of the journal *De Nieuwe Stijl* (1965–1966), which the editors considered to be 'international avant-garde'. Armando's influence on art and literature in the Netherlands was rather significant between the years of 1954 and 1966 due to his activities: as an editor of the *Haagse*

Post he was in a position to exercise influence on the selection and reception of artistic and literary works.

This also raises the question of how far the double-talented writer Armando was influenced in his choices and preferences by his other artistic discipline. According to Hans Sleutelaar (poet, journalist, and co-author of *The SS Men*) the relationship between the artistic movements Cobra and the Hollandse Informele Groep is comparable with that between the literary movements De Vijftigers and *De Nieuwe Stijl*. Sleutelaar claims that *De Nieuwe Stijl* and Nul had a decidedly positive attitude to society, unlike De Vijftigers, which was critical of social developments.[6] The same claim also emerges from Armando's recollections:

> Well, what was our ideology? To begin with it was about opposition to De Vijftigers. When I, as an older man, look back on it: a desperate attempt to *embrace* consumer society. When I look back on it: it really was desperate. Our aim was for an urban hardness (as in: just bring it all on), an amoral stance: everything is good, build a wall, don't show disgust. I was hard too at that time. Not a nice person. (Meijer 2003: 161, emphasis in original)[7]

In Armando's opinion, De Vijftigers paid too much attention to the irrational, and 'logical or grammatical links were viewed as inertia' (Bril 1989).[8]

As for their artistic premises, for the Nul artists anything could be art, with coincidence playing a major role in their work. Anja de Feijter concludes, summarizing an article by Frank Gribling, that the development from Informeel to Nul is a move 'in the direction of greater anonymity or objectivity' (2008: 164).[9] Although ZERO was a very heterogeneous group,[10] there was nonetheless significant common ground shared by all the artists, which had to do with 'a reduction, concentration, and innovation of artistic styles', with which the artists distanced themselves from the Abstract Expressionists and Informal Painting.[11] The concepts of reduction, concentration and innovation of artistic styles can also be used to describe innovations in the literary movements of the time.

It is worth taking another, closer look at the rifts in art and literature, in which Armando was actively involved. In art, this means Cobra and the Informele Groep, in literature the two experimental journals *Gard Sivik* — with its Flemish and Dutch editors — and *De Nieuwe Stijl*, which had no editors from Flanders.

Informal art was initially a synonym for 'lyrical abstraction': a 'spontaneous, non-representative current in painting that took paint as a material as its starting point' (quoted in De Feijter 2008: 164).[12] Whereas Cobra stuck to representation and the artists valued spontaneity and expression (the term 'gestural painting' was used in 1960), this played an ever-smaller role among the artists of the Informele Groep, for whom coincidence became more important, referring to greater anonymity and objectivity (De Feijter 2008: 164).[13] A key word to characterize the art of the Informals, besides non-representative and formless, is *artless* (Armando: 'an art that is no longer an art', 'Credo I', Armando 1958–1959: 810). A point of dispute was the question whether the work could be anonymous, and whether neutrality was possible, which Schoonhoven and Armando imply is impossible. As Armando explains: 'Of course it depends on what you choose' (quoted in De Feijter 2008:

166),[14] and Armando's choice was always that of violence and aggression (see Brems 2006: 234). Armando later voiced the opinion that a large proportion of Nul art is based on 'journalistic principles' (quoted in De Feijter 2008: 167).[15] He states:

> After a while I wasn't excited enough about making Nul works. One cause of that was that I had so little personal contribution to make. I could have had the paintings made for me, as it were. [...] I left after the second Nul exhibition in the Stedelijk Museum in 1965. [...] [F]or me the facts were exhausted. (quoted in De Feijter 2008: 167)[16]

As will become clear in this chapter, the basic principles that the artist Armando applied at this time show major similarities with the premises he used to compile *The SS Men*.

Alexander Kluge

Alexander Kluge was born on 14 February 1932 as the son of a doctor in Halberstadt. After his parents' divorce, Kluge went to live with his mother in Berlin. He studied law, history and church music at the universities of Marburg, Freiburg, and Frankfurt am Main. He obtained a Ph.D. in law in 1956. Kluge did his training as a legal counsellor to the Frankfurt *Institut für Sozialforschung* [Institute for Social Research], where he befriended Theodor W. Adorno.

In the 1960s, Kluge gained fame mainly as a film director. His first short film *Brutality in Stone* (1960) was presented at the Oberhausen film festival. In 1963 he founded his own film production company 'Kairos-Film'. His essay films *Yesterday Girl* (1996, *Abschied von gestern*) and *Artists under the Big Top: Perplexed* (1968, *Die Artisten in der Zirkuskuppel: ratlos*) won awards at the Venice film festival and established his fame in the world of arthouse cinema. Already *Brutality in Stone* reveals (experimental) documentary as the basso continuo of Kluge's oeuvre, as it is a kind of mock-version of the ill-famed *Wochenschau*, Hitler's format of televised news-journals (shown in cinema). In Kluge and Schamoni's short film, the monumental and sublime architecture of the infamous *Parteigelände* [the Nazi party rally grounds] in Nuremberg is undercut by a soundtrack veering in many directions.

In 1962, Kluge co-initiated (with Edgar Reitz and Peter Schamoni) and acted as spokesperson of the Oberhausen Manifesto, which famously declared 'daddy's cinema' to be dead. The manifesto opposed the escapist tendencies of mainstream movie production, which had become apolitical and ahistorical after World War II. But at a deeper level, the Oberhausen manifesto also targeted underlying funding structures that stifled innovation. New German Cinema gained renown because some of the young directors involved went on to earn critical acclaim at film festivals abroad (Schlöndorff in France, Kluge in Venice). The location, Oberhausen, was tied to the local Short Film Festival, but it also echoed the harsh realities of the industrial production of the *Ruhrgebiet*. Oberhausen was the birthplace of a neo-realist independent German cinema modelled on the aesthetic principles of the French *Nouvelle Vague*: filming without a script; documentary orientation;

personal choice of then-unknown, recurring actors; anti-illusionism. Another moniker for this trend is post-Brechtian cinema. Together with Edgar Reitz, Kluge taught at the Ulm *Hochschule für Gestaltung Ulm*. Funded partially with money from *the Geschwister Scholl-Stiftung* (the legal heirs to the Munich-based resistance group *Weiße Rose*, one of the few attempts to destabilize Hitler), the *Hochschule für Gestaltung Ulm* aimed at a progressive pedagogical project. There is some debate as to how the Oberhausen signatories' stance relates to their actual film production and what films fulfil best the promise of a new cinema (see Eue 2012; Eue and Gass 2012; Schubert and Maus 2012; Eue et al. 2016). Of course, the later falling-apart of the Oberhausen group is only one version of the perennially contested identity of the movement of contestation itself. It is useful to point out that Kluge himself has acted as a key player in shaping the shifting collective memory of this revolution in cinema, by providing eyewitness accounts (and iconic images). It is safe to say that Alexander Kluge was at the heart of a revolutionary movement, pushing for the renewal of German cinema in the 1960s and beyond. Given Kluge's academic background and theoretical ambitions, some have situated Kluge not at the heart, but rather at the head of New German Cinema.[17]

Although every avant-garde manifesto claims to make *tabula rasa* in order to instigate the new, there are a number of decisive influences that anticipate the spirit of the Oberhausener Manifesto. In autobiographical accounts, Kluge singles out quite a number of artistic tendencies, to wit: the journal *Filmkritik*, and the BRD *Nachtstudio* manned by Helmut Heißenbüttel and Alfred Andersch. In music, the 1960s saw the rise of experimental music as embodied by the *Kranichsteiner Kammerensemble*, the Siemens studio (Martini, Reitz), Karlheinz Stockhausen, as well as the Italian composer and conductor Bruno Maderna (1920–1973). At the time, these composers were young Turks at the helm of an avant-garde that was to transform post-war music and conduction practices. The Darmstadt School is associated with Luciano Berio, Pierre Boulez, Luigi Nono, and Karlheinz Stockhausen. The Oberhausener shared with them the gesture of openly confronting the powerful continuity of anti-modernism, epitomized in the towering figure of Herbert von Karajan. Alexander Kluge is similar to these avant-garde musicians in that he started out from pedagogy and that he went through the institutions (of education and of broadcasting) rather than delegitimizing them. These references will leave their traces, not only on Kluge's own soundtracks (e.g. the experimental composer Helmut Lachenmann's music opening Kluge's 2008 *News from Ideological Antiquity: Marx — Eisenstein — Das Kapital*). In fact, the *Hochschule für Gestaltung Ulm* bought and housed the original Siemens studio in the 1960s. Mostly, the wish to start anew translates in a defiant, confrontational habitus and in Kluge's approach towards 'exploding' (Boulez) literature, the artistic canon, and its conventional genre borders.

Kluge published his first volume of prose texts *Case Histories* in 1962, and his book *The Battle* appeared in 1964. It is important to note that Kluge's literary work has always closely interacted with his work in other media. In fact, the books that he published in the 1960s were mainly companions to his essay films. Kluge is wildly unorthodox in his conviction that the visual cannot subsist without the support of the textual and vice versa. In hindsight, Kluge's literary work of the 1960s is somewhat atypical of his later work in the sense that it does not yet feature the explicit intermediality that rose to the surface with the publication of *New Histories* (1977, *Neue Geschichten*) and that has grown into the hallmark of his writing. In the following section, we will explore how and to what extent both artists' background and creative multi-talent has left traces in their poetics.

2. Round Two: Poetology

Armando

The content and strategy of the Nul-Groep in particular, and the journals *Gard Sivik* (1955–1964) and *De Nieuwe Stijl* (1965–1966), all belonging to the neo-avant-garde, are related to that of the historical avant-garde: all three of them are active across borders and critical of other, competing movements. In his 1959 manifesto 'Credo 1', Armando contends e.g. that the innovation they claim to initiate is an international phenomenon and that they are in conflict with De Vijftigers (quoted in De Feijter 2008: 176). They also aim for a radical renewal of the arts, experiment with materials, forms, techniques and principles (such as ready-mades), as well as publish manifestos in which the use of military imagery is striking (see Van den Berg and Dorleijn 2002: 6). This is about more than just making new art; it is also a matter of extending their power by eliminating opponents and establishing positions by means of provocation and polemics. Armando played a leading role in this, in accordance with his pseudonym, which means 'arming oneself' (Beekman 2010: 1). In his 1964 text 'An international novelty' ('Een internationale primeur'), Armando discusses his poetics, using important key words such as reality (he pointedly uses a capital letter) and authenticity, and refers to other media:

> Not moralising or interpreting (artifying) Reality, but intensifying it. Starting point: a consistent acceptance of Reality. Interest in a more autonomous manifestation of Reality, which can already be seen in journalism, TV reports and film. Working method: isolating, annexing. In other words: authenticity. Not on the part of the maker, but that of the information. The artist, who is no longer an artist: a cool, objective eye. (Armando 1964: n.p.)[18]

What Armando calls 'Working method' shows similarities with his views as a Nul artist.

De Nieuwe Stijl also includes manifestos by foreign artists (Günther Uecker, Mack, Piero Manzoni, Lucio Fontana), with the aim of emphatically legitimising the literary and artistic positions of the Dutch artists. Reality must become art, a view that recurs in many contributions: those of the Dutch artists (Schoonhoven), Mack and Fontana (in *Das weiße Manifest*). For Armando, reality as a 'ready-made', as a quotation, becomes poetry, and as an interview, it becomes prose, as it does in *The SS Men*. Most Nul art, in Armando's view, is based on journalistic principles, which time and again leads to the question whether art is still art and documentary literature or literary reports are still literature, whether the artist is no longer an artist or, conversely, to quote Joseph Beuys, whether everyone is an artist. There are not only areas of overlap with Beuys's view here, but also significant parallels between Armando's art and that of Beuys's student Anselm Kiefer, who also constantly refers to German history in his work. In retrospect, Armando assesses himself in the years of *De Nieuwe Stijl*:

> Yes, we were a group — shock troops who deliberately blinkered their vision and in that way made history. I was strict, a fanatic. I stood in the thick of life, and I am still curious about everything. *De Vijftigers*, what a bunch of bohemians they were, which meant that a great deal of reality escaped them, a large amount of richness. (Meijer 2003: 162)[19]

The SS Men was considered the climax and concluding act of *Nieuwe Stijl* poetics. After that, Armando was to change tack, although his fascination for the motifs of violence and war remained: in earlier work such as 'Boxers' (1962, 'boksers') and later collections such as *From Berlin* (1982), in which he records German war memories, or *Notes About the Enemy* (1981, *Aantekeningen over de vijand*) and *The Street and the Shrubbery* (1988). He explains his fascination with states of war as follows: 'I love "Ausnahmesituationen" [exceptional situations] and boxing is one such situation, as is war', and he compares boxing to art: 'violence, subdued by rules, restrained violence. What else remains than to stylize, to aestheticize, to excuse violence' (1983: 34).[20] As we have already seen, Armando is concerned with the intensification of reality and with authenticity, and he believes that in situations such as states of war, people show their true selves.

On the basis of this perspective, we would like to develop two points: we would like to make it clear that the way in which Armando uses concepts such as authenticity, and the opposition between friend and foe and 'frapper le bourgeois' has similarities with views that Carl Schmitt developed in *The Concept of the Political* (1927, *Der Begriff des Politischen*), which we will use as a critical touchstone in order to clarify the development (or the lack thereof) in the works of both Armando and Kluge. Carl Schmitt was a legal theorist and a towering protagonist of the Conservative Revolution, well-known for his critique of liberalism and of modern understandings of statehood. He joined the National-Socialist Movement and became its prime legal thinker. After the war, he retained influence over various journalists and high school teachers. He was a Catholic and a nationalist. His influence on left-Heidegerrians like Nancy, Lefort, Badiou, Laclau and others like Giorgio Agamben cannot be overestimated. According to Helmut Lethen, Schmitt's *Concept* in particular is to be analysed 'as a cultural-historical event'; Lethen connects Schmitt's ideas with 'avant-garde tendencies' (2000: 136).[21] We are not concerned with demonstrating that Armando has studied Schmitt, but that Schmitt's views clarify Armando's worldview, whereas for Kluge, they represent a position that needs to be overcome. The second point is the sublime, which will be linked — along with the fragment, a form favoured by Armando — to early German Romanticism (*Frühromantik*), a period to which Armando regularly refers.

According to Schmitt's *Concept*, human beings only encounter authenticity in danger zones and people only gain an identity if they find something for which they are prepared to fight and die (Lethen 2000: 128–46). Schmitt argues that in liberal society, the world of the inauthentic, the capacity for seriousness has been lost. The opposite to a liberal society is a society based on motifs from myths, and Armando often links authenticity to myths in his work: to basic elements of human existence (birth and death), anonymous characters (the enemy, the perpetrator and the victim, who can switch roles and embody actions); elsewhere the basis of Armando's stories is an existing myth, through which actions such as wars, like natural phenomena, become events over which human beings have no influence. For Schmitt, the natural state of aggression, unlike for Thomas Hobbes, is a permanent phenomenon that is not suppressed by the state and cannot be softened by the civilization process. Schmitt is not alone in the belief that the 'seriousness of life is the criterion that forms the authentic, and identity is only to be found in the sphere of pain and in the shadow of death': similar views can also be found in 'avant-garde tendencies and literary groups with extreme political views' (Lethen 2000: 137).[22]

The second point relates to the sublime. In *The SS Men*, it is striking that Armando and Sleutelaar mainly pay attention to the experience of Dutch members of the SS in exceptional situations, wartime, combat operations or horrific experiences, and Armando also states in later interviews that he believes it is precisely then that people's true nature becomes visible, a pessimistic conviction that is fruitful for artistic purposes but controversial from various philosophical perspectives. Lethen rightly asks why 'Lebensernst' [seriousness in life] and authenticity are frequently linked to extreme situations, war, and dictatorship (2000: 145).[23]

The descriptions of these extreme situations can be considered to present sublime experiences. These are confrontations with things that are overwhelming (impressive, dangerous or horrific), and not just in witnessing natural phenomena such as mountains or waterfalls (examples that Immanuel Kant gives), but, because the content of these experiences is not static, also in extreme situations in wartime. In *The Critique of Judgment* (1790, *Die Kritik der Urteilskraft*), Kant describes the sublime as a gulf between the powers of the imagination and the mind, comparing the experience to falling into the abyss. These feelings release the individual from his or her ties to the civil order, with the result that the sublime isolates the individual. It removes the borders of finitude, the 'I' conceives of this removal as a release and exaltation and discovers within the self a sense of the infinite. Then reason intervenes, and the natural phenomena are rendered innocuous by means of ideas. This phase generates pleasure, because one discovers that one can measure oneself against nature and elevate oneself above it. Humans have two sides: they are gifted with reason and subjected to nature (Kant 1974: 102–05).

In scholarship on Armando, the link between his work and the sublime is rarely made. Joke J. Hermsen is one of the exceptions. In a lecture entitled *On Beauty* (*Over Schoonheid*) that Armando gave in 1987, she claims, he made it clear that 'he is concerned with sneaking horrific, terrifying beauty into the region of art that is beyond good and evil, "resulting in the sublime, the *Erhabene*, as the artistic restraining of the horrendous"' (1999: 338).[24]

Both the content and form of Armando's work can be linked to the sublime. It is clear from interviews, as well as from the content of *The SS Men*, that Armando attaches great significance to the sublime, a theme that was discussed extensively in early German Romanticism. Armando places the aesthetic technique of the collage in opposition to isolation and intensification: 'Collage meant: opposing things to each other. We aimed to use isolation to suddenly intensify pieces of reality' (Meijer 2003: 162).[25] Intensification, concentration on a moment, refers to a sublime experience.

Another point is form, meaning Armando's preference for the fragment and the fragmentary, something he has in common with Kluge, although for Kluge, the fragment is no longer the herald of unspoken totality. The German writer Novalis, an early Romantic, claimed that fragments only have a transitory value and that they are thus eminently suitable as 'seismographs of the present' (Fetscher 2001/2010: 561). To be able to capture the sublime in words, the early German Romantics chose a form that emphasizes the ineffable or that which cannot be represented, namely the incomplete (Fetscher 2001/2010: 560–61).[26] In *The SS Men*, Armando and Sleutelaar indicate that their interest is in sublime experiences among those interviewed. They opt for the fragment rather than the whole by concentrating on merely a few decisive years in the lives of the interviewees. In the fragments from the biographies, transgressions of boundaries and — less often — sublime experiences are highlighted. Moreover, the term fragments — Armando uses the word 'flarden' — returns in his collections *From Berlin* and *Rulers* (*Machthebbers*), in which he quotes German memories of the Second World War.

What is striking is not simply the connection between the fragment and the avant-garde, but also the link to the sublime: the avant-garde aspect of early Romantic fragments, Fetscher claims, 'therefore lies in their deployment as a rapid reaction force' and 'the stylistic ideal of early Romantic fragments was sublime impertinence.' Sublimity: through 'participation in the attributes of the dynamic sublime. They are lighting strikes, agile, fast, energetic, targeting the infinite. As a method of transforming the sublime into art, they opt to accentuate the unrepresentable as incompleteness'. Friedrich Schlegel even believed that 'incompleteness [...] gives the sublime a greater allure' (Fetscher 2001/2010: 561).[27]

Kluge

A decisive moment in the development of Kluge's poetology is the encounter with Adorno and Critical Theory. Kluge befriended Adorno during his time as a legal intern at the *Institut für Sozialforschung* in Frankfurt. Kluge has it that actually Adorno tried to deter him from engaging in artistic activity, both literary and cinematic. The 'ban' on literary production bespeaks Adorno's conviction that, in the wake of a highly selective high-modernist canon of literary works (Proust and Beckett), nothing more remained to be done. Kluge's interest in film, on the other hand, was to be *abgeklärt* [cooled down] by helping him to a position as assistant to Fritz Lang in order to witness the industrial nature of film production. When Kluge published his first films and books, these indeed flouted some of Adorno's strict standards of high-modernist canon. Instead of the indirectness of negativity, the documentary basso continuo of Kluge's art may seem to tackle reality straight-on and somewhat similarly to the political, anti-aesthetic documentary theatre of Peter Weiss, Heinar Kipphardt, and Rolf Hochhuth (which Adorno opposed.)

Kluge is now generally perceived as the narrator of Critical Theory of the Frankfurt School. However, Kluge's documentary poetics goes against the grain of some of the central tenets of Critical Theory. In *The Use and Abuse of Cinema: German Legacies from the Weimar Era to the Present* (2015), Eric Rentschler addresses the legacy of Adorno's thought in Kluge's work, while also pointing out an important difference, stating that 'in his redemptive relationship to mass culture (despite his acute awareness of its regressive potential), Kluge does not share Adorno's dismissive determinism regarding industrialized amusement' (2015: 265). According to Rentschler, Kluge is in this respect 'much closer to Walter Benjamin' than to Adorno. Most importantly, Walter Benjamin credited the new media of his age, photography, radio and a particular type of (documentary) film, as practised by the historical avant-garde (Vertov, Joris Ivens), with emancipatory potential. In fact, Benjamin was more open to popular culture than other representatives of Critical Theory; he was a close friend of Bertolt Brecht, whose *Threepenny Opera* resorted to popular formats like cabaret in order to drive home its message. Benjamin's point of view resonates strongly with Kluge's attempt to establish a proletarian version of Critical Theory's definition of *Öffentlichkeit* [the public sphere], a *Gegenöffentlichkeit* [counter-public sphere]. It is important to note that in the 1950s, Benjamin was not the household name that he is now; in fact, his legacy was salvaged through Adorno's edition of his works in 1955 as well as Kluge's relentless attempts to create art in the spirit of Benjamin and the historical avant-garde.

Kluge's poetological writings mostly concern film. In these writings on film, Kluge has documented his orientation towards the historical avant-garde in more explicit ways. His *Cinema Stories* (*Kinogeschichten*) detail many hidden affiliations to lesser-known representatives of experimental documentary forms during the Weimar era, e.g. the essay film by Hans Richter (1888–1976), a German painter, graphic artist, avant-gardist, film-experimenter, and producer who claimed to have filmed the first abstract film. One could argue that Kluge quarrels with, but ultimately abides by Adorno's principle of negativity: the trauma of the past is shown through indirection. Indeed, it is not uncommon for Kluge's films and stories to pay an extraordinary amount of attention to circumstances and bystanders (e.g. demolition workers in the street, firemen, waiters, waitresses), before central events or actors are brought into focus. This leads up to a process of bricolage that indeed escapes both Adorno and the programmatic New German Cinema (most importantly: its tendency towards melodrama) and to a polymath writing style quite sui generis.

It is useful to mention Kluge's cooperation with the sociologist Oskar Negt and the body of theoretical work that ensued from this cooperation. In 1972, Negt and Kluge published the first part of their philosophical work *Public Sphere and Experience* (*Öffentlichkeit und Erfahrung*). Devin Fore links the open and collaborative structure of the work with that of Deleuze and Guattari's *A Thousand Plateaus* (*Mille plateaux*). With this work, Kluge and Negt formulated a rejoinder to Adorno's and

Habermas' (ultimately pessimistic) take on the structural evolution of *Öffentlichkeit*, against the stalemate of dogmatic Marxist theory in favour of a development in which both theory and artistic practice are attuned to the needs of the proletariat. A lot of importance is allotted to the oral transmission and generation of knowledge and insight, as exemplified in the television interviews with Negt and in the ever-growing body of television work since 1986.

The avant-garde nature of Kluge's filmic and literary work resides in harking back to the historical avant-garde. Some of the techniques that now signal documentary distance were very much part of *cinéma impure* that Kluge does not cease to reference. The most striking aspect of Kluge's artistic production is indeed its heterogeneity. Kluge abides by the standards of *New Objectivity* (*Neue Sachlichkeit*), but also exceeds them by emphasizing the potential and the prime importance of emotions. In the age of the image, Kluge's involvement in television production gives him extensive power for self-fashioning and literary positioning. Just as Armando's *Sufferings of Gentlemen*, Kluge may have jeopardized their literary-artistic credentials by forging an alliance with (commercial) television or other media. Transformative power resides even in popular cultural formats, but this emancipatory potential has to be wrestled free by relentless questioning. In this regard, he is on a par with Armando's uncompromising interview technique at the root of *The SS Men*. At the same time, Kluge sees any dialogue, any interview (in whatever context or medium) as agonistic. In this regard, more work needs to be done on the acoustic dimensions of Kluge's universe. Younger authors like Joachim Bessing, adherents of a more loose type of pop-literature documentary, new journalist writing, attend to the controlling, exhortative nature of Kluge's questioning voice, which they interpret as a sign of the unceasing presence of Kluge as the author. When Kluge sticks to the inaudibility of the authorial voice-over, he signals a willingness to remain in charge of signification[28] (Bessing 2016: n.p.).

While Bessing's account is very sympathetic, others see this critical interview style as meddlesome and domineering. We submit that it is useful to recast these acoustic gestures in terms of boxing, as the involuntary moves of shadowing and foreshadowing that are required to 'touch' reality. The metaphor of boxing as a trope for documentary realism has an impressive legacy: Brecht was very fond of boxing, to the extent that he saw in it a model for the democratization of theatre. Fascination for archaic sports like boxing is also a hallmark of New Objectivity. Likewise, Kluge does not remain passive as an interviewer but rather works toward the truth through anticipation and confrontation.

Whereas Armando by and large seems to have given up on the documentary paradigm altogether in favour of a new theology of art, with the epiphany of violence as its sublime, the post-1960s' Kluge has transcended the documentary avant-garde in a more theoretical direction. Kluge concedes that Walter Benjamin is not just the proponent of a second Enlightenment in Adorno and Horkheimer's vein. In Benjamin's theological thought, he argues, there is a certain proximity to Carl Schmitt and to the esotericism of other thinkers of the Far Right. Benjamin is not just a progressive Marxist critic, as the author pondering configurations and the magic of mimetic language, he also harbours an esoteric streak. This discussion, however, is still absent from Kluge's early literary production. Kluge's work from the 1960s, rather, is motivated by a reading of Benjamin as a materialist open to new media and avant-garde innovations of artistic production. Kluge's programmatic film essays use Benjamin to establish the idea of independent film production as an emancipatory force. Romantic notions such as the fragment as profane absolute and the sublime are ditched in the effort to increase, by way of documentation, the speakability of horrific historical events (rather than to hint at their unspeakability). Since 2000, Kluge's documentary writing has become much more autobiographical and subjective in nature. Although Carl Schmitt is not of much relevance for Kluge, his name figures more prominently in the writings that refer to the esoteric flipside of Frankfurt School (Jewish) thought. Schmitt's political theology, although at odds with the upbeat optimism about enlightenment and art's capacity to bring the truth to light, is shown to be present in the more apocryphal parts of Critical Theory. This does not turn Kluge into an (implicit) adherent of Schmitt like Armando; he uses Schmitt (and similar far-right thinkers) to illustrate that intellectual biographies could have gone in different directions at crucial moments in time.

3. Round Three: Reception

Armando

Many scholars and critics believe that there is a rupture in Armando's work: his work in the period 1951–1963, collected in his *Collected Poems* (1964, *Verzamelde gedichten*), is considered realistic, and his Romantic period is considered to begin with the collection *Heaven and Earth* (1971, *Hemel en aarde*). Others refer to his entire oeuvre as Romantic, citing the following characteristics: his work is said to have a 'mythic nature', paratexts such as book covers with pictures by Albrecht Altdorfer and Caspar David Friedrich, and 'the mottos taken from the works of late Romantics such as Hofmannsthal, Novalis, Hölderlin, Rilke, and George point in that direction, particularly those of Ernst Jünger' (Beekman 1985: 8).[29] Comments by Armando himself also have a great influence on his image as a Romantic: 'I have always been a Romantic in terms of my mentality. The reality I notated was a glacial one, but had to do with the Romantic reality of the *Industrialgesellschaft* [industrial society]' (Meijer 2003: 164).[30]

The question is whether critics refer explicitly to the paratexts in their reviews and to the mythical nature of Armando's work, attempting to describe its Romanticism. In an article on exactly this question, Trudie Favié presents the results of her research into 149 reviews of 20 of Armando's publications from the period 1964–1994. Ten of those publications 'have one or more mottos, the lion's share of which are taken from the Romantics', but although Beekman claims this is reason enough for critics to call Armando's work Romantic, only six of the 149 reviews devote any attention to the mottos. Since there is even less attention for the book covers, Favié (1996: 216) feels 'Beekman overvalues the role that the critics place on mottos and book covers.'[31] Furthermore, critics closely situate Armando's work to writers such as Friedrich Nietzsche, Richard Wagner, Heinrich Heine, and Friedrich Hölderlin — without giving examples from the text (Favié 1996: 217) — , another dominant frame of historical reference being that of Dutch-language writers publishing around the time of World War I, such as Adriaan Roland Holst, and a few German-speaking expressionists (Ernst Toller, August Stramm, Georg Trakl) (Favié 1996: 218).

Critics do pay attention to the use of language in his work: Armando uses formal language alongside colloquial speech, and his work includes ungrammatical constructions and non-Dutch expressions (in many cases German ones). Critics such as J.F. Vogelaar, Kees Fens, and J. Bernlef react negatively to Armando's archaic language, and Vogelaar also criticises 'the mythical conception' of Armando's work: 'the commonplace, as apparently deep as it is actually meaningless, that victim and perpetrator lurk within one person' (quoted in Beekman 1985: 10).[32] The motif of violence often meets with negative reactions and, according to Favié, is associated with Romanticism without further explanation.[33] Louis Ferron, an author in whose work National Socialism plays a major role, is the first to comment on the 'aesthetiziation of evil' in Armando's work (Favié 1996: 222).[34] No references to the sublime can be found in the reviews; Pieter de Nijs does imply the sublime, claiming that Armando feels attracted 'to the immensity' of German Romantic paintings. He describes their concept of nature as 'the timeless and endlessly self-renewing beauty', as 'a treacherous beauty because nature is imperturbable' (Favié 1996: 224).[35]

Critics see 'violence, crime, power' as dominant motifs in Armando's work (Schouten 1986: 201).[36] Schouten is of the opinion that Armando has two aims: opposition to an 'academic, intellectualist approach to society, and the numbing of society itself, or as he tends to call it, 'coca-colazation' (Schouten 1986: 202).[37] To realize these aims, myths form the basis of his poems (the Bible; basic elements such as earth, water, fire, sky), 'characters are abstracted', and he makes use of cycles, also based on seasons or elements, in which characters become types (the enemy, master and servant in *Sufferings of Gentlemen*) and can switch roles (perpetrator and victim); historical events are described from a timeless perspective, thus gaining mythical status, and the places described become metaphors and are anthropomorphised (as in the 'guilty landscape') (Beekman 1985: 56).[38]

If we look at the reviews in response to the publication of *The SS Men*, it is striking that reviews after publication of the first edition were negative. Reviewers at the time found it irresponsible for the authors to publish the words of former members of the SS without commentary, claiming that they thus gained a platform for their National Socialist propaganda. It is striking that only one reviewer (Peter Berger, 1967, in *Het Vaderland*) assigns *The SS Men* to a literary genre. He too is negative: 'It is a novel that is no longer a novel, a non-fiction novel [...] that transforms reality into a myth'; he claims: 'Sleutelaar asks for a total aesthetic in the language of the Nazis: Wollt ihr die totale Poesie? And his response is a total aesthetic of a book that necessarily has to be about Nazis, as the impossible novelistic characters of reality' (Berger, quoted in Bril 1990).[39] According to Schouten, some critics claimed that 'it should not have been allowed to be published, because the writers did not take a position and did not challenge the enemy at all' (Schouten 1986: 201).[40]

Favié notes on the basis of her research that the reviewers read the book as a historical work, 'paying no attention to the aspects of literary history in the text or to use of language or rhetorical elements [...]' (Favié 1996: 215).[41] In his foreword to the sixth edition, Joost de Vries (2012: 9) situates the tone of the criticism in the context of the 1960s and writes that there was great interest in World War II from 1960 onwards: *The Rise and Fall of the Third Reich* by William L. Shirer was a bestseller, Lou de Jong presented the programme *The Occupation* (*De Bezetting*) from 1960 onwards with 'spoken testimonies',[42] but in the episode about Dutch members of the SS and collaborators, their testimonies were not broadcast as direct speech. Reviewers in the 1960s needed a clear-cut distinction between right and wrong, perpetrator and victim.

Alexander Kluge

Critical reception of Alexander Kluge's literary work was not favourable right from the start. In a spontaneous critique of Kluge's reading in front of the Gruppe 47, Günter Grass put down Kluge as a pretentious priest-like know-it-all. Another member of the group, Marcel Reich-Ranicki, was very critical of Kluge's writing style. Because Kluge rendered the border between fact and fiction, he even accused Kluge of being a 'charlatan'. In a very insightful review, Hans Magnus Enzensberger (1978) labelled Kluge as a 'heartless' writer. This clarified Kluge's relationship to New Objectivity, but did little to make him popular with non-academic audiences. A moot point in the reception of his films has been the very specific type of authorship inherent in Kluge's version of *Autorenkino* [author's cinema]. An early review by Peter Handke, a representative of the younger generation of contestation, singles out this experience (this review was never reprinted as part of Handke's edited works):

> They demand that the spectator seeks out connections and thereby restrict his freedom: instead of letting images just be images, they become an image puzzle. Instead of just looking at something and then really seeing it, one is expected to relate images to sentences. (Handke 1969: 32)

It is interesting to look back at these negative reviews because they reveal to what extent Kluge's artistic project ran counter to the norms propagated by the Gruppe 47. Whereas the Gruppe 47 was founded in the name of a firm belief in the possibility to make a fresh start, Kluge meant to show the continuities between the historical and the post-war avant-garde. On the other hand, experimental documentary formats have become so ubiquitous nowadays that it amazes to see so much resistance to them.[43]

In 1986, Kluge won the Kleist prize. Helmut Heißenbüttel's presence on the jury may have helped him to gain recognition for an oeuvre that was at the time still puzzling to many readers. Kluge's place in literary history has become much clearer since W.G. Sebald's favourable review of his writings in 1997. In his widely noted *On the Natural History of destruction* (1997 [1997], *Luftkrieg und Literatur*), Sebald blamed the bulk of post-war German literature (including the Gruppe 47) for having failed to come to terms with the traumatic aftermath of World War II in an aesthetically valid way. Notable exceptions to this (rather wholesale) indictment are, according to Sebald, Alexander Kluge, and Hubert Fichte. In 2003, Kluge's literary work was honoured with the Büchner prize, the most important literary award to be earned in the German context.

Kluge's work is sui generis. One could perhaps compare him to Arno Schmidt, because of his encyclopaedic tendencies and their preoccupation with German history (however, for a shift in Kluge's scope, see Martens 2014); and beyond this, Thomas Pynchon comes to mind (for the close alliance between literature and science). Similar polymath and genre-crossing tendencies are to be found in the non-fictional works of Friedrich Kittler and Peter Sloterdijk. Interpreters have drawn on practices and traditions that predate the modernism-avant-garde divide and likened Kluge's work to early modern collection practices (*historia litteraria*), encyclopaedism, the combination of which may turn his work into a prime specimen of overdetermined postmodern intertextuality. The filmmakers of the *Neue Berliner Schule* [New Berlin School] (Christian Petzold, Thomas Arslan) sometimes refer to his aesthetics, as well as neo-documentary authors such as Kathrin Röggla.

In Dutch literature, Kluge tallies with Armando in terms of their shared multimedial production and their preoccupation with the aesthetic of violence. In view of counterfactual scenarios and the usage of analogies, also Louis Ferron comes to mind as a feasible sparring-partner, although Kluge does not write novels.

As one of the leading figures of New German Cinema, Kluge has been the object of intensive attention in studies of neo-avant-garde film. Scholarly interest in his literary work has never been as strong, but has been steadily on the rise since at least 1978. Kluge's rise to wider prominence as a literary author actually dates to the late 1990s through Sebald's aforementioned treatise and its declaration of debt to Kluge's documentary writing style. From this retrospective angle, it has become easier to articulate Kluge's proximity to other neo-avant-garde literary authors such as Arno Schmidt, Rolf Dieter Brinkmann, and Helmut Heißenbüttel, and his being a precursor of current authors of mega-novels like Thomas von Steinaecker and Dietmar Dath. In the Dutch-speaking context, Alexander Kluge's literary work is as yet unavailable in translation. Partial translations of Kluge's work were published in the journal *Raster*; Kluge's documentary procedure, as well as his theoretical formulation of the New Left, may have aroused the interest of Jacq F. Vogelaar and Anthony Mertens (1980). In this journal, Kluge's work was initially presented as a specimen of a Marxist-materialist aesthetics. But later on, critics like Cyrille Offermans aligned Kluge more with postmodernism. Daniël Rovers, a critic and novelist and co-translator of David Foster Wallace, presented Alexander Kluge in the literary journal *Yang*. Alexander Kluge's literary work is now widely available in English translation. Due to the dimensions of the material, most translations opt for a selection of specific stories deemed of interest to non-German audiences.

4. Round Four: Literary Practice

Armando

If we apply Bart Vervaeck's criteria (2003: 146–47) for the techniques of experimental prose, Armando only qualifies in terms of the final point: 'the use of different levels of narrative, alternating narrative voices and focalizations and the surreal dimensions of their prose'.[44] What characterises Armando's work is its fragmentary nature: short notes or *flarden* [scraps], which we have linked to early Romanticism and the sublime.

Constant motifs in Armando's oeuvre are the *place* and the *landscape*, which are expressed in his literary work and in the film *History of a Place: Concentration Camp Amersfoort*. Besides the fact that both artists make films, Armando's interest in the history of places also provides a significant parallel between him and Kluge, whose film *The Female Patriot (Die Patriotin)* appeared in 1979: a film in which a woman travels around with a shovel to dig up Germany's history, reveal all its traces and, as it transpires — another significant likeness between the two artists: a film consisting largely of fragments. In Kluge's opinion, history consists of several stories and can only be told in a set of fragments that refuse totalization. Armando personifies nature, holding it responsible for the events during the war. Nature and elements in nature, particularly the trees and the forest, are silent witnesses to the horrifying events, sharing in the guilt because they did not intervene. This is expressed, for example, in the title *Guilty Landscape* (1986, *Schuldig landschap*). His fascination for violence can be explained with a biographical reference to his youth in Amersfoort, where he lived close to Amersfoort concentration camp. There he came into contact with violence, its victims and its perpetrators, learning that the two can exchange roles.

As we have seen, quotations play a major role in Armando's work, for example in ready-mades that he included in his *Collected Poems* (1964, *Verzamelde gedichten*), in reports and interviews, and in the 'Cycle "Boxers"' ('Cyclus "boksers"'). The works known as the boxing poems, as he says himself, are made up entirely of quotations, including slips of the tongue. An example is the poem 'Cycle "Boxers"', where we also find the motif violence: 'nelis got a glass jaw, hasn't he? || well nail him right in the throat | cut his fucking breath off || , a feint one or two little jabs | I come from the left he comes from the right | I go inside I catch him, | down he goes on his arse for three grand, || isays: undo my gloves. water. | esays: control yourself. | isays: undo my gloves. water. | esays: control yourself. | isays: take your fucking self-control and | stuff it. water.' (Armando 2012)[45]

He also uses the technique of quotations in the book *The SS Men*, which consists of interviews with seven anonymous men and one woman. Armando and Sleutelaar deliberately sought out people who had not distanced themselves from their actions. In an interview, they describe their method: all conversations were typed out, amounting to a total of about '2500 folio sheets'. Then they removed the questions and information they believed to be superfluous and authorized that version (Armando and Sleutelaar 2012: 13).[46] They view themselves as editors, not judging or condemning the interviewees, and they claim that that is precisely what critics hold against them. They themselves are of the opinion that their position as interviewers is neutral, but given the difference in the amount of material between the book publication and the typed version, they must have selected fragments from the conversations and intervened by putting certain sentences in italics, including photographs from the period, isolating statements, adding paragraphs, by 'montage, selection and ordering' (Bril 1990)[47] and by choosing mottos.[48]

Armando and Sleutelaar's attention is focused on autobiographical motifs and those that have become taboo: a stereotypical image of masculinity characterised by hardness, discipline, ambition, danger, adventure, life and death, the ability to bear pain, existing as a human machine (consider the boxer), camaraderie, and pressure, in which only the strongest survive — elements that can become addictive for some. One of the former SS members is quoted as saying the following:

> In a storm attack like that you are actually in a kind of trance. You're gone. You're gone. You no longer have any thoughts. Nothing. No... All that is left is action. [...] You are no longer yourself. Your own self isn't there, you see. It has gone. [...] Some of the boys did go mad. [...] (Armando and Sleutelaar 2012: 61–62)[49]

As a quotation, this is not merely a direct allusion to authenticity, a central concept in Schmitt's ideas, which we referred to earlier, but also to an experience of the sublime. The relationship between Armando's idea of authenticity and his biography can be seen, for example, in what he has to say about the extraordinary situation of the war, a period in which naked, bare humans became visible, whom he believes are humans as they really are: 'For me 40–45 was: life without masks. After the war, everyone could go back to playing their little roles — not in the war, then they were forced to be who they were' (Meijer 2003: 158).[50] Sleutelaar says in the interview with Bril that he associates the stories with folk tales, like fairy tales: 'They are full of unexpected twists of fate, hard blows. There are winners and losers; good and evil are clearly indicated [...]' (Bril 1990).[51] The genre of the folk tale has similarities to myth due to these motifs, and these motifs are characteristic of an anti-liberal society in Schmitt's work.

The interviews can also be seen as a portrait of a generation, the interviewers that experienced the war as children but were too young to be able to make a choice. The members of the SS chose to participate actively and to go and fight. They have that in common with other members of their generation who joined the resistance, although they chose an opposing ideology. Representatives of both groups used violence but afterwards only the members of the resistance were officially rewarded for this. The testimonies of the people who made the 'wrong' choice recur again and again in Armando's work: in *Rulers, From Berlin, Turmoil of War* (1986, *Krijgsgewoel*) and *We Were So Wonderfully Young* (1999, *We waren zo heerlijk jong*), people from the generation before Armando's also recount their wartime experiences. After the war, it is decided who will be hero or villain, victim or perpetrator, friend or foe, but Armando and Sleutelaar make it clear that these are not clearly delineated opposites.

Martin Bril, who published an interview in 1990 with Armando ('the ideologist of the Nieuwe Stijl') and Sleutelaar ('its great organiser') in the *Haagse Post*, claims

rigid official language used in the documents themselves. The very word *Ordnung* [organization] is part of the official language control with which the Nazi state managed to shield its ideologically motivated crimes as purely formal, bureaucratic processes, for which Victor Klemperer (1998 [1957]) coined the term *Lingua Tertii Emperii* or LTI. Kluge casts these crimes as (temporary) breakdowns in the routines of a capitalist logic. The narrator refrains from rendering the protagonists' thoughts and feelings transparent. This omission may impart a sense of emblematization of events as in allegorical, Baroque literature. On the other hand, given the fairly generic nature of group dynamics (rather than the historicity of abstruse ideologies), one gets the impression that the events could repeat themselves even under different circumstances. One could compare this with Armando's conviction that anyone is capable of (or even tempted towards) killing, provided the circumstances facilitate or necessitate this anthropologically sedimented behaviour. If the underlying habitus is framed in terms of sociology or the history of mentalities: cultures of male bonding seem to transcend specific political or psychological motivations.

Kluge's striving for objectivity will culminate in his *Air Raid* (1977, *Der Luftangriff auf Halberstadt*). In this seminal text, Kluge encircles the bombing of his hometown both from the point of view of strategic planners and victims. He does so without foregrounding his own experience as an eyewitness and a survivor of these events. One may have the impression that the view from above is slightly more absurd, self-serving and cruel. But Kluge does not take sides, the strategic blindness of both the view from below and from above, as well as the similarities between victims and perpetrators are pinpointed.

5. Final Round

Alexander Kluge and Armando are among the most multifaceted artists of their generation: they are active in a large number of fields. At first glance, the similarities between the two are great: both are strongly influenced by World War II, and both had a traumatic experience during the war — the Amersfoort concentration camp for the young Armando, and the air raid on Halberstadt for Kluge. Armando's poetics are informed by ideas from early Romanticism in Germany (in terms of his preference for the fragmentary and the sublime), the historic avant-garde and the views of Carl Schmitt. Furthermore, there are major parallels in the 1960s between his literary ideas (*Gard Sivik* and *De Nieuwe Stijl*) and his artistic ones, as formulated by the Hollandse Informele Groep and the Nul movement. Likewise, *The SS Men*, the collected interviews with Dutch people who volunteered to join the German SS, is an excellent example of Armando's poetics in which the focus is on authenticity, the fragmentary, and the sublime. The themes of *The SS Men* continue to recur in his work with minor variations: a cult of masculinity, fascination with World War II, perpetrators and victims, and violence. A particular difference between Kluge and Armando has to do with their development: some Dutch critics rightly state that there is virtually no change in Armando's work and that he continues to repeat himself. Kluge has remained far more flexible, gaining an important position as an intellectual in recent decades.

One can link Armando with Kluge when one highlights specific traits of the former's protean identity over others. Anton Kaes (1987: 69–70) links Kluge, mainly on the basis of movies like *The Female Patriot*, to Romanticism. Despite Kluge's documentary aesthetics that stresses the long-lasting impact of the *longue durée*, a decisionist potential of the individual is indeed made visible in the interstices of the narration, in its interruptions, in moments of *kairos* that return confidence and sovereignty to the individual. Kluge's literary production of the 1960s is strongly objective. But as of 2000, one can witness a return of the autobiographical subject in his texts. If Romanticism is to play a role in his literary practice, then it is a self-reflexive and ironic appropriation. In the case of Armando, early documentary beginnings give way to an unabashed aesthetics of the sublime. Armando's preoccupation with the perpetrator leads up to the diagnosis of the ubiquitous nature of violence thinly veiled by civilization.

To some extent, Kluge too focusses on the planning of perpetrators, but his worldview is that of comedy rather than of tragedy. To give an example: Armando's *Diary of a Perpetrator* (1973, *Dagboek van een dader*) reproduces Caspar David Friedrich's painting *The Chasseur in the Forest* (1814, *Der Chasseur im Walde*) on its cover. Kluge's *The Female Patriot* reproduces the same painting, however, with a subtext: 'Napoleonic heavy infanterist, Kellerman's brigade, already at Valmy, in front of the entrance to a forest East of the Elbe. Sceptical' (1979: 122).[57] By pointing out the anonymous soldier's rank in the hierarchy and part of his history, in addition to an exact geographical location, Kluge effectively destroys the allegorical nature of the painting as well as the mythical grandeur of the forest. However, this anti-aesthetical, documentary procedure is supplemented by an ironic re-entry of literary speculation. The attribution 'sceptical', unwarranted by clues in the painting and heavily in contrast with the nationalist reception of Friedrich, clearly transcends the non-fictional realm and points to a putative judgment of the soldier's inner state, once more dissolving (ideologically connoted) resolve into doubt. The very way in which the meaning of this iconic and sublime painting is abducted, points once more to the legacy of the historical avant-garde, to Surrealism and Dada (see Malkmus 2009; for an insightful overview over the debate on where to situate the avant-garde politically, see Bohrer 2000).

Contrary to Armando's work, the characters featured in Kluge's stories are not motivated by an archetypical drive for violence. They are epitomes of the banality of evil rather than of its sublimity. Both artistic strategies have as a common outcome that the boundaries between good and bad are blurred. But they differ in the amount of weight attributed to individual agency. Whereas Armando's notion of authenticity ties in with notions of sublime experience, Kluge's paradox subjective documentary works towards both the demythologization of sublime experience and the deconstruction of autobiography. Both authors have played a seminal role in *Vergangenheitsbewältigung* [working through the past] in both Germany and the Netherlands, they have thwarted attempts to turn a blind eye to recent history. At first sight, Kluge may seem as preoccupied with the *state of emergency* as Armando himself. In Kluge's work, there are indeed various stand-ins for the role that Carl Schmitt came to play in the twentieth century: Heidegger, Ernst Jünger, even

Walter Benjamin to some extent represent the fascination with the terrible or violence as a mythic apriori untouched by civilization and as an opportunity to be seized by the truly great. Unlike Armando, Kluge seems to be (increasingly) in search of alternative outcomes of catastrophic events, and deals with these thinkers by bringing into contact extremes, by pointing out the spatial and/or biographical contiguity between apparent opponents. This indeed turns what are at first glance unlikely bedfellows into productive sparring-partners.

Works Cited

'0-Institute / ZERO Foundation' [n.d] <http://www.4321zero.com> [accessed 30 May 2019]

ALPHEN, ERNST VAN. 2000. *Armando: Shaping Memory* (Rotterdam: NAi Publishers)

ARMANDO. 1958–1959. ['Credo 1'], in Hans Sleutelaar, Gust Gils, René Gysen et al., 'Om het ongerijmde', *Maatstaf*, 16.9–10: 810–11. <HTTPS://WWW.DBNL.ORG/TEKST/_maa003195801_01/_maa003195801_01_0121.php> [accessed 25 June 2019].

——. 1964. 'Een internationale primeur', *Gard Sivik* 7.33, n.p.

——. 1996. *From Berlin*, trans. by Susan Massotty (London: Reaktion Books)

——, and HANS SLEUTELAAR. 2010. 'Die SSer: Niederländische Freiwillige im Zweiten Weltkrieg erzählen', trans. by Marlene Müller-Haas, *Schreibheft*, 70: 118–41

——, and HANS SLEUTELAAR. 2012. *De SSers: Nederlandse vrijwilligers in de Tweede Wereldoorlog*, preface by Joost de Vries, 6th edn (Amsterdam: De Bezige Bij)

——. 2015. 'Cycle Boxers', trans. by Paul Vincent <http://www.literaturefromthelowcountries.eu/armando> [accessed 30 May 2019]

BANDEILI, ANGELA. 2014. *Ästhetische Erfahrung in der Literatur der 1970er Jahre: Zur Poetologie des Raumes bei Rolf Dieter Brinkmann, Alexander Kluge und Peter Handke* (Bielefeld: transcript)

BEEKMAN, KLAUS. 1985. 'Armando', *Kritisch literatuur lexicon*, 18 (August)

——. 2010. 'Armando', *Kritisch literatuur lexicon*, 116 (February)

BERG, HUBERT F. VAN DEN, and GILLES J. DORLEIJN. 2002. 'Avantgarde! Voorhoede? Ter Inleiding', in *Avantgarde! Voorhoede? Vernieuwingsbewegingen in Noord en Zuid opnieuw beschouwd*, ed by Hubert F. van den Berg and Gilles J. Dorleijn (Nijmegen: Vantilt), pp. 5–15

BESSING, JOACHIM. 2016. '2016 — The Year Punk Broke. 17.2' <http://www.waahr.de/kolumnen/joachim-bessing/172> [accessed 30 May 2019]

BOHRER, KARL HEINZ. 2000. 'Sprachen der Ironie — Sprachen des Ernstes: Das Problem', in *Sprachen der Ironie: Sprachen des Ernstes*, ed. by Karl Heinz Bohrer (Frankfurt a/M: Suhrkamp), pp. 11–35

BORK, G.J. VAN, ET AL. 2015. 'readymade', in *Algemeen letterkundig lexicon* <http://www.dbnl.org/tekst/dela012alge01_01/dela012alge01_01_02711.php> [accessed 30 May 2019]

BRECHT, BERTOLT. 1989 [1957]. 'Vergnügungstheater oder Lehrtheater?', in *Schriften zum Theater: Über eine nicht-aristotelische Dramatik,* ed. by Siegfried Unseld (Frankfurt a/M: Suhrkamp), pp. xx–yy.

BREMS, HUGO. 2006. *Altijd weer vogels die nesten beginnen: Geschiedenis van de Nederlandse literatuur 1945–2005* (Amsterdam: Bert Bakker)

BRIL, MARTIN. 2015. 'Dubbelgesprek met Armando [1990]' <http://www.hanssleutelaar.nl/interviews/dubbelgesprek-met-armando> [accessed 30 May 2019]

——. 2017. 'Gesprek met Martin Bril [1989]' <https://www.hanssleutelaar.nl/interviews/gesprek-met-martin-bril/> [accessed 30 May 2019]

Corrigan, Timothy. 2011. *The Essay Film: From Montaigne, After Marker* (Oxford: Oxford University Press)

Eco, Umberto. 2004. 'Les semaphores sous la pluie', in *On Literature*, trans. by Martin McLaughlin (Orlando: Harcourt), pp. 180–200

Enzensberger, Hans Magnus. 1978. 'Ein herzloser Schriftsteller', *Der Spiegel*, 1: 81–83 <https://www.spiegel.de/spiegel/print/d-40693842.html> [accessed 30 May 2019]

Eue, Ralph. 2012. *Provokation der Wirklichkeit: 50 Jahre Oberhausener Manifest — das Wiener Symposium* (Vienna: Synema)

——, and Lars Henrik Gass. 2012. *Provokation der Wirklichkeit: Das Oberhausener Manifest und die Folgen* (Munich: edition text + kritik)

——, Alexandra Hesse, Jana Koch, Stefanie Schmitt, and Christian Schulte. 2016. *CHIFFRE OBERHAUSEN: Suchbewegungen zwischen Ästhetik, Politik und Utopie des Neuen Deutschen Films* (Hamburg: Vorwerk 8)

Favié, Trudie. 1996. 'Armando in de kritiek: Op welke gronden leest de literaire kritiek het werk van Armando als romantisch?', *Voortgang*, 16: 209–32

Feijter, Anja de. 2008. 'De geschiedenis van *Gard Sivik*: De overgang van een experimentele naar een nieuw-realistische poetica in Nederland en Vlaanderen', in *Een of twee Nederlandse literaturen? Contacten tussen de Nederlandse en Vlaamse literatuur sinds 1830*, ed. by Ralf Grüttemeier and Jan Oosterholt (Leuven: Peeters), pp. 157–82

Fetscher, Justus. 2001/2010. 'Fragment', in *Ästhetische Grundbegriffe (ÄGB)*, ed. by Karlheinz Barck et al., 7 vols (Stuttgart: Metzler/), II: Dekadent — Grotesk, pp. 551–88

Goedegebuure, Jaap. 2002. 'Het verschrikkelijke wonder: Over de Tweede Wereldoorlog en de Nederlandse literatuur na 1945', *Literatuur*, 19: 66–76

Handke, Peter. 1969. 'Augsburg im August: trostlos — Peter Handke über Alexander Kluges *Die Artisten in der Zirkuskuppel: ratlos*', *Film*, 7.1: 32

Hermsen, Joke J. 1999. 'Unheimlich mooi: Over (ge)weldadige kunst (Armando, Dumas, Heidegger)', *Tirade*, 43: 336–51

Huitker, Astrid. 2004. 'Tussen norm en experiment: De museale presentatie van Nul-kunst', *Kunstlicht*, 25.1/2: 48–53

Kaes, Anton. 1987. *Deutschlandbilder: Die Wiederkehr der Geschichte als Film* (Munich: edition text + kritik)

Kant, Immanuel. 1974. *Kritik der Urteilskraft*, ed. by Karl Vorländer (Hamburg: Meiner)

Klemperer, Victor. 1998 [1957]. *LTI: Notizbuch eines Philologen*, 17th edn (Leipzig: Reclam)

Kluge, Alexander. 1967. *The Battle*, trans. by Leila Vennewitz (New York: McGraw)

——. 1979. *Die Patriotin: Texte, Bilder 1–6* (Hamburg: Zweitausendeins)

——. 1986. *Lebensläufe* (Frankfurt a/M: Suhrkamp)

——. 1988. *Case Histories*, trans. by Leila Vennewitz, Modern German Voices Series (New York: Holmes & Meier)

——. 2007. *Cinema Stories*, trans. by Tim Brady (New York: New Directions)

——, and Gerhard Richter. 2012. *December: 39 stories — 39 Pictures*, trans. by Martin Chalmers (London: Seagull)

——. 2014. *Air Raid*, trans. by Martin Chalmers (London: Seagull)

——. 2015. *30 April 1945: The Day Hitler Shot Himself and Germany's Integration with the West Began*, translated by Wieland Hoban, The German List (London: Seagull)

——, and Gerhard Richter. 2016. *Dispatches from Moments of Calm*, trans. by Nathaniel McBride, The German List (London: Seagull)

Lethen, Helmut. 2000. 'Carl Schmitt: *Der Begriff des Politischen* (1927)', in *Jahrhundertbücher: Große Theorien von Freud bis Luhmann*, ed by Walter Erhart and Herbert Jaumann (Munich: Beck), pp. 128–46

Malkmus, Bernhard. 2009. 'Intermediality and the Topography of Memory in Alexander Kluge', *New German Critique*, 36.2 (107): 231–52

MARTENS, GUNTHER. 2014. 'Distant(ly) reading Alexander Kluge's distant writing', in *Vermischte Nachrichten*, ed. by Richard Langston, Gunther Marthens, Christian Schulte, Rainer Stollmann, and Vincent Pauval, Alexander-Kluge-Jahrbuch 1 (Göttingen: Vandenhoeck & Ruprecht unipress), pp. 29–41

MEIJER, ISCHA. 2003. 'Armando, Hans Sleutelaar, Cornelis Bastiaan Vaandrager, Hans Verhagen', in *De interviewer en de schrijvers,* ed. by Connie Palmen (Amsterdam: Prometheus), pp. 154–67

MERTENS, ANTHONY. 1980. 'Alexander Kluge: Berichten van het slagveld', *Raster,* 13: 44–47

PÖRSCHMANN, DIRK, and MARGRIET SCHAVEMAKER. 2015. 'New Encounter with a Forgotten Avant-garde', in *ZERO: The International Art Movement of the 50s and 60s,* ed. by Dirk Pörschmann and Margriet Schavemaker (Cologne: König), pp. 14–17

RENTSCHLER, ERIC. 2015. *The Use and Abuse of Cinema: German Legacies from the Weimar Era to the Present* (New York: Columbia University Press)

SCHMITT, CARL. 1991 [1932]. *Der Begriff des Politischen* (Berlin: Duncker & Humblot)

SCHOUTEN, ROB. 1986. 'Armando 1929', in *'t Is vol van schatten hier...,* ed. by Anton Korteweg and Murk Salverda, 2 vols (Amsterdam: De Bezige Bij/Nederlands Letterkundig Museum en Documentatiecentrum), II, pp. 201–03 < https://www.dbnl.org/tekst/kort006isv001_01/kort006isv001_01_0192.php> [accessed 30 May 2019]

SCHUBERT, PETER, and MONIKA MAUS. 2012. *Rückblicke: Die Abteilung Film — Institut für Filmgestaltung an der HFG Ulm 1960–1968* (Detmold: Rohn)

SCHÜTTE, WOLFRAM. 1992. 'Sein Name: eine Ära. Rückblicke auf den späten Fassbinder', in *Rainer Werner Fassbinder,* ed. Peter W. Jansen and Wolfram Schütte (Frankfurt a/M: Fischer), pp. 12–123

SEBALD, WINFRIED G. 1999 [1997]. *Luftkrieg und Literatur: Mit einem Essay zu Alfred Andersch* (Munich: Hanser)

VERVAECK, BART. 2003. 'Hoe zwart was mijn dal? Realiteit en fictie in het Nederlandstalige proza van de jaren vijftig,' *Spiegel der Letteren,* 45.2: 121–53

VOGT, LUDGERA. 2012. 'Der montierte Lebenslauf: Soziologische Reflexionen über den Zusammenhang von Kluges Lebensläufen und der Form des Biographischen in der Moderne', in *Die Schrift an der Wand — Alexander Kluge: Rohstoffe und Materialien,* ed. by Christian Schulte (Göttingen: Vandenhoeck & Ruprecht unipress), pp. 161–78

VRIES, JOOST DE. 2012. 'Voorwoord', in Armando and Hans Sleutelaar, *De SS'ers,* pp. 7–9

'ZERO: The international art movement of the 1950s and 1960s'. 2018. <https://www.kulturstiftung-des-bundes.de/cms/en/projekte/bild_und_raum/archiv/zero.html> [accessed 30 May 2019]

Notes to Chapter 5

1. Armando was an actor in the television series and theatre play *Sufferings of Gentlemen* (*Herenleed*), for which he wrote the scripts in collaboration with Cherry Duyns. Together with Hans Verhagen, he also made the documentary *The History of a Place: Concentration Camp Amersfoort* (1978, *De geschiedenis van een plek: Concentratiekamp Amersfoort*).

2. ZERO had a major exhibition in renowned museums in 2014–2015 and is considered to be among the largest and most significant artistic movements of the post-1945 period. The exhibitions were held in: New York, Solomon R. Guggenheim Museum (1 September 2014 — 25 January 2015); Berlin, Martin Gropius Bau (21 March — 8 June 2015); and Amsterdam, Stedelijk Museum (5 July — 4 October 2015).

3. For example, *From Berlin* (Armando 1996) appeared in English, offering a selection from Dutch publications. Two prose titles were published in German (the 1987 collection *The Warmth of Aversion* [*Die Wärme der Abneigung*], and *The Street and the Shrubbery* [1992, *Straße und Gestrüpp*; Dutch: *De straat en het struikgewas*]). Other translations into German include a selection of his

fables in catalogues of his exhibitions (2000–2002), a selection of fables and fragments from 1996 to 2003 in the journal *Am Erkner* (a total of about ten pages), and a publication in *Akzente* in 1998 (five pages). Two bilingual publications have also appeared in the Dutch-speaking world: *Die schuldige Landschaft*, trans. by Anne Stolz (Amsterdam: Voetnoot), 1998 — the title refers to his most important theme — and *De stilte — Die Stille*, trans. by Marlene Müller-Haas (Ghent: Ergo Pers), 2010. A fragment from *The SS Men* appeared as late as 2010 in the German literary journal *Schreibheft* (Armando and Sleutelaar 2010: 118–41).

4. Huitker (2004: 49) testifies that the *Nul-Groep* were judged more critically in the Netherlands than abroad, because influential critics did not support the group in the way that Pierre Restany did in France.

5. The website 'o-Institute / ZERO Foundation', which recently appeared online, introduces the members in detail.

6. See also Hugo Brems (2006: 232), who said that '[t]he modern consumer society was no strange, inimical environment for them [Armando and the artists of the Nul-Groep], but the natural world of the artist' ('De moderne consumptiemaatschappij was voor hen [Armando en de kunstenaars van de *Nul*-groep] geen vreemde, vijandige omgeving, maar de vanzelfsprekende wereld van de kunstenaar').

7. 'Tja, wat was onze ideologie. In de eerste plaats ging 't om het afzetten tegen de Vijftigers. Als ik er, als oudere heer, op terugkijk: een wanhopige poging om de consumptiemaatschappij te *bejahen*. Als ik erop terugkijk: inderdaad wanhopig. Een grootsteedse hardheid streefden we na (zo van: laat 't allemaal maar op je afkomen), amoreel: alles is goed, een muur opbouwen, geen walging tonen. Ik was ook hard in die tijd. Geen prettig mens.'

8. 'grammaticaal-logische verbanden werden als inertie beschouwd'

9. 'in de richting van grotere anonimiteit of objectiviteit'

10. 'ZERO was never a group, never had a fixed membership, never formed a contoured structure, and was too diverse to present a clear image. ZERO remains difficult to pin down, and art historians who cling to rigid categories have a difficult time categorizing it' (Pörschmann and Schavemaker 2015: 17).

11. 'The most essential aspects of the artistic ZERO practices may be described as a reduction, concentration, and innovation of artistic styles, by which the artists cut themselves loose from the prevalent art of that era' (Pörschmann and Schavemaker 2015: 14).

12. 'lyrische abstractie'; 'spontane, voorstellingsloze schildertrant, die uiting van de verf als materie'

13. 'geste-schilderkunst'

14. 'een kunst die geen kunst meer is'; 'Het gaat dan natuurlijk wel om wat je kiest'

15. 'journalistieke principes'

16. 'Het maken van de Nul-werken vond ik op den duur ook niet spannend genoeg meer. Dat had mede als oorzaak dat ik nog maar zo weinig persoonlijke inbreng had. Ik kon ze bij wijze van spreken laten maken. [...] Ik ben in 1965 bij de tweede Nul-tentoonstelling in het Stedelijk Museum opgestapt. [...] [B]ij mij waren de feiten uitgeput.'

17. See for instance Wolfram Schütte (1992: 82), who calls Kluge the 'kombinatorische Intelligenz', the combinational brains of the New German Cinema.

18. 'Niet de Realiteit be-moraliseren of interpreteren (ver-kunsten), maar intensiveren. Uitgangspunt: een konsekwent aanvaarden van de Realiteit. Interesse voor een meer autonoom optreden van de Realiteit, al op te merken in de journalistiek, tv-reportages en film. Werkmethode: isoleren, annexeren. Dus: authenticiteit. Niet van de maker, maar van de informatie. De kunstenaar, die geen kunstenaar meer is: een koel, zakelijk oog.'

19. 'Ja, we waren een groep — een stoottroep die bewust de oogkleppen opzet, op die manier geschiedenis maakt. Ik was streng, fanatiek. Ik stond in het volle leven, ik ben nog steeds naar alles nieuwsgierig. Die Vijftigers, dat waren toch bohémiens, waardoor een groot deel van de realiteit hun ontging, een groot stuk rijkdom.'

20. 'Ik hou van *Ausnahmesituationen* en daar is boksen er één van, en oorlog'; 'geweld, gedempt door regels, gekluisterd geweld. Wat blijft ons anders over dan het geweld te stileren, te esthetiseren, te verontschuldigen'

21. 'als kulturhistorisches Ereignis, das den Zeitraum 1927 bis 1933 umfaßt'; 'Strömungen der Avantgarde'
22. '"Ernst des Lebens" das Kriterium des Authentischen bildet und Identität nur in Sphären des Schmerzes und im Schatten des Todes zu haben ist'; 'In Strömungen der Avantgarde, in der Literatur der verschiedenen Lager des politischen Extremismus'. Jaap Goedegebuure (2002: 68) makes an attempt to explain why the influence of the historic avant-garde in the Netherlands was only acknowledged after 1945: 'It is an accepted idea among historiographers that Dutch literature only connected after 1945 with the artistic innovations that had already occurred in most European countries between 1910 and 1922' ('Het is een aanvaard idee onder geschiedschrijvers dat de Nederlandse literatuur pas na 1945 aansluiting vond bij de artistieke vernieuwingen die zich in de meeste Europese landen al tussen 1910 en 1922 hadden voltrokken'). He cites the 'anti-modernist attitude of dominant critics such as Ter Braak, Du Perron and Marsman' as an explanation, and claims that little attention was paid 'to the fact that the shock of a war experienced at first hand had swept away the foundations of a world view and a representation of reality that had been taken for granted for centuries' (2002: 68; 'anti-modernistische optreden van dominante critici als Ter Braak, Du Perron en Marsman'; 'naar de omstandigheid dat de schok van een aan den lijve ervaren oorlog het fundament had weggeslagen onder een wereldbeeld en een werkelijkheidsrepresentatie die eeuwenlang als vanzelfsprekend hadden gegolden').
23. The novel *All Souls' Day* (*Allerzielen*, 1998) by Cees Nooteboom is an interesting case in point; *All Souls' Day* is not merely a novel about Berlin, but a roman à clef in which Herman van Dodeweerd appears as Victor Leven (Nooteboom exchanges the Dutch word for 'death' to 'life' in his character's name), a man who views the present day from the perspective of the Third Reich, with a negative attitude to Germany and Germans and an even more negative attitude to the Dutch. Nooteboom — and the reader may wonder whether this is intentional — sketches a negative image of this character, as a grumpy old man constantly occupied by the past.
24. 'het hem erom gaat de afschuwelijke, vreeswekkende schoonheid in het voorbij goed en kwaad gelegen gebied van de kunst binnen te loodsen, "met als resultaat het sublieme, het *Erhabene*, als het artistieke aan banden leggen van het verschrikkelijke"'. See also Van Alphen (2000).
25. 'Collage betekende: het tegenover elkaar zetten van dingen. Wij wilden stukken realiteit door isoleren plotseling intensiveren.'
26. 'nur einen transitorischen Werth'; 'Seismographen der Gegenwart'; 'das Undarstellbare als Unvollendbares zu akzentuieren'
27. 'liegt daher in ihrer Bestimmung zur "schnellen Eingreiftruppe"; 'das Stilideal der frühromantischen Fragmente war die erhabene Frechheit'; Erhabenheit: durch die 'Teilhabe an den Attributen des Dynamisch-Erhabenen. Sie sind Blitze, agil, schnell, energisch, zielen aufs Unendliche. Als Methode, das Erhabene künstlerisch umzusetzen, wählen sie die, das Undarstellbare als Unvollendbares zu akzentuieren'; 'Unvollendung giebt dem Erhabenen [...] einen höhern Reiz'.
28. 'Alexander Kluge macht die für ihn typischen Geräusche des atemlosen Folgens in Gedanken, also er markiert, weil er selbst nicht zu Wort kommt, durch hörbar gemachte Respiration eine Art Schluckaufgeräusch, das die Stationen seines gedanklichen Voranschreitens anzeigt wie Pfosten; er signalisiert seinen Gesprächspartnern, dass er schweigenderweise trotzdem vorankommt, gedanklich noch dabei ist, gleichzuziehen mit seinem Gegenüber [...].'
29. Beekman defines 'late Romanticists' very broadly. The original text reads: 'mythische karakter'; 'de motto's, ontleend aan het werk van laat-Romantici als Von Hofmannsthal, Novalis, Hölderlin, Rilke en George in die richting wijzen en vooral die van Ernst Jünger'.
30. 'Ik ben altijd romanticus geweest qua mentaliteit. Die genoteerde werkelijkheid van mij was onderkoeld, maar had te maken met de romantische werkelijkheid van de *Industrialgesellschaft*.'
31. 'hebben een of meer, voor het leeuwendeel aan romantici ontleende motto's'; 'Beekman heeft de rol die de kritiek aan de motto's en omslagafbeeldingen zou toekennen overgewaardeerd'
32. 'de mythologische conceptie'; 'de even diepzinnig ogende als nietszeggende gemeenplaats dat slachtoffer en dader in één persoon schuil gaan'
33. Favié lists several characteristics of Romanticism: 'an aesthetic current in which imagination, the powers of the imagination, myth and symbol play a primary role. It is characterised by the

following airs of opposites: utopian dreams of the future and nostalgia for the past; revival of Christianity and the loss of all believe; nihilism and the fervent search for truth; old religions and new ideologies', 'nature is experienced as transcendent; higher qualities are ascribed to it. Awe of nature is expressed in art as "the sublime" ("das Erhabene")' (Favié 1996: 214; 'een esthetische stroming waarbinnen verbeelding, verbeeldingskracht, mythe en symbool een primaire rol spelen. Kenmerkend zijn de volgende oppositieparen: utopische toekomstdromen tegenover nostalgie naar het verleden; herleving van het christendom tegenover verlies van alle geloof; nihilisme tegenover fervent zoeken naar waarheid; oude religies tegenover nieuwe ideologieën'; 'De natuur wordt als transcendent ervaren, aan haar worden hogere kwaliteiten toegekend. Ontzag voor de natuur komt in de kunst tot uiting in "het sublieme" ("das Erhabene").')

34. 'esthetisering van het kwaad'.

35. 'tot het mateloze'; 'de tijdloze en zich eindeloos vernieuwende schoonheid. [...] een verraderlijke schoonheid omdat de natuur onverstoorbaar is'. Favié adds: 'It would be interesting to investigate the extent to which Armando's oeuvre or poetics, and also the metaphor of the 'guilty landscape' that De Nijs considers sublime, display features of the sublime. However, this requires a clear definition of the concept. If it is considered to be a Romantic characteristic, the relation between the metaphysical and the sublime in Armando's work will also need to be investigated' (Favié 1996: 224); 'Het zou interessant zijn na te gaan in hoeverre Armando's oeuvre of poëtica, en ook de door De Nijs subliem geachte metafoor van het 'schuldige landschap', kenmerken vertonen van het sublieme. Hiervoor is echter een duidelijke afbakening van het begrip nodig. Wanneer het als romantisch kenmerk wordt aangemerkt, zal ook de relatie metafysisch-subliem in het werk van Armando nader onderzocht moeten worden.').

36. 'geweld, misdaad, macht'

37. 'academistische, intellectualistische benadering van de maatschappij, en de vervlakking van de maatschappij zelf, of zoals hij het pleegt uit te drukken "de coca-colazation"'

38. 'personages worden geabstraheerd'

39. 'Het is een roman die geen roman meer is, een non-fiction novel [...] die de werkelijkheid tot een mythe omvormt'; 'Sleutelaar vraagt naar de totale esthetica in de taal van de nazi's: Wollt ihr die totale Poesie? En zijn antwoord is een totaal esthetisch boek dat noodzakelijk over nazi's moet gaan, als onmogelijke romanfiguren van de realiteit.'

40. '[dat] het niet uitgegeven had mogen worden, omdat de schrijvers geen partij kozen en de vijand helemaal niet in de rede vielen'

41. 'waarbij aan literair-historische aspecten van de tekst noch aan taalgebruik of retorische elementen aandacht wordt besteed [...]'

42. 'sprekende getuigen'.

43. On Kluge's position within the tradition of essay film, see: Corrigan 2011.

44. 'ingebedde vertellers en verhalen, verspringende focalisaties en versmeltende ervaringsmodaliteiten'

45. 'heeft nelis een glazen kin? || priem hem precies op z'n strot | godverdomme geen asem meer || , een schijnstootje een paar plaagstootjes | ik kom van links hij komt van rechts | ik ga binnendoor ik pak'm, | hij gaat op z'n kont voor 3 rojen || zeg: maak m'n handschoenen los. water, | zegt: toon zelfbeheersing. | zeg: maak m'n handschoenen los. water, | zegt: toon zelfbeheersing. | zeg: krijg de kelere-kanker met je zelfbeheersing. water'

46. '2500 foliovellen'

47. 'montage, de selectie en de volgorde'. The following subjects are covered in each interview in more or less the same order: youth, parental home, school, economic situation in the 1930s, opinions about Communism and National Socialism, reason for membership of the SS, political and military training, differences between Germany and the Netherlands, fighting in the Soviet Union or South-Eastern Europe, the period after 1945 and any punishment and imprisonment, opinions about the murder of Jews and other minorities, anti-Semitism, justification of their own actions, and reunions of former SS members after 1945.

48. The mottos in *The SS Men* refer to important motifs in the book, specifically the question of right and wrong: 'Where a crime begins, comradeship ends' ('Wo ein Verbrechen beginnt, hört die Kameradschaft auf'), from *Der Freiwillige*, members' newsletter for the Hiag [mutal support group for former members of the SS], 1966. Firstly, this emphasises the motif of *Kameradschaft*

[camaraderie], a basic tenet of the SS, and secondly it implies that the SS did not commit any crimes in World War II, because if they had the SS would never have existed. It is clear from the second motto, a quotation from ex-Chancellor Konrad Adenauer, that right and wrong are relative from a Chancellor's perspective, because Adenauer justifies wrong actions: 'The men of the SS were soldiers like any others. Make it clear for once and for all to the rest of the world that the SS has nothing to do with the secret service and the Gestapo. Make it clear to people for once and for all that the SS did not shoot any Jews, but was feared most by the Soviets for its outstanding soldiers' (Adenauer, speech in Hannover, 1953; 'Die Männer der Waffen-SS waren Soldaten wie alle andere auch. Machen Sie einmal dem Ausland klar, dass die Waffen-SS nichts mit Sicherheitsdienst und Gestapo zu tun hat. Machen Sie einmal den Leuten deutlich, dass die Waffen-SS keine Juden erschossen hat, sondern als hervorragende Soldaten von den Sowjets am meisten gefürchtet war'). The third motto, a quotation from the German philosopher Johann Gottlieb Fichte, is about heroes and the chosen, a statement that is extremely well suited to the members of the SS: 'Only such souls that already have strength within them elevate war to heroism: the ignoble relish robbery and repression of the weak and helpless; it raises heroes and cowardly thieves, and the latter probably in larger numbers'. Original text: 'Nur solche Seelen erhebt der Krieg zum Heroismus, welche schon Kraft in sich haben; den Unedlen begeistert er zum Raube und zur Unterdrückung der wehrlosen Schwäche; er erzeugte Helden und feige Diebe, und welches wohl in grösserer Menge?' (Fichte, *Beiträge zur Berichtigung der Urteile des Publikums über die Französische Revolution*, 1793).

49. '*Met zo'n stormaanval ben je eigenlijk in een soort roes. Je bent weg. Je bent weg. Je hebt geen gedachten meer. Niks meer. Nee... Er is alleen nog maar een handeling. [...] Je bent jezelf niet meer. Je eigen ik is er niet, hoor. Dat is weg. [...] Er zijn wel jongens krankzinnig geworden. [...]*'

50. ''40–'45 was voor mij: het leven zonder maskers. Na de oorlog kon iedereen weer een rolletje gaan spelen — in de oorlog niet, toen waren ze gedwongen te zijn wie ze waren.'

51. 'Die zitten vol onverwachte wendingen van het lot, harde slagen. Er zijn winnaars en verliezers, goed en kwaad zijn heel duidelijk aangegeven [...]'.

52. 'de ideoloog van de Nieuwe Stijl'; 'de grote organisator ervan', 'het hoogtepunt'; 'verhevigde werkelijkheid'

53. Eco discusses hypotyposis or evidentia in terms of four strategies: denotation; minute description; enumeration or accumulation; and description with reference to personal experience. He also briefly references 'hypotyposis as one of the figures that leads to the production of the sublime' (2004) in postmodernism.

54. 'Manfred Schmidt wurde am 21. Februar 1926 vorzeitig in Thorn (Westpreußen) als Sohn des prakt. Arztes Manfred Schmidt und seiner Frau Erika, geb. Scholz, geboren. Er besuchte die deutsche Volksschule seiner Heimatstadt und später das Realgymnasium. Von dort meldete er sich Ostern 1943 zur Luftwaffe. Als die Einheit geschlossen in die Waffen-SS überführt werden sollte, desertierte er zusammen mit seinem Freund K. und rettete sich in die Schweiz. Sie nahmen die Tour über den Bodensee, wo sein Freund K. jemand kannte und ein verstecktes Boot besaß.' (Kluge 1986: 115)

55. 'Auch in die Dramatik ist die Fußnote und das vergleichende Blättern einzuführen.' (Brecht 1989: 70)

56. 'organisatorischer Aufbau eines Unglücks'

57. 'Napoleonischer schwerer Chasseur, Brigade Kellermann, schon bei Valmy dabei, vor dem Eingang eines ostelbischen Waldes. Zweiflerisch.'

CHAPTER 6

❖

Rolf Dieter Brinkmann and Patrick Conrad: Pop Poetry, Intermediality and Literary Countercultures in Flanders and Germany

*Thomas Ernst (Universiteit van Amsterdam/Universiteit Antwerpen) &
Hans Vandevoorde (Vrije Universiteit Brussel)*

In 1966 a Dutch translation of Guy Debord's 'The Situationists and the New Forms of Action in Art and Politics' (1963, 'Les Situationnistes et les nouvelles formes d'action dans la politique ou l'art') was published in the Dutch journal *Randstad*. It is a seminal text that outlines the revolutionary stance of the Situationists. It goes on to criticize the fashionable neo-Dada movement of the time as a form of reactionary art and counterposes it to the total negation of Situationism. This catalogue text by Debord was written for a project in the Danish *Galerie EXI* that he describes in a letter to J.V. Martin (2006: 644–46). It was an exhibition consisting of three parts: a fallout shelter; 'Destruction of the RSG-6', whose very construction is exposed as the ultimate gesture of an elite trying to save their own skin; and then, negating the shelter, an information centre on revolt and an exhibition of artworks with titles in the form of political proclamations and abstract art with Debord's directives printed on the works.

The way in which Situationism attempted to unite politics and art represents the most extreme form of social and art criticism in the 1960s. However, the *Zeitgeist* of that time is more often characterized by less radical catchphrases such as protest, sexual emancipation, and agitation. The most fervent expressions of this spirit were the protest against the Vietnam War and the student revolts of May 1968, Woodstock and flower power, free love and drugs. In Belgium and Germany, that counterculture spirit was artistically expressed in documentary prose, the discovery and popularity of the beat poets, collective poetry performances, visual poetry (which was usually critical of society), and the more noncommittal sound poetry. In the visual arts, the iconic embodiments of the 1960s were happenings and pop art and its derivations. Situationism played only a marginal role in this vast assortment.[1] The Situationists criticized not only the establishment, but also happenings and other such artistic developments in a practically neo-anarchist and very Marxist manner. Situationism pushed the boundaries of artistic and social *engagement* and showed that other forms of art were much tamer and more noncommittal in their positioning or even directly in conflict with the criticism of consumer culture.[2] The pop artists and so-called new realists, in particular, were, after all, embracing that culture, while paying lip service to criticizing the constrictions brought about by the influence of money and consumption.

International political and artistic movements have to translate their concepts into specific national or regional contexts. In the case of the global pop artists movement and its ambivalent relation to the capitalist consumer society, the content of conceptual binaries like *overground* vs. *underground* or *hegemonic culture* vs. *counterculture* changes as they get adjusted in light of different cultural systems. We plan to illustrate these processes, straddled by so many artists, by examining the work of two poets who transferred North-American pop cultural aesthetics to Europe: the Flemish poet Patrick Conrad (born 1945) and the German poet Rolf Dieter Brinkmann (1940–1975). We will especially be focusing on their attitude toward political *engagement* in the arts and demonstrating how these openly apolitical artists were forced to nonetheless take a critical position, which was thus necessarily ambivalent and far less revolutionary than the position of the Situationists. A central element of these aesthetics consists of specific strategies of intermediality, as we will show.

1. Institutional, Biographical and Geographical Contexts

Rolf Dieter Brinkmann: From 'New Realism' to Intermedial Experiments

'I hate old poets' ('Ich hasse alte Dichter'; 1968c: 38), the subtitle of an essay by a 28-year-old Rolf Dieter Brinkmann, gives us a first impression of the innovative and subversive ambition, if not aggressive character of the West-German author. In his essay, he comments on — amongst others — the works of Leslie A. Fiedler, Jim Morrison, Marshall McLuhan, and Andy Warhol. Today, all of them are famous. Back in 1968, however, most literary critics found it difficult to accept that these artists and thinkers could or should affect contemporary literature.

At that time, the societal importance of German literature, even its general legitimation was at stake. In 1967, the Gruppe 47, the former centre of the German literary system and a central tool of cultural democratization in Germany after World War II, with amongst its members the later Nobel-prize winners Heinrich Böll and Günter Grass, organized its last convention. In November 1968 the famous *Kursbuch 15* was published with Karl Markus Michel's and Hans Magnus Enzensberger's epochal essays: Michel threw 'a wreath on the grave of literature', and Enzensberger declared the more journalistic and documentary texts as the ones society needed instead of literature: 'for example Günter Wallraff's reports from German factories, Bahman Nirumand's book on Persia, Ulrike Meinhof's columns, Georg Alsenheimer's report from Vietnam'[3] (1968: 196). These aesthetic demands were realized on stage in the so-called *Dokumentarisches Theater* [Documentary Theatre] by writers like Heinar Kipphardt and Peter Weiss. The Dortmunder

Gruppe 61 and authors like Max von der Grün, Erika Runge and Günter Wallraff published realistic or documentary novels and reports.

Beyond and, to a certain extent, even against these institutionalized contexts and their documentary or directly political aesthetics, Rolf Dieter Brinkmann worked on a different aesthetics with a stronger international orientation. Before he was ran over by a car in London in 1975 and died thus only 35 years young, he had left several marks on German literary history.

Firstly, in his early 20s he published a number of poems and stories that are connected to the Kölner Schule and Dieter Wellershoff's concept of New Realism. In his novel *No One Knows Anymore* (1968, *Keiner weiß mehr*) he exceeded this realism by using 'obscene language' and writing openly about sexuality — so openly that his publisher decided to add a cautionary note to ensure that the books would never fall into the hands of younger people (see Figure 6.1).

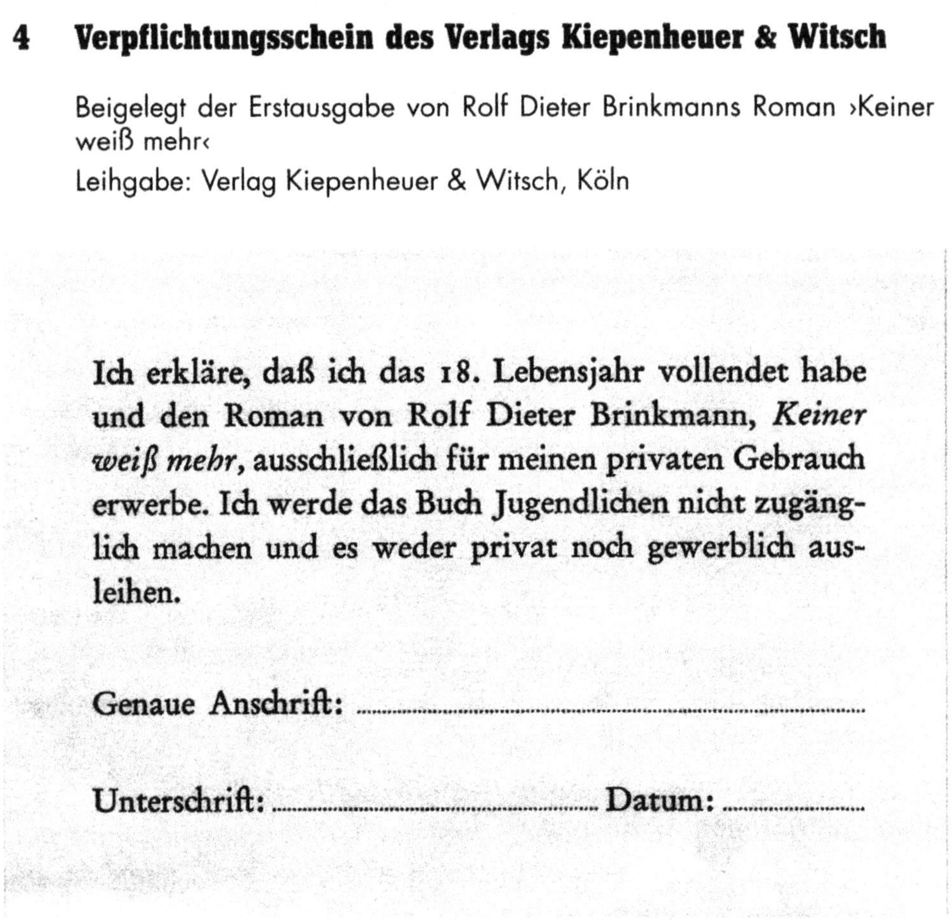

4   Verpflichtungsschein des Verlags Kiepenheuer & Witsch

Beigelegt der Erstausgabe von Rolf Dieter Brinkmanns Roman ›Keiner weiß mehr‹
Leihgabe: Verlag Kiepenheuer & Witsch, Köln

Ich erkläre, daß ich das 18. Lebensjahr vollendet habe und den Roman von Rolf Dieter Brinkmann, *Keiner weiß mehr*, ausschließlich für meinen privaten Gebrauch erwerbe. Ich werde das Buch Jugendlichen nicht zugänglich machen und es weder privat noch gewerblich ausleihen.

Genaue Anschrift: ....

Unterschrift: .... Datum: ....

FIG. 6.1. Cautionary note in Rolf Dieter Brinkmann's *Keiner weiß mehr*
(scan from Bentz 1998: 249)

Secondly, in 1969 Brinkmann became the most important agent of the cultural transfer of American Beat- and pop-literature to Western Germany. As an editor and translator he published several anthologies of mainly American Beat Poetry, prose, essays and interviews, like *Lunch Poems and other Poems* (*Lunch Poems und andere Gedichte*, translations of poems by Frank O'Hara), *ACID: New American Scene* (*ACID: Neue amerikanische Szene*, ed. with Ralf-Rainer Rygulla) and *Silver Screen: New American Poetry* (*Silver Screen: Neue amerikanische Lyrik*, with texts from Charles Bukowski, William S. Burroughs, Gerard Malanga, Michael McClure, Frank Zappa, and others).

Thirdly, in 1968 and 1969 his own poetics became profoundly inspired by these Beat- and pop-influences from the United States. In his volumes of poems, *Godzilla* and *The Pilots* (*Die Piloten*), Brinkmann used strategies of intermediality and intertextual references to other media and pop culture. At the end of 1971, however, he distanced himself from this phase of his work.[4]

Fourthly, in the late 1960s and in the early 1970s, Brinkmann started experimenting with radio plays, audio-montage and video recordings (Super 8 and other formats). Between 1970 and 1974, some of his radio plays and readings were broadcast by the *Westdeutscher Rundfunk*.

As Brinkmann died at an early age, some of his most influential and especially intermedial works were only published posthumously: the volume of material *Rome, Views* (1979, *Rom, Blicke*) recounting his stay in Rome as a fellow of Villa Massimo; the 5-CD-box *Words Sex Cut* (*Wörter Sex Schnitt*) with five hours of audio-material (2005, ed. by Herbert Kapfer and Katarina Agathos); and the movie *Brinkmann's Anger — Director's Cut* (2007, *Brinkmanns Zorn — Director's Cut*, ed. by Harald Bergmann).

We will focus on Brinkmann's cultural transfer of media theories and literary aesthetics from the United States to Western Germany and the intermedial and pop-related poetics of his poetry around 1968/69 (and thus on the second and third entry in the list above), since this focus will make him comparable with Flemish artist Patrick Conrad and his writings at that time. This approach to Brinkmann might not be new, as since the late 1990s scholars have already focused on Brinkmann's relation with American pop culture and his status as the 'father of German pop literature'. Recently, researchers like Markus Fauser, Dirk Niefanger, and Sibylle Schönenborn have been working on the *Metzler-Handbuch Rolf Dieter Brinkmann* and specifically aim to broaden the academic focus on his œuvre (see Fauser 2014: 12; Fauser 2015). Nevertheless, the confrontation of Brinkmann's and Conrad's specific adaptation of pop aesthetics will help us to read Brinkmann's works of 1968 and 1969 from a new, comparative view.

Patrick Conrad: From Neo-Experimentalism to Decadentism

Patrick Conrad chose to navigate a 'middle way' between mimetic poetry (incorporated by new forms of realism) and the neo-avant-garde (frequently using intermedial practices in order to undermine mimetic representations).[5] In the wake of the language experimentation of the 1950s, it was difficult for him and others to forge new aesthetic paths, and in the early 1960s Dutch poetry evolved in two directions; it was either very matter-of-fact (the New Realism of journals such as *Barbarber, Gard Sivik 2*, and *De Nieuwe Stijl*), or it was extremely experimental, such as the jazz-influenced poetry produced in Flanders (the poets of the journal *Labris*; Willy Roggeman). Conrad's middle way seemingly combines pop art elements *with* language experimentation, making it come across as less radical, which, somewhat surprisingly, made it immediately more noticeable and appreciated.

Brinkmann's provocative poems have a great deal in common with the poets showcased in the somewhat aggressive Dutch journal *De Nieuwe Stijl*: that same disregard for the distinction between high and low, that same anti-conventionality and lowbrow, even coarse humour. Brinkmann lifted his posture from the American literary scene. For his part, Conrad turned toward the Decadents and embraced a new *fin de siècle*: for his drawings, Aubrey Beardsley became the point of reference. This Decadentism adds a retro accent to the pop culture we see reflected in Conrad's poems as part of a deliberate counterculture attitude (Pay 1975: 431). A component of that attitude was the embrace of pop music, which Conrad refers to when he names the Beatles as one of his greatest inspirations:

> But after the Beatles, our entire way of living, thinking, making music — actually the entire culture — changed, and to an extent not yet seen in this century. [...] It was a factory, but a very useful one. Just look at the visual arts, such as pop art; everything changed with the Beatlemania phenomenon. [...] The Beatles unleashed those elements of playfulness, humour and psychedelia.[6] (Pay 1975: 427–28)

In the 1970s Conrad even introduced literature in pop music, in the LP *Happy As In the Presence Of a Woman* (1973, *Gelukkig als in het bijzijn van een vrouw*), which includes a performance by the Belgian blues singer Roland (Marreyt 2013). The Belgian poet Gust Gils was also experimenting with songs at that time.

Closely affiliated with the pop music at the time was pop art, with its use of modern materials (such as plexiglass) and popular topics, from Mick Jagger (Andy Warhol) to Coca Cola bottles, soup cans, ice-cream, tires, saws, targets, and flags. The term *global pop art* ('Global Pop Symposium' 206) has recently come into use to indicate that the movement involved more than just the Americans. In Belgium pop art took on an erotic tone with painters such as Pol Mara (1920–1998), who illustrated the cover for Conrad's novella *The Little Death of Kasper Q* (1971, *De kleine dood van Kasper Q*), and Evelyne Axell (1935–1972).[7]

The erotic subject matter in *The Little Death of Kasper Q* — a title that may refer to *la petite mort* in the work of Georges Bataille — ranges from lesbianism and paedophilia to sadism and sodomy (with a gorilla). Kasper behaves like a dandy in a highly artificial world. This Decadentism in Conrad's work increases in the 1970s. In the early 1970s, Conrad was one of the co-founders of the *Pink Poets*, a neo-Decadent group of poets who embraced a highly mannered form of poetry but were all individually quite different (Buelens 2001: 982): the hermeticism of Michel Bartosik and Wilfried Adams differs wildly from the neo-Baroque poems of Jan de Roek, Nic van Bruggen and Patrick Conrad. Van Bruggen, in turn, considered himself much more intimate than the theatrical Conrad (Roggeman 1980: 94). The *Pink Poets* viewed themselves as a neo-Dada group, a joke, even though poetically and formally, there is little about their work that is reminiscent of Dada. They were more of a neo-Romantic movement, further represented in Dutch by prose writers such as Jan Siebelink and the *Joyce & Co.* collective (Brems 2005: 358–62). This neo-Romantic turn in Conrad's poetry is illustrated in his collection *Conrad life on stage: Gedichten 1963–1973*, where new drawings in Beardsley style have been added.

But let us go back to Germany in 1968, when young writers discussed whether their literature should become *postmodern* and *pop*, concepts that were just imported from the US and controversial to the literary scene. In these debates, Rolf Dieter Brinkmann plays a central role.

2. Poetological Positions

At the end of June 1968, Leslie A. Fiedler presented his 'Case for Post-Modernism' and for a new literature at an international symposium in Freiburg on *For and Against Contemporary Literature in Europe and America* (*Für und wider die zeitgenössische Literatur in Europa und Amerika*). The weekly newspaper *Christ und Welt* invited him to present his theses; Fiedler's essay 'The Age of New Literature: The Rebirth of Critique' ('Das Zeitalter der neuen Literatur: Die Wiedergeburt der Kritik'), as published on 13 September 1968, became the cornerstone of his famous essay 'Cross the border, close the gap', which was published in December 1969 in, ironically enough, *Playboy* magazine (see Luckscheiter 1998: 369–73). His *Christ und Welt*-essay, translated into German, was the starting point of the so-called 'Fiedler-debate'.

Fiedler's plea for a new post-modern and pop-cultural literature was met with both praise and criticism by five younger German authors and critics whom *Christ und Welt* had asked to react to Fiedler.[8] Especially Martin Walser's essay 'Myths, Milk, and Mettle' ('Mythen, Milch und Mut') responded critically to Fiedler: while he welcomed his critique of traditional art and literature, at the same time he questioned his aesthetic programme. Walser was afraid that Fiedler only replaced 'popes of classicism' with 'popes of pop, conforming to market laws'[9] (1968: 59) and he rejected his American mysticism from an enlightened and socialist standpoint as a representative of the Gruppe 47, the SDS (Socialist German Student's Association) and *littérature engagée*: 'Art is dead, long live not anti-art [...] but rather democratic literature'[10] (1968: 60).

Brinkmann's contribution to the Fiedler-debate, his essay 'Attack on the Monopoly: I Hate Old Poets' ('Angriff aufs Monopol: Ich hasse alte Dichter'), is a fundamental critique of the former reactions from his German colleagues. In the subtitle, which is a quotation from Gregory Corso, he marks his opposition to 'the Ugly, Cynical Old Males of the Cultural Establishment'[11] (1968c: 70). Brinkmann describes the debate on Fiedler as a cultural war between a traditional European-occidental hegemony and an innovative development of American culture — with writers like Burroughs or Pynchon. Whilst Brinkmann asks whether rigid national views are still helpful, and Fiedler attacks the cultural monopoly of the occident, according to Brinkmann, German authors are basically blinded and even racist:

'There is a general deep-rooted ignorance and aversion against all that is "alien" to "our species".' (Brinkmann 1968c: 69).[12] By contrast, Brinkmann suggests that his German readers can learn something from these American tendencies on both aesthetic and infrastructural levels: on the one hand, he describes how the potential of literature as a medium could help discover human subjectivity in a mass and consumer society; on the other hand, he gives examples of authors who work as versatile artists and demonstrates how pre-official or underground literary scenes are implemented in the United States.

In opposition to political authors like Erich Fried or Peter Weiss, who had just published their critical texts *and Vietnam and (und Vietnam und)* respectively *Viet Nam Discourse (Viet Nam Diskurs)* on the Vietnam war (see Fried 1966; Weiss 1968), as well as authors like Martin Walser and Günter Grass, who were connected with political movements and parties, Brinkmann rejected such forms of political literature and actions that would merely 'create insanity, in the name of humanity'[13] (Brinkmann 1968c: 74). Through several harsh comments Brinkmann already showed his strong opposition to political movements and literary institutions; from 1970 onward he strengthened this role as an outsider of the literary system (in 1968/69 he participated in a happening on the 'final solution to the student problem' ('Endlösung der Studentenfrage') in Cologne, and in Berlin he publicly announced to critic Marcel Reich-Ranicki that he would shoot him if the book in his hand were a machine gun; see Bentz 1998: 244; Keppler-Tasaki 2012: 215).

In his essay, Brinkmann generally adheres to Fiedler's understanding of post-modernism, looking for a different concept of a societal change that uses new media and new forms of literature. In Brinkmann's view, 'the new man' can thrive in mass communication, popular culture and media like movies, music, and drugs. This '"new" human of the second half of the twentieth century'[14] rises through 'the conquest of the inner space: through an adventure of the mind, the extension of the mental capabilities of human beings' (1968c: 76).[15]

The way in which Brinkmann adapts this approach to his own poetics is highly significant. His focus on the medial broadening of literature strengthens the presence of the moment, mobility, intermedial and intertextual references to material like movie posters, newspaper headlines, comics or songs. In his essay 'The Movie in Words' ('Der Film in Worten'), written in February 1969 and published in his anthology *ACID: New American Scene (ACID: Neue amerikanische Szene)*, Brinkmann elaborates on this intermedial view. The title of the essay harks back to a quote by Jack Kerouac and exemplifies Brinkmann's poetics of mixing: 'There are blends — pictures, interwoven with words; sentences, newly arranged to pictures and contexts of picture (imaginations); LPs, designed like books ... etc.' (1969a: 384).[16] Whilst at that time in Europe political writing is mainly linked to the literary reflection upon political topics, to Brinkmann his specific usage of technical possibilities 'creates a fraction of liberated reality'[17] (Brinkmann 1969a: 384),[18] and helps the underprivileged to subvert the hegemonic categories of knowledge. In his essays, he uses this strategy as well, when interrupting his argument and explaining that he is just listening to a *The Doors*-LP and perhaps should stop writing and enjoy

FIG. 6.2. Cover of *ACID: Neue amerikanische Szene*, ed. by
Rolf Dieter Brinkmann and Ralf-Rainer Rygulla, published in 1969 by März
(Brinkmann and Rygulla 1969a: cover).

the song, or that he should stop writing and walk to the city centre to figure out what is going on in the cinemas — thereby downplaying the role of literature as *Leitmedium* [key medium] (see 1968c: 66; 1969a: 394). In his plea for intertextual strategies he even recommends deliberate plagiarism (1969a: 390) and collaborative ways of writing.[19]

Such intermedial strategies and collaborative forms of writing require a change of literary institutions and traditional concepts of authorship. Brinkmann mentions multi-talented artists like John Perreault, Gerard Malanga, Tom Veitch, und Anne Waldman (see 1969a: 386), who question the traditional idea that a literary author should mainly or only be a writer. These expanded forms of literary production and authorship need alternative networks and publishing companies, too. Brinkmann distinguishes an official from a pre-official literary scene in the United States and describes the anthology *ACID* (see Figure 6.2) as an attempt to make translations of 'pre-official US-works' available in Germany. Brinkmann himself has at that time already published in both alternative and official German publishing companies like Oberbaumpresse on the one hand and Kiepenheuer & Witsch on the other, and he knows that the official publishing companies will take over the most interesting underground authors anyway (see Brinkmann and Rygulla 1969d: 417). In his essay he recommends the Edition Voltaire from Bernward Vesper and later terrorist Gudrun Ensslin as an outstanding German example of pre-official literary institutions. The publisher of *ACID*, Jörg Schröder's company März Verlag, was established in 1969 as a demerger from the Melzer Verlag, and became famous for its pop cultural, pornographic and subversive publications before becoming insolvent in 1974 (see Bandel, Kalender, and Schröder 2011; Ott 1998).

But how does Brinkmann connect this poetological position to his own poetry? Poetry is, as Brinkmann writes in a foreword of *The Pilots*, 'the most convenient form to conserve spontaneous events and motions, to fix the sensitivity of a certain moment concretely as a snap-shot' (1968c: 185).[20] A writer has to be unscrupulous and write down spontaneous perceptions of every-day-life. In contrast to the majority of established German authors who are focused on stylistic issues, Brinkmann follows Frank O'Hara's rule that 'simply everything one sees or is dealing with can become a poem, if one observes it closely enough and describes it directly, even if it is just lunch' (Brinkmann 1968b: 187).[21]

This spontaneous way of writing leads to a significant paradox of reception, according to Brinkmann, since some readers do not value his poems as poetry: 'They said that these [poems] are simple, everyone could understand them, which, at the same time, made my poems incomprehensible to them' (1968c: 186).[22] This paradox would already be an example of Brinkmann's play with literary genres and the reader's perception, as we will later see in the analyses of exemplary poems. Thus spontaneity, directness and a specific form of simplicity are key characteristics of Brinkmann's new realism, which we will now confront with the extreme masquerades in Conrad's work and his poetical defence of illusionism.

Patrich Conrad's Defence of the Lie

In one of his rare writings on poetry, his acceptance speech for the 'Ark Prize of the Free Word' ('Ark Prijs van het Vrije Woord') in 1969, Conrad advocated the lie. The lie — which, to him, is nothing else than imagination (Pay 1975: 425) — has a liberating, healing effect: 'Lying that frees him of reality, largely grotesque and burlesque, while at the same time making the boring everyday more or less bearable'[23] (Conrad 1969: 486).

The lie is primarily important in terms of constructing an I, an identity. The poet puts on his mask. He creates, according to Conrad, an 'imaginary biography' (1969: 486) or 'dream autobiography' (Roggeman 1975: 109), just as his predecessor Karel van de Woestijne constructed a 'symbolic biography'. And just as that *fin de siècle* poet did at a certain stage in his life, Conrad too fled from the banality of reality into an artificial world of aestheticism, hyper-refinement and pleasure. He revels in complication and presents himself as a dandy. To him — just as for Brinkmann — poetry and life are ultimately the same thing: 'In shaping all the facets of my life, I am a poet, and literature is *one* of the means to briefly pinpoint that life is literature, but there are also others' (Pay 1975: 426).[24]

Such a poet may not seem very socially engaged. Indeed, in interviews Conrad rails against the notion of commitment: 'It's true, I generally find what people refer to as "political *engagement*" tasteless. I think it's totally useless for someone here to write poems about the war in Vietnam' (Roggeman 1975: 113–14).[25] Though he himself had once succumbed to the weight of history, as becomes evident in his poem 'A Doll by Patrick Conrad with Pola Negri Playing Eleonora' (1966) with its direct references to Vietnam ('Everything, meaning this, too, | takes place in | Viet-Nam'), according to Conrad poetry should not be used as 'a weapon' (Pay 1975: 429) in the battle against war.

That curious, intermedial poem was published as a special edition with artwork consisting of four pages and we present it here as a case study. There are actually several of Conrad's poem cycles from 1966 to 1968 that can be classified as innovative because of their intermediality. Conrad introduces elements of comic writing in the cycle *Rose My Camel* (1965, *Rose mon chameau*). In the poem 'Babi Yar', which appeared in the neo-avant-garde journal *De Tafelronde* in 1968,

> Victorian gentlemen with stiff collars, cut-out female nudes, hand-drawn phallic flowers and Beatles quotes ("When you say hello, I say goodbye")[26] printed in *Yellow Submarine* font in speech bubbles produce a subtext that is sometimes absurd and sometimes ironic in a story filled with Freudian allusions, with a guest appearance by Charles Baudelaire. (Buelens 2001: 987)[27]

This intermediality combined with sexual provocations seems to be the most interesting parallel between Conrad and Brinkmann as an analysis of some of their poems will show.

3. Critical Reception

Rolf Dieter Brinkmann

During his lifetime, the reception of Brinkmann's work was ambivalent: on the one hand, important critics like Marcel Reich-Ranicki (1968) looked beyond the personal animosities and praised his talent from early on (see also Piwitt 1979 for posthumous praise). On the other hand, Brinkmann's provocative behaviour and difficult private situation made him an outsider to the literature business, especially from 1970 onwards, when Brinkmann decided to withdraw from the public sphere and into silence (1995b: 218). In his review of *Rome, Views*, Hermann Peter Piwitt states in 1979: 'The ones who posthumously praise him with literary prizes and even profoundly interpret the poems of the 16-year-old, should ask themselves, where they were when, as in his final days, he was living from one borrowed hundred-mark-note to the next' (Piwitt 1979: 327).[28]

The first two decades after Brinkmann's death are characterized by a reserved reception. We see rather personal approaches to his life and works and attempts to make new materials available (Brinkmann 1995a; Geduldig/Sagurna 1994), alongside some early attempts to analyse his œuvre systematically: a special issue of *Text + Kritik* in 1981, a commentary of his work published in the Sammlung Metzler series in 1989 (Arnold 1981; Späth 1989), some articles and only a few monographs, which are mainly interested in the usage of material from other arts and from everyday life (Urbe 1985; Groß 1993). Significantly, just after the historical changes of 1989/90 and the temporary disappearance of socialist utopias, Brinkmann's literature plays an important role in three publications on the political power of literature beyond the Gruppe 47 and *littérature engagée*: Klaus Briegleb, Martin Hubert, and Gundel Mattenklott deal with 'ways of writing in emptiness' (Briegleb 1993: 154),[29] a literary aestheticization of politics (Hubert 1992), and the potentials of a literature from the margins (Mattenklott 1992)[30] when analyzing Brinkmann's aesthetics.

From the end of the 1990s onwards, the reception of Brinkmann and his work changes in a remarkable way. Jörgen Schäfer's dissertation *Pop-Literatur: Rolf Dieter Brinkmann und das Verhältnis zur Populärkultur in der Literatur der sechziger Jahre* plays a key role in this change (1998). An influential critical analysis by Jost Hermand in 1971 on *Pop International* was mainly responsible for the fact that the literary institutions of Western Germany did not respond favourably to Brinkmann's conception of pop literature in the 1970s and 1980s (although authors like Hubert Fichte, Elfriede Jelinek, Diedrich Diederichsen, or Rainald Goetz are examples of pop authors at that time; see Hermand 1971). Starting in 1995 with *Faserland* by Christian Kracht and *Soloalbum* by Benjamin von Stuckrad-Barre, a very successful boom of pop literature caught the attention of the German literary market for some years. Suddenly, critics and literary scholars had to deal with this phenomenon and its history, which usually took them back to Rolf Dieter Brinkmann's import of pop culture aesthetics from the United States to Germany. Monographs and volumes on German pop literature became countless, and most of them were focusing on Brinkmann as the founder or at least an important distributor of this tradition

(Schäfer 1998; Ullmaier 2001; Baßler 2002; Ackermann and Greif 2003; Schäfer 2003; Schumacher 2003; Hecken 2009; McCarthy 2015b; Stahl 2015). This specific reception of Brinkmann as an initiator of German pop literature is responsible for his increasing importance in writings on German literary history since 1998.

Yet, we should be aware that Markus Fauser, on occasion of Brinkmann's seventy-fifth birthday in 2015, published an article with the angry title 'He Never Was the God-Father of Pop'.[31] According to Fauser, Brinkmann's work is much broader than the 'very short phase' of his engagement with pop, 'only a small part of his poems was influenced by pop'.[32] And indeed, at the latest since 1998, the expanding research on Brinkmann also discusses the following topics: the intermediality of Brinkmann's texts and especially their text-picture-relations (Strauch 1998; Röhnert 2007; von Steinaecker 2007; von Petersdorff 2009; Fauser 2011); Brinkmann's aesthetics of empirical writing and his relation with space, objects and every-day-life (Bandeili 2014); his specific concepts of subjectivity and consciousness (Herrmann 1999; Bauer 2002; Okun 2005); the 'intercultural Brinkmann' — Brinkmann as a traveller or artist in London and Rome, as an intercultural mediator between the United States and Germany, and as an author who uses language differences in his poems (Kramer 2000; Kramer 2003; Kramer 2010; Dembeck 2013; see also Schlösser 1987); and finally as a subcultural, subversive or neo-avant-garde author (Bentz 1998; Ackermann and Greif 2003; Ernst 2006; Ernst 2013). Most researchers focus on his novel *No One Knows Anymore* (1968, *Keiner weiß mehr*; see Bandeili 2014; Irsigler 2013; Rauen 2010), his late material volume *Rome, Views* (1979, *Rom, Blicke*; see Bandeili 2014; Herrmann 1999), his poetry (Kohlroß 2000; Kramer 2010; Röhnert and Geduldig 2012) and his acoustic works (Selg 2001; Schumacher 2006; Binczek 2012). In our paper, we deal with three essays and two volumes of poetry from 1968 and 1969, which for the scope of our analysis constitutes a representative part of Brinkmann's oeuvre.

Patrick Conrad

The reception of Conrad's poetry is far less sensational than Brinkmann's. It is only recently that Conrad's thrillers have been awarded literary accolades and his poetry collected in one monumental volume *As* (2015), leading to a renewed interest in his work. Conrad's early collections met with a positive reception in small circles and quickly received awards. It was seen as mannerist poetry.[33] After the flamboyant actions of the *Pink Poets* in the 1970s, however, public interest in his work waned. Still, in many ways (e.g., his mania for citation, highly mannered style, etc.), Conrad can be seen as a predecessor of the postmodern poets who emerged in Flanders in the second half of the 1980s (e.g. Dirk van Bastelaere and Peter Verhelst). He never again ventured into political poetry. In the unabashedly autobiographical poems of *Chronicles* (1998, *Annalen*), it is only surreptitiously and pessimistically that he alludes to the relationship of the present to the past:

> Because he who thought yesterday that he could think
> Tomorrow with cut off tongue
> Will be trembling and counting his balls
> In the night of a window-less cell[34] (Conrad 1998: 34)

4. Literary Practices

Rolf Dieter Brinkmann: Godzilla *(1968) and* The Pilots *(1968)*

It certainly is problematic to consider Rolf Dieter Brinkmann's œuvre as a whole as experimental, especially since Brinkmann worked in different media and used various aesthetic strategies. Karsten Herrmann, who asked the question how Brinkmann's literature could be described as 'experimental', looked at the way Brinkmann makes use of neo-avant-garde strategies and techniques like cut-up and fold-in, multimediality, montages of texts, collages of images and collages of images and texts. According to Herrmann, Brinkmann's use of these techniques in his posthumously published volumes of material and collages [Material- und Collagebänden] like *Rome, Views* (1979), *Explorations of the Specification of the Sense of Rebellion* (1987, *Erkundungen für die Präzisierung des Gefühls für einen Aufstand*) or *Cuts* (1988, *Schnitte*) adheres less strictly to the tradition of the historic avant-garde or experimental German writers of the 1960s like Helmut Heissenbüttel, Jürgen Becker, and Alexander Kluge (Herrmann 1999: 194). Rather he is 'in his works of montage and collage [...] definitely influenced by American trends' (Herrmann 1999: 194–95).[35]

In Brinkmann's works, the transfer and adaptation of this 'North-American Postmodernism'[36] (Herrmann 1999: 209–24), with its use of every-day materials, the connection and expansion of art and life, its experiments with images and perception and its popularization of literature, intensifies in 1968 and 1969. His translation of Frank O'Hara's *Lunch Poems* and his anthologies of the 'new American scene' and 'new American poems' respectively — *ACID: New American Scene* (edited with Ralf-Rainer Rygulla) and *Silver Screen: New American Poetry* — are published in 1969; these influences by American postmodernism inspire his volumes of poetry, *Godzilla: Poems* and *The Pilots: New Poems*, both published in 1968. An analysis of these volumes will help us to understand Brinkmann's literary experiments and how they are inspired by American postmodernism. We will consider to what extent Brinkmann's 'pop-period (1967–1969)'[37] (Röhnert and Geduldig 2012: 95–290) shows a specific awareness and influence of the global pop artists movement.

Godzilla: Poems *(1968)*

Godzilla is a collection of seventeen poems printed on twenty-two cuttings from magazines. The cuttings show prints of smiling female underwear models or, mostly, parts of their half-naked bodies (see Figure 3 for an example). The collection was originally published in an edition of 200 copies with a changing choice of coloured cuttings (see Urbe 1985: 99) and later reprinted in black and white (see Brinkmann 1968a). This specific combination of erotic poems and cuttings from magazines with half-naked female body-parts on them is practised by Tom Clark and Sherry Barba, too, as Brinkmann and Rygulla show in their anthology *ACID* (Clarke 1969; Barba 1969). The title of the volume, *Godzilla*, refers to Ishirō Hinda's 1954 horror movie, in which the legendary monster attacks Japan's cities and population, jolted by atomic bomb tests.

Gedicht

Hier, wo es nichts mehr
zu sagen gibt, hört man
auf zu reden und fängt
an abzukauen. Eine alte

Blume, die aus Papier ge-
dreht ist, fällt um wie
eine alte Blume, die nicht
aus Papier gedreht ist

und unter einem Licht
das von Osram ist wie
ein Licht, das nicht
von Osram ist, macht

man weiter an derselben
Stelle wie ..... Und kann
vor lauter Beschäftigtsein
nicht ..... reden und vor

..... Gefühl nicht mehr
..... wenn man abkaut und
..... einen abkauen läßt
..... ohne polizeiliche

.....nehmigung. Wir bleiben
..... beschäftigt.

Godzilla und der Vogel

Ein Vogel ist kein Selbst-
bedienungsautomat, auch
kein Gummitier, sagte er

aber als ich ihn dort
hüpfen sah ohne wegzu-
fliegen, wußte ich, daß

er „piep" machen würde
wenn ich ihm auf den Kopf
träte. Und der Vogel machte

„piep!"

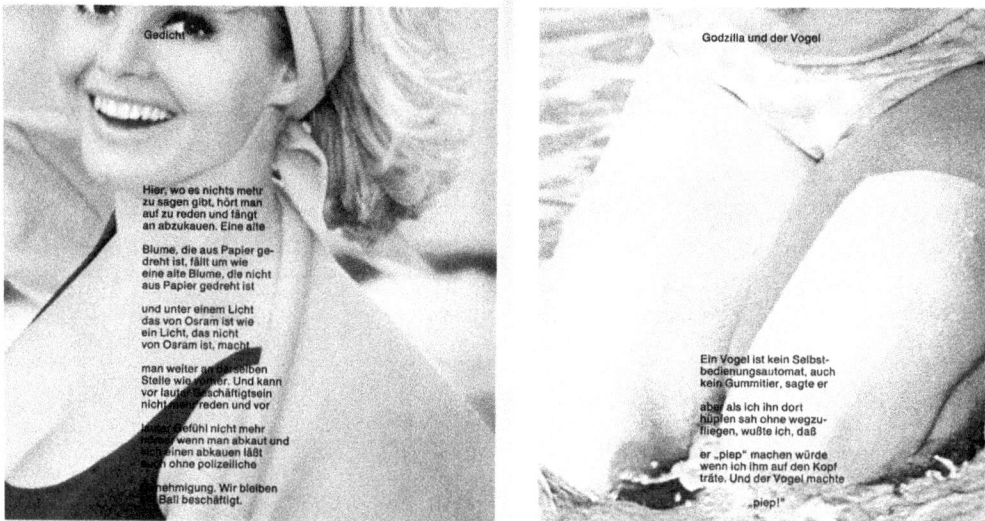

FIG. 6.3. Rolf Dieter Brinkmann, 'Gedicht' and 'Godzilla und der Vogel' [Poem; Godzilla and the Bird] from *Godzilla* (Brinkmann 1968a: 176–77)

This intermedial setting provokes a range of dichotomies, like civilization vs. nature, the beauties vs. the beast, the shaved female bodies vs. the hairy monster or the sexual female objects vs. the implied view of the male monster or reader. Brinkmann contrasts the promises of tamed lust and capitalized satisfaction in the sterile and artificial advertising magazines on the one hand with the natural sexual desires of his (male) readers. In this constellation, his intermedial poems become the central space to reflect on the impact and meaning of mass media communication on the imagination of bodies and eroticism. The specific achievement of this setting 'can be seen in a purposeful act of subversion of the ready-made material: the confrontation of a "clean" public projection of lust with a disinhibited libidinous phantasy' (Röhnert 2007: 321).[38]

The construction of gender and sexuality in this intermedial setting is ambivalent. On the one hand, the female bodies are fragmented — they mostly appear as faceless torsos — , which could be considered as a recurring act of violence against the integrity of women. But on the other hand, here the object of reflection is not the real female body but its mediatized version in the advertising world: 'In the advertising world, females stay real as a photo' (Fliethmann 2012: 125).[39] And the setting also subverts forced binary structures of gender and sexuality: superficially we might associate the implied male gaze on these photos with Godzilla's desires (whose gender obviously is related to male stereotypes), but at the same time we have to cope with Godzilla's indeterminate sex.

The poems of *Godzilla* address the bigoted principles of a capitalist consumer society in which eroticism and lust are no more than trimmed products. Its second poem, 'Meditation on Porn' ('Meditation über Pornos'), starts with the lines: 'This cunt is good | This cunt is good | This cunt is good | This cunt is good'

(Brinkmann 1968a: 162).[40] It verbalizes the objectification and commercialization of the main female sexual organ and how '[t]he direct honesty of "dirty speech" helps to make a decision on the offered good' (Späth 1989: 49).[41] Here, the vagina is attributed the status of a mass produced consumer good, and the poem reproduces the expected reaction of male consumers ('we') to such products ('here we cum' ['hier spritzen wir ab']). But in this alienating context, the language still allows for a moment of subversion, since nature and uncontrollability find their way back into the scenery. Incidentally, 'we' find an unforeseen niche of 'natural rest' on the next page that comforts 'us':

> Slowly sprouts
> again some hair at the
> verge of a wrinkle. We
> lie down in its
>
> shadow.
> (Brinkmann 1968a: 162)[42]

The next poem, 'Romance I' ('Romanze I'), states already in the first line the replaceability of the female subject: 'The lady isn't one. XYZ.'[43] This can be linked to the exchangeable illustrated female body that the poem is printed on, but it can also be read as pointing at the mutation or transition of gender and sexual identities in pop cultural settings:

> The lady isn't one. XYZ. The
> balls are moving. One goes
> dancing and comes back
>
> changed.
> (Brinkmann 1968a: 163)[44]

And not only female bodies change, as 'Romance I' shows us, the centre of male power and potency mutates into a consumer's product, too:

> Now something in
> his trousers becomes stiff and clots
> to toothpaste.
> (Brinkmann 1968a: 163)[45]

The unnatural mutation of sperm into toothpaste hints at the transformation of natural desire into a discourse of hygiene while at the same time inducing male impotence. Moreover, this transformation is connected to Godzilla as the mutated monstrosity of male lust under capitalist conditions. And still other natural parts of the human body become the subject of transition and destruction as in 'Godzilla telefoniert nicht so gern' [Godzilla does not like to phone]: this poem deals with pubic hair and overcomes the impossibility of using the word 'Schamhaar' [pubic hair] in a poem, which Brinkmann bemoans in his essay 'On Poetry and Sexuality' ('Über Lyrik und Sexualität').[46] 'Godzilla' as 'he' ('er') announces 'her' ('ihrer') on the phone that an act of brutality ('vom Körper abgerissen', parted from the body) will follow and bring death to at least her pubic hair — which he 'enjoys' ('vergnügt'; Brinkmann 1968a: 173).

'Celluloid 1967/68' is the longest poem of *Godzilla*, the title being an intertextual reference to Heißenbüttel's experimental prose *Celluloid 1959/60*. The poem reflects critically on the objectification and quantification of lust in Hollywood movies:

> The reproduction takes place
> immediately using an obscure formula:
> one time Coca Cola, two times
> Kim Novak, three times the guy from Hol-
> lywood, four times George Hamilton, five
> times Senta Berger, eight times Tony Curtis
> nine times the tits of Jayne Mansfield
> [...] I mean when
> this is not enough, I mean
> from
> left
> below
> towards
> right
> above
> till
> the image is full of their white
> flesh and you can personally
> jack off.
> (Brinkmann 1968a: 171–72)[47]

The objectification of female bodies and the emptiness of male masturbation under the regime of capitalist cultural industries are described directly in this poem. Again, Brinkmann plays with the reproducibility of images, here with images of Hollywood and movie stars. His words measure up the frame of a television ('from left below towards right above') by forming a chiastic structure in combination with the typesetting (from left above to right below), and thus exposing the on-screen borderlines of lust in movie productions. In the first lines of the poem, he describes openly how stars like Kim Novak, George Hamilton, Senta Berger, and Raquel Welch perform the 'real sex' that they are not allowed to have on this screen — a single poem as a medium of truth beyond the lies of a mass medium like the movies.

The Pilots: New Poems (1968)

Compared to *Godzilla*, Brinkmann's volume *The Pilots* displays a broader scope thematically and aesthetically and an even stronger link with the global pop artists movement and especially American writers and movies. In his foreword, Brinkmann explicitly dedicates this collection of poems to Frank O'Hara, who was 'a passionate moviegoer'[48] and who taught him how to produce poems out of everyday life situations (Brinkmann 1968b: 187). The cover consists of a collage in the style of the famous cover of *Sgt. Pepper's Lonely Hearts Club Band* by The Beatles (1967). Thomas von Steinaecker describes it as a 'psychedelic landscape of flower power'[49] (2007: 113) with pictures of naked women, pop stars and friends and family of Brinkmann, and himself as being part of it. In the speech bubble that pops up from Brinkmann's image, he gives his collection its neo-Romantic motto: 'It is not enough to **love** art. One must **be** art!' (see Röhnert 2007: 326).

The Pilots is a tripartite with each part being introduced by a (translated) comic strip that is taken from Joe Brainard's series *C-Comics*, which is more a parody or meta-reflection of the commercial comics (Brinkmann 1968b: 188, 216, 247; Röhnert 2007: 326). The sixty poems are replete with references to iconic American places like Washington, DC, Beverly Hills, and Hollywood (Brinkmann 1968b: 218, 231, 232), American products like Coca Cola, chewing gum, or popcorn (Brinkmann 1968b: 193–94, 199, 215, 241–42, 255), American singers and alternative bands like Frank Sinatra and The Fugs (Brinkmann 1968b: 198, 200), and especially American movie characters like Batman, Mary Poppins, or Bonnie & Clyde (Brinkmann 1968b: 207, 211, 244, 267) and movie stars like Liz Taylor, Ava Gardner, Charlie Chaplin, Humphrey Bogart, Jerry Lewis, Johnny Weismüller, Ursula Andress, Raquel Welch, Jane Russel, and Marilyn Monroe (Brinkmann 1968b: 217, 222, 224–25, 231, 232, 235, 237). Besides these numerous references to American movie and pop culture, the poems deal with 'the private world, everyday life' ('die Welt des Privaten, des Alltags') — and these different lines of motives are combined in various ways (Röhnert 2012: 98).

Since we are aiming at comparing Brinkmann's pop poems with Conrad's works and are especially interested in how both authors are political in their non-political approach to literary aesthetics, we will limit our analysis to some poems that deal with political topics. We will see that Brinkmann's approach to a new form of political writing in *The Pilots* expresses indifference.

A first example can be read as a complete and even sarcastic denial of any political content of literature. In the poem 'Political poem after a sleepless night' ('Politisches Gedicht nach einer schlaflosen Nacht'; (Brinkmann 1968b: 253), the title of which relates directly to the *littérature engagée*, the lyrical I describes waking up in the morning, seeing his kid defecate on his potty and starting to defecate himself:

> I am
>
> sitting down and start
> shitting, too
> and all talks are
>
> finally finished
> (Brinkmann 1968b: 253)[50]

The political potential of poetry is in the most literal sense dropped in an intimate and private situation. However, at the end, the lyrical I tells about his dream of a toothless, naked woman who apparently has not been able to poo for years:

> [...] on the dirty
> Towel from last night
>
> Leans smiling a
> Naked woman
> Toothless and naked
>
> Toothless and naked

> And smiling. (She
> Finally wants after
> Years once again
> To shit properly,
> I presume.)
> (Brinkmann 1968b: 254)[51]

Here, a glimpse of the horrifying situation of the Vietnamese people under the circumstances of war shines through, as in the poem 'Cheap' ('Billig', see Brinkmann 1968b: 205), too. In 'Cheap', Brinkmann reacts to the compelling political situation at the time of the Vietnam War, describing two old men who apparently make a deal in their function as statesmen, whilst the meaning of ketchup changes from being a symbol of western wealth to the death-bringing weapons of the war (see Späth 1989: 53):

> And somebody is falling as li-
> quid ketchup like a red
> string from heaven
> (Brinkmann 1968b: 205)[52]

Whilst the political references in these lines remain rather vague, the poem 'Farewell, Dr. Wilhelm Reich; dedicated to the police of Berlin' ('Lebewohl Dr. Wilhelm Reich [der Berliner Polizei gewidmet]') is 'apparently Brinkmann's most direct contribution to the political conflicts of his time' (Späth 1989: 51).[53] Here, against the background of the brutal incidents during the Berlin demonstrations against the Shah of Persia and Axel Cäsar Springer's media house, the poem cynically asks the police about their attitude towards the demonstrators: 'WHY DIDN'T YOU KILL THEM?'[54] (Brinkmann 1968b: 257). Its reference to Wilhelm Reich (and thus to his work *Mass Psychology of Fascism*) and its suggestion to the policemen that they could torture the demonstrators 'to quickly | get rid of some pressure'[55] (Brinkmann 1968b: 257) describes Germany as a pre-fascist society and its executive as a fascist institution, performing uncontrolled violence.

Much more complex and rather *pars pro toto* for Brinkmann's general literary attitude towards society is his poem 'Ra-ta-ta-ta for [orig. für] Bonnie & Clyde etc.'. The poem refers to Arthur Penn's gangster movie which started screening in Germany at the end of 1967. Brinkmann already relates to this movie in the introduction of *The Pilots*, contrasting the 'spookiness' of the German cultural institutions and their 'endless cry for style' with the noise, violence and aggression of this movie: 'What did Warren Beatty say to the owners of German cinemas when Bonnie and Clyde started screening? "When the final scene with the fire of the machine gun is shown you have to turn the volume all the way up!"' (Brinkmann 1968c: 186).[56]

The 'Ra-ta-ta-ta' in the title helps onomatopoetically to imagine the burst of a machine gun — which already contrasts sharply with the highbrow tone of traditional poetry. The unrhymed tiercets (with an added closing line) support a heavy reading speed that is underlined by the words, too: 'The movie is running on and Bonnie is running | on and Clyde is running on und we || are running with them' (Brinkmann 1968b: 244).[57] It is noticeable that only three times an enjambment cuts words into two, the compound nouns 'female cinema ushers' and 'machine gun fire': 'Platz- || anweiserinnen', 'Maschinen- | gewehrfeuer' and 'Platzanweiser- /| innen'. The cutting of these specific words allows for the imagination of destroyed bodies.

But the poem is rather ironic in its description of the cinema experience with 'us' watching *Bonnie and Clyde* on the screen and their squirting blood just being red jelly. Interpretations of 'Ra-ta-ta-ta für Bonnie & Clyde etc.' are as ambiguous as the poem itself: whilst Keppler-Tasaki (2012: 214) doubts that this poem 'could be fully explained in reading it only as critical of the state'[58] and that its rebellious playfulness is comparable to Bonnie and Clyde, who 'do not find a political line but stumble joyfully and hysterically from situation to situation',[59] Jan Röhnert (2007: 331) reads the poem only as a 'parody of the use of special effects in commercial cinema'.[60] At the same time, though, he discusses whether the poem, in its profundity, creates a paralysis amongst 'us' moviegoers (and readers) (Röhnert 2007: 332).

These different readings of a poem that sends aggressive ('Ra-ta-ta-ta') as well as meta-reflective, playful and even sweet ('red jelly') signals hint at a central criticism of Brinkmann's pop poems that is most prominently reproduced by the author himself: on the one hand these poems successfully take the changed media situation and the global pop artists movement and its aesthetic strategies as the starting point of an ambiguous and media-reflective cultural production that explores intermedial settings of literary writing, but on the other hand their societal and especially critical impact remains rather harmless. In 1971, Brinkmann distances himself from this part of his œuvre (see footnote 4). In his posthumously published book *Rome, Views* (1979), for instance, Brinkmann appears much more frequently as an angry writer who condemns Western civilization in general.

Patrick Conrad: 'A Doll by Patrick Conrad with Pola Negri Playing Eleonora' (1966)

'A Doll by Patrick Conrad with Pola Negri Playing Eleonora' (a translation has been added at the end of this chapter, alongside a reprint of the original poem) appeared in 1966 as a special edition published by Monas, founded by Henri-Floris Jespers, and was also included, without the accompanying collage, in *Mercantile Marine Engineering*, which came out a year later. In a later edition of 1973, *Conrad life on stage*, the collage was replaced by a drawing in the style of Beardsley (Conrad 1973: 90-91, see Figure 6.4). These two publications are symptomatic of the tension between elite and mass culture that the poet was struggling with at the time. The special edition (250 printed copies) stands in stark contrast to the paperback edition on cheap paper published in a series called *The Gallows* (De Galge).

The collage, very much a persiflage of Eugène Delacroix's well-known picture *La Liberté guidant le peuple* (1830)[61] and John Heartfield's photomontage (1936), depicts a tortoise-like helmet over an American soldier's forehead (see Figure 6.5). The information presented is redundant: the word 'Vietnam' appears repeated in three places — at the bottom, in the middle and at the top; the Polish-American actress Pola Negri (1898–1987) appears in various poses; and the skeleton on which she appears to be perched at the top echoes the replicated heads at the bottom that look like those of Auschwitz survivors. The pyramid-shaped image is crowned, with some irony, by an American flag. Some elements are time-bound, such as the playbill for several old-fashioned musicals (*Bohemian Girl*; *White Cat*; *The Devil in Love*) and the poster for the opening of the Union Pacific transcontinental railroad in 1869. The stamped date at the centre of the collage, 21 March 1966, has its own significance. As the Dutch investigative journalist Willem Oltmans, who was based in the US at the time, wrote in his *Diaries* (*Memoires 1964–1966*), that was the day the *Times* reported that the land war was accelerating (2001: 309). The word 'Viet Doll' ('Viet Pop'), drawn on the playbill, is literally repeated in the poem. The poem and the visual text thus interact, deliberately creating an intermedial artwork. In fact, the poem acquires a much more political message through the association with the collage.

Hugo Brems (1972; 1981) has previously pointed out the fragmented nature of Conrad's early poetry, which paradoxically was eventually combined with storytelling aspects. Similar to other Conrad poems of that time, 'A Doll' is highly narrative. It depicts an actual situation: a man and a woman live in '(the only, perhaps, and probably last) stone | manor in Asia'. In section one of the poem, the woman, Eleonora, is described like a doll: her skin is 'tough as plastic or celluloid' and she can spread her arms and legs apart elastically. The house's garden is given a specific location in the 'mossy triangle of Khamkeut-Khammouane-Napé', somewhere in Laos. The intrusion of history is represented typographically by the two indented stanzas: these make direct mention of 'Viet-Nam', a B-52 bomber and American G.I.s.

One of the recurring themes in Conrad's early work that is prominent in this poem and occurs immediately in this first section is the process of hardening and petrification that even sexuality is subject to. The house is made of stone, while the natural surroundings are 'mossy' and bestial, and thus alive. The closing lines of this section are enigmatic, with the wordplay in 'husks: husks, helmets: helmets' also evoking both the hard and the soft. The shattered heavens foreshadow the doll's 'pieces' in the third section of the poem. The second section describes how Eleonora continues to slowly evolve into a doll. Even the capital Saigon is fake: made of neon. 'The vacant gaze of napalm eyes' is almost a premonition of the famous photo from 1972 of a naked young girl fleeing down the road after a napalm attack. In the third section, '(Eleonora Murdered)', the doll is broken, 'smashed and blood-/ less'. In the first of four three-line stanzas, she is only described in the past tense. And by the last of those stanzas, the doll has been overgrown by forest vegetation, as well as manmade material. The poem ends with a line in English from Oscar Wilde's *Poems in Prose* (1894), which in this context is surely meant as an ironic provocation: 'And there was silence in the house of Judgement'. The irony stems from the fact that the destruction of the inanimate doll mirrors the fate of the dead person in Wilde's prose poem. In punishment for his sins, 'the Man' is sent first to hell and then to heaven, but God is left speechless by the Man who refuses to acknowledge his plight and says that he has always lived in hell and has never been able to imagine heaven. The righteousness of God's judgement is thus questioned, just as the destruction of Eleonora is — and maybe of the people bombed by the Americans.

In terms of content this tripartite poem fits with Conrad's fascination for violence, as demonstrated for instance in his interest in movie stars, such as Marilyn Monroe, Jayne Mansfield, and Françoise Dorleac, all of whom 'died in a violent manner' (Roggeman 1975: 110) and died prematurely,[62] as well as for the female body, often described in vegetative or animal terms. The Stefan George motif of an artificial garden, which recurs in Conrad's short novel *Kasper Q*, is characteristic of his neo-Decadent inspiration. Another artificial element is the doll, an item which appears in other poems from that time as well, such as 'Nickelodeon' (1967):

> Photo:
> Crawling with light and make-up (Sarah?) a doll
> chaste in brocade and silver-stilled velvet
> with ancient gestures and the eyes the mouth
> mute hollows full of shadows and shades.[63] (1973: 113)

And in the poem 'Villa of roses' (1967, 'Villa des roses'), the woman is scoffed at: 'O tottering leprous doll with pox!'[64] (122). That woman turns out to be Eleonora Duse, the famous actress and mistress of the poet and playwright Gabriele d'Annunzio. She — or the cousin of the narrator in Poe's story — could be the source for the Eleonora named in 'A Doll'.

L'histoire montre que les guerres se divisent en deux catégories: les guerres justes et les guerres injustes.
MAO TSÉ TOUNG

FIG. 6.4. Illustration from Patrick Conrad, *Life on stage: Gedichten 1963–1973*
(1966: 90-91, © Patrick Conrad)

Dolls, puppets and mannequins figured prominently in the work of the Dada and Surrealist artists (e.g. in the work of Bauhaus artist Oscar Schlemmer) and, of course, also in pop art (e.g. Kienholz). They represent a negation of the humanity of the human figure. Marcel van Acker, the fictitious artist in Conrad's eponymous novel from 2009, takes up taxidermy at a certain point (241) and creates his own wax museum of people he has killed. The mummification or 'dollification' of human beings represents a negative process; when the doll of the poem is destroyed on top of that, it is like a double form of dying.

Is it a protest poem because of this? Not explicitly. Without the collage (as it appears in the Monas edition and the complete poems *As. Gedichten 1963–2014*, that were published in 2015) the poem could be considered no more than a free-form hermetic reflection on past events, whereas with the cartoon-like drawing that accompanies it in *Conrad life on stage*, the poem almost becomes a sort of *fin de siècle* story that is completely de-historicized. With the collage, however, the poem *is* openly critical, as previously mentioned. The paratext also amplifies those critical overtones: the specified setting that precedes the poem suggests that *all* poetry is politically tainted, given that 'everything' takes place in Vietnam, and Mao's motto ('History shows that wars are divided into two kinds, just and unjust') rings in the reader's ears and is used here ironically to allude to the 'just' war that the Americans, too, claim to be fighting. But what is both disconcerting and original is the false environment and unreal human (a doll) associated with the Vietnam theme, which to some extent convey very personal connotations.

The general consensus regarding Conrad's early poetry, in particular, is that it is impersonal (Jespers 1967), and more philosophical than psychological (Cartens 1995: 17). Cartens emphasizes the artificiality of this poetry:

> Conrad's poems are highly artificial. They are calculated, *constructed*, shaped; they evince tremendous erudition and a passion for gambling with all the cards of existence. They are not the jottings of a tortured soul looking to empty itself on paper in order to find acknowledgment and recognition among readers.[65] (1995: 16)

The viewpoint and the wording of the poems are nevertheless subjective,[66] so that a singular pathos emerges that one could call rhetorical because of its self-awareness as a construction. Conrad achieves that rhetorical/self-reflective pathos through various means, such as his use of inversion ('He with she lives'; 'in a subdued Saigon once a vibrant neon bush'; 'for so long the sun has been fixed') and alliteration that emerges as one of Conrad's most recognizable style principles, the typographical mark of indentation (which was lost in the collections but restored in the new 2015 edition), and his use of irony, as previously pointed out, in the montage, motto and closing citation. One final means by which the poem reveals its construction is the montage, or rather, collage. 'Writing a poem is about gathering the fragments, the elements of a puzzle, and there is only one unique way they will fit together correctly'[67] (Pay 1975: 431), Conrad says. This assembly indicates that the pathos has been orchestrated.

The notion of montage brings us to film. According to his friend Van Bruggen (Roggeman 1980: 94), Conrad revelled in theatricality and outward appearance, and the films he started making in the 1980s, mostly, would appear to be the inevitable culmination of that. The poet himself acknowledges that everything is in service of film: 'My experiments in poetry, illustration, a bit in prose, in human contact, the theatrical aspect I try to bring to poetry — all of that is, in the end, preparation for arriving at film' (Pay 1975: 435).[68]

Of all the elements that lead to pathos, the lyrical I would appear to be less objectified and impersonal than has been asserted in scholarship so far. Subjectivity is not absent from this supposedly I-less poetry. Conrad himself says that he was always looking at himself in a mirror: 'Writing poems and looking at yourself in a mirror are essentially the same thing, for that matter' (Pay 1975: 433).[69] But the mirror presents an incomplete image, warped by the fact that what is being represented is almost a projection, as on a stage. In much of his work, Conrad constructs alter egos, personas, so that even the most autobiographical of his poetry — such as his late collection *Chronicles* — is infected with poses.

FIG. 6.5. Illustration from Patrick Conrad, *Een pop van Patrick Conrad met Pola Negri in de rol van Eleonora* (Conrad 1966, © Patrick Conrad)

5. Conclusion: A Comparison of Patrick Conrad and Rolf Dieter Brinkmann

The confrontation of Flemish writer Patrick Conrad and German author Rolf Dieter Brinkmann and their aesthetics and poems written in 1968/69 revealed similarities as well as differences. In a similar manner both writers are part of the counterculture and repeatedly distance themselves from literary institutions. Both refuse to follow the concept of *littérature engagée* (writing novels on political topics, speaking in public as an intellectual). Rather, they develop more formal and media-oriented concepts of how literature could have social impact — they experiment with intermediality and adapt principles of filmic editing, or staging, to produce their poems. Both writers use pop-cultural elements (music, movie stars, visual arts) to eradicate the distinction between 'high' and 'low' literature, they write openly about sexuality and focus specifically on the female body and its *Warencharakter* [commodity character] in a consumer society.[70] As a result, neither is afraid of provoking the petty bourgeois, traditionalist and political authors. Finally, both stand for the idea that every-day-life and literary work coincide.

At the same time, there are obvious differences between Conrad and Brinkmann. Conrad chooses the lie and an elitist, dandyish posture and thus, despite his many references to pop culture, for *Hochkultur* [high culture]. Brinkmann's poetics in 1968/69, and especially his poetry, are more related to every-day-experiences and the search for an incorrupt perception (although his attitude towards 'reality' changes in his later work and so does his self-staging as a rebel, dandy, or loner). They draw on two different traditions: Brinkmann follows in the spirit of American postmodernism and its movie, music and pop culture, whereas Conrad goes further back in time to *fin de siècle* culture. Rather than renounce hermeticism, he uses it as an escape mechanism.

Brinkmann and Conrad both distance themselves from the prevailing bourgeois culture of the 1960s, but Conrad is definitely less polemical. Their criticism does not translate into action. And yet their so-called apoliticism is at times openly punctuated by a — albeit half-hearted — political perspective on reality. This discrepancy is typical of a great deal of Conrad's poetry and the so called Flemish 'mannerism' ('Maniërisme'; Jespers 1967) of the 1960s. It also proves typical for the poetry of Brinkmann and the tendencies of *Neue Subjektivität* [New Subjectivity]. Both aesthetic trends have never been able to close the gap between literature and society.

This becomes apparent when we compare our two poets with Situationism. Asger Jorn, who went from being a Cobra artist to a Situationist, was one of the first to reference the standard work on mannerism by Gustav R. Hocke, *Die Welt als Labyrinth* (1957), and to denote mannerism as a counter movement to classicism or formalism (De Groof 2007: 237). In his view, the new art transcends that opposition by viewing art as a process which is about more than merely providing answers to the questions of how (mannerism) and what (formalism), but also addressing where, when, why and so forth. It establishes a unity between mankind and the world and thus also between artist and reality. Something both Conrad and Brinkmann have never achieved.

Translations

Patrick Conrad

A Doll by Patrick Conrad with Pola Negri Playing Eleonora
1966

Everything, meaning this, too,
takes place in
Viet-Nam.

1.

He with she lives
far beyond the rice and the eucalyptus
    the mud and the buffaloes
in (the only, perhaps, and probably last) stone
manor in Asia.

No ore hardens from the sap of her skin
tough as plastic or celluloid:
Eleonora's skin a layer on her body.

Deeper in the mossy triangle of Khamkeut-Khammouane-Napé
(The patience is that of tigers, panthers and rust)
the oaks are even taller than the beeches
and the few plants growing in her moist garden
are, in fact, animals.

Like nothing so much as a polished piece in some costly collection
  — she spreads arms and legs mechanically open flexible
wider than a normal woman —
heaving she bends rubber receiving.

      Submissive and
      made-up: Eleonora
      in Viet-Nam.

      1 B-52 above and
      7 G.I.'s between:
      watchful hedges.

(And the drought and the tornadoes and the bombs from the heavens
and Eleonora's dusky skin a plague in the oil-slick night
and sometimes a book. On photography.)

Husks: husks, helmets: helmets:
like the heavens' fractured reflection in the shatters
of her mirror.

2.

On the surface, irreversibly,
in a subdued Saigon once a vibrant neon bush,
Eleonora becomes a doll with excruciating slowness.

Yet where the wet light falls, torn, in green flashes

and the muck sucks up the soles like slime,
where only ever drops but no rains come,
on the other side of the horse: a child, a tie,
with the vacant gaze of napalm eyes like blinded blossoms.

Surrounded by deep darkness and the wafting dust of rooms,
Eleonora petrifies inside her pink bark, motionless and bitter,
as in those far-off lands
for so long the sun has been fixed
somewhere at the base of silence.

3. (Eleonora Murdered)

Eleonora was a caressing night, a caressing night
that once stroked her velvet loins protectively
even forgotten even just before her death.

> And breaks both the
> thighs and the calves
> of plaster.

> Smashed and blood-
> less: Eleonora a
> Viet-Doll.

Smouldering and wilting her hollow pieces lie dust-caked
in the treacherous jungle, covered at length by
iron, furious ferns and a brackish silence.

And there was silence in the House of Judgment. (Oscar Wilde)

Een pop van Patrick Conrad met Pola Negri in de rol van Eleonora

Alles dus ook dit
speelt zich af in
Viët-Nam.

I.

Hij met haar woont
ver achter de rijst en de eucalyptus
        de modder en de buffels
in (het enige misschien en weliswaar het laatste) stenen
herenhuis van Azië.

In geen erts verharden de sappen van haar huid
die echter taai is als plastiek of celluloïde:
Eleonora's huid een laag op haar lichaam.

Verder in de mossige driehoek Kahmkeut-Kanmon-Napé
(Het geduld is dat van tijgers, panters en roest)
zijn de eiken nog hoger dan de beuken
en in haar klamme tuin groeien slechts enkele planten
die eigenlijk dieren zijn.

Eerder als een effen voorwerp uit een dure verzameling

— ze spreidt armen en benen mechanisch open soepel
verder dan een normale vrouw —
hijgend buigt ze rubber, krijgend

> Onderdanig en
> geverfd: Eleonora
> in Viët-Nam.

> 1 B-52 boven en
> 7 G.I.'s tussen:
> de waakzame heesters.

(En de droogte en de tornado's en de bommen uit de hemel
en de schemerhuid van Eleonora een zwerm in de oliedikke avond
en soms een boek. Over fotografie.)

Halmen: halmen, helmen: helmen:
zoals de hemel verbrokkeld ligt in de scherven van haar spiegel.

2.

Aan de oppervlakte, onherroepelijk,
in het gebluste Saïgon dat was een bruisende neonstruik
wordt Eleonora haast onmerkbaar traag een pop.

Waar gescheurd echter het natte licht hangt in groene flarden
en het slijk de zolen zuigt als slijm,
waar slechts de druppel maar nooit de regen komt,
aan de ander zijde van het paard: een kind dat is een draad
met als blinde bloemen de bleke blik der napalmogen.

Midden de hoge duisternis en het vlokkige stof der kamers
versteent Eleonora roerloos bitter in haar roze schors,
zoals in die verre landen
sinds lang de zon zich bevindt
ergens op de bodem van de stilte.

3. (Moord op Eleonora)

Eleonora was een strelende nacht, een strelende nacht
die ooit beschermend op haar fluwelen lenden drukte
juist voor haar dood zelfs vergeten.

> En breekt zowel de
> dijen als de kuiten
> van gips.

> Verbrijzeld en bloedloos:
> Eleonora een
> Viët-Pop.

Smeulend en verslenst liggen haar holle brokken stofferig
in het gevaarlijke woud bedekt weldra door
ijzer, snelle varens en een ziltige stilte.

And there was silence in the House of Judgment. (Oscar Wilde)

(© Patrick Conrad)

Works Cited

ACKERMANN, KATHRIN, and STEFAN GREIF. 2003. 'Pop im Literaturbetrieb: Von den sechziger Jahren bis heute', in *Pop-Literatur*, ed. by Heinz Ludwig Arnold and Jörgen Schäfer, pp. 55–68

ARNOLD, HEINZ LUDWIG (ed). 1981. *Rolf Dieter Brinkmann, Text + Kritik*, 71 (Munich: text + kritik)

——, and JÖRGEN SCHÄFER (eds). 2013. *Pop-Literatur, Text + Kritik*: Sonderband x (Munich: Boorberg)

BANDEL, JAN-FREDERIK, BARBARA KALENDER, and JÖRG SCHRÖDER. 2011. *Immer radikal, niemals consequent: Der MÄRZ-Verlag — erweitertes Verlegertum, postmoderne Literatur und Business Art* (Hamburg: Philo Fine Arts)

BANDEILI, ANGELA. 2014. *Ästhetische Erfahrung in der Literatur der 1970er Jahre: Zur Poetologie des Raumes bei Rolf Dieter Brinkmann, Alexander Kluge und Peter Handke* (Bielefeld: transcript)

BARBA, SHERRY. 1969. 'Für verheiratete Frauen und noch einen Bekannten', in *ACID: Neue amerikanische Szene*, ed. by Rolf Dieter Brinkmann and Ralf-Rainer Rygulla (Darmstadt: März), p. 228

BASSLER, MORITZ. 2002. *Der deutsche Pop-Roman: Die neuen Archivisten* (Munich: Beck)

BAUER, THOMAS. 2002. *Schauplatz Lektüre: Blick, Figur und Subjekt in den Texten R.D. Brinkmanns* (Wiesbaden: DUV)

BENTZ, RALF. 1998. 'Avantgarde und Subkultur', in *PROTEST!*, ed. by Ralf Bentz et al., pp. 181–263

BENTZ, RALF, SABINE BRTNIK, CHRISTOPH KÖNIG, HELMUTH KIESEL, ROMAN LUCKSCHEITER, ULRICH OTT, and BRIGITTE RAITZ (eds). 1998. *PROTEST! Literatur um 1968* (Marbach am Neckar: Deutsche Schillergesellschaft)

BINCZEK, NATALIE. 2012. 'Das Material ordnen: Rolf Dieter Brinkmanns akustische Nachlassedition *Wörter Sex Schnitt*', in *'High' und 'low': Zur Interferenz von Hoch- und Populärkultur in der Gegenwartsliteratur*, ed. by Thomas Wegmann and Norbert Christian Wolf (Berlin: de Gruyter), pp. 57–81

BREMS, HUGO. 1972. 'Twee dichters', *Dietsche Warande & Belfort*, 117.9: 701–06

——. 1981. 'Alles immers is weerkaatsing', in Hugo Brems, *Al wie omziet: Opstellen over Nederlandse poëzie, 1960–1980* (Antwerp: Elsevier), pp. 82–91

——. 2005. *Altijd weer vogels die nest beginnen: Geschiedenis van de Nederlandse literatuur 1945–2005* (Amsterdam: Bert Bakker)

BRIEGLEB, KLAUS. 1993. *1968: Literatur in der antiautoritären Bewegung* (Frankfurt a/M: Suhrkamp)

BRINKMANN, MALEEN (ed.). 1995A. *Sonderheft Rolf Dieter Brinkmann*, Rowohlt Literaturmagazin 36 (Reinbek bei Hamburg: Rowohlt)

——. 1995B. 'Editorische Notiz', in *Sonderheft Rolf Dieter Brinkmann*, ed. by Maleen Brinkmann, pp. 216–18

BRINKMANN, ROLF DIETER. 1968A [1980].[71] 'Godzilla', in Rolf Dieter Brinkmann, *Standphotos*, pp. 159–82

——. 1968B [1980]. 'Die Piloten', in Rolf Dieter Brinkmann, *Standphotos*, pp. 183–280

——. 1968C [1994]. 'Angriff aufs Monopol: Ich hasse alte Dichter', in *Roman oder Leben*, ed. by Uwe Wittstock, pp. 65–77

——. 1969A. 'Der Film in Worten', in *ACID*, ed. by Rolf Dieter Brinkmann and Ralf-Rainer Rygulla, pp. 381–99

——. 1969B. 'Über Lyrik und Sexualität', *Streit — Zeit — Schrift*, 7.1 (Pornographie: Dokumente, Analysen, Fotos, Comics): 65–70

——, and RALF-RAINER RYGULLA (eds.). 1969C. *ACID: Neue amerikanische Szene* (Darmstadt: März)

——, and RALF-RAINER RYGULLA. 1969D. 'Nachbemerkung der Herausgeber', in *ACID*, ed. by Rolf Dieter Brinkmann and Ralf-Rainer Rygulla, pp. 417–19

——. 1979. *Rom, Blicke* (Reinbek bei Hamburg: Rowohlt)

——. 1980. *Standphotos: Gedichte 1962–1970* (Reinbek bei Hamburg: Rowohlt)

——. 1987. *Erkundungen für die Präzisierung des Gefühls für einen Aufstand: Reise Zeit Magazin (Tagebuch)* (Reinbek bei Hamburg: Rowohlt)

BUELENS, GEERT. 2001. *Van Ostaijen tot heden: Zijn invloed op de Vlaamse poëzie* (Nijmegen: Vantilt)

CARTENS, DAAN. 1995. 'Inleiding', in *Dichters van nu 6: Bloemlezing uit de poëzie van Patrick Conrad*, ed. by Daan Cartens (Ghent: PoëzieCentrum), pp. 5–38

CLARKE, TOM. 1969. 'Sonett', in *ACID*, ed. by Rolf Dieter Brinkmann and Ralf-Rainer Rygulla, p. 111

CONRAD, PATRICK. 1966. *Een pop van Patrick Conrad met Pola Negri in de rol van Eleonora* (Antwerp: Monas)

——. 1967. *Mercantile Marine Engineering* (Antwerp: De Galge)

——. 1969. '[Dankwoord]'; 'De Arkprijs 1969', *Nieuw Vlaams Tijdschrift*, 22.5: 485–87

——. 1973. *Conrad life on stage: Gedichten 1963–1973* (Brussels: Manteau)

——. 1998. *Annalen* (Ghent: PoëzieCentrum)

——. 2009. *Leven & werk van Marcel van Acker* (Antwerp: Houtekiet)

——. 2015. *As: Gedichten 1963–2014* (Ghent: PoëzieCentrum)

DEBORD, GUY. 2006. *Oeuvres* (Paris: Gallimard)

DE GROOF, PIET. 2007. *Le Général situationniste : Entretiens avec Gérard Berréby & Danielle Orhan* (Paris: Allia)

DEMBECK, TILL. 2013. '"No pasaran" — Lyrik, Kulturpolitik und Sprachdifferenz bei T.S. Eliot, Paul Celan und Rolf Dieter Brinkmann', *Arcadia*, 48.1: 1–41

ENZENSBERGER, HANS MAGNUS. 1968. 'Gemeinplätze, die Neueste Literatur betreffend', *Kursbuch*, 15: 187–97

ERNST, THOMAS. 2006. 'Literarische Grenzüberschreitungen: Die Grundlegung der Popliteratur durch Rolf Dieter Brinkmann — Für und Wider', in *Grenzüberschreitungen — zwischen Realität und Utopie*, ed. by Verena Di Pasquale et al. (Münster: Westfälisches Dampfboot), pp. 120–37

——. 2013. *Literatur und Subversion: Politisches Schreiben in der Gegenwart* (Bielefeld: transcript)

FAUSER, MARKUS. 2014. 'Einleitung', in *Medialität der Kunst: Rolf Dieter Brinkmann in der Moderne*, ed. by Markus Fauser (Bielefeld: transcript), pp. 7–15

——. 2015. 'Er war kein Urvater des Pop: Rolf Dieter Brinkmann zum 75. Geburtstag', *literaturkritik.de*, 4, 10 January 2016 <http://www.literaturkritik.de/public/rezension.php?rez_id=20381> [accessed 30 May 2019]

FIEDLER, LESLIE A. 1994 [1968]. 'Überquert die Grenze, schließt den Graben!', in *Roman oder Leben*, ed. by Uwe Wittstock, pp. 14–39

FLIETHMANN, AXEL. 2012. 'Godzilla [Gedichtzyklus]', in *Rolf Dieter Brinkmann*, ed. by Jan Röhnert and Gunter Geduldig, 1, pp. 120–29

FRIED, ERICH. 1966. *und vietnam und: 41 Gedichte* (Berlin: Wagenbach)

GEDULDIG, GUNTER, and MARCO SAGURNA (eds). 1994. *too much — Das lange Leben des Rolf Dieter Brinkmann* (Aachen: Alano)

'Global Pop Symposium'. 2016. Tate Modern <http://www.tate.org.uk/whats-on/tate-modern/conference/global-pop-symposium> [accessed 30 May 2019]

GROSS, THOMAS. 1993. *Alltagserkundungen: Empirisches Schreiben in der Ästhetik und in den späten Materialbänden* (Stuttgart: Metzler)

HECKEN, THOMAS. 2009. *POP: Geschichte eines Konzepts 1955–2009* (Bielefeld: transcript)

HERRMANN, KARSTEN. 1999. *Bewußtseinserkundungen im 'Angst- und Todesuniversum': Rolf Dieter Brinkmanns Collagebücher* (Bielefeld: Aisthesis)

HERMAND, JOST. 1971. *Pop International: Eine kritische Analyse* (Frankfurt a/M: Athenäum)

HUBERT, MARTIN. 1992. *Politisierung der Literatur — Ästhetisierung der Politik: Eine Studie zur literaturgeschichtlichen Bedeutung der 68er-Bewegung in der Bundesrepublik Deutschland* (Frankfurt a/M: Lang)

IRSIGLER, INGO. 2013. '"Der Entwicklungsroman ist verreckt": Versperrte Räume in der Prosa des Neuen Realismus', in *Raumlektüren: Der Spatial Turn und die Literatur der Moderne*, ed. by Tim Mehigan and Alan Corkhill (Bielefeld: transcript), pp. 277–96

JACOBS, CARL. 2015. *Pop Art in Belgium! 1963–1970* (Brussels: Mercatorfonds)

JESPERS, HENRI-FLORIS. 1967. 'Maniërisme en moderne sensibiliteit', in Patrick Conrad, *Mercantile Marine Engineering*, pp. 133–47

KEPPLER-TASAKI, STEFAN. 2012. 'Ra-ta-ta-ta für Bonnie & Clyde etc.', in *Rolf Dieter Brinkmann*, ed. by Jan Röhnert and Gunter Geduldig, 1, pp. 205–15

KOHLROSS, CHRISTIAN. 2000. *Theorie des modernen Naturgedichts: Oskar Loerke, Günter Eich, Rolf Dieter Brinkmann* (Würzburg: Königshausen & Neumann)

KRAMER, RAINER. 2000. *Auf der Suche nach dem verlorenen Augenblick: Rolf Dieter Brinkmanns innerer Krieg in Italien* (Bremen: Temmen)

——. 2003. 'Von Beat bis "Acid": Zur Rezeption amerikanischer und britischer Literatur in den sechziger Jahren', in *Pop-Literatur*, ed. by Heinz Ludwig Arnold and Jörgen Schäfer, pp. 26–40

——. 2010. 'Westwärts — und zurück: Zu London-Texten von Jörg Fauser und Rolf Dieter Brinkmann', in *Angermion: Yearbook für Anglo-German Literary Criticism, Intellectual History and Cultural Transfers*, ed. by Rüdiger Görner (Berlin: de Gruyter), pp. 51–68

LUCKSCHEITER, ROMAN. 1998. 'Plädoyer für eine Postmoderne', in *PROTEST!*, ed. by Ralf Bentz et al., pp. 363–78

MARREYT, STEVE. 2013. '"En geen mens die het merkte": Over Patrick Conrads elpee *Gelukkig als in het bijzin van een vrouw*', *Zacht Lawijd*, 12.1: 58–77

MATTENKLOTT, GUNDEL. 1992. 'Literatur von unten — die andere Kultur', in *Gegenwartsliteratur seit 1968*, ed. by Klaus Briegleb and Sigrid Weigel (Munich: dtv), pp. 153–81

McCARTHY, MARGRET. 2015A. *German Pop Literature: A Companion* (Berlin: de Gruyter)

——. 2015B. 'Introduction', in *German Pop Literature*, ed. by Margret McCarthy, pp. 9–45

MICHEL, KARL MARKUS. 1968. 'Ein Kranz für die Literatur', *Kursbuch*, 15: 169–86

OKUN, KIRSTEN. 2005. *Unbegrenzte Möglichkeiten: Brinkmann — Burroughs — Kerouac* (Bielefeld: Aisthesis)

OLTMANS, WILLEM. 2001. *Memoires 1964–1966* (Breda: Papieren Tijger) <https://www.dbnl.org/tekst/oltm003memo08_01/> [accessed 30 May 2019]

OTT, ULRICH. 1998. 'MÄRZ', in *PROTEST!*, ed. by Ralf Bentz et al., pp. 339–60

PAY, LUC. 1975. 'Een gesprek met Patrick Conrad: La fête perpétuelle', *Dietsche Warande & Belfort*, 123.6 (1975): 424–37

PIWITT, HERMANN PETER. 1979. 'Rauschhafte Augenblicke: Über Rolf Dieter Brinkmann — Rom, Blicke', *Der Spiegel*, 38: 252–57 <https://www.spiegel.de/spiegel/print/d-39868548.html> [accessed 30 May 2019]

RAUEN, CHRISTOPH. 2010. 'Entwicklungsroman und "Zwei-Drittel-Gesellschaft": Rolf Dieter Brinkmanns *Keiner weiß mehr* im Kontext ästhetischer und sozialer Normalisierung', in *Neue Perspektiven auf Rolf Dieter Brinkmann: Orte — Helden — Körper*, ed. by Thomas Boyken, Ina Cappelmann, and Uwe Schwagmaier (Munich: Fink), pp. 91–106

REICH-RANICKI, MARCEL. 1968. 'Außerordentlich (und) obszön: Über Rolf Dieter Brinkmanns Roman "Keiner weiß mehr" und die hohe schriftstellerische Kunst, die Kluft zwischen Obsession und Distanz zu überwinden', *Die Zeit*, 26 April 1968 <https://www.zeit.de/1968/17/ausserordentlich-und-obszoen> [accessed 30 May 2019]

RÖHNERT, JAN. 2007. 'A German Poet at the Movies: Rolf Dieter Brinkmann', in *Processes of Transposition: German Literature and Film*, ed. by Christiane Schönfeld and Hermann Rasche (Amsterdam: Rodopi), pp. 223–34

——. 2012. 'Einleitung', in *Rolf Dieter Brinkmann*, ed. by Jan Röhnert and Gunter Geduldig, 1, pp. 95–100

——, and GUNTER GEDULDIG (eds). 2012. *Rolf Dieter Brinkmann: Seine Gedichte in Einzel-interpretationen*, 2 vols (Berlin: de Gruyter)

ROGGEMAN, WILLEM M. 1975. 'Patrick Conrad', in *Beroepsgeheim: Gesprekken met schrijvers 1* (The Hague: Nijgh & Van Ditmar), pp. 105–16

——. 1980. 'Nic van Bruggen', in *Beroepsgeheim: Gesprekken met schrijvers 3* (Antwerp: Soethoudt), pp. 88–96

RYGULLA, RALF-RAINER. 1995. 'Frank Xerox' wüster Traum und andere Kollaborationen', in *Sonderheft Rolf Dieter Brinkmann*, ed. by Maleen Brinkmann, pp. 51–55

SCHÄFER, JÖRGEN. 1998. *Pop-Literatur: Rolf Dieter Brinkmann und das Verhältnis zur Populärkultur in der Literatur der sechziger Jahre* (Stuttgart: Metzler)

——. 2003. '"Mit dem Vorhandenen etwas anderes als das Intendierte machen": Rolf Dieter Brinkmanns poetologische Überlegungen zur Pop-Literatur', in *Pop-Literatur*, ed. by Heinz Ludwig Arnold and Jörgen Schäfer, pp. 69–80

SCHLÖSSER, HERMANN. 1987. *Reiseformen des Geschriebenen: Selbsterfahrung und Weltdarstellung in Reisebüchern Wolfgang Koeppens, Rolf Dieter Brinkmanns und Hubert Fichtes* (Cologne: Böhlau)

SCHUMACHER, ECKHARD. 2003. *Gerade Eben Jetzt: Schreibweisen der Gegenwart* (Frankfurt a/M: Suhrkamp)

——. 2006. '"Schreiben ist etwas völlig anderes als Sprechen": Rolf Dieter Brinkmanns Originaltonaufnahmen', in *Abfälle: Stoff- und Materialpräsentationen in der deutschen Pop-Literatur der 6oer Jahre*, ed. by Dirck Linck and Gert Mattenklott (Hannover: Wehrhahn), pp. 75–90

SELG, OLAF. 2001. *Essay, Erzählung, Roman und Hörspiel: Prosaformen bei Rolf Dieter Brinkmann* (Aachen: Shaker)

SPÄTH, SIBYLLE. 1989. *Rolf Dieter Brinkmann* (Stuttgart: Metzler)

STAHL, ENNO. 2015. 'An Alternative History of Pop', in *German Pop Literature*, ed. by Margret McCarthy, pp. 47–80

STRAUCH, MICHAEL. 1998. *Rolf Dieter Brinkmann: Studie zur Text-Bild-Montagetechnik* (Tübingen: Stauffenberg)

THE BEATLES. 1967. *Sgt. Pepper's Lonely Hearts Club Band* (Parlophone (UK)/Capitol (US))

TITZ, SUSANNE, LIESBETH DECAN, and JEAN ANTOINE. 2011. *Evelyne Axell 1964–1972* (Tielt: Lannoo)

ULLMAIER, JOHANNES. 2001. *Von Acid nach Adlon und zurück: Eine Reise durch die deutsch-sprachige Popliteratur* (Mainz: Ventil)

URBE, BURGLIND. 1985. *Lyrik, Fotografie und Massenkultur bei Rolf Dieter Brinkmann* (Frankfurt a/M: Lang)

VON PETERSDORFF, DIRK. 2009. 'Intermedialität und neuer Realismus: Die Text-Bild-Kombinationen Rolf Dieter Brinkmanns', in *Literatur intermedial: Paradigmenbildung von 1918–1968*, ed. by Wolf Gerhard Schmidt and Thorsten Valk (Berlin: de Gruyter), pp. 361–77

VON STEINAECKER, THOMAS. 2007. *Literarische Foto-Texte: Zur Funktion der Fotografien in den Texten Rolf Dieter Brinkmanns, Alexander Kluges und W.G. Sebalds* (Bielefeld: transcript)

WALSER, MARTIN. 1994 [1968]. 'Mythen, Milch und Mut', in *Roman oder Leben*, ed. by Uwe Wittstock, pp. 58–60

WEISS, PETER. 1968. *Diskurs über die Vorgeschichte und den Verlauf des lang andauernden Befreiungskrieges in Viet Nam als Beispiel für die Notwendigkeit des bewaffneten Kampfes der Unterdrückten gegen ihre Unterdrücker sowie über die Versuche der Vereinigten Staaten von Amerika, die Grundlagen der Revolution zu vernichten* (Frankfurt a/M: Suhrkamp)

WITTSTOCK, UWE (ed.). 1994. *Roman oder Leben: Postmoderne in der deutschen Literatur* (Leipzig: Reclam)

Notes to Chapter 6

1. Nevertheless, Situationist groups in Germany like *SPUR, Kommune 1* or *Subversive Aktion,* and figures like Dieter Kunzelmann or Fritz Teufel are still famous for their actions and happenings between art, politics and life — like the 'pudding-assassination' in April 1967 or the flyers on the fire-catastrophe in the Brussels Inno store ('Why are you burning, consumer?' ['Warum brennst du, Konsument?'], on 22 and 24 May 1967). As to the art in the Low Countries, it is important to note that one of the pioneers of Situationism, Piet de Groof, was active in Belgium in the 1950s under his pen name, Walter Korun. But he was relieved of his duties by Debord because he aspired to a military career.

2. Although the Situationists' actions from the late 1950s influenced the *nouveau réalistes* and pop artists — with the former, for instance, eventually building a labyrinth originally conceived by the Situationist International (De Groof 2007: 242) — the Situationists became scornful of these groups in the 1960s.

3. '[...] beispielsweise Günter Wallraffs Reportagen aus deutschen Fabriken, Bahman Nirumands Persien-Buch, Ulrike Meinhoffs [sic] Kolumnen, Georg Alsenheimers Bericht aus Vietnam' (all translations by T.E. and H.V.). In 1968, Meinhof was still working as a journalist, she only became a member of the terrorist group *Rote Armee Fraktion* [Red Army Fraction] in 1970.

4. In a letter to his wife Maleen Brinkmann he wrote (1987: 321): 'Do not forget that for me the whole rebellion with pop, underground, the people there, the Leftists, etc., etc. [...] is gone, and I am angry with myself, since I have been naïve in many respects. [...] I felt confused, and now this confusion is going away. And all this has to do with this imprecise, insecure state I was in, to begin with financially' ('Vergiß auch nicht, daß die ganze Rebellion mit Pop, Untergrund, den Leuten dort, den Linken usw. usw. [...] vorbei ist für mich, und mein Ärger mich oft selber meint, weil ich naiv in vielem gewesen bin. [...] Da ist eine Menge Verwirrung bei mir auch passiert, und die geht jetzt weg. Und das hängt doch aauch [sic] alles [...] zusammen [...] mit diesem ungenauen, unsicheren Zustand, schon allein finanziell.').

5. Geert Buelens in this context refers to Conrad's characterization by Paul de Vree, who placed him between the Surrealism and the New Realism of the *Gard Sivik* group (2001: 986).

6. 'Maar na de Beatles is de hele manier van leven, van denken, van muziek maken, is eigenlijk de hele cultuur veranderd, en wel op een manier zoals het in deze eeuw nog niet was gebeurd. [...] Het is een fabriek geweest, maar een zeer nuttige. Kijk naar de plastische kunsten, de pop-art bijvoorbeeld, alles is veranderd met het Beatlemania-fenomeen. [...] De Beatles hebben het speelse, de humor en de roes gelanceerd.'

7. Regarding Axell, see Titz, Decan and Antoine (2011). The new interest in her work and of other Belgian pop artists is also shown by Jacobs (2015) and by the poster of one of her works for the international exhibition on pop art in the Philadelphia Museum of Arts (2016), which sparked some controversy because of its sexual implications.

8. Before Brinkmann positioned himself on 15 November 1968, essays by Jürgen Becker and Helmut Heißenbüttel (4 October 1968), Reinhard Baumgart (11 October 1968), Martin Walser (18 October 1968) and Hans Egon Holthusen (25 October 1968) were published (Wittstock 1994: 11–77).

9. 'Klassizismus-Päpste'; 'Pop-Päpste. Marktgesetzen gehorchend.'

10. 'Die Kunst ist tot, es lebe aber nicht die Anti-Kunst [...], sondern die demokratische Literatur.'

11. '[...] die häßlichen, zynischen alten Männer des Kulturbetriebs [...]'.

12. 'Es herrscht eine generelle, tiefverwurzelte Ignoranz und Abneigung gegen alles "art-fremde".'

13. '[...] Irrsinn hervorbringen, im Namen der Humanität'.

14. '[...] "neue" Mensch der zweiten Hälfte des 20. Jahrhunderts'.

15. '[...] die Eroberung des inneren Raums: durch ein Abenteuer des Geistes, die Erweiterung der psychischen Möglichkeiten des Menschen'.

16. 'Vermischungen finden statt — Bilder, mit Wörtern durchsetzt, Sätze, neu arrangiert zu Bildern und Bild-(Vorstellungs-)zusammenhängen, Schallplattenalben, aufgemacht wie Bücher ... etc.'.

17. '[...] schafft ein Stückchen befreite Realität'.

18. See also the quotes of Barthes in Brinkmann and Rygulla 1969b: 418; and Brinkmann 1969a: 384–85.

19. From 1967 to 1970, Brinkmann was working on collaborations using techniques of the historic and international avant-garde like cadavre exquis, cut-up and fold-in with artist Berndt Höppner and writer Ralf-Rainer Rygulla (see Brinkmann 1995a: 57–69; Rygulla 1995: 54–55; and Brinkmann 1995b: 217).

20. '[...] die geeignetste Form [...], spontan erfaßte Vorgänge und Bewegungen, eine nur in einem Augenblick sich deutlich zeigende Empfindlichkeit konkret als snap-shot festzuhalten'.

21. '[...] schlechthin alles, was man sieht und womit man sich beschäftigt, wenn man es nur genau genug sieht und direkt genug wiedergibt, ein Gedicht werden kann, auch wenn es sich um ein Mittagessen handelt'.

22. 'Sie sagten, das hier sei ja alles einfach, man könne es ja verstehen, und das wiederum macht ihnen meine Gedichte unverständlich.'

23. 'Leugen die hem enerzijds bevrijdt van de dikwijls groteske, burleske werkelijkheid, en hem anderzijds de saaie alledaagsheid min of meer draaglijk maakt.'

24. 'Ik ben in de hele vormgeving van mijn leven een dichter, en één van de middelen om dat leven even te fixeren is de literatuur, maar er zijn er ook andere.'

25. 'Wat men noemt "politiek engagement" vind ik dikwijls wansmakelijk, ja. Ik vind dat het helemaal geen zin heeft wanneer hier bij ons iemand gedichten gaat schrijven over de oorlog in Vietnam.'

26. In fact, the song-text runs as follows: 'You say Goodbye and I say Hello'.

27. 'Victoriaanse heren met stijve boord, uitgeknipte naakte vrouwen, getekende fallische bloemen en in *Yellow Submarine*-lettertype gedrukte Beatlescitaten in de tekstballon ("When you say hello I say goodbye" [...] voor een soms absurde, soms ironische subtekst bij het met freudiaanse allusies en een gastoptreden van Charles Baudelaire gelardeerde verhaaltje.'

28. 'Die, die ihn postum mit Preisen ehren und bereits die Gedichte des 16jährigen tiefsinniger Deutung unterziehen, sollten sich lieber fragen, wo sie denn waren, als er, wie zuletzt, von einem geliehenen Hundertmarkschein zum andern lebte.'

29. 'Schreibweisen in der Leere'.

30. 'Literatur von unten'.

31. 'Er war kein Urvater des Pop.'

32. 'sehr kurze Phase'; '[...] nur ein kleiner Teil seiner Gedichte war davon angeregt'.

33. The term was introduced by Jespers (1967).

34. 'Omdat wie gisteren dacht dat hij mocht denken | Morgen met afgesneden tong | Knikkend zijn kloten zal tellen | In de nacht van een cel zonder raam'.

35. '[...] in seinen Montage- bzw. Collagearbeiten [...] eindeutig durch die US-amerikanische Linie beeinflußt'.

36. 'nordamerikanische Postmoderne'.

37. 'Pop-Periode (1967–1969)'.

38. 'Seine spezifische Leistung ist im Akt gezielter Subversion des vorgefundenen Materials zu sehen: der Gegenüberstellung "sauberer" öffentlicher Lust-Projektion und enthemmter libdinöser Phantasie.'

39. 'Die Frau in der Werbung bleibt echt als Foto.'

40. 'Diese Fotze ist gut | Diese Fotze ist gut | Diese Fotze ist gut | Diese Fotze ist gut'.

41. 'Mit der direkten Ehrlichkeit der "dirty speech"' wird hier das Urteil über die angebotene Ware gefällt [...].'

42. '[...] langsam sprießt | wieder etwas Haar am | Rand einer Falte. Wir | ruhen uns in seinem || Schatten aus.'

43. 'Die Dame ist keine. XYZ.'

44. 'Die Dame ist keine. XYZ. Die | Eier bewegen sich. Man geht | tanzen und kommt verändert || zurück.'

45. 'Jetzt wird etwas in | der Hose steif und gerinnt | zu Zahnpasta.'
46. Brinkmann writes: 'Whilst movies and advertising images shyly show pubic hair, poets obviously do not dare to enrich their delicate artistic creations of language and thoughts by using the word *pubic hair*.' ('Während bereits in Filmen oder auf Reklamebildern zaghaft Schamhaar gezeigt wird [...], wagt es der Lyriker offensichtlich nicht, sein zartes, kunstvoll-apartes Sprach- und Gedankengebilde durch das Wort *Schamhaar* zu bereichern.'; Brinkmann 1969b: 67)
47. 'Die Vermehrung geschieht nach einer | undurchsichtigen Formel sofort auf | der Stelle: einmal Coca-Cola, zwei Mal | Kim Novak, drei Mal der Kerl aus Hol- | lywood, vier Mal George Hammilton [*sic*], fünf | Mal Senta Berger, acht Mal Tony Curtis | neun Mal die Titten von Jane [*sic*] Mansfield | [...] ich meine, wenn | das nicht ausreicht, ich meine | von | links | unten | nach | rechts | oben | bis | das Bild voll ist von ihrem wei- | ßen Fleisch und du dir persönlich | einen runter holen kannst.'
48. 'ein leidenschaftlicher Kinogänger'.
49. '[...] psychedelischen Blumen-Landschaft [...] Flower-Power'.
50. 'Ich || setze mich hin und fange | auch zu scheißen an | und alle Gespräche sind || endgültig beendet [...]'.
51. '[...] | an das dreckige | Handtuch von gestern abend || lehnt lächelnd eine | nackte Frau | zahnlos und nackt || zahnlos und nackt | und lächelnd. (Sie | möchte endlich nach || Jahren wieder einmal | richtig scheißen, nehme | ich an.)'
52. '[...] und jemand fällt als flüs- | siges Ketchup wie ein roter | Faden vom Himmel'.
53. '[...] wohl Brinkmanns offenster Beitrag zu den gesellschaftlichen Auseinandersetzungen seiner Zeit'.
54. 'WARUM SCHLAGT IHR SIE NICHT TOT?'.
55. 'um schnell noch | den Druck loszuwerden'.
56. 'Gibt es etwas, das gespenstischer wäre als dieser deutsche Kulturbetrieb mit dem fortwährenden Ruf nach Stil etc.? [...] Wie sagte Warren Beatty zu den deutschen Kinobesitzern beim Start von Bonnie und Clyde: "Bei der Schlußszene mit dem Maschinengewehrfeuer müßt ihr den Ton ganz aufdrehen!"'
57. 'Der Film läuft weiter und Bonnie läuft | weiter und Clyde läuft weiter und wir || laufen alle mit.'
58. '[...] dass "Ra-ta-ta-ta" in einer nur staatskritischen Deutung aufgehen würde'.
59. 'Schon im Film finden Bonnie und Clyde [...] keine politische Linie, sondern taumeln heiter-hysterisch von Situation zu Situation'.
60. 'Parodie auf den Einsatz von Spezialeffekten im kommerziellen Kino'.
61. We thank Dirk De Geest for the suggestion.
62. See also the collection *The Tears of Mary Pickford* (*De tranen van Mary Pickford*, 1991) and *The Life & Work of Marcel van Acker* (*Leven & werk van Marcel Van Acker*, 2009).
63. 'Foto: | Krioelend van licht en make-up (Sarah?) een pop | zedig in brokaat en zilverstil fluweel | met oude gebaren en de ogen de mond | stomme kuilen vol schaduwen en schimmen.'
64. 'O wankelende melaatse pop met pokken!'
65. 'Conrads gedichten zijn in hoge mate artificieel. Ze zijn doordacht, *gemaakt*, gevormd, ze verraden een enorme eruditie en speelzucht met alle kaarten van het bestaan. Het zijn geen spatten van een gekweld gemoed dat papier zoekt om herkenning én erkenning bij lezers.'
66. Jespers observed as early as 1967 that Conrad, 'under the pressure of circumstances in life, evolved [...] toward a more soulful lyricism' (Jespers 1967: 145; 'onder de druk van omstandigheden uit het leven, evolueerde [...] naar een meer gevoelsgerichte lyriek').
67. 'Een gedicht schrijven is de brokstukken, de elementen van een puzzel verzamelen, en die passen slechts op één unieke manier juist in elkaar.'
68. 'Mijn experimenten in de poëzie, de grafiek, een beetje ook in het proza, in het menselijk contact, het theatrale aspect dat ik de poëzie tracht te geven, dat zijn tenslotte allemaal voorbereidingen om tot een film te komen.'
69. 'Gedichten schrijven en jezelf in een spiegel bekijken is trouwens uiteindelijk hetzelfde.'
70. Cf. the poem 'The Cunts and Cardinals of the Middelheim Museum' (1970, 'De kutten en de kardinalen van het Middelheim') and the Bataille-esque accumulation of 'perversities' in *The Little Death of Kasper Q: A Long Short Story* (1)971.

71. Brinkmann's literary and poetological publications of 1968 and 1969 that are quoted from later volumes got a different abbreviation, which will help the reader to contextualize the texts properly.

INDEX

❖

www.ingramcontent.com/pod-product-compliance
Lightning Source LLC
Chambersburg PA
CBHW080541090426
42734CB00016B/3173